THE WICKED + THE DIVINE

VOL. 1, THE FAUST ACT

GILLEN

McKELVIE

WILSON

COWLES

KIERON GILLEN
WRITER

JAMIE MCKELVIE
ARTIST

MATTHEW WILSON
COLOURIST

CLAYTON COWLES
LETTERER

HANNAH DONOVAN
DESIGNER

CHRISSY WILLIAMS
EDITOR

DEE CUNNIFFE
FLATTER

NATHAN FAIRBAIRN
GUEST COLOURIST #4, PP 1-2

IMAGE COMICS, INC.
Robert Kirkman, CHIEF OPERATING OFFICER
Erik Larsen, CHIEF FINANCIAL OFFICER
Todd McFarlane, PRESIDENT
Marc Silvestri, CHIEF EXECUTIVE OFFICER
Jim Valentino, VICE-PRESIDENT
Eric Stephenson, PUBLISHER
Corey Murphy, DIRECTOR OF SALES
Jeff Boison, DIRECTOR OF PUBLISHING PLANNING & BOOK TRADE SALES
Jeremy Sullivan, DIRECTOR OF DIGITAL SALES
Kat Salazar, DIRECTOR OF PR & MARKETING
Emily Miller, DIRECTOR OF OPERATIONS
Branwyn Bigglestone, SENIOR ACCOUNTS MANAGER
Sarah Mello, ACCOUNTS MANAGER
Drew Gill, ART DIRECTOR

Jonathan Chan, PRODUCTION MANAGER
Meredith Wallace, PRINT MANAGER
Briah Skelly, PUBLICITY ASSISTANT
Sasha Head, SALES & MARKETING PRODUCTION DESIGNER
Randy Okamura, DIGITAL PRODUCTION DESIGNER
David Brothers, BRANDING MANAGER
Addison Duke, PRODUCTION ARTIST
Vincent Kukua, PRODUCTION ARTIST
Tricia Ramos, PRODUCTION ARTIST
Jeff Stang, DIRECT MARKET SALES REPRESENTATIVE
Emilio Bautista, DIGITAL SALES ASSOCIATE
Chloe Ramos-Peterson, ADMINISTRATIVE ASSISTANT
imagecomics.com

GILLEN McKELVIE WILSON COWLES

THE

WICKED

+

DIVINE

THE

VOL. 1, THE FAUST ACT

THE WICKED + THE DIVINE, VOL. 1, THE FAUST ACT
Fourth printing. June 2016.
ISBN: 978-1-63215-019-6
Newbury Cover A ISBN: 978-1-63215-986-1
Newbury Cover B ISBN: 978-1-63215-987-8
Forbidden Planet/Big Bang Cover ISBN: 978-1-63215-995-3
Fried Pie Cover ISBN: 978-1-63215-992-3

Published by Image Comics Inc. Office of publication:
2001 Center Street, Sixth Floor
Berkeley, California 94704
United States of America

For information regarding the CPSIA on this printed material call:
(203) 595 3636 and provide reference # RICH - 684672.

Representation: Law Offices of Harris M. Miller II, P.C.
rights.inquiries@gmail.com

This book was designed by Hannah Donovan and Jamie McKelvie,
set into type by Hannah Donovan in London, United Kingdom,
and printed and bound in The United States.

The text face is Gotham, designed and issued by Hoefler & Co. in 2000.

The paper is Liberty 60 matte.

"Ah, Faustus,

Now hast thou but one bare hour to live,

And then thou must be damn'd perpetually!

Stand still, you ever-moving spheres of Heaven,

That time may cease, and midnight never come"

Christopher Marlowe
Doctor Faustus

"BOOM, BOOM, BOOM, BOOM"

Vengaboys
'Boom, Boom, Boom, Boom!!', *The Party Album!*

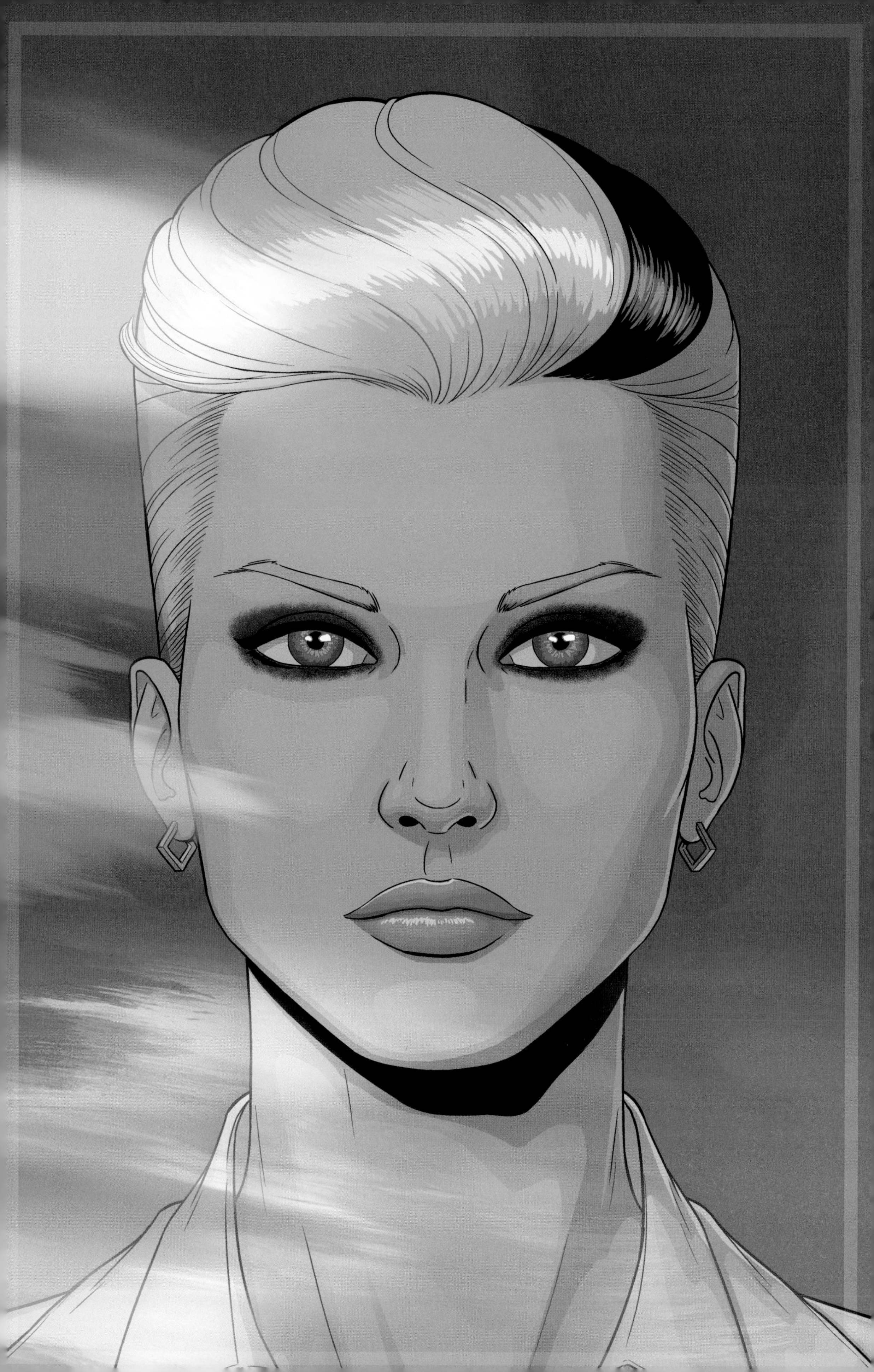

ONCE AGAIN

31 DECEMBER 1923

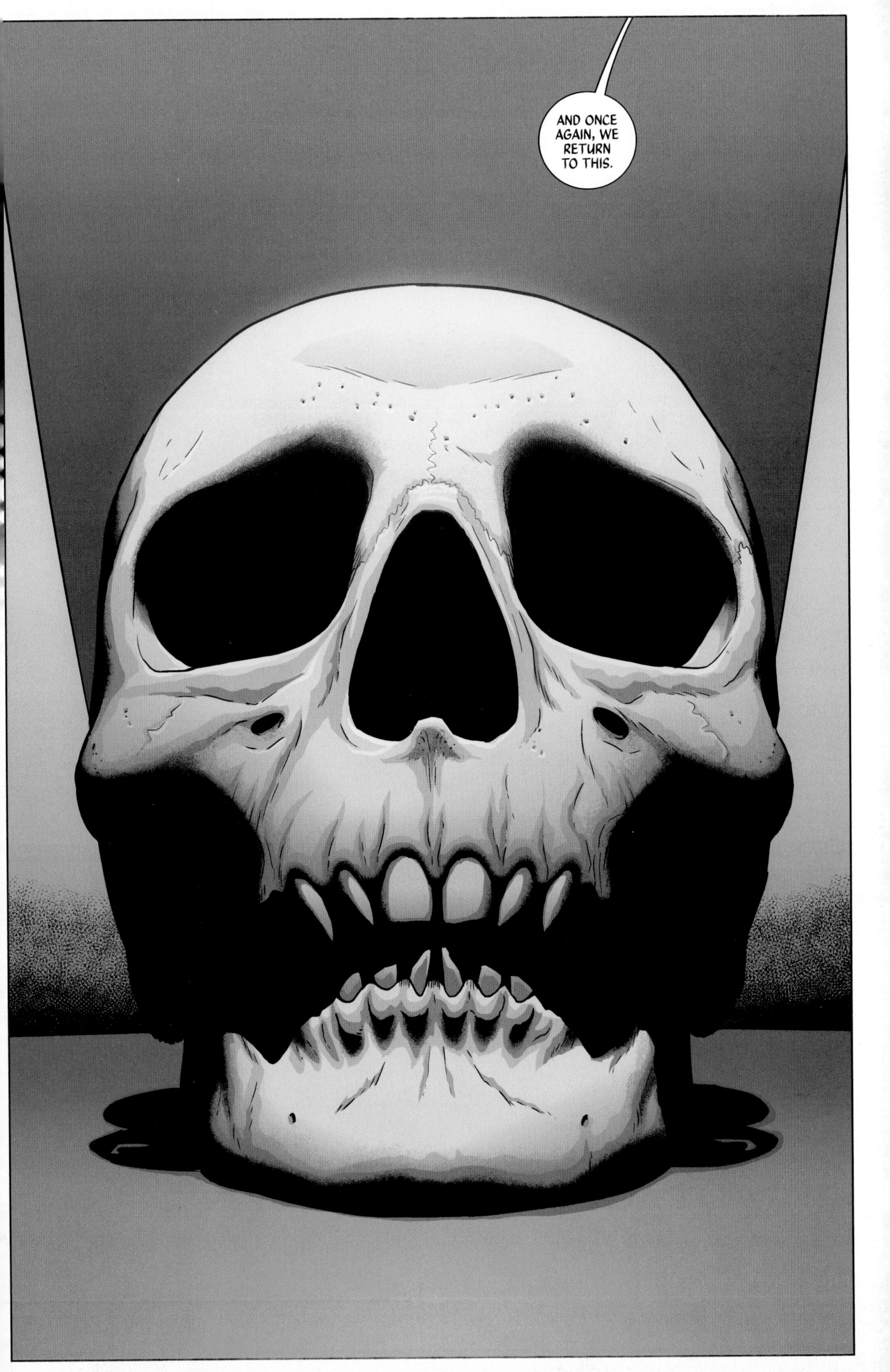
AND ONCE AGAIN, WE RETURN TO THIS.

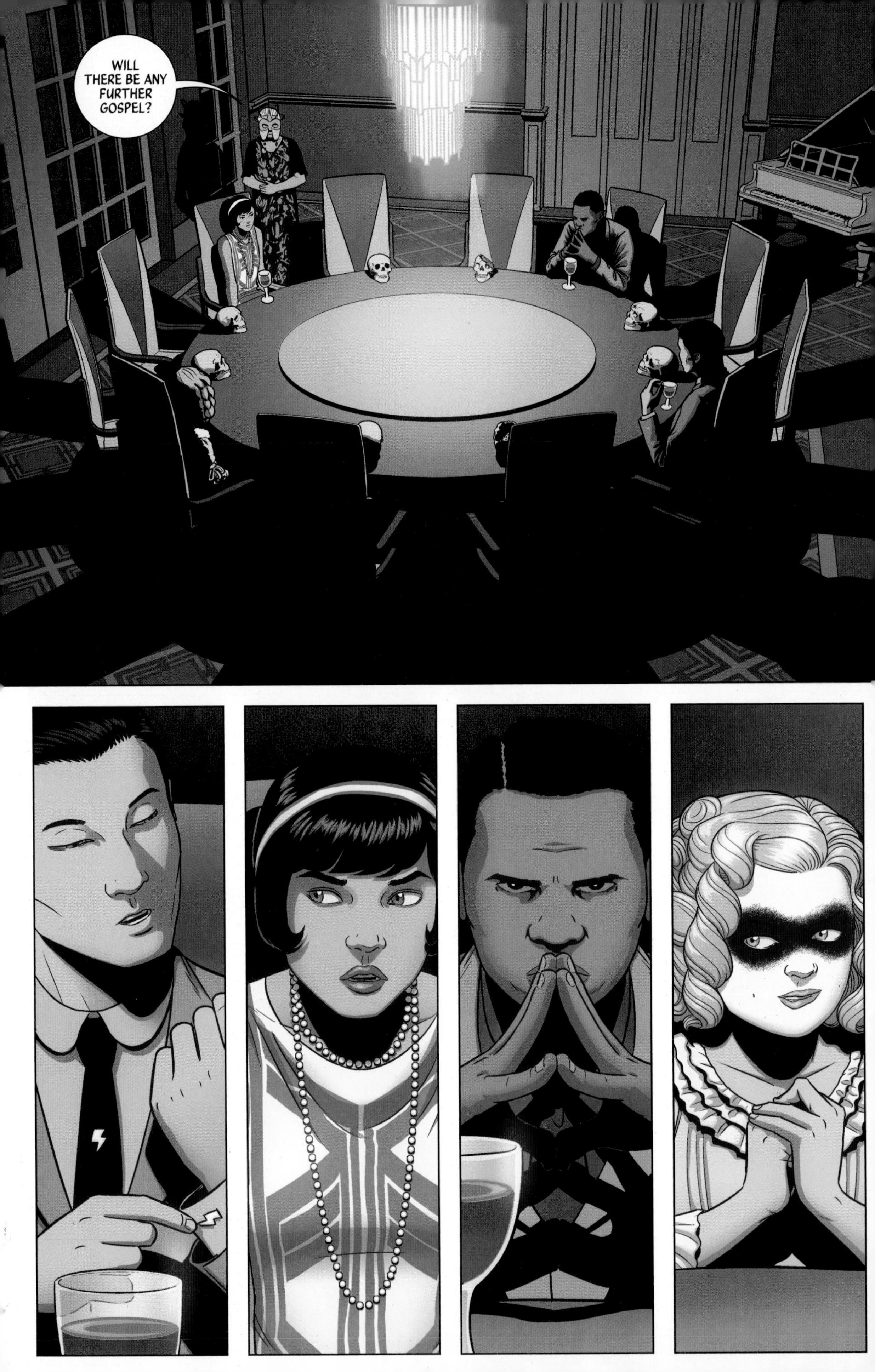
WILL THERE BE ANY FURTHER GOSPEL?

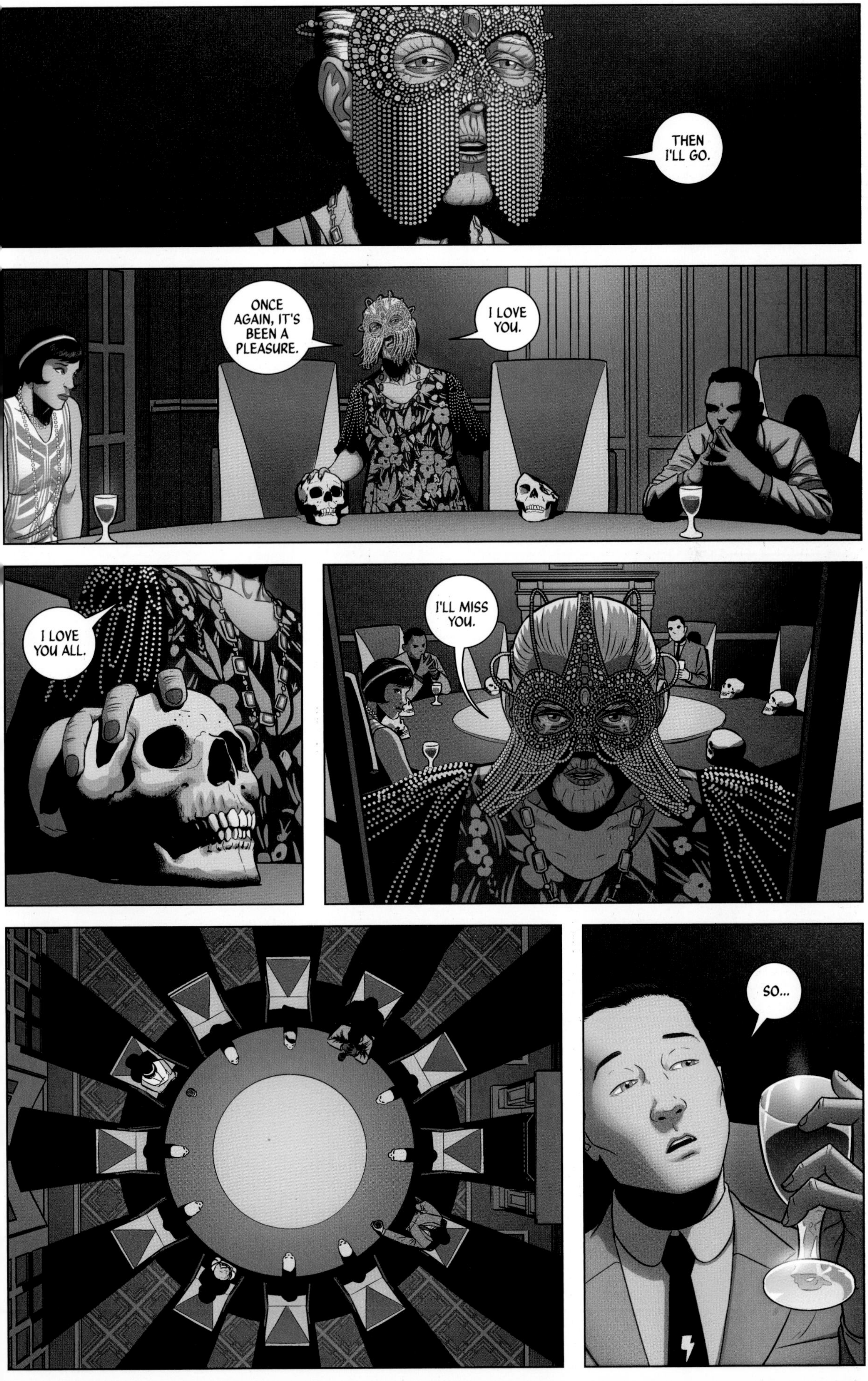
THEN I'LL GO.
ONCE AGAIN, IT'S BEEN A PLEASURE.
I LOVE YOU.
I LOVE YOU ALL.
I'LL MISS YOU.
SO...

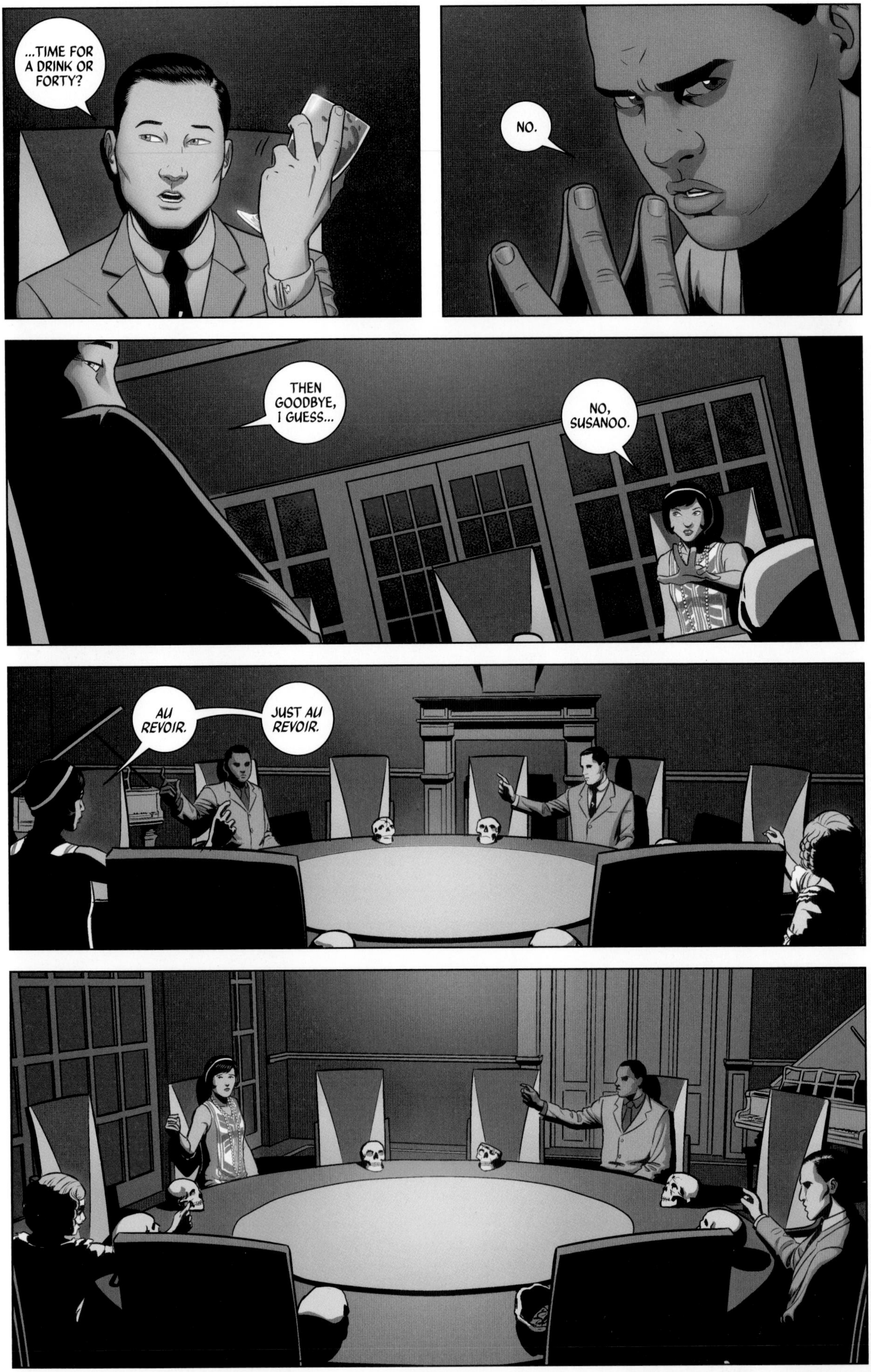
...TIME FOR A DRINK OR FORTY?
NO.
THEN GOODBYE, I GUESS...
NO, SUSANOO.
AU REVOIR.
JUST AU REVOIR.

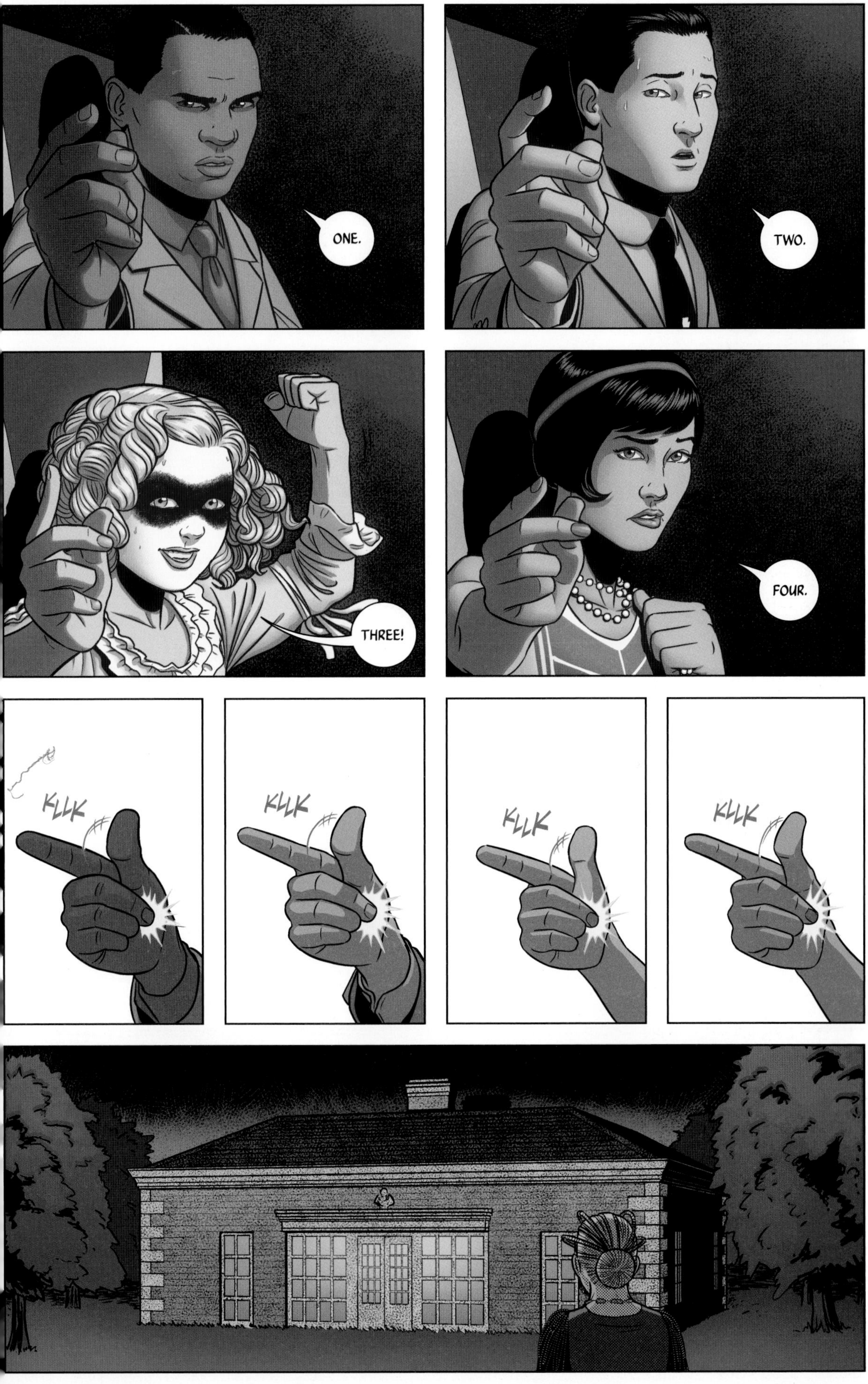
ONE.
TWO.
THREE!
FOUR.
KLLK
KLLK
KLLK
KLLK

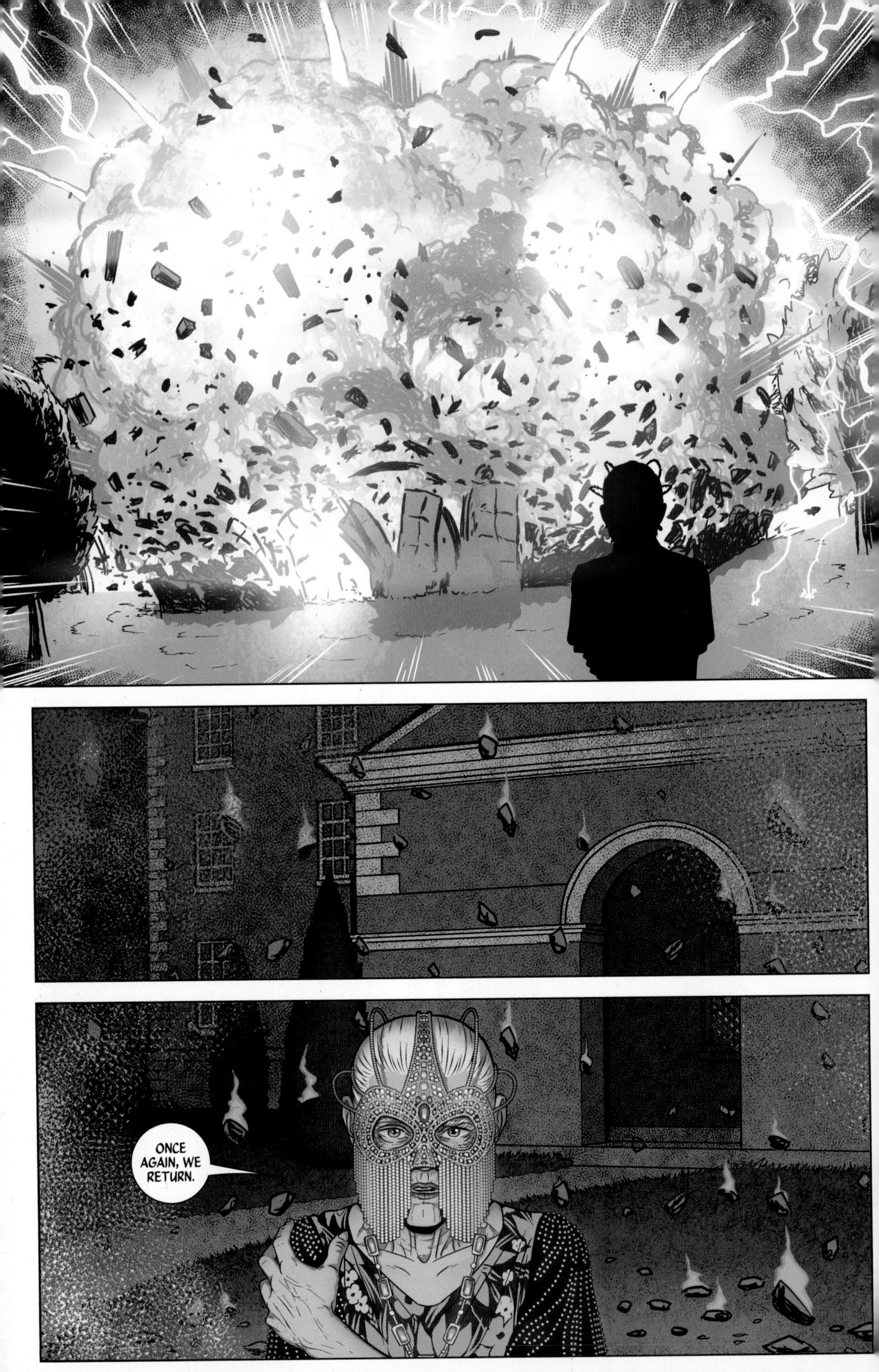
ONCE AGAIN, WE RETURN.

1–2–3–4

1 JANUARY 2014

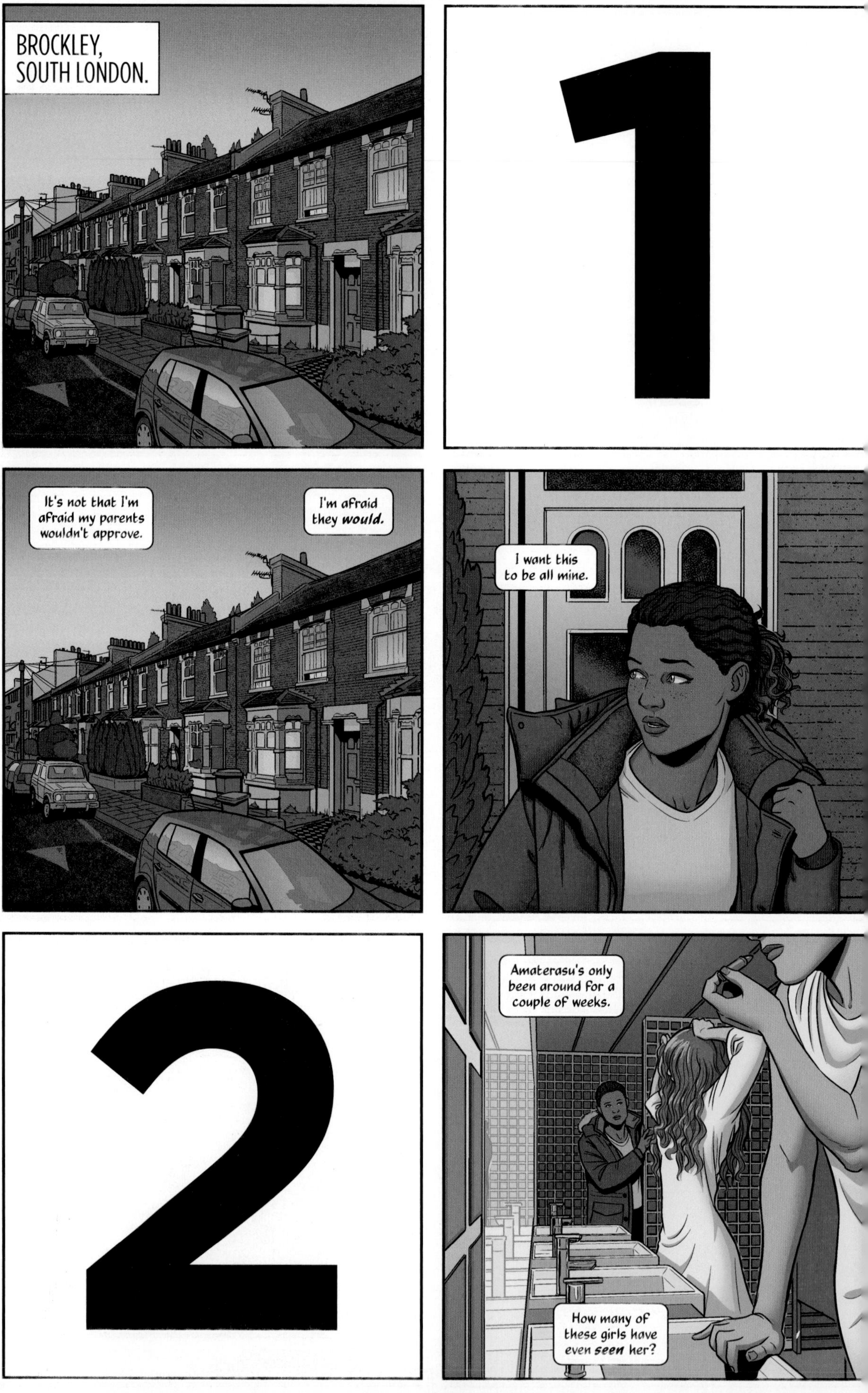
BROCKLEY, SOUTH LONDON.
1
It's not that I'm afraid my parents wouldn't approve.
I'm afraid they *would.*
I want this to be all mine.
2
Amaterasu's only been around for a couple of weeks.
How many of these girls have even *seen* her?

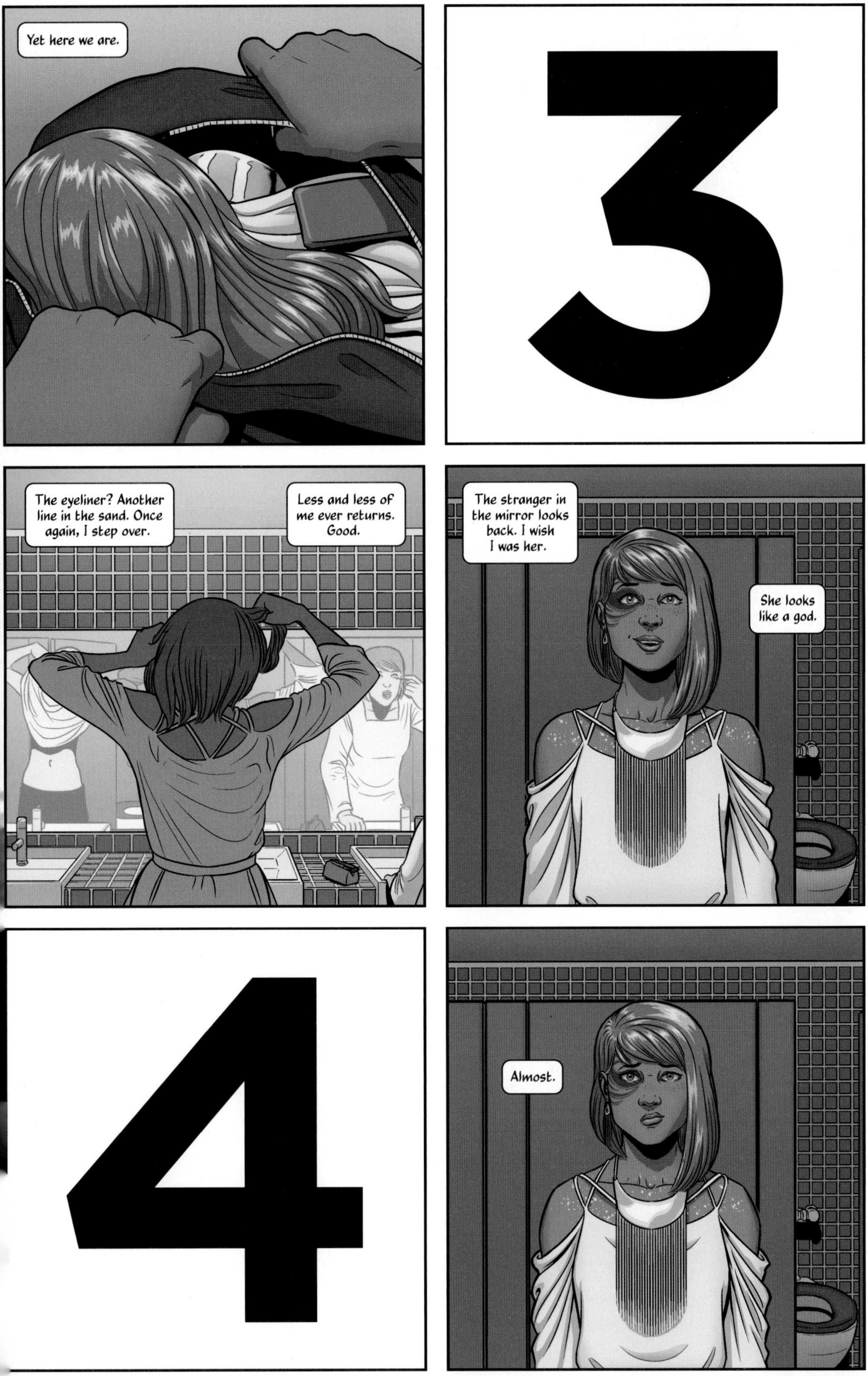
Yet here we are.
3
The eyeliner? Another line in the sand. Once again, I step over.
Less and less of me ever returns. Good.
The stranger in the mirror looks back. I wish I was her.
She looks like a god.
4
Almost.

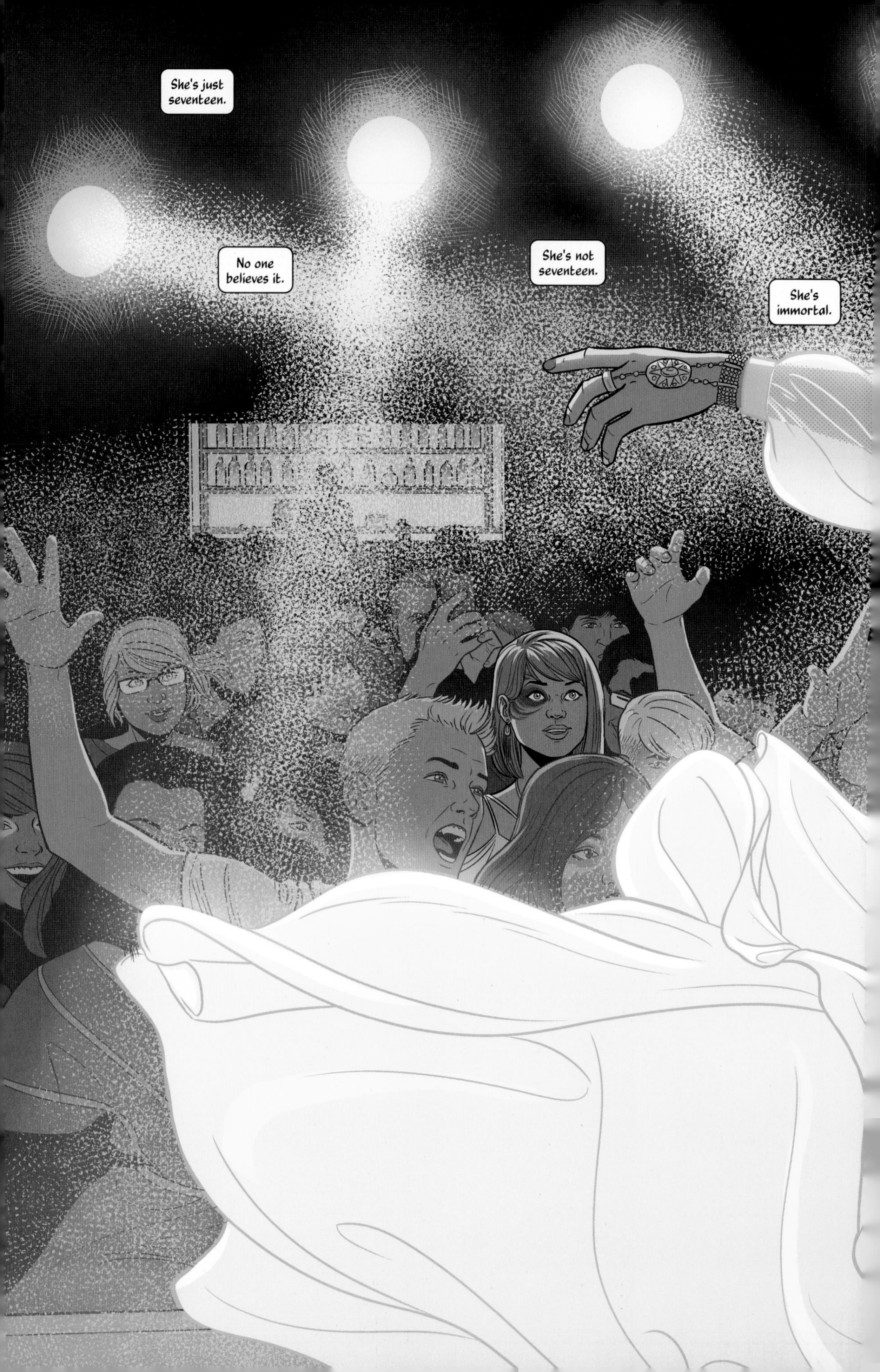
She's just seventeen.
No one believes it.
She's not seventeen.
She's immortal.

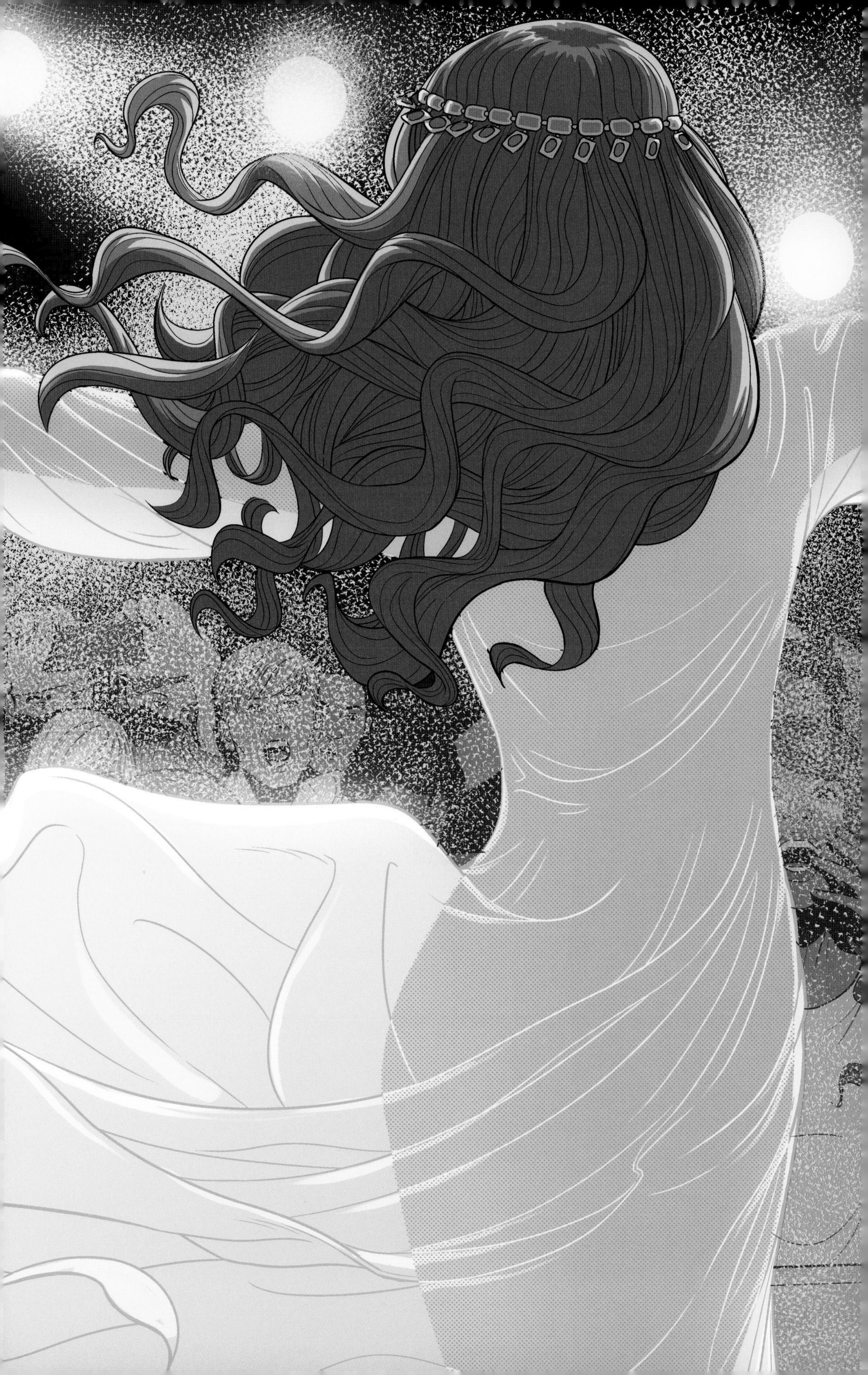

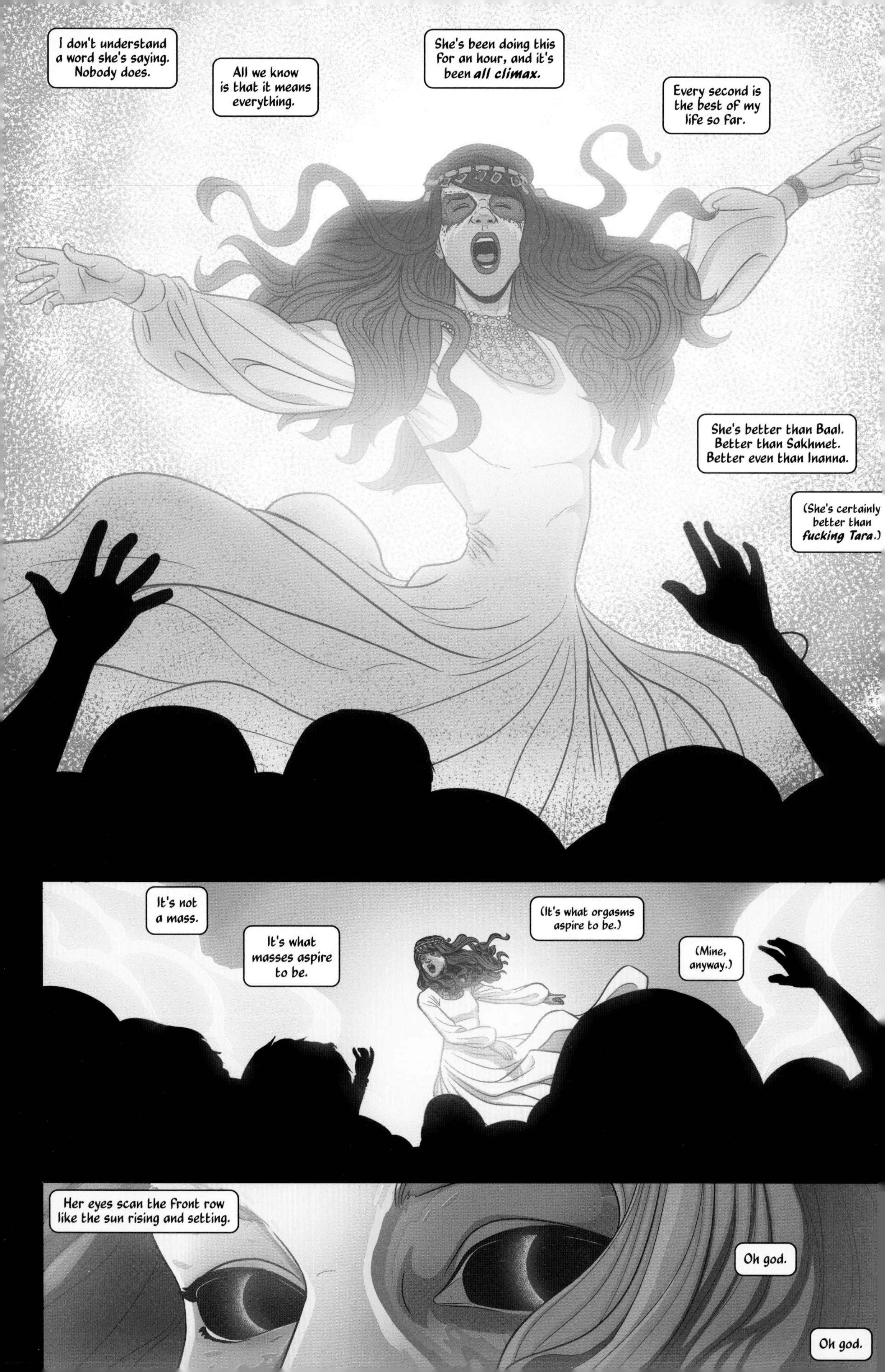

I don't understand a word she's saying. Nobody does.
All we know is that it means everything.
She's been doing this for an hour, and it's been *all climax.*
Every second is the best of my life so far.
She's better than Baal. Better than Sakhmet. Better even than Inanna.
(She's certainly better than *fucking Tara*.)
It's not a mass.
It's what masses aspire to be.
(It's what orgasms aspire to be.)
(Mine, anyway.)
Her eyes scan the front row like the sun rising and setting.
Oh god.
Oh god.

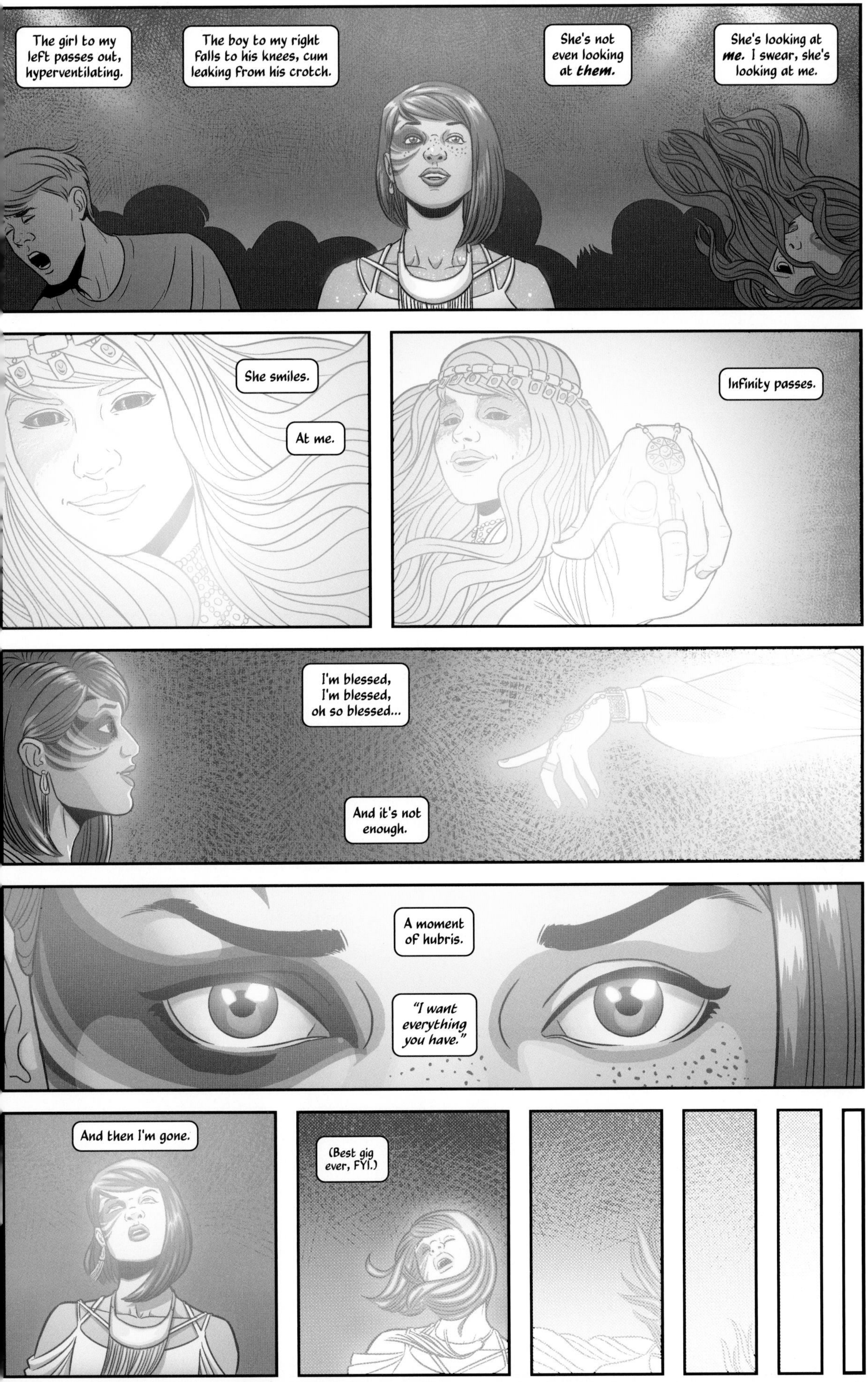
The girl to my left passes out, hyperventilating.
The boy to my right falls to his knees, cum leaking from his crotch.
She's not even looking at *them.*
She's looking at *me.* I swear, she's looking at me.
She smiles.
At me.
Infinity passes.
I'm blessed, I'm blessed, oh so blessed...
And it's not enough.
A moment of hubris.
"I want everything you have."
And then I'm gone.
(Best gig ever, FYI.)

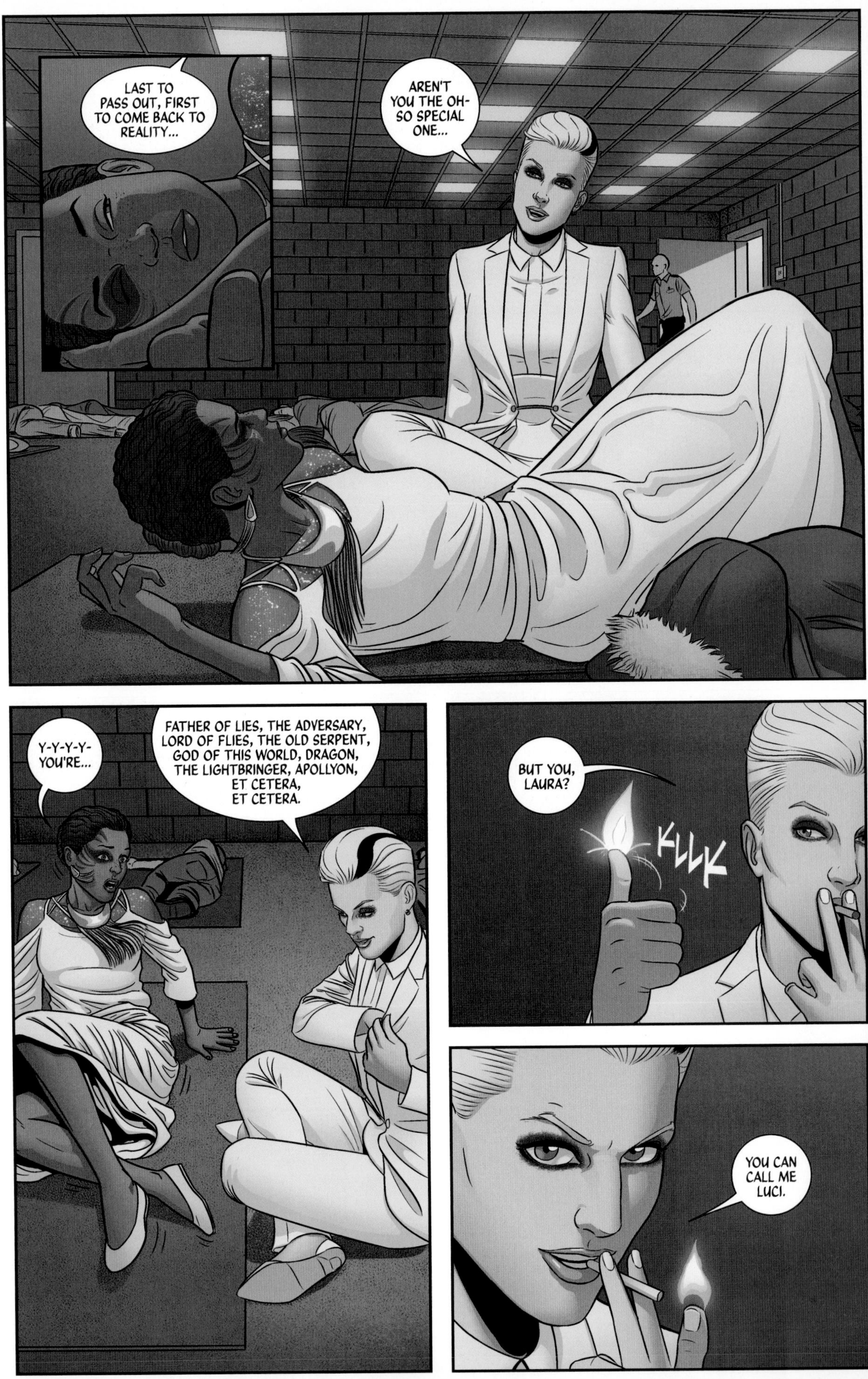
LAST TO PASS OUT, FIRST TO COME BACK TO REALITY...
AREN'T YOU THE OH-SO SPECIAL ONE...
Y-Y-Y-Y-YOU'RE...
FATHER OF LIES, THE ADVERSARY, LORD OF FLIES, THE OLD SERPENT, GOD OF THIS WORLD, DRAGON, THE LIGHTBRINGER, APOLLYON, ET CETERA, ET CETERA.
BUT YOU, LAURA?
KLLK
YOU CAN CALL ME LUCI.

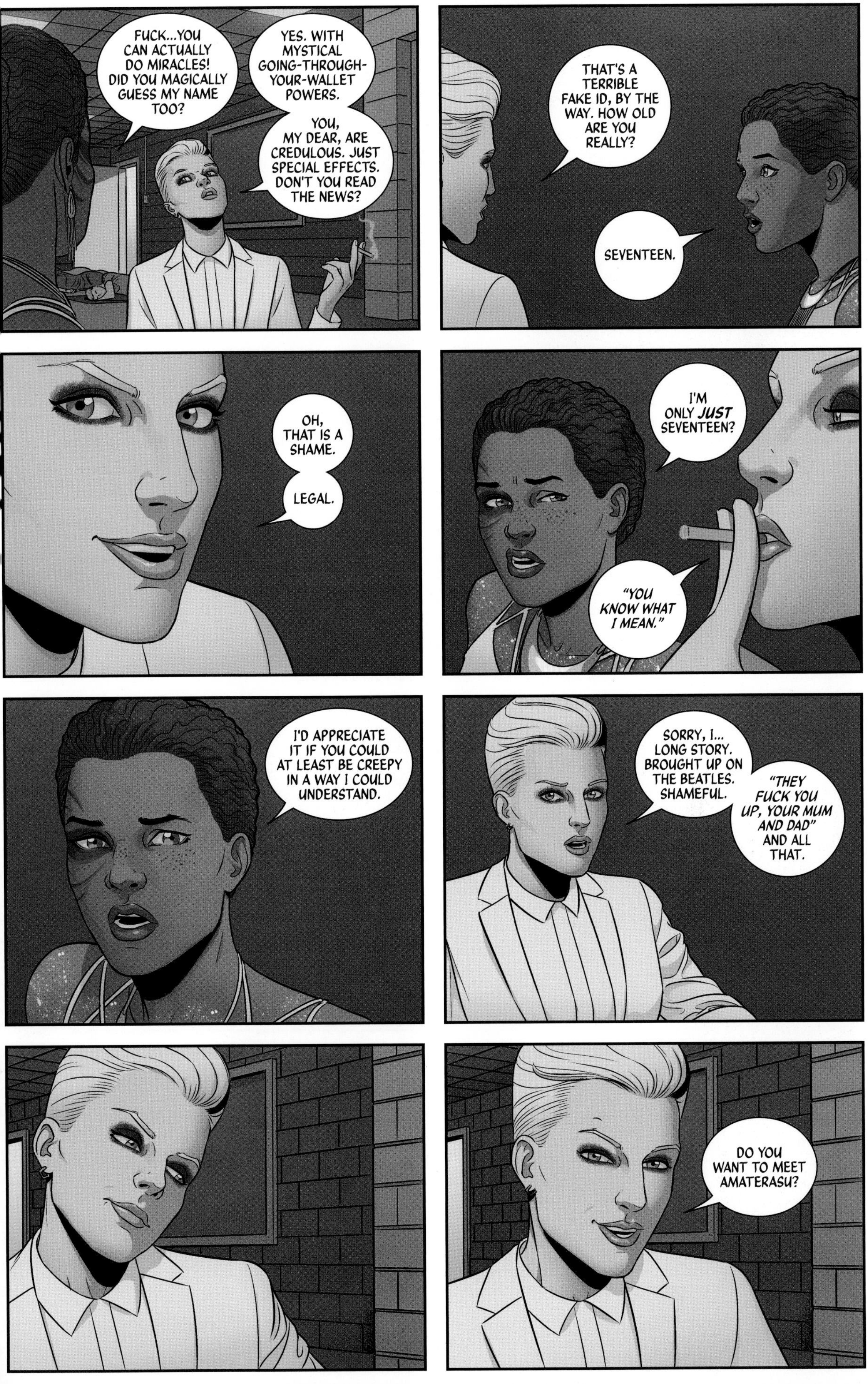
FUCK...YOU CAN ACTUALLY DO MIRACLES! DID YOU MAGICALLY GUESS MY NAME TOO?
YES. WITH MYSTICAL GOING-THROUGH-YOUR-WALLET POWERS.
YOU, MY DEAR, ARE CREDULOUS. JUST SPECIAL EFFECTS. DON'T YOU READ THE NEWS?
THAT'S A TERRIBLE FAKE ID, BY THE WAY. HOW OLD ARE YOU REALLY?
SEVENTEEN.
OH, THAT IS A SHAME.
LEGAL.
I'M ONLY *JUST* SEVENTEEN?
"YOU KNOW WHAT I MEAN."
I'D APPRECIATE IT IF YOU COULD AT LEAST BE CREEPY IN A WAY I COULD UNDERSTAND.
SORRY, I... LONG STORY. BROUGHT UP ON THE BEATLES. SHAMEFUL.
"THEY FUCK YOU UP, YOUR MUM AND DAD" AND ALL THAT.
DO YOU WANT TO MEET AMATERASU?

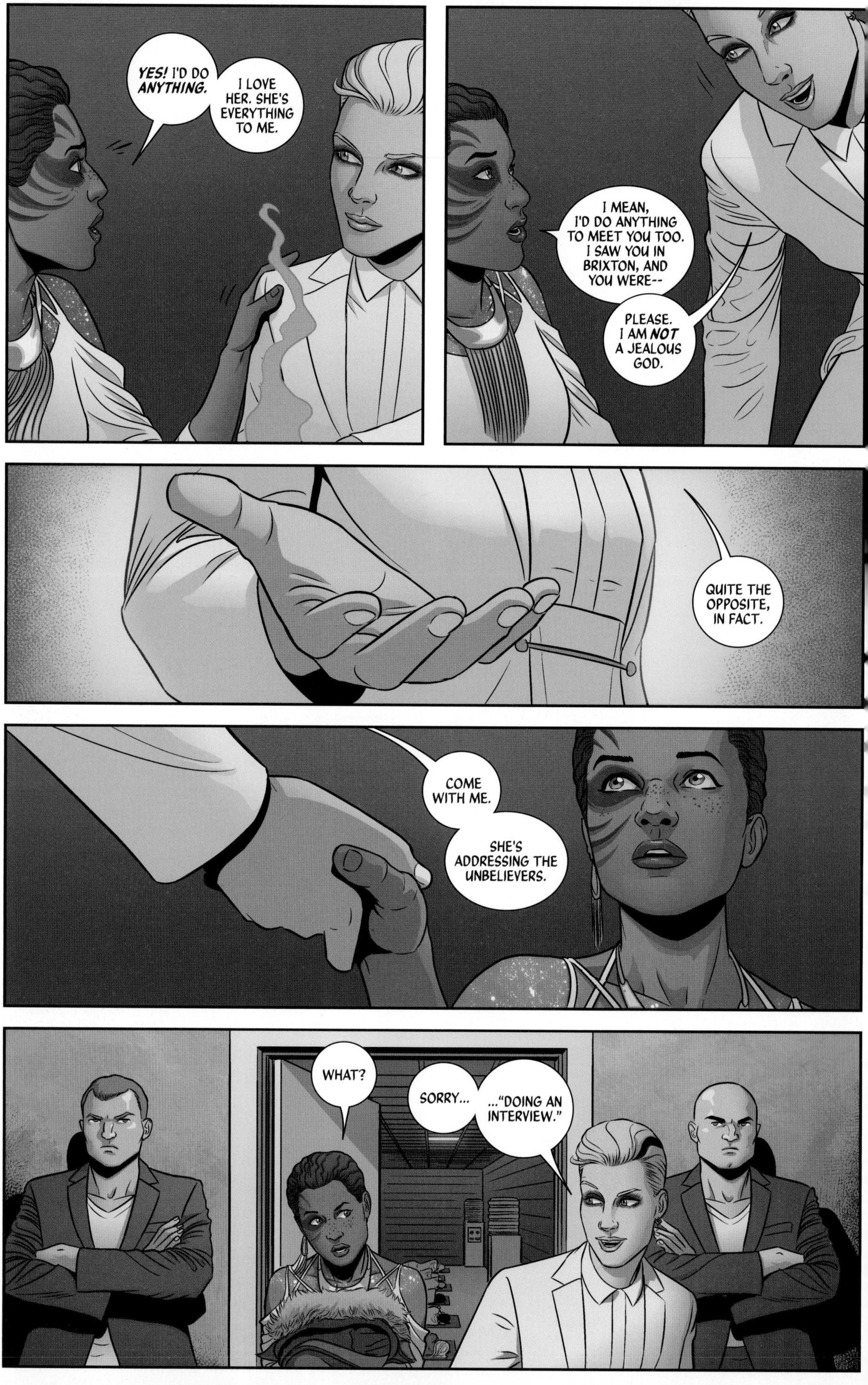
YES! I'D DO ANYTHING.
I LOVE HER. SHE'S EVERYTHING TO ME.
I MEAN, I'D DO ANYTHING TO MEET YOU TOO. I SAW YOU IN BRIXTON, AND YOU WERE--
PLEASE. I AM NOT A JEALOUS GOD.
QUITE THE OPPOSITE, IN FACT.
COME WITH ME.
SHE'S ADDRESSING THE UNBELIEVERS.
WHAT?
SORRY...
..."DOING AN INTERVIEW."

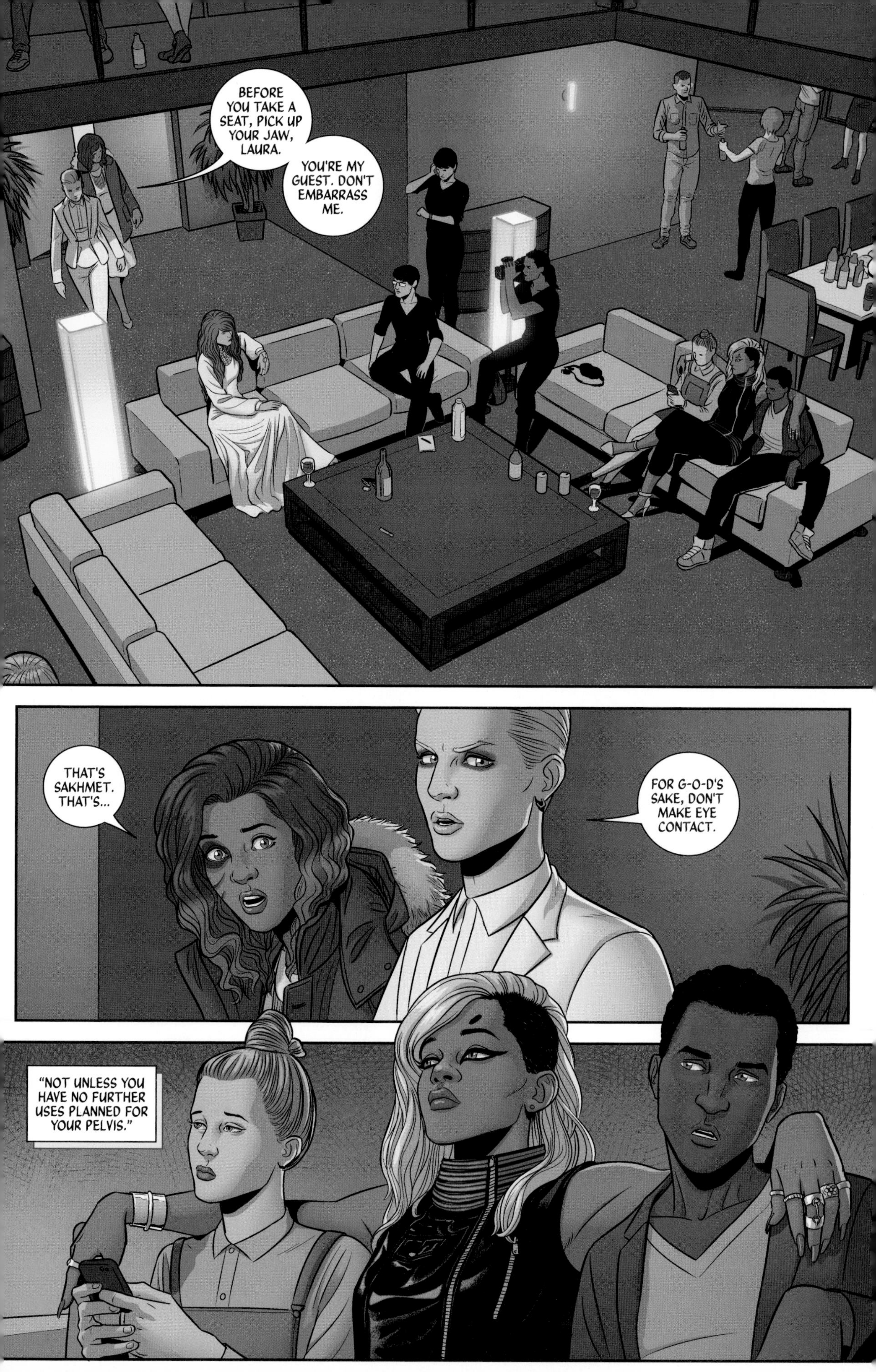
BEFORE YOU TAKE A SEAT, PICK UP YOUR JAW, LAURA.
YOU'RE MY GUEST. DON'T EMBARRASS ME.
THAT'S SAKHMET. THAT'S...
FOR G-O-D'S SAKE, DON'T MAKE EYE CONTACT.
"NOT UNLESS YOU HAVE NO FURTHER USES PLANNED FOR YOUR PELVIS."

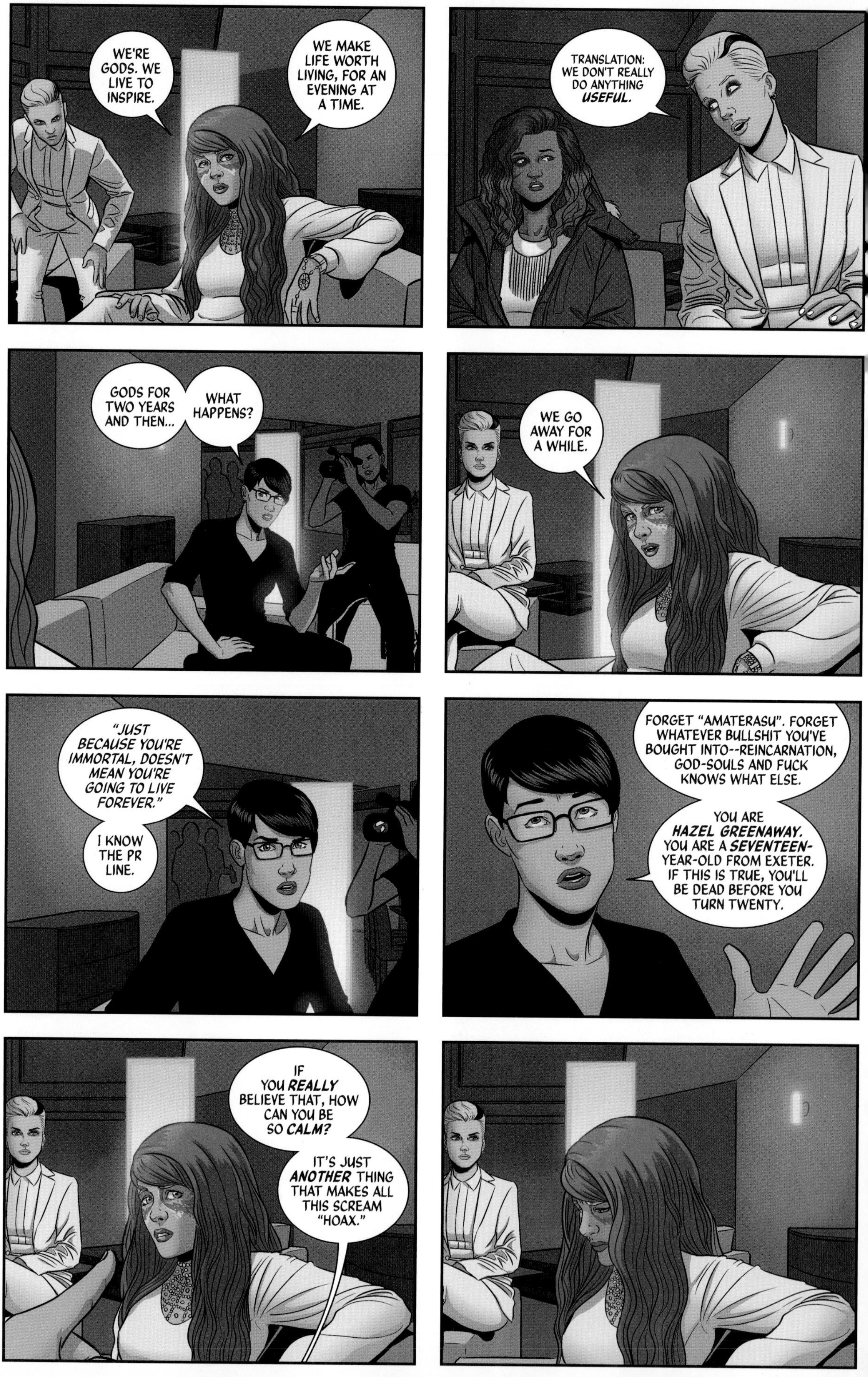
WE'RE GODS. WE LIVE TO INSPIRE.
WE MAKE LIFE WORTH LIVING, FOR AN EVENING AT A TIME.
TRANSLATION: WE DON'T REALLY DO ANYTHING *USEFUL.*
GODS FOR TWO YEARS AND THEN...
WHAT HAPPENS?
WE GO AWAY FOR A WHILE.
"JUST BECAUSE YOU'RE IMMORTAL, DOESN'T MEAN YOU'RE GOING TO LIVE FOREVER."
I KNOW THE PR LINE.
FORGET "AMATERASU". FORGET WHATEVER BULLSHIT YOU'VE BOUGHT INTO--REINCARNATION, GOD-SOULS AND FUCK KNOWS WHAT ELSE.
YOU ARE ***HAZEL GREENAWAY.*** YOU ARE A ***SEVENTEEN-***YEAR-OLD FROM EXETER. IF THIS IS TRUE, YOU'LL BE DEAD BEFORE YOU TURN TWENTY.
IF YOU ***REALLY*** BELIEVE THAT, HOW CAN YOU BE SO ***CALM?***
IT'S JUST ***ANOTHER*** THING THAT MAKES ALL THIS SCREAM "HOAX."

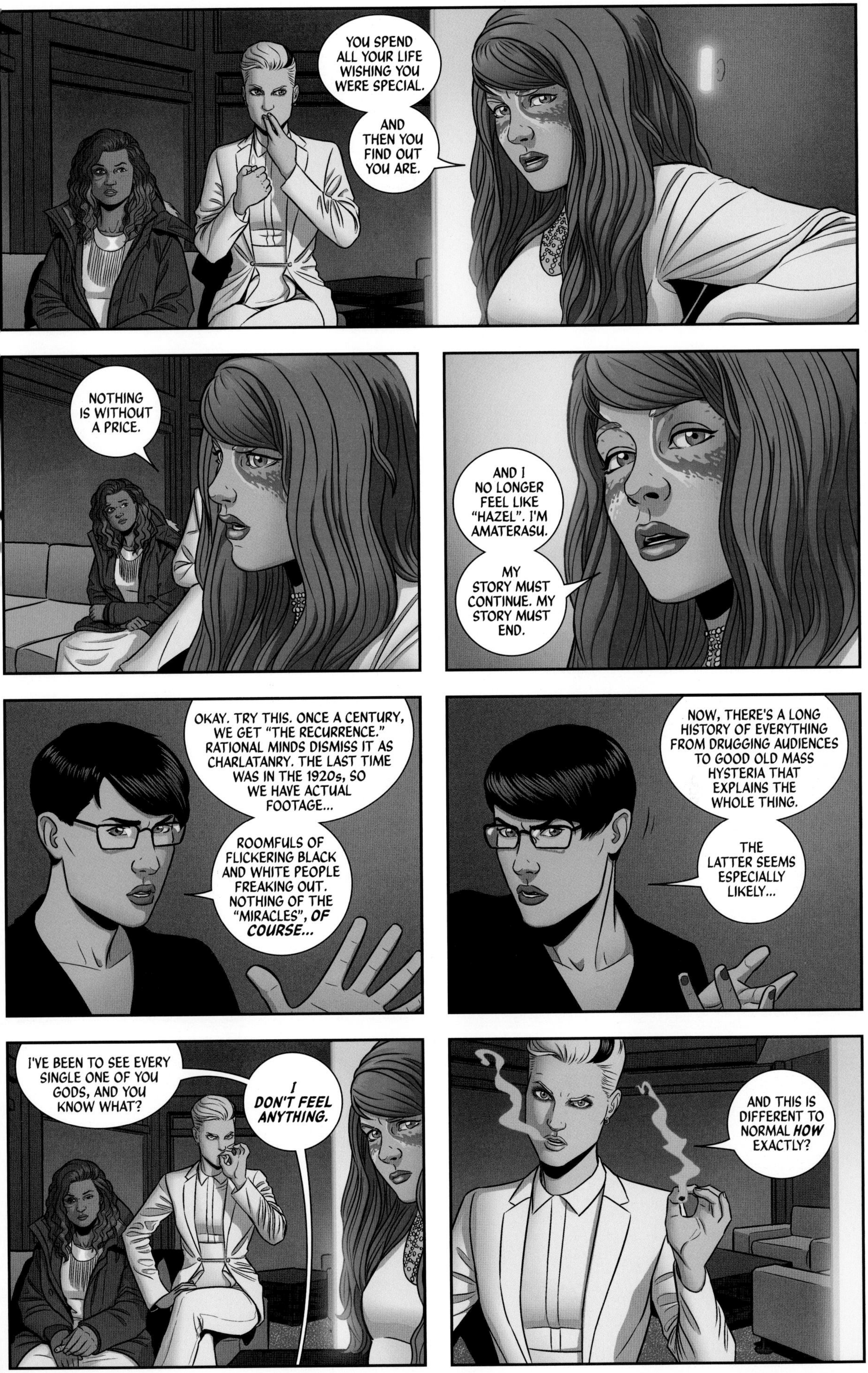
YOU SPEND ALL YOUR LIFE WISHING YOU WERE SPECIAL.
AND THEN YOU FIND OUT YOU ARE.
NOTHING IS WITHOUT A PRICE.
AND I NO LONGER FEEL LIKE "HAZEL". I'M AMATERASU.
MY STORY MUST CONTINUE. MY STORY MUST END.
OKAY. TRY THIS. ONCE A CENTURY, WE GET "THE RECURRENCE." RATIONAL MINDS DISMISS IT AS CHARLATANRY. THE LAST TIME WAS IN THE 1920s, SO WE HAVE ACTUAL FOOTAGE...
ROOMFULS OF FLICKERING BLACK AND WHITE PEOPLE FREAKING OUT. NOTHING OF THE "MIRACLES", OF COURSE...
NOW, THERE'S A LONG HISTORY OF EVERYTHING FROM DRUGGING AUDIENCES TO GOOD OLD MASS HYSTERIA THAT EXPLAINS THE WHOLE THING.
THE LATTER SEEMS ESPECIALLY LIKELY...
I'VE BEEN TO SEE EVERY SINGLE ONE OF YOU GODS, AND YOU KNOW WHAT?
I DON'T FEEL ANYTHING.
AND THIS IS DIFFERENT TO NORMAL HOW EXACTLY?

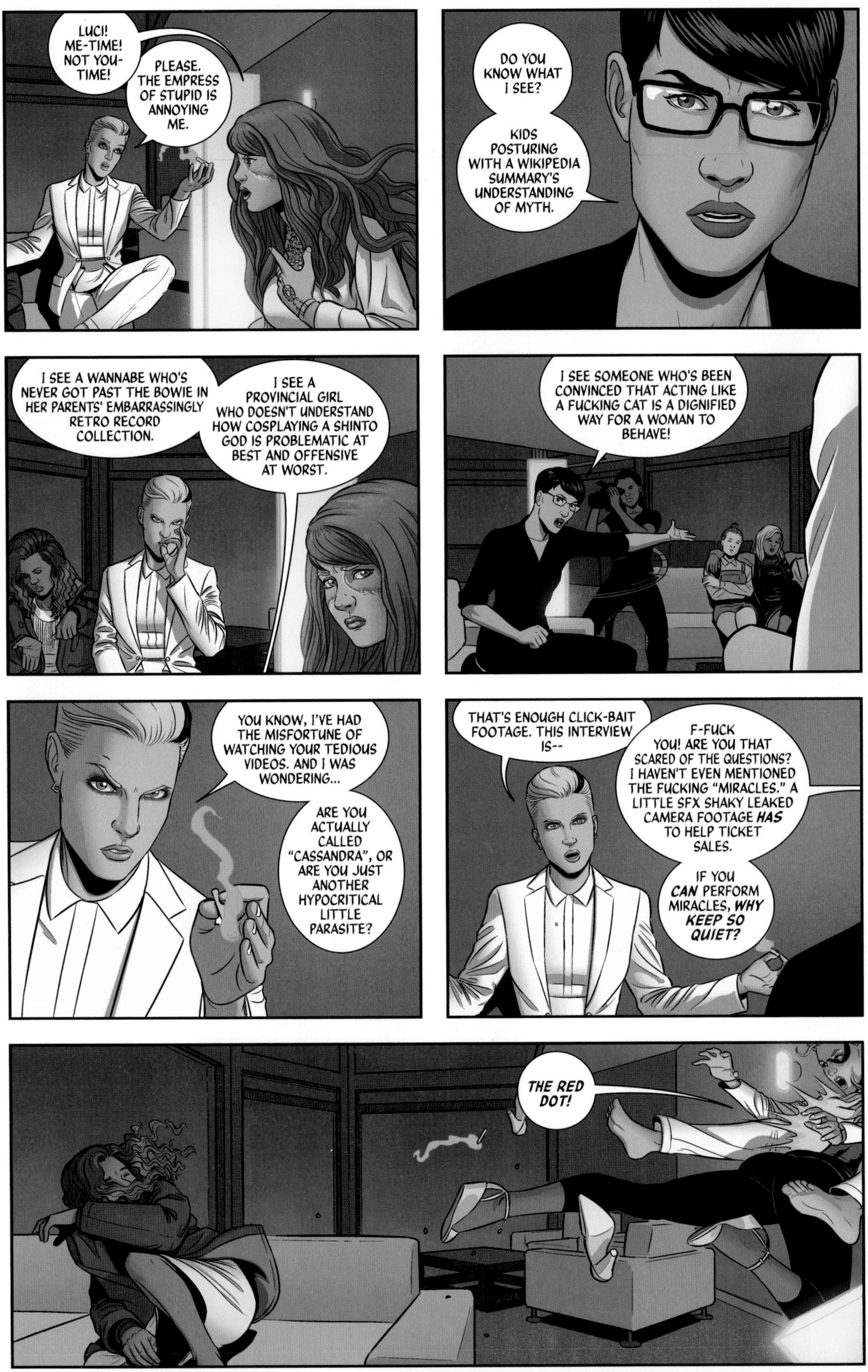

LUCI! ME-TIME! NOT YOU-TIME!
PLEASE. THE EMPRESS OF STUPID IS ANNOYING ME.
DO YOU KNOW WHAT I SEE?
KIDS POSTURING WITH A WIKIPEDIA SUMMARY'S UNDERSTANDING OF MYTH.
I SEE A WANNABE WHO'S NEVER GOT PAST THE BOWIE IN HER PARENTS' EMBARRASSINGLY RETRO RECORD COLLECTION.
I SEE A PROVINCIAL GIRL WHO DOESN'T UNDERSTAND HOW COSPLAYING A SHINTO GOD IS PROBLEMATIC AT BEST AND OFFENSIVE AT WORST.
I SEE SOMEONE WHO'S BEEN CONVINCED THAT ACTING LIKE A FUCKING CAT IS A DIGNIFIED WAY FOR A WOMAN TO BEHAVE!
YOU KNOW, I'VE HAD THE MISFORTUNE OF WATCHING YOUR TEDIOUS VIDEOS. AND I WAS WONDERING...
ARE YOU ACTUALLY CALLED "CASSANDRA", OR ARE YOU JUST ANOTHER HYPOCRITICAL LITTLE PARASITE?
THAT'S ENOUGH CLICK-BAIT FOOTAGE. THIS INTERVIEW IS--
F-FUCK YOU! ARE YOU THAT SCARED OF THE QUESTIONS? I HAVEN'T EVEN MENTIONED THE FUCKING "MIRACLES." A LITTLE SFX SHAKY LEAKED CAMERA FOOTAGE ***HAS*** TO HELP TICKET SALES.
IF YOU ***CAN*** PERFORM MIRACLES, ***WHY KEEP SO QUIET?***
THE RED DOT!

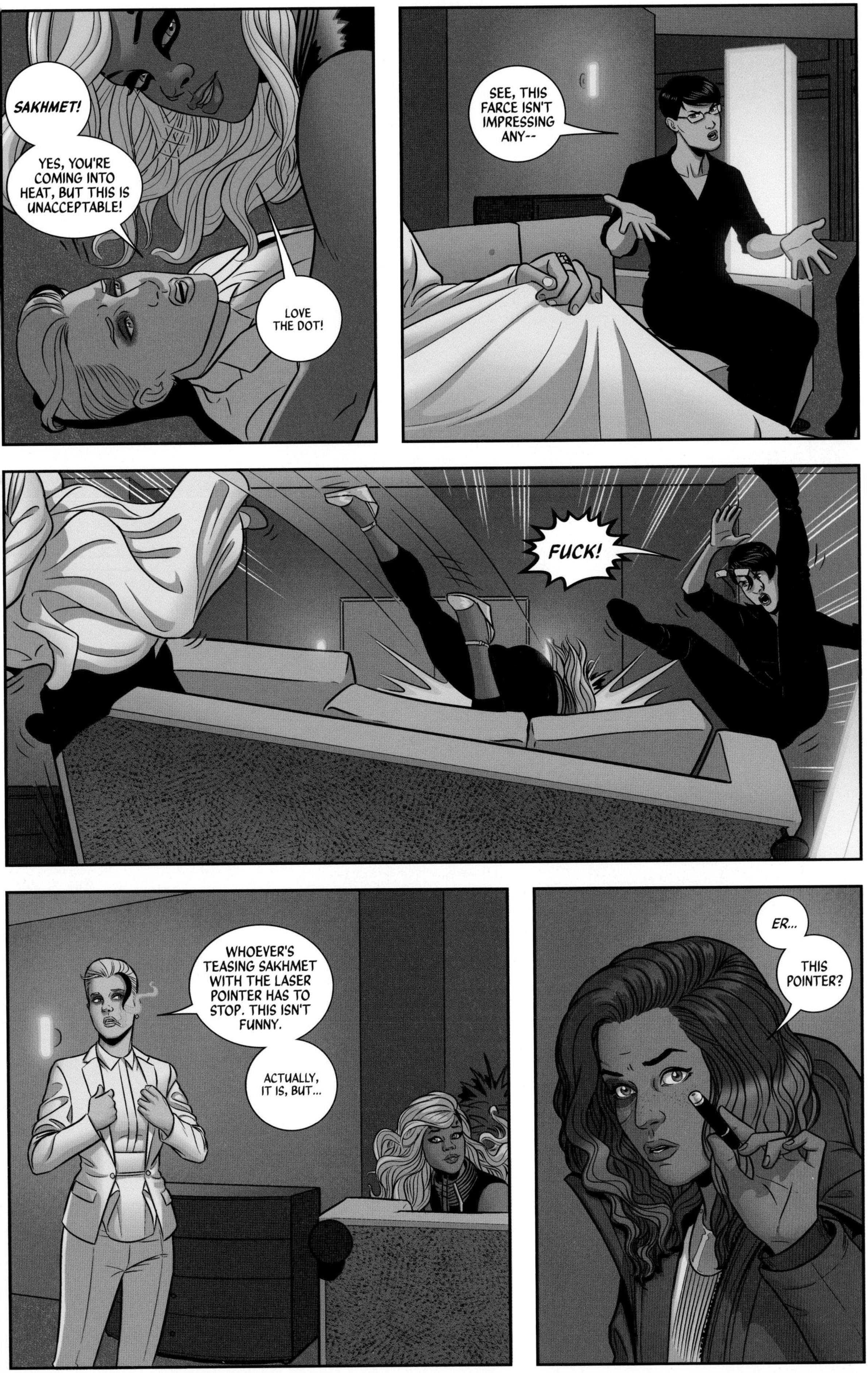
SAKHMET!
YES, YOU'RE COMING INTO HEAT, BUT THIS IS UNACCEPTABLE!
LOVE THE DOT!
SEE, THIS FARCE ISN'T IMPRESSING ANY--
FUCK!
WHOEVER'S TEASING SAKHMET WITH THE LASER POINTER HAS TO STOP. THIS ISN'T FUNNY.
ACTUALLY, IT IS, BUT...
ER...
THIS POINTER?

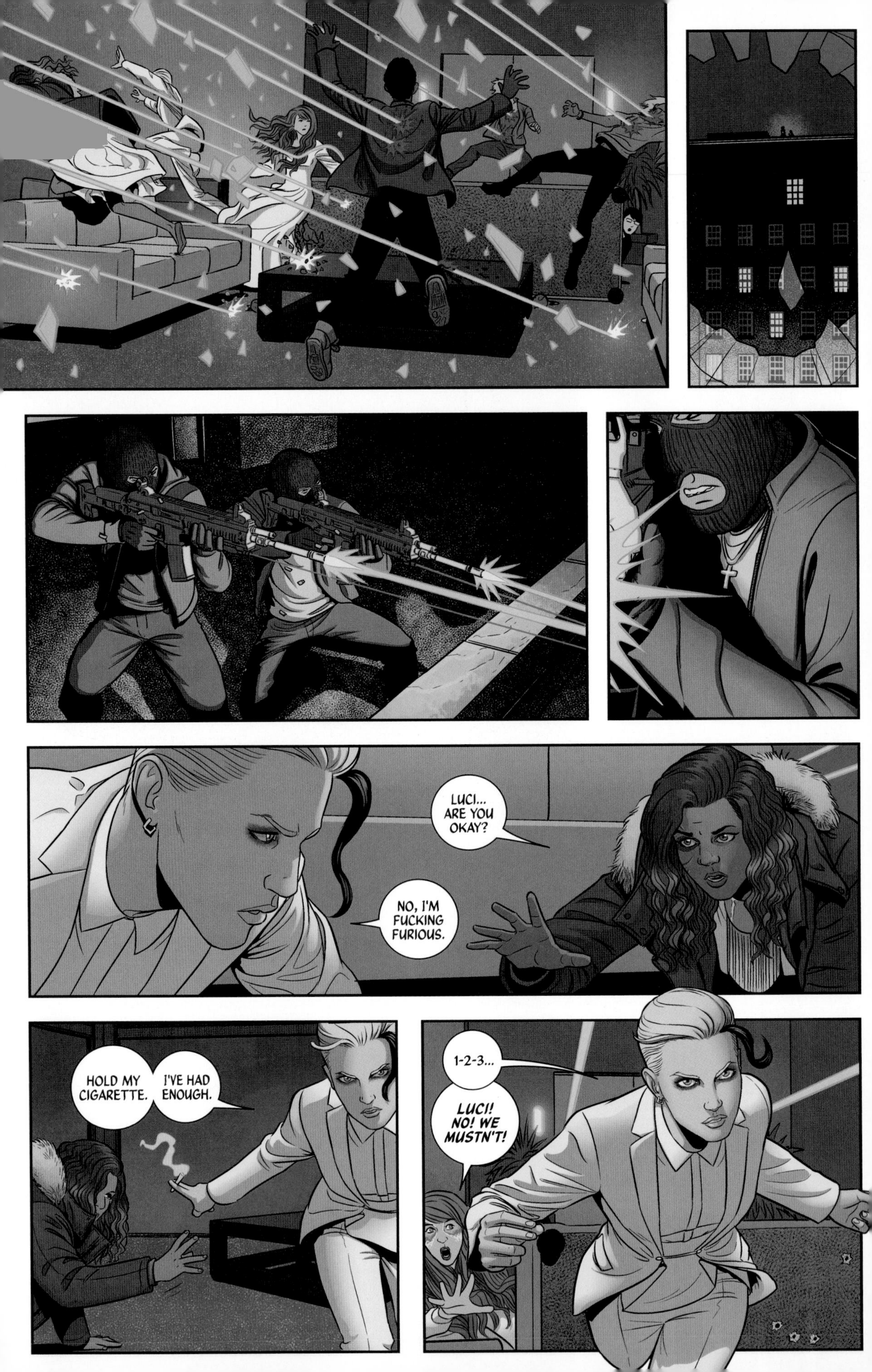
LUCI... ARE YOU OKAY?
NO, I'M FUCKING FURIOUS.
HOLD MY CIGARETTE.
I'VE HAD ENOUGH.
1-2-3...
LUCI! NO! WE MUSTN'T!

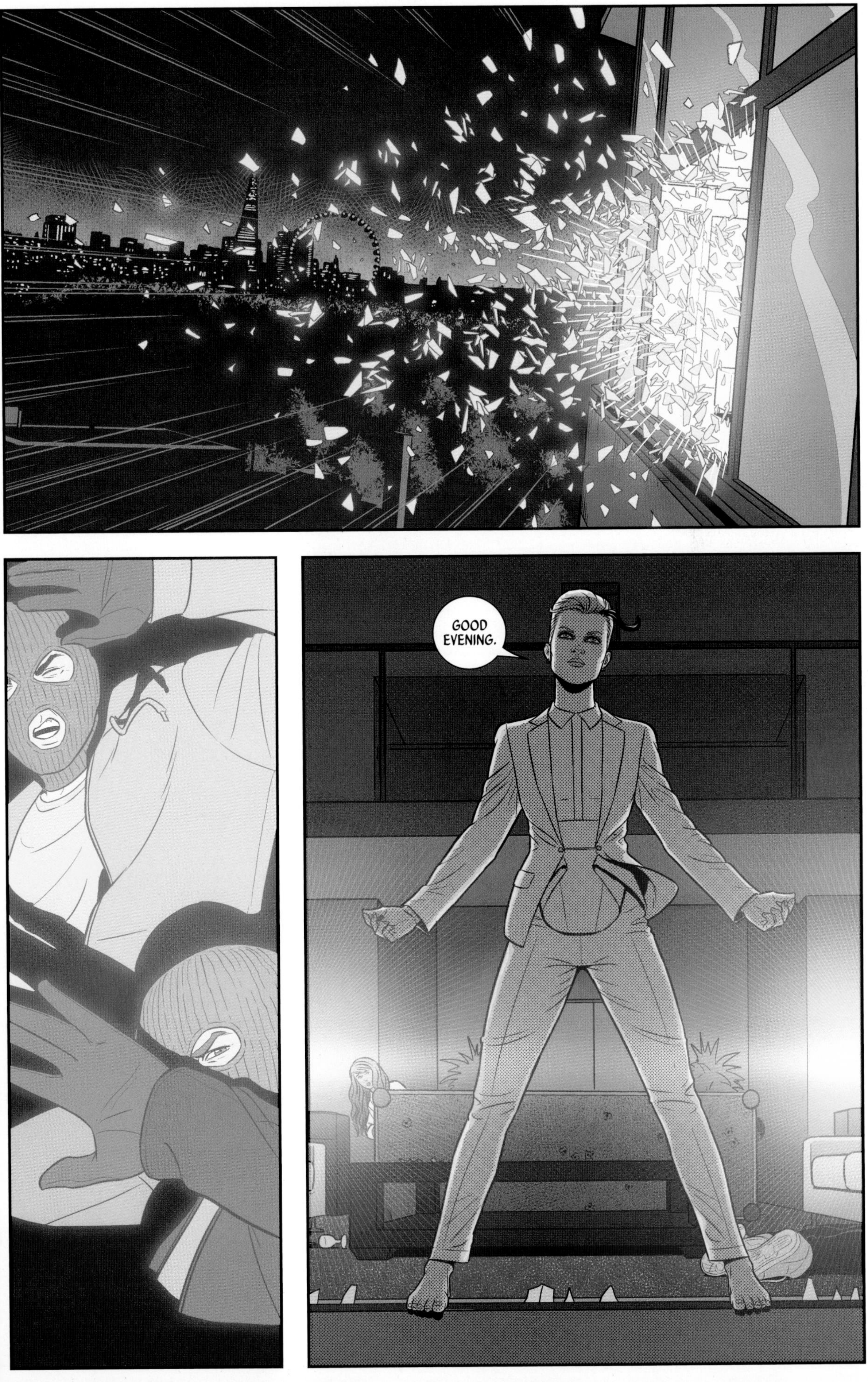
GOOD EVENING.

DIE, LUCIFER!
HEY, YOU GUESSED MY NAME.
KLLK
KLLK

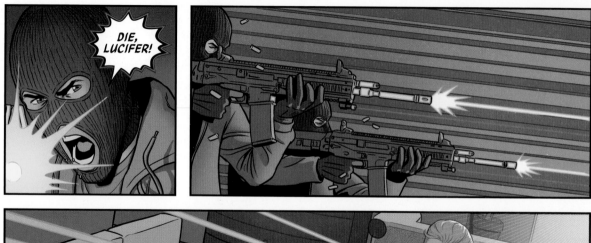

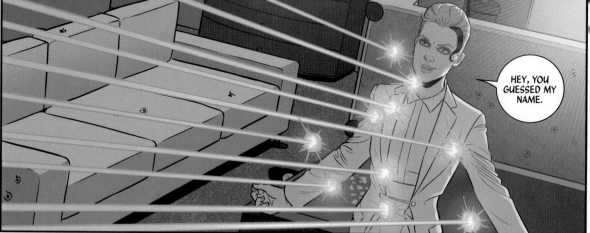

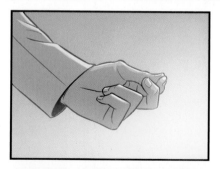

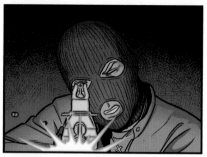

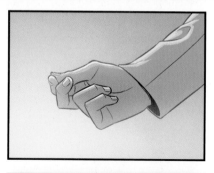

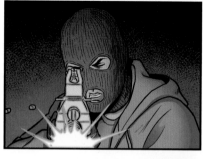

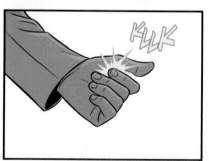

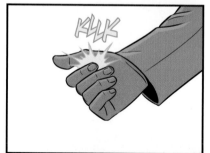

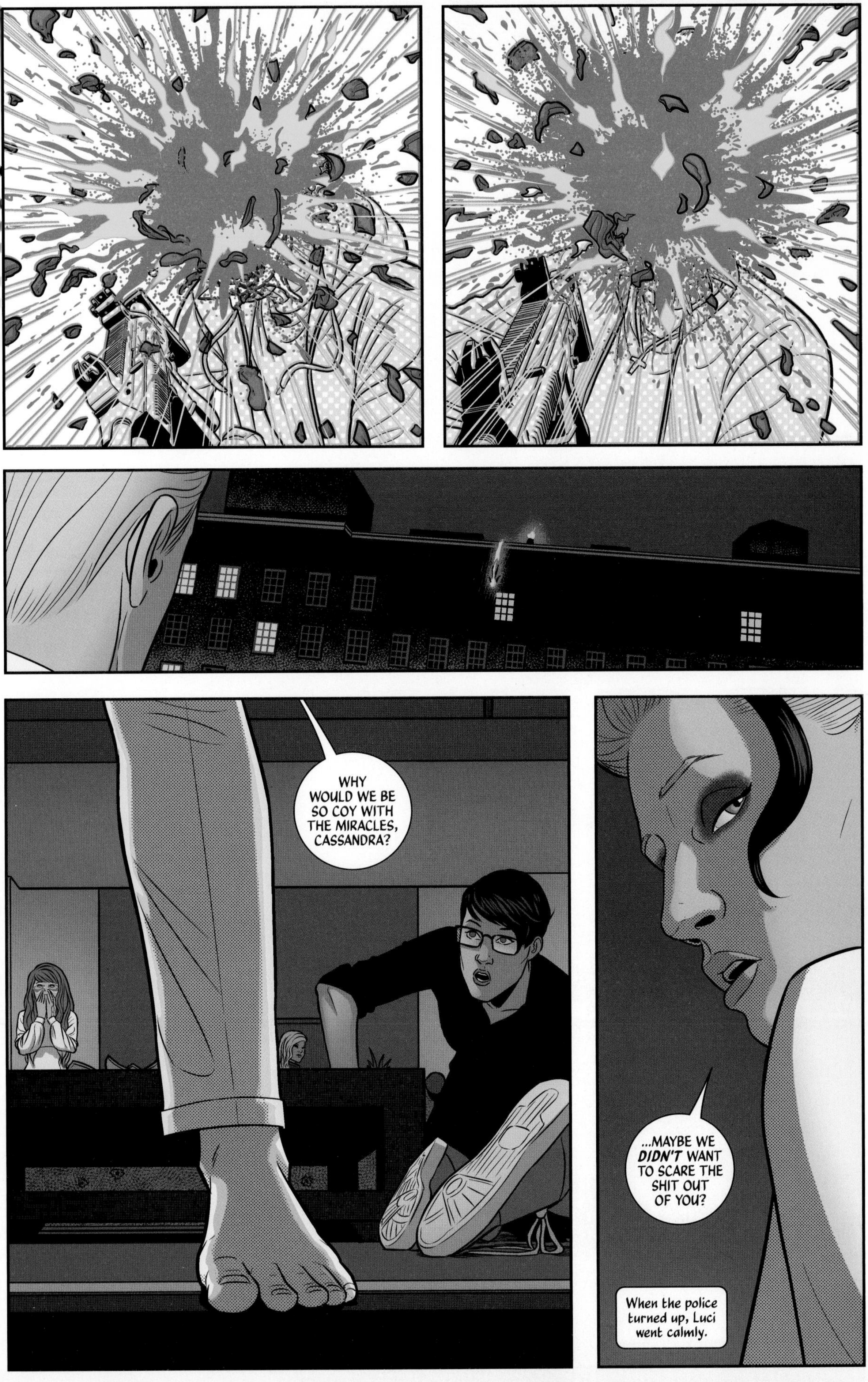
WHY WOULD WE BE SO COY WITH THE MIRACLES, CASSANDRA?
...MAYBE WE *DIDN'T* WANT TO SCARE THE SHIT OUT OF YOU?
When the police turned up, Luci went calmly.

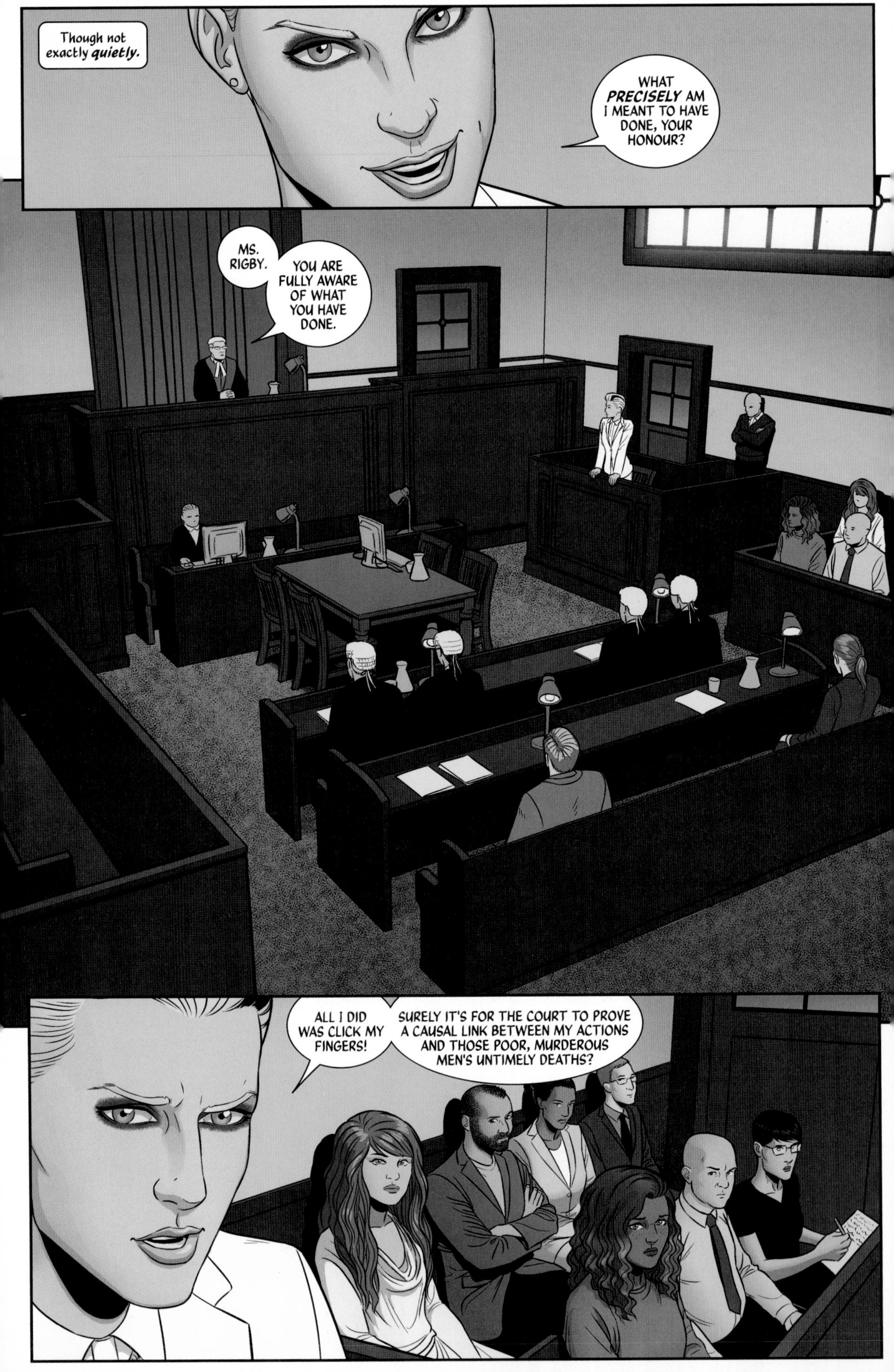

Though not exactly *quietly*.
WHAT *PRECISELY* AM I MEANT TO HAVE DONE, YOUR HONOUR?
MS. RIGBY.
YOU ARE FULLY AWARE OF WHAT YOU HAVE DONE.
ALL I DID WAS CLICK MY FINGERS!
SURELY IT'S FOR THE COURT TO PROVE A CAUSAL LINK BETWEEN MY ACTIONS AND THOSE POOR, MURDEROUS MEN'S UNTIMELY DEATHS?

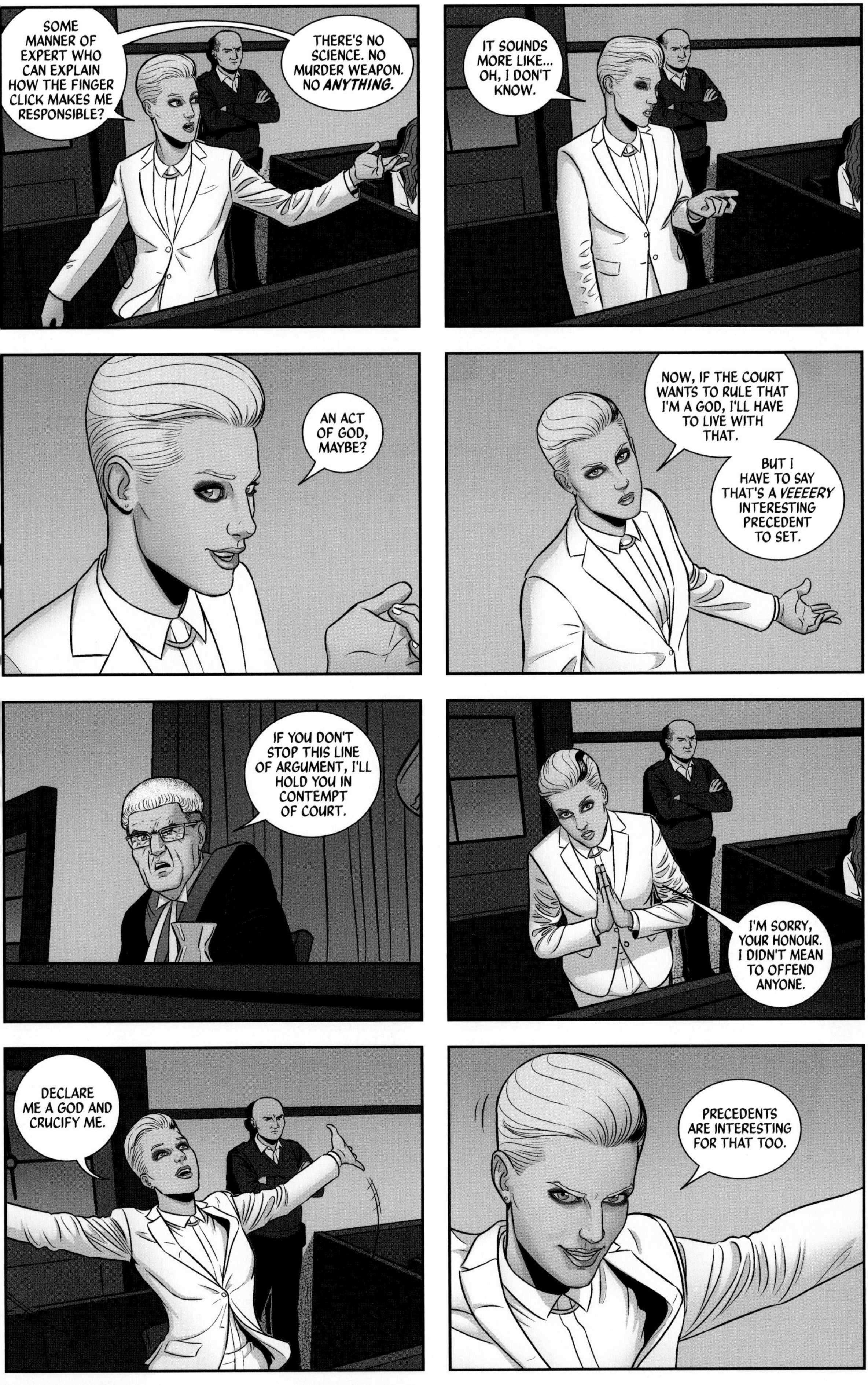
SOME MANNER OF EXPERT WHO CAN EXPLAIN HOW THE FINGER CLICK MAKES ME RESPONSIBLE?
THERE'S NO SCIENCE. NO MURDER WEAPON. NO *ANYTHING.*
IT SOUNDS MORE LIKE... OH, I DON'T KNOW.
AN ACT OF GOD, MAYBE?
NOW, IF THE COURT WANTS TO RULE THAT I'M A GOD, I'LL HAVE TO LIVE WITH THAT.
BUT I HAVE TO SAY THAT'S A *VEEEERY* INTERESTING PRECEDENT TO SET.
IF YOU DON'T STOP THIS LINE OF ARGUMENT, I'LL HOLD YOU IN CONTEMPT OF COURT.
I'M SORRY, YOUR HONOUR. I DIDN'T MEAN TO OFFEND ANYONE.
DECLARE ME A GOD AND CRUCIFY ME.
PRECEDENTS ARE INTERESTING FOR THAT TOO.

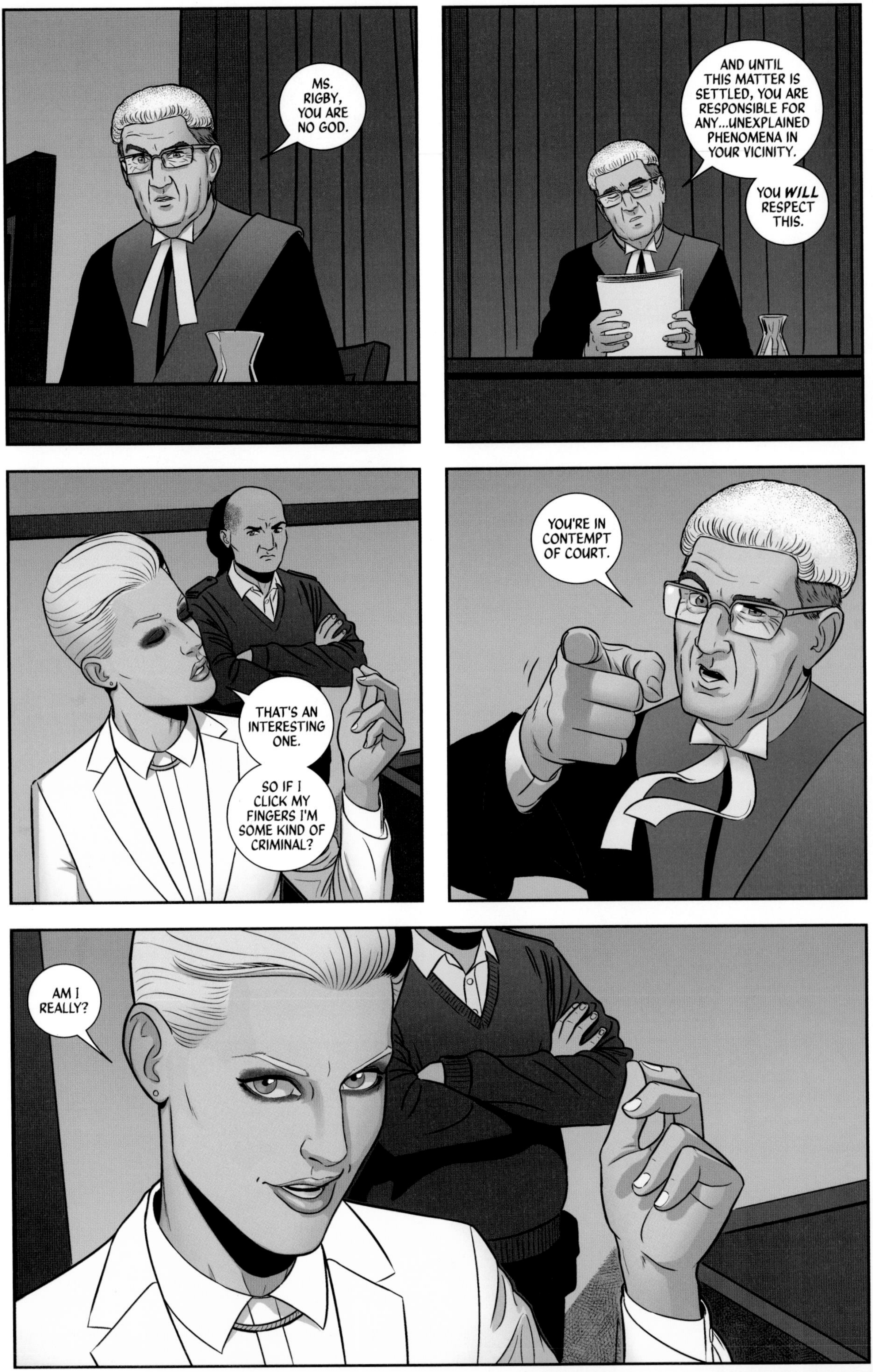
MS. RIGBY, YOU ARE NO GOD.
AND UNTIL THIS MATTER IS SETTLED, YOU ARE RESPONSIBLE FOR ANY...UNEXPLAINED PHENOMENA IN YOUR VICINITY.
YOU *WILL* RESPECT THIS.
THAT'S AN INTERESTING ONE.
SO IF I CLICK MY FINGERS I'M SOME KIND OF CRIMINAL?
YOU'RE IN CONTEMPT OF COURT.
AM I REALLY?

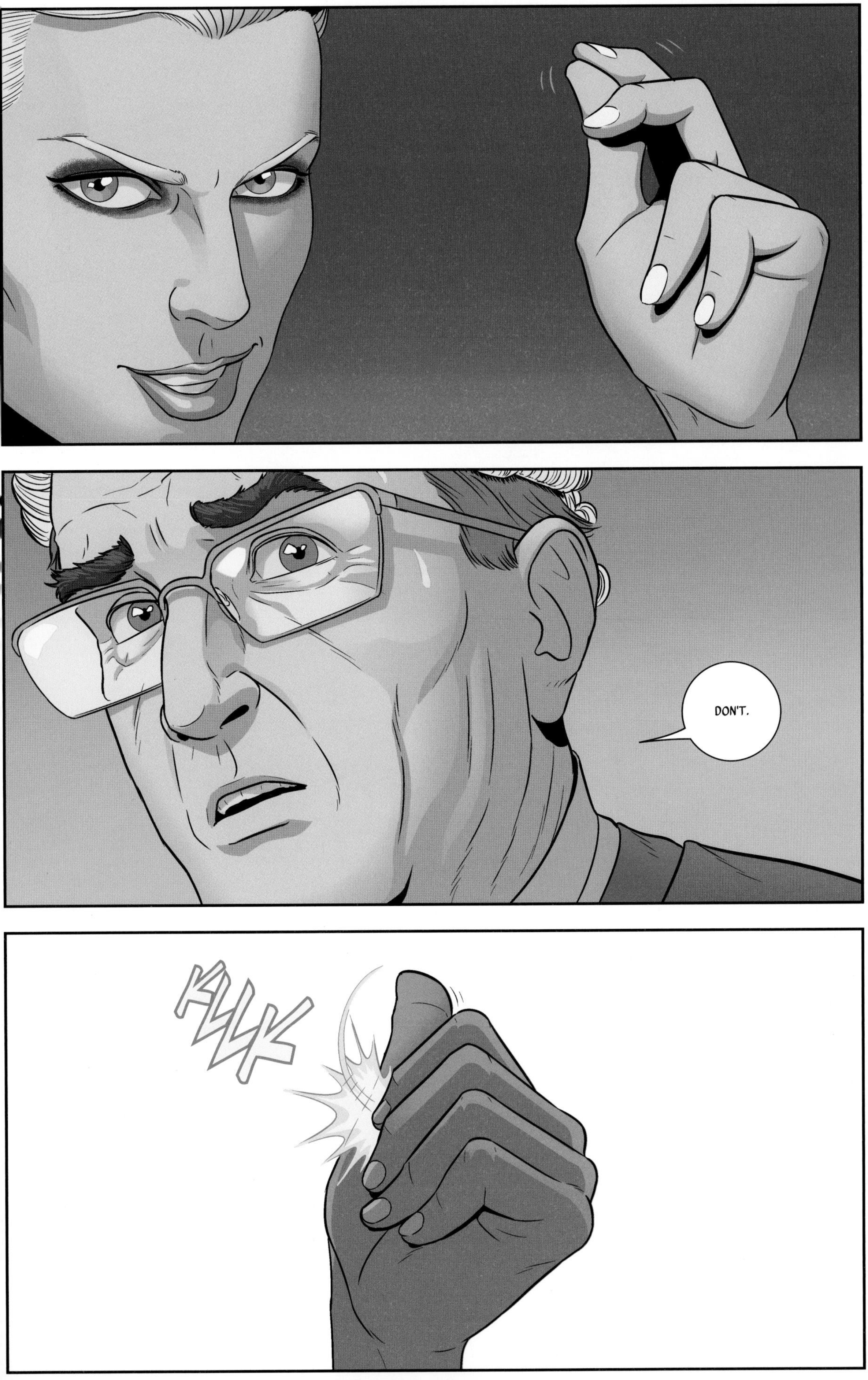
DON'T.

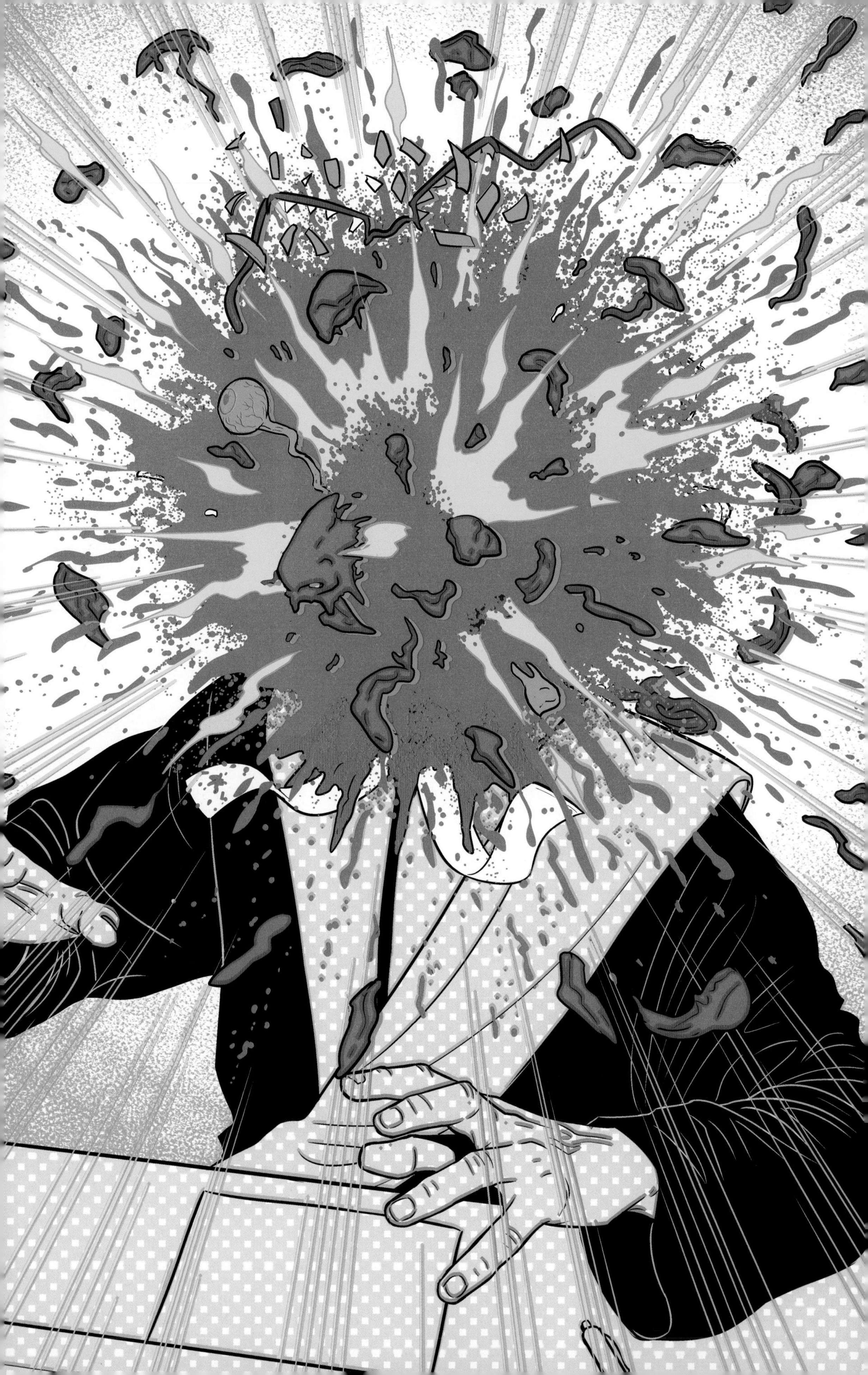

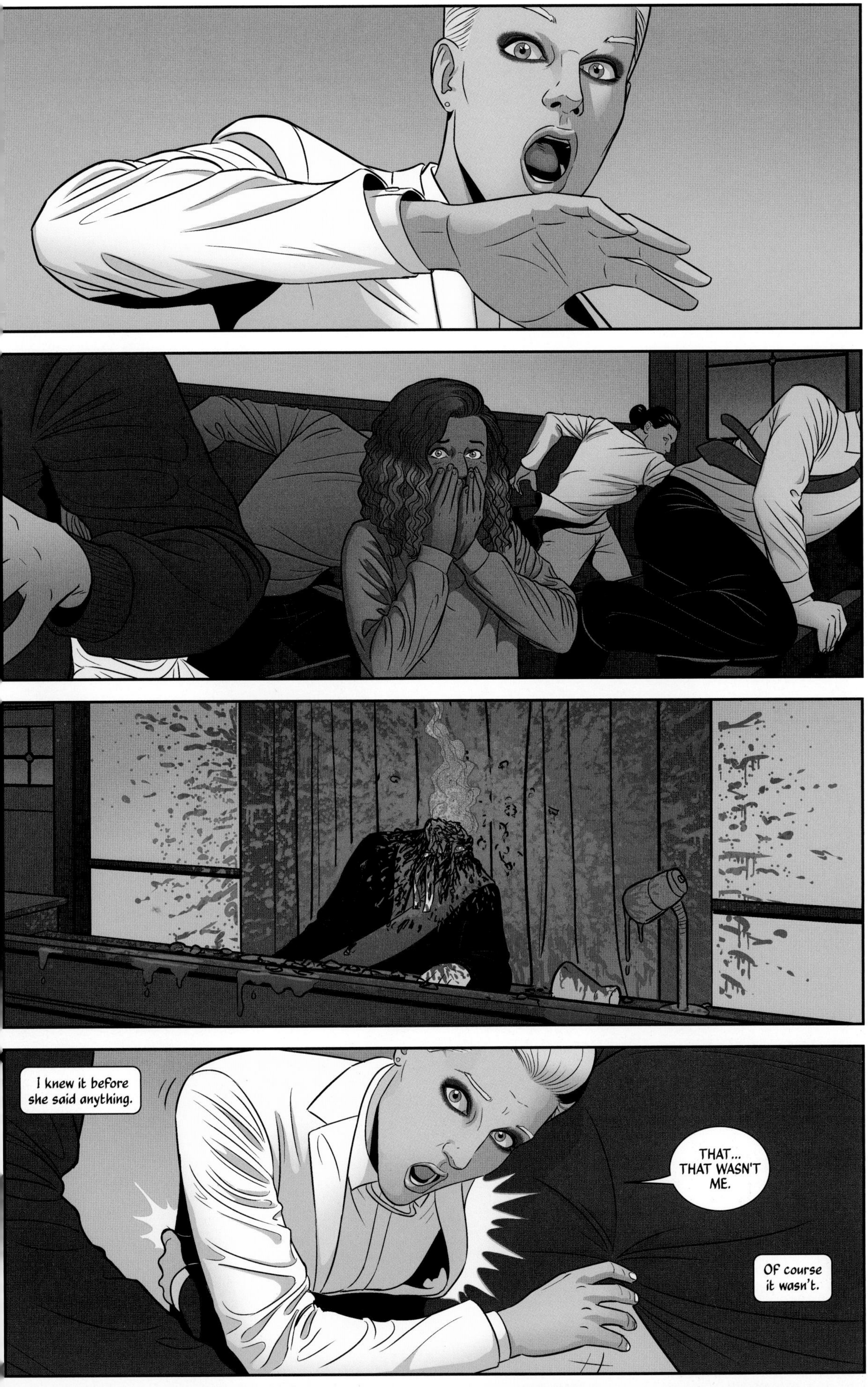
I knew it before she said anything.
THAT... THAT WASN'T ME.
Of course it wasn't.

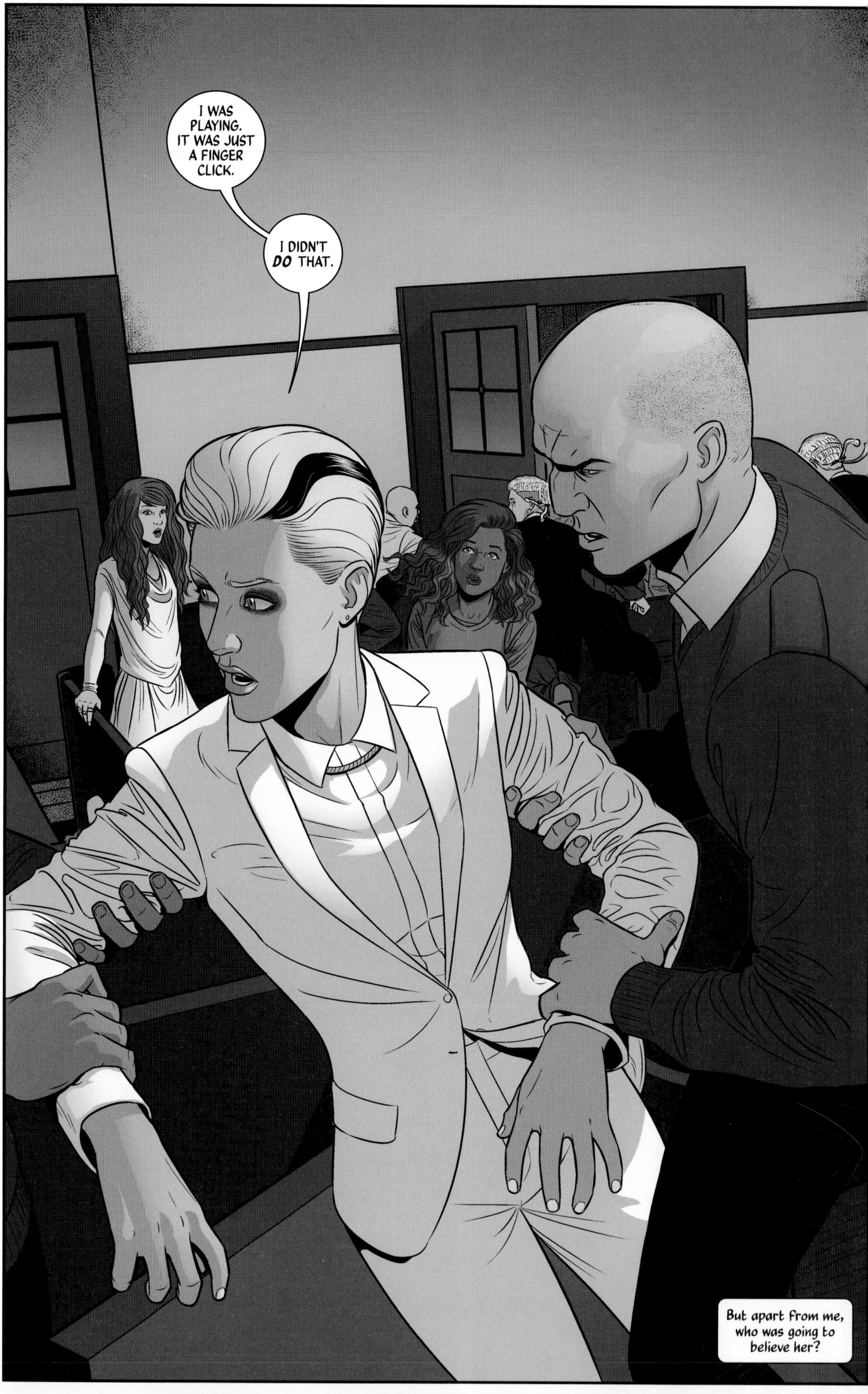
I WAS PLAYING. IT WAS JUST A FINGER CLICK.
I DIDN'T *DO* THAT.
But apart from me, who was going to believe her?

THE
WICKED
+
DIVINE
THE

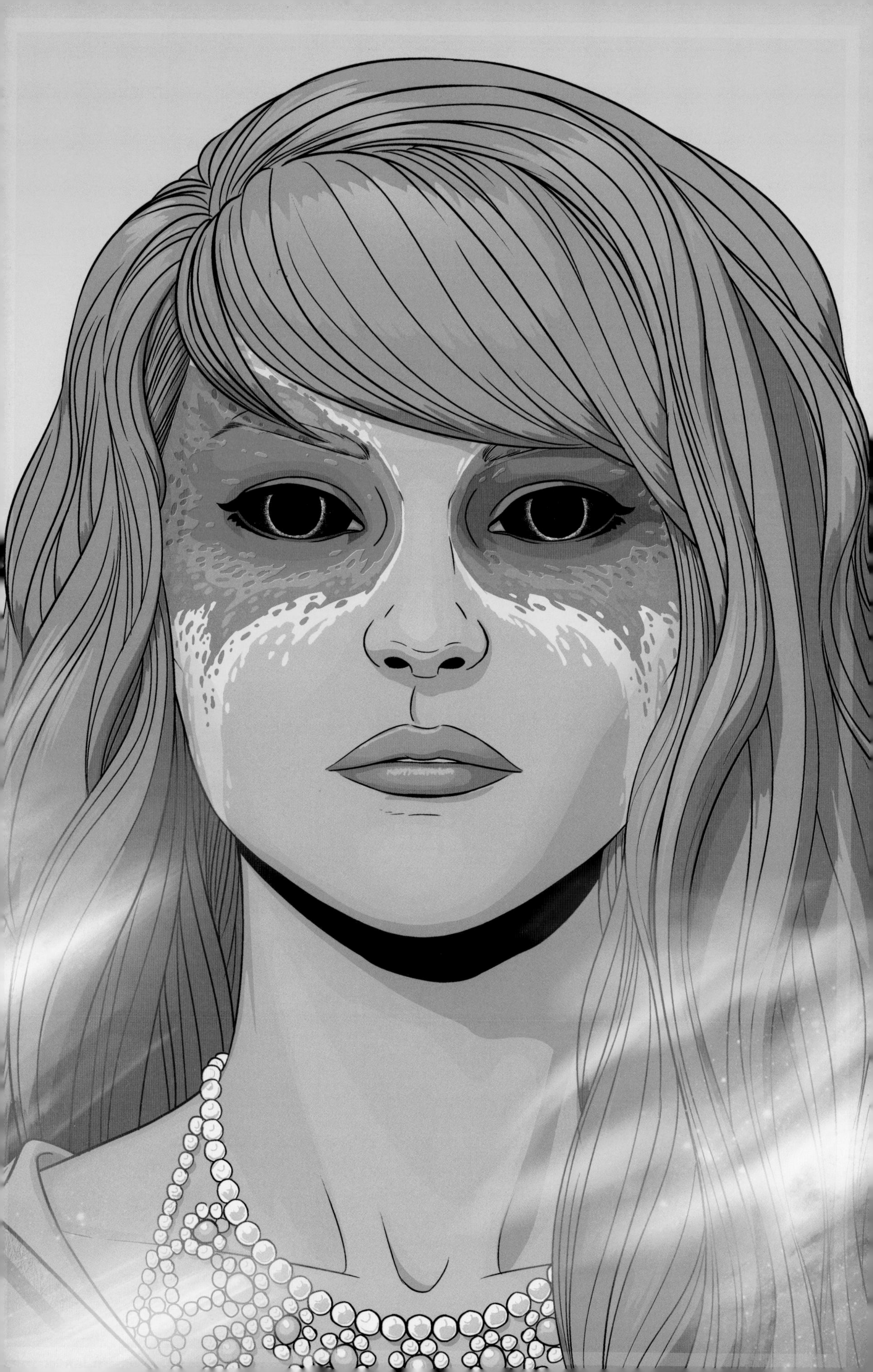

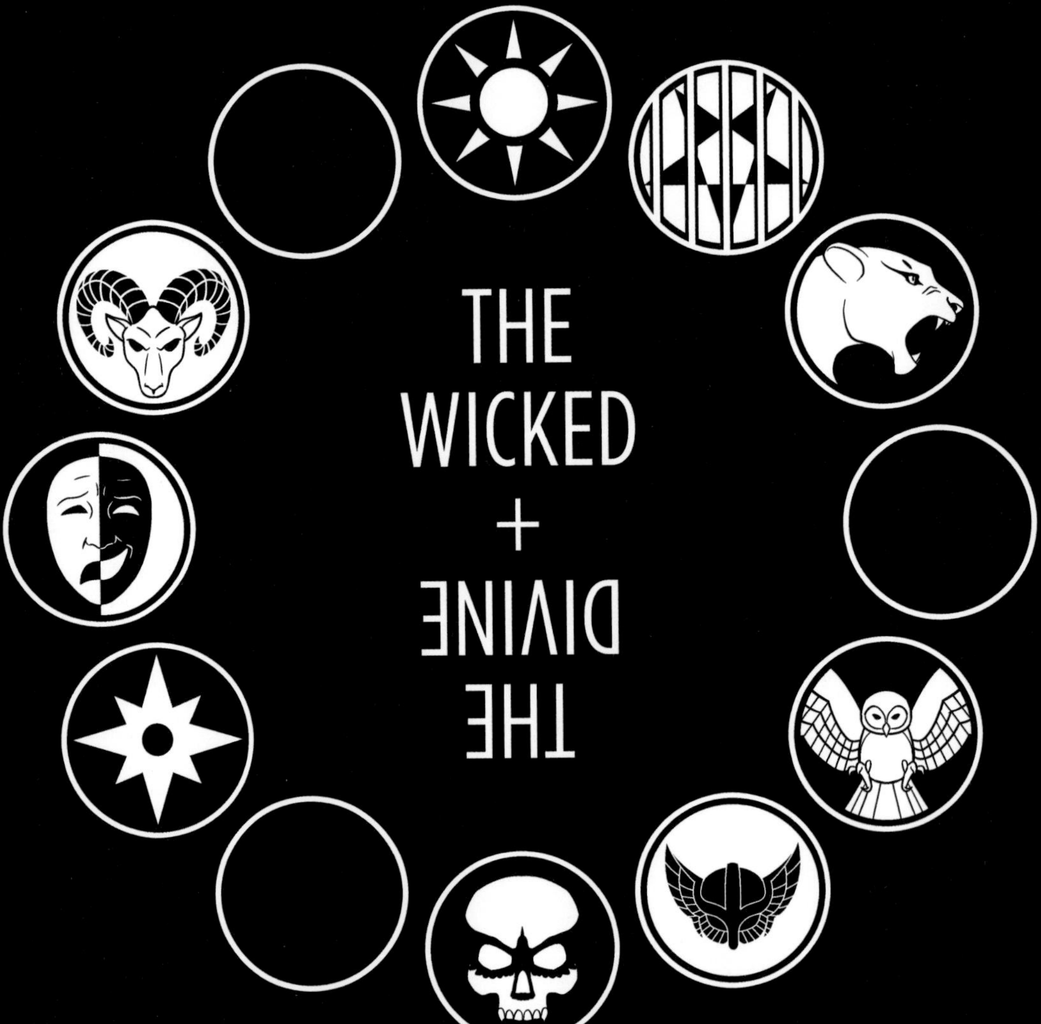
THE
WICKED
+
THE
DIVINE

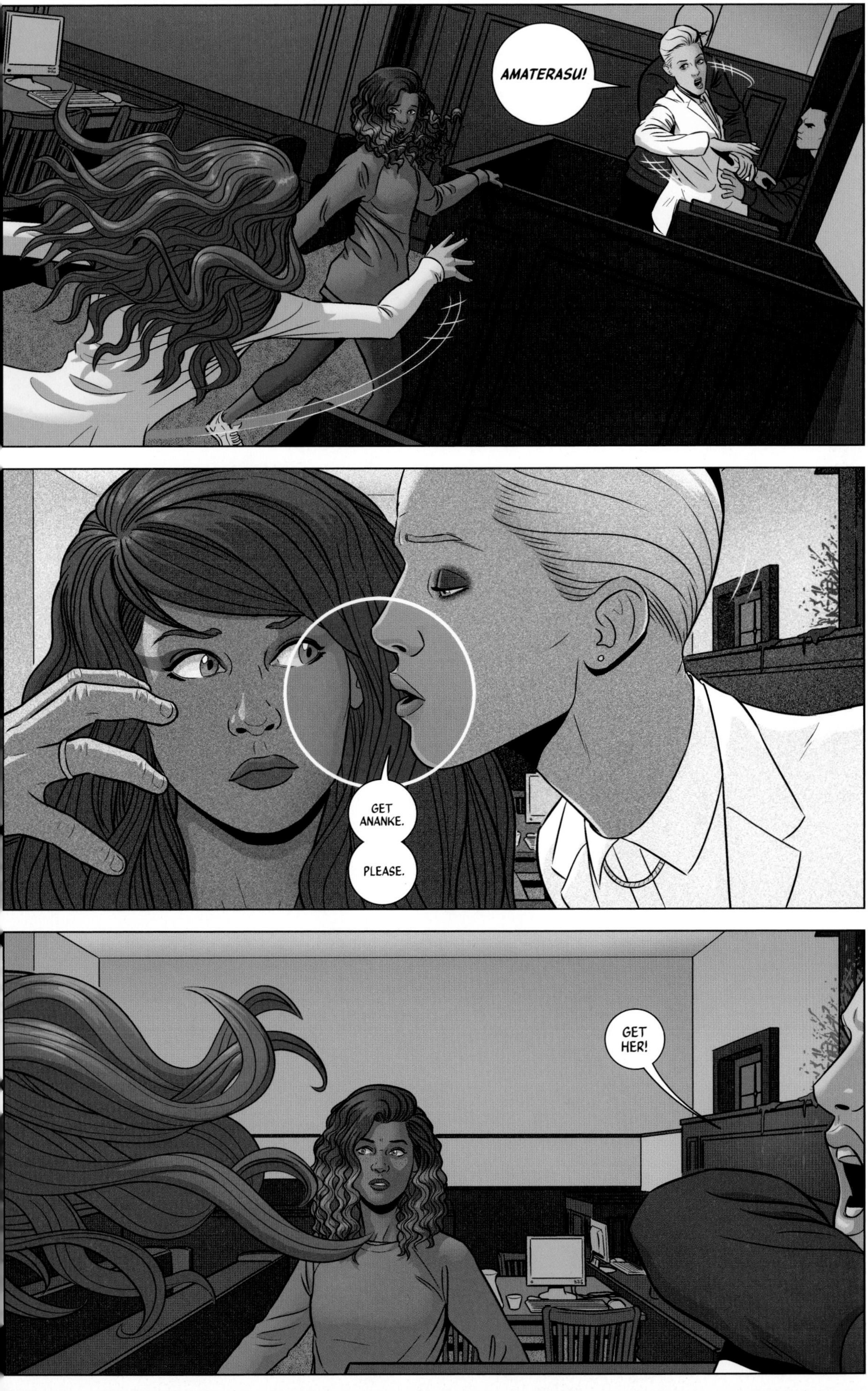
AMATERASU!
GET ANANKE.
PLEASE.
GET HER!

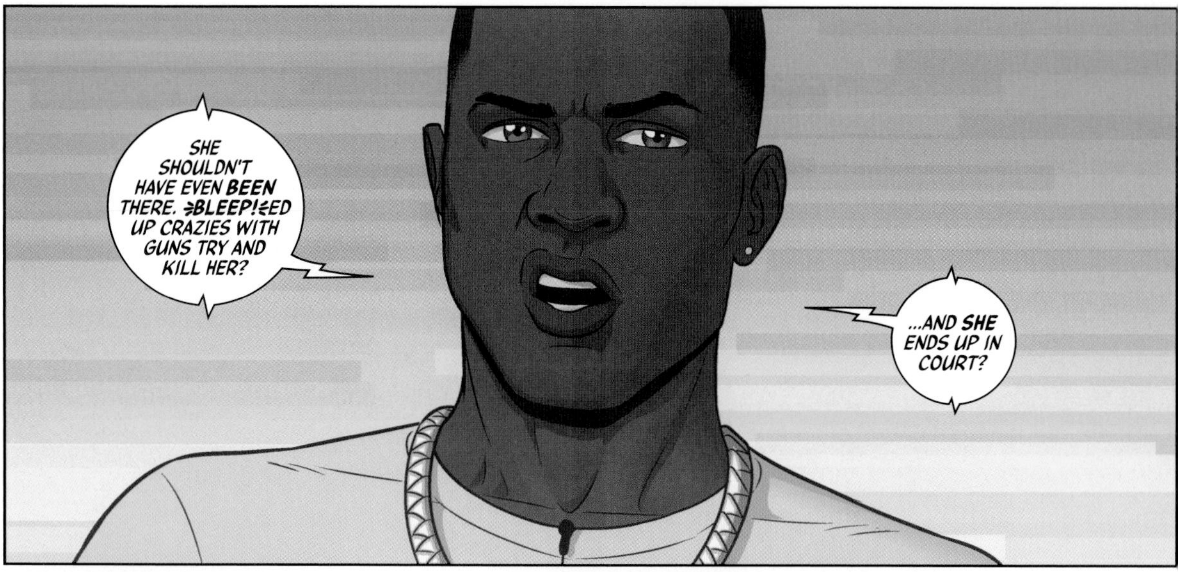
SHE SHOULDN'T HAVE EVEN BEEN THERE. ≯BLEEP!≮ED UP CRAZIES WITH GUNS TRY AND KILL HER?
...AND SHE ENDS UP IN COURT?

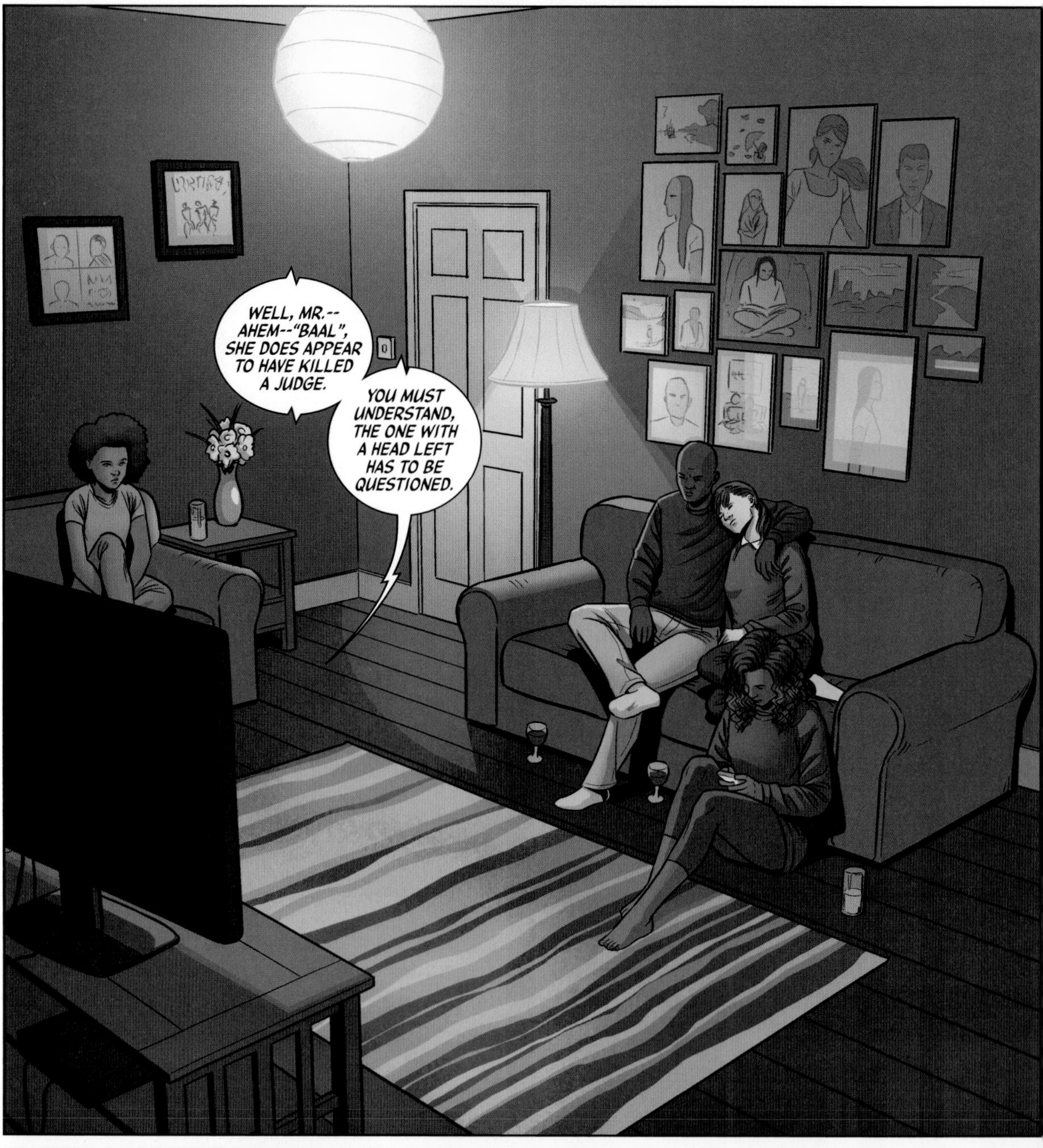
WELL, MR.--AHEM--"BAAL", SHE DOES APPEAR TO HAVE KILLED A JUDGE.
YOU MUST UNDERSTAND, THE ONE WITH A HEAD LEFT HAS TO BE QUESTIONED.

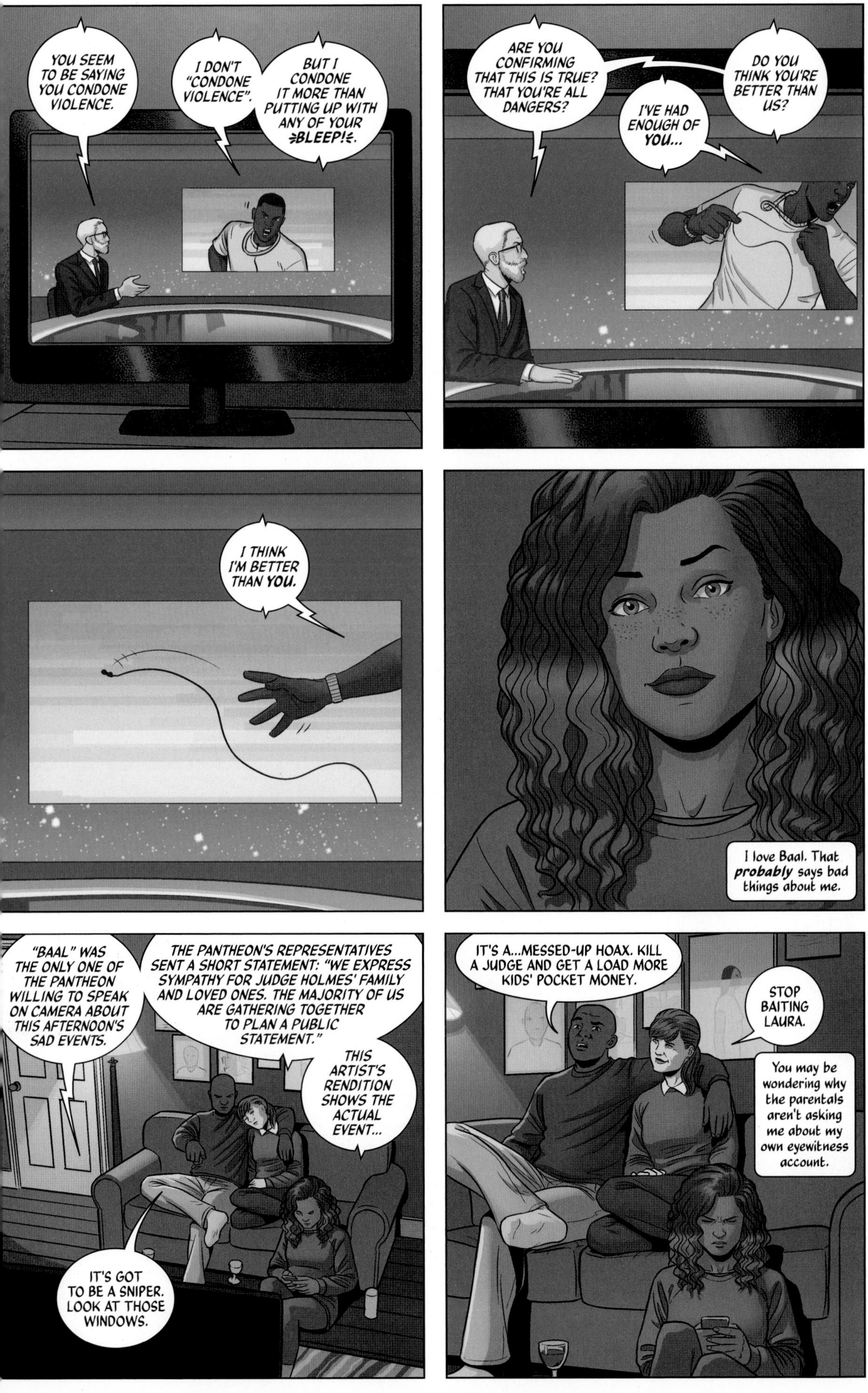
YOU SEEM TO BE SAYING YOU CONDONE VIOLENCE.
I DON'T "CONDONE VIOLENCE".
BUT I CONDONE IT MORE THAN PUTTING UP WITH ANY OF YOUR BLEEP!.
ARE YOU CONFIRMING THAT THIS IS TRUE? THAT YOU'RE ALL DANGERS?
DO YOU THINK YOU'RE BETTER THAN US?
I'VE HAD ENOUGH OF YOU...
I THINK I'M BETTER THAN YOU.
I love Baal. That probably says bad things about me.
"BAAL" WAS THE ONLY ONE OF THE PANTHEON WILLING TO SPEAK ON CAMERA ABOUT THIS AFTERNOON'S SAD EVENTS.
THE PANTHEON'S REPRESENTATIVES SENT A SHORT STATEMENT: "WE EXPRESS SYMPATHY FOR JUDGE HOLMES' FAMILY AND LOVED ONES. THE MAJORITY OF US ARE GATHERING TOGETHER TO PLAN A PUBLIC STATEMENT."
THIS ARTIST'S RENDITION SHOWS THE ACTUAL EVENT...
IT'S GOT TO BE A SNIPER. LOOK AT THOSE WINDOWS.
IT'S A...MESSED-UP HOAX. KILL A JUDGE AND GET A LOAD MORE KIDS' POCKET MONEY.
STOP BAITING LAURA.
You may be wondering why the parentals aren't asking me about my own eyewitness account.

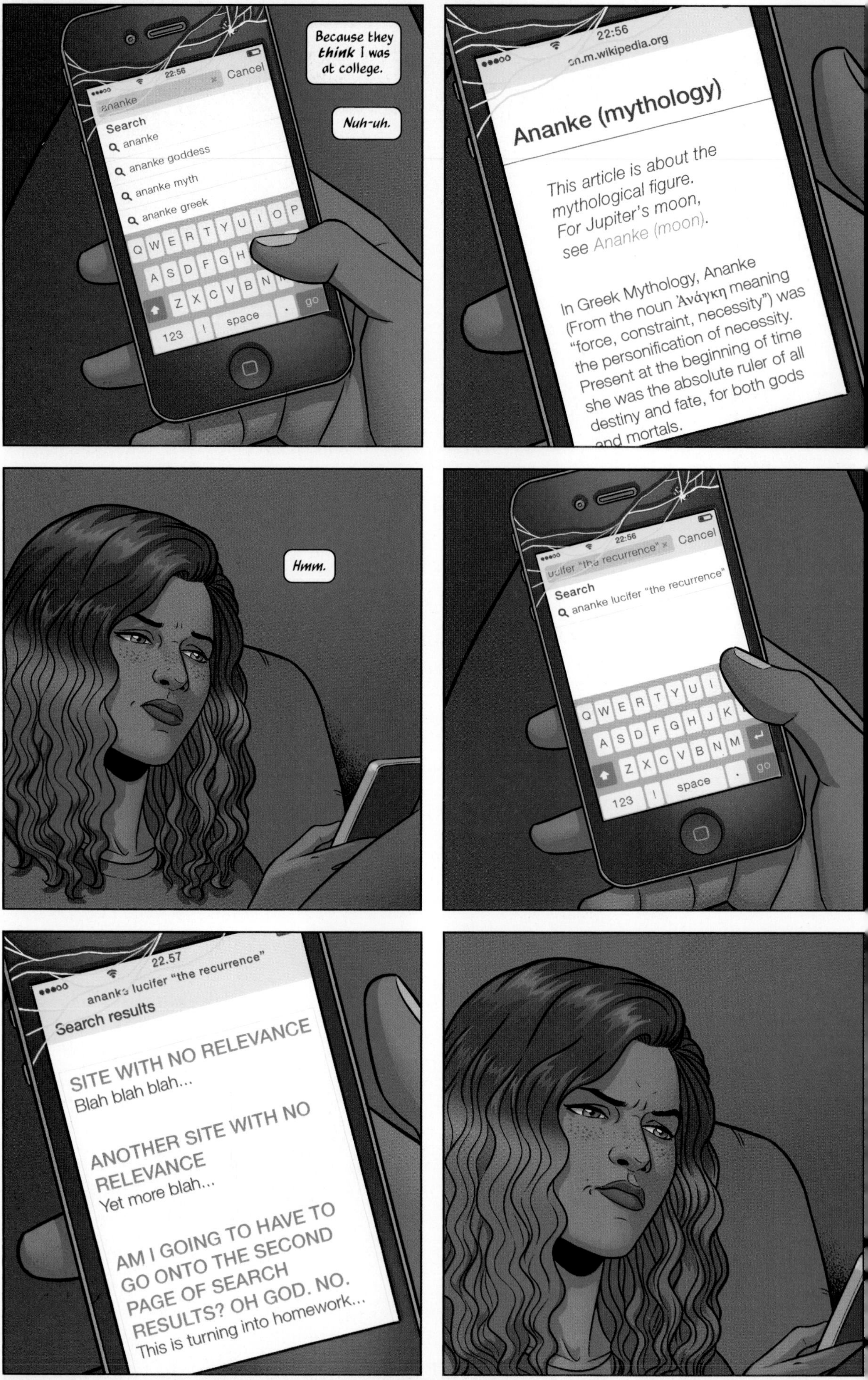
22:56
ananke
Cancel
Search
ananke
ananke goddess
ananke myth
ananke greek
Because they *think* I was at college.
Nuh-uh.
22:56
en.m.wikipedia.org
Ananke (mythology)
This article is about the mythological figure. For Jupiter's moon, see Ananke (moon).
In Greek Mythology, Ananke (From the noun Ἀνάγκη meaning "force, constraint, necessity") was the personification of necessity. Present at the beginning of time she was the absolute ruler of all destiny and fate, for both gods and mortals.
Hmm.
22:56
Cancel
Search
ananke lucifer "the recurrence"
22.57
ananke lucifer "the recurrence"
Search results
SITE WITH NO RELEVANCE
Blah blah blah...
ANOTHER SITE WITH NO RELEVANCE
Yet more blah...
AM I GOING TO HAVE TO GO ONTO THE SECOND PAGE OF SEARCH RESULTS? OH GOD. NO.
This is turning into homework...

THE NO-PINKIE
PINKIE SWEAR

ONE WEEK LATER

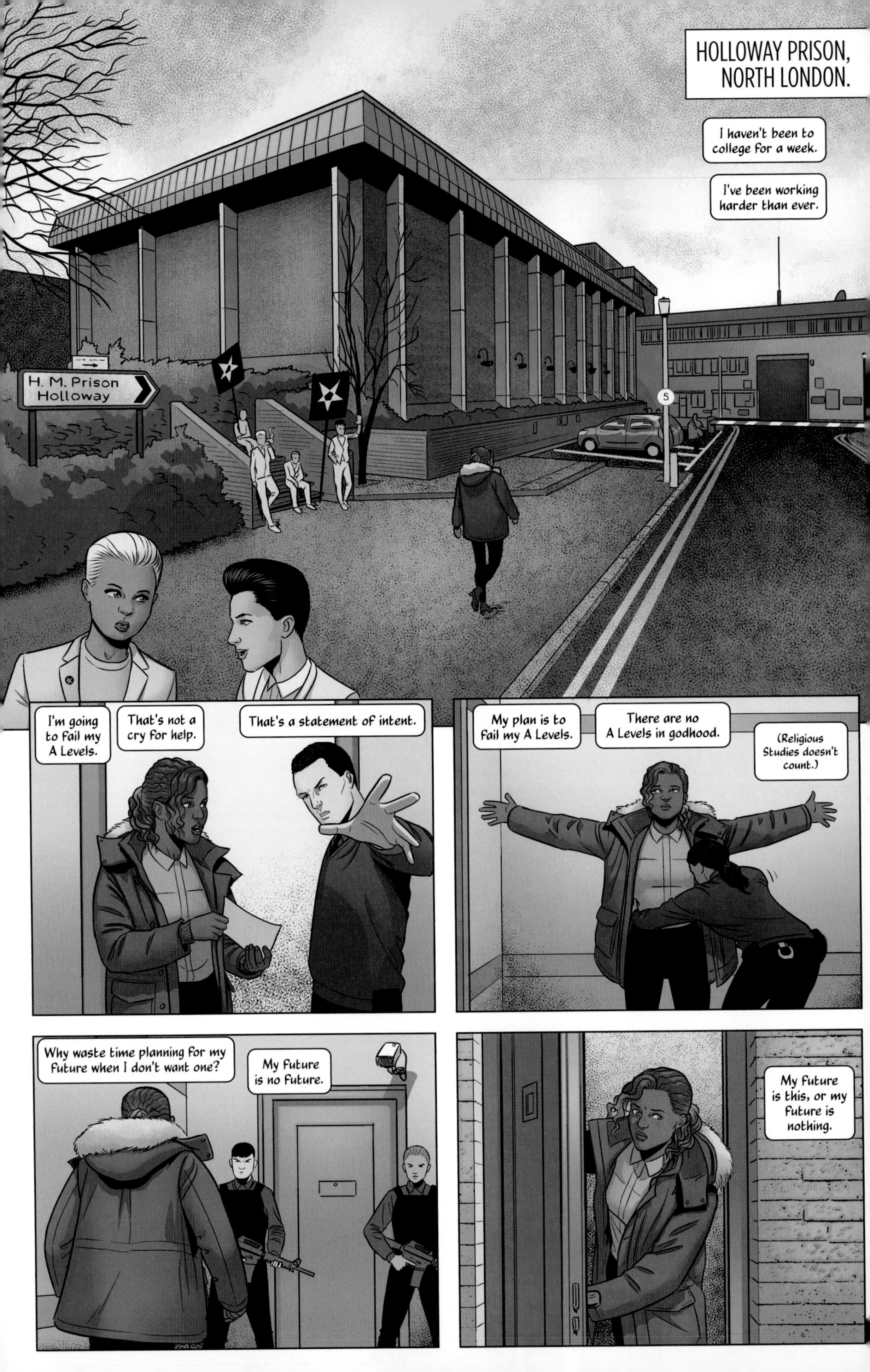
HOLLOWAY PRISON, NORTH LONDON.
I haven't been to college for a week.
I've been working harder than ever.
H. M. Prison Holloway
5
I'm going to fail my A Levels.
That's not a cry for help.
That's a statement of intent.
My plan is to fail my A Levels.
There are no A Levels in godhood.
(Religious Studies doesn't count.)
Why waste time planning for my future when I don't want one?
My future is no future.
My future is this, or my future is nothing.

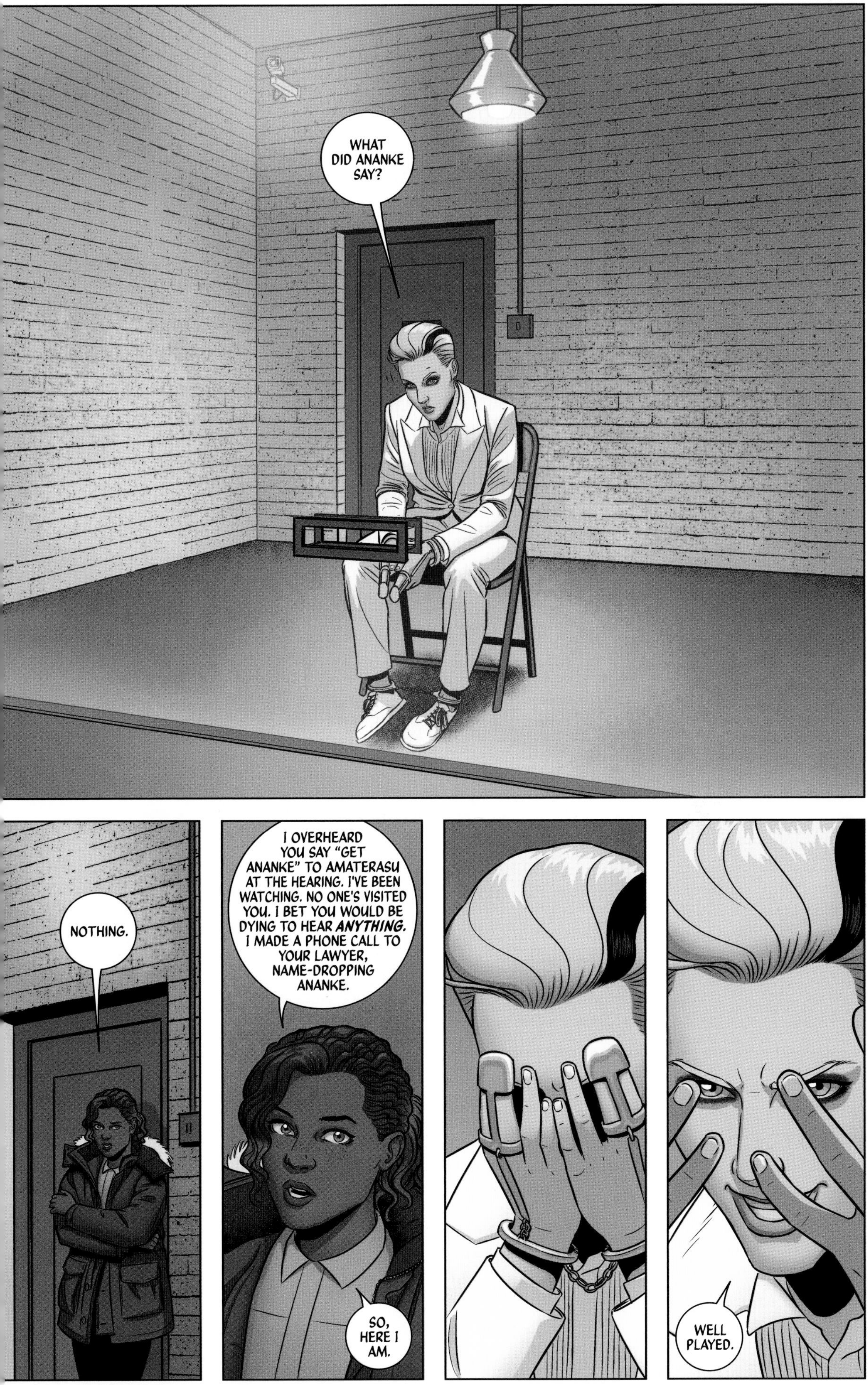
WHAT DID ANANKE SAY?
NOTHING.
I OVERHEARD YOU SAY "GET ANANKE" TO AMATERASU AT THE HEARING. I'VE BEEN WATCHING. NO ONE'S VISITED YOU. I BET YOU WOULD BE DYING TO HEAR ANYTHING. I MADE A PHONE CALL TO YOUR LAWYER, NAME-DROPPING ANANKE.
SO, HERE I AM.
WELL PLAYED.

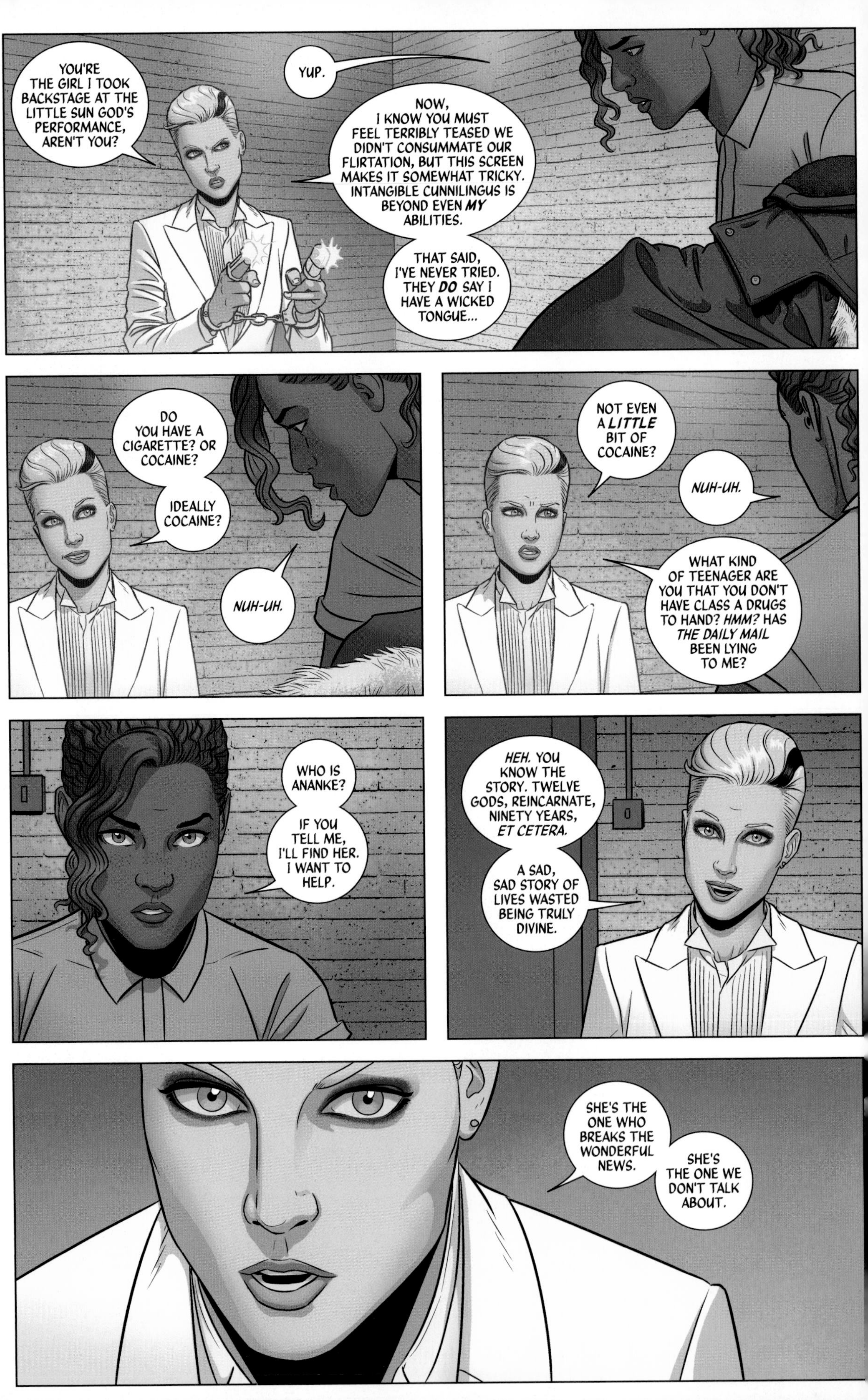
YOU'RE THE GIRL I TOOK BACKSTAGE AT THE LITTLE SUN GOD'S PERFORMANCE, AREN'T YOU?
YUP.
NOW, I KNOW YOU MUST FEEL TERRIBLY TEASED WE DIDN'T CONSUMMATE OUR FLIRTATION, BUT THIS SCREEN MAKES IT SOMEWHAT TRICKY. INTANGIBLE CUNNILINGUS IS BEYOND EVEN *MY* ABILITIES.
THAT SAID, I'VE NEVER TRIED. THEY *DO* SAY I HAVE A WICKED TONGUE...
DO YOU HAVE A CIGARETTE? OR COCAINE?
IDEALLY COCAINE?
NUH-UH.
NOT EVEN A *LITTLE* BIT OF COCAINE?
NUH-UH.
WHAT KIND OF TEENAGER ARE YOU THAT YOU DON'T HAVE CLASS A DRUGS TO HAND? *HMM?* HAS *THE DAILY MAIL* BEEN LYING TO ME?
WHO IS ANANKE?
IF YOU TELL ME, I'LL FIND HER. I WANT TO HELP.
HEH. YOU KNOW THE STORY. TWELVE GODS, REINCARNATE, NINETY YEARS, *ET CETERA.*
A SAD, SAD STORY OF LIVES WASTED BEING TRULY DIVINE.
SHE'S THE ONE WHO BREAKS THE WONDERFUL NEWS.
SHE'S THE ONE WE DON'T TALK ABOUT.

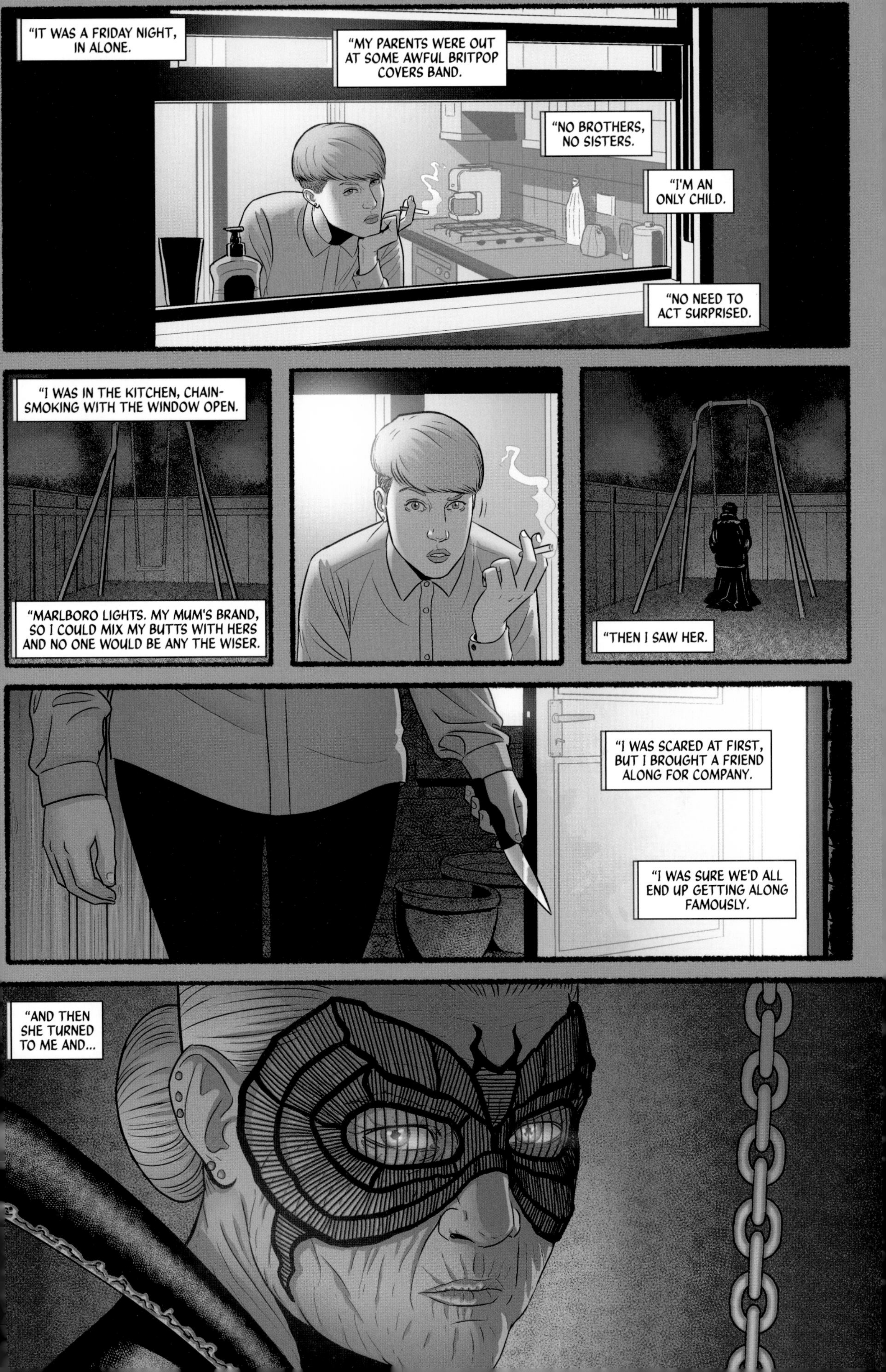
"IT WAS A FRIDAY NIGHT, IN ALONE.
"MY PARENTS WERE OUT AT SOME AWFUL BRITPOP COVERS BAND.
"NO BROTHERS, NO SISTERS.
"I'M AN ONLY CHILD.
"NO NEED TO ACT SURPRISED.
"I WAS IN THE KITCHEN, CHAIN-SMOKING WITH THE WINDOW OPEN.
"MARLBORO LIGHTS. MY MUM'S BRAND, SO I COULD MIX MY BUTTS WITH HERS AND NO ONE WOULD BE ANY THE WISER.
"THEN I SAW HER.
"I WAS SCARED AT FIRST, BUT I BROUGHT A FRIEND ALONG FOR COMPANY.
"I WAS SURE WE'D ALL END UP GETTING ALONG FAMOUSLY.
"AND THEN SHE TURNED TO ME AND...

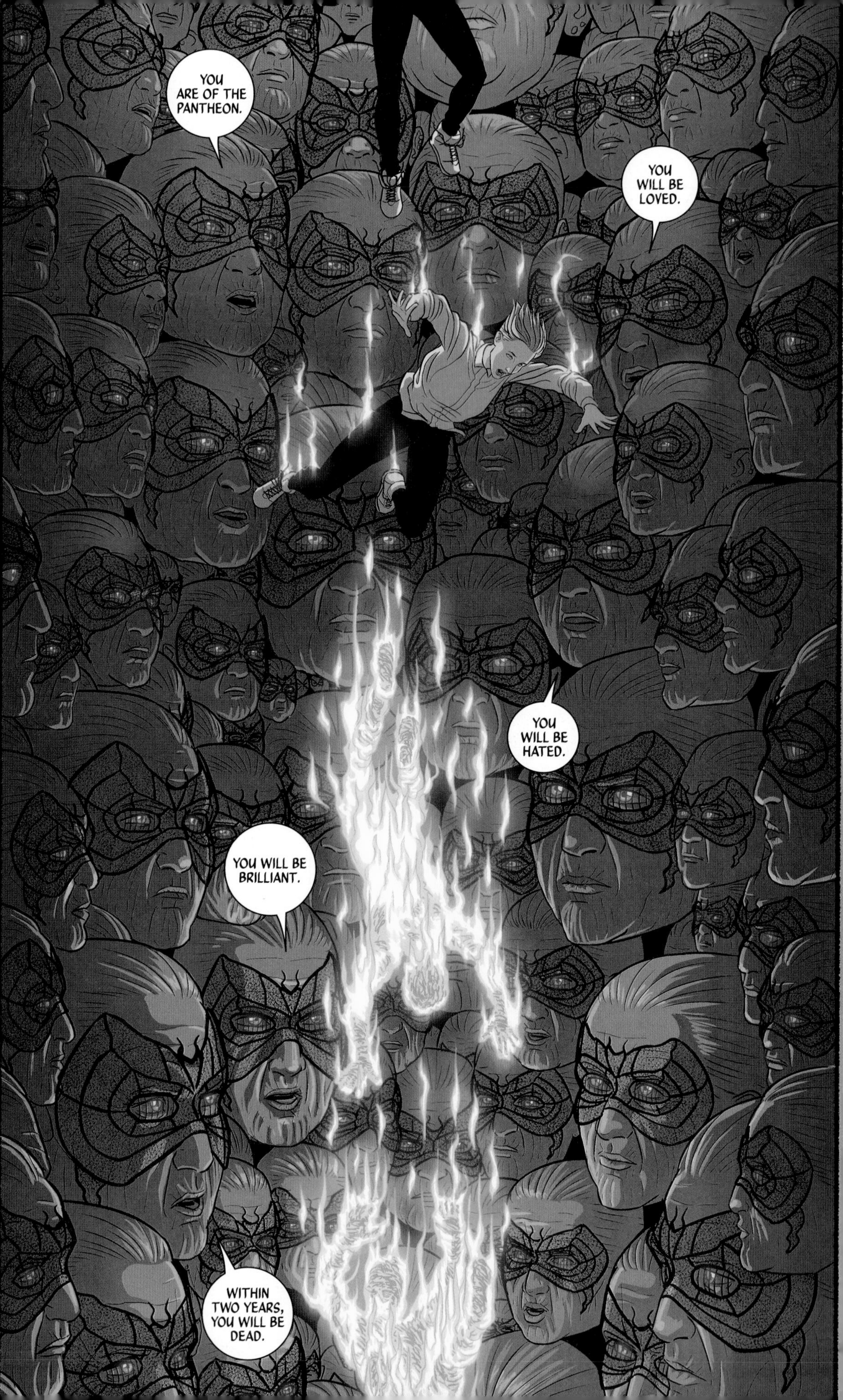
YOU ARE OF THE PANTHEON.
YOU WILL BE LOVED.
YOU WILL BE HATED.
YOU WILL BE BRILLIANT.
WITHIN TWO YEARS, YOU WILL BE DEAD.

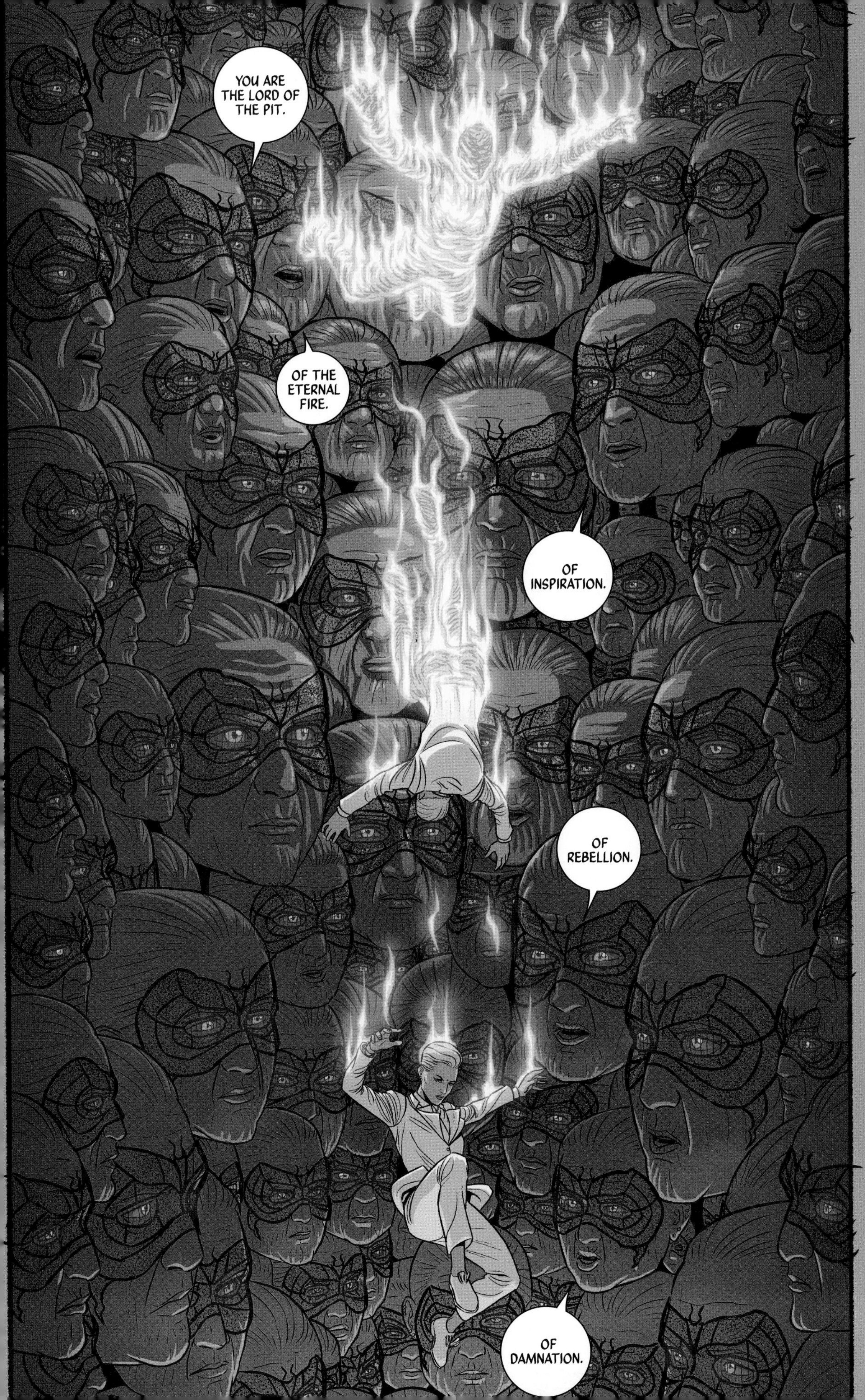
YOU ARE THE LORD OF THE PIT.
OF THE ETERNAL FIRE.
OF INSPIRATION.
OF REBELLION.
OF DAMNATION.

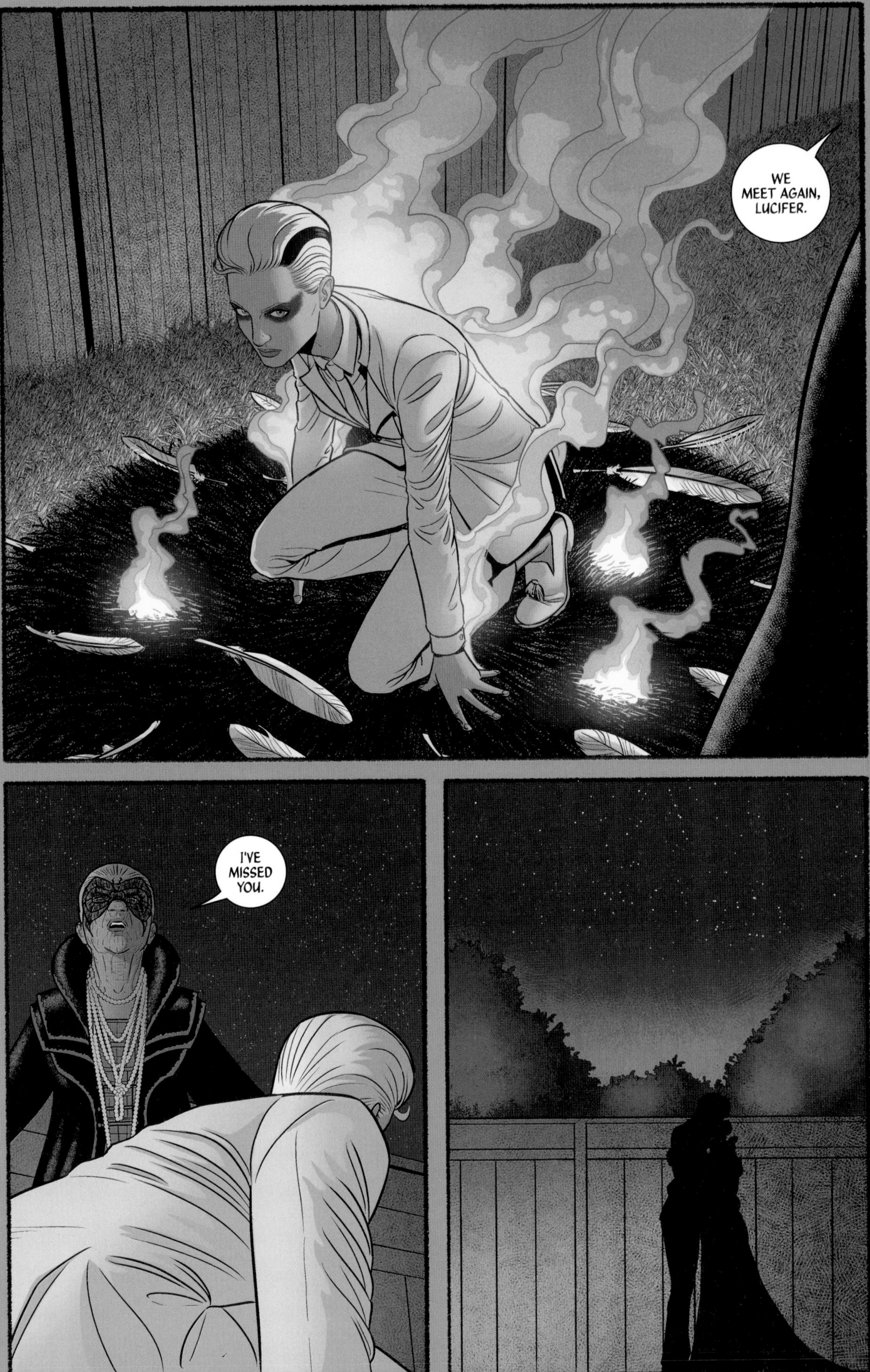
WE MEET AGAIN, LUCIFER.
I'VE MISSED YOU.

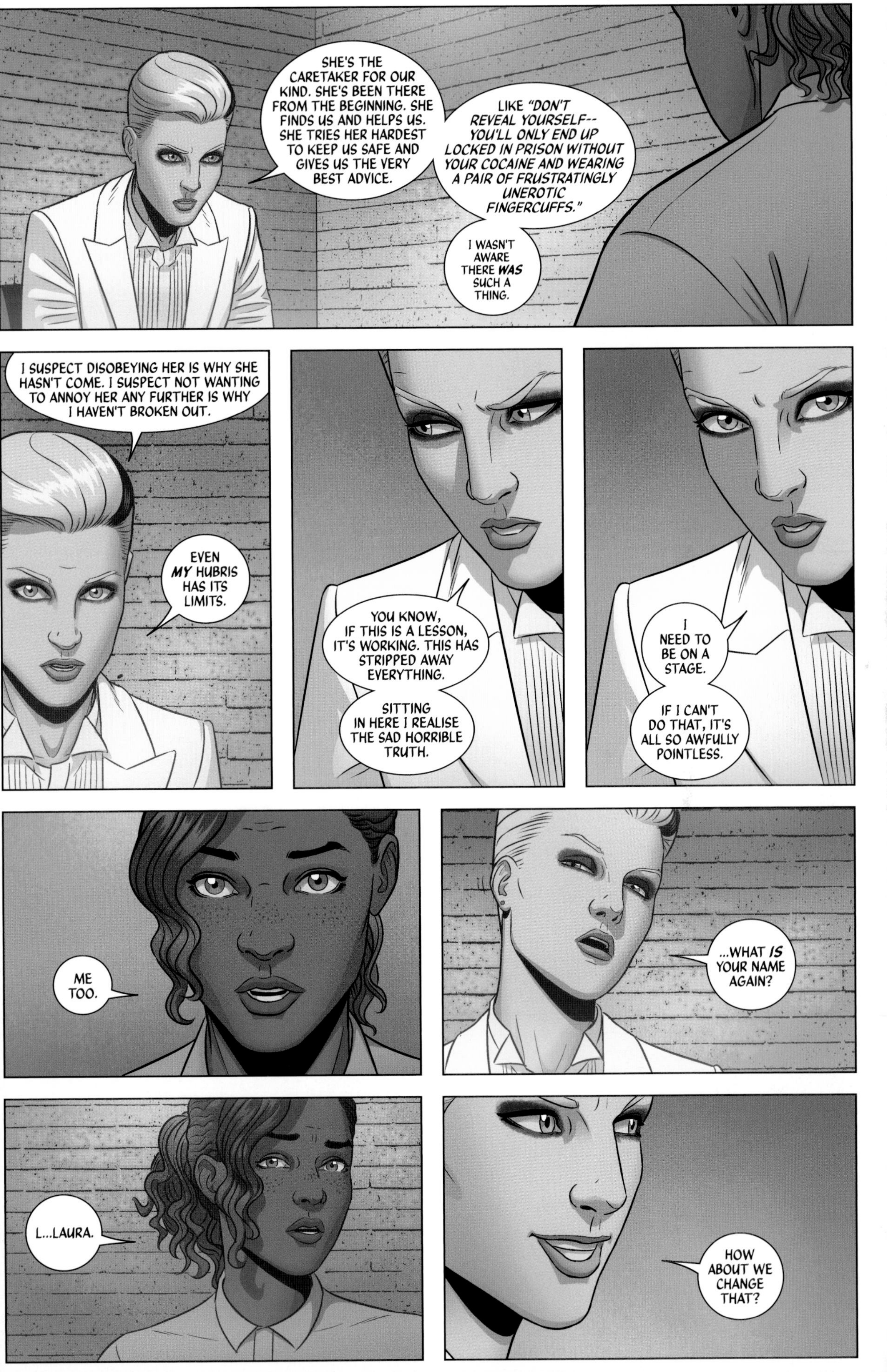
SHE'S THE CARETAKER FOR OUR KIND. SHE'S BEEN THERE FROM THE BEGINNING. SHE FINDS US AND HELPS US. SHE TRIES HER HARDEST TO KEEP US SAFE AND GIVES US THE VERY BEST ADVICE.
LIKE "DON'T REVEAL YOURSELF-- YOU'LL ONLY END UP LOCKED IN PRISON WITHOUT YOUR COCAINE AND WEARING A PAIR OF FRUSTRATINGLY UNEROTIC FINGERCUFFS."
I WASN'T AWARE THERE *WAS* SUCH A THING.
I SUSPECT DISOBEYING HER IS WHY SHE HASN'T COME. I SUSPECT NOT WANTING TO ANNOY HER ANY FURTHER IS WHY I HAVEN'T BROKEN OUT.
EVEN *MY* HUBRIS HAS ITS LIMITS.
YOU KNOW, IF THIS IS A LESSON, IT'S WORKING. THIS HAS STRIPPED AWAY EVERYTHING.
SITTING IN HERE I REALISE THE SAD HORRIBLE TRUTH.
I NEED TO BE ON A STAGE.
IF I CAN'T DO THAT, IT'S ALL SO AWFULLY POINTLESS.
ME TOO.
...WHAT *IS* YOUR NAME AGAIN?
L...LAURA.
HOW ABOUT WE CHANGE THAT?

LUCIFER IMPLIES DEMONS. I HAVE NONE AS OF YET, BUT I PROBABLY SHOULD INITIATE A FEW...

DAMNATION IS *DELIGHTFUL*. EVERYONE SHOULD TRY IT.

CAN YOU DO THAT? TURN ME INTO... SOMETHING LIKE YOU?

YES, OF COURSE I CAN. LOOK AT WODEN AND HIS CHEERILY RACIST ARMY OF ETHNIC MONO-CULTURED VALKYRIE FUCK BUDDIES.

I JUST HAVEN'T FOUND ANYONE WICKED ENOUGH TO DESERVE IT YET.

HELP ME AND THAT SOMEONE IS YOU.

I... WHY ME?

BECAUSE LUCIFER IS IN HELL. AND YOU'RE THE ONLY ONE WHO CAME.

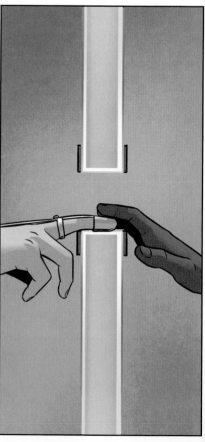

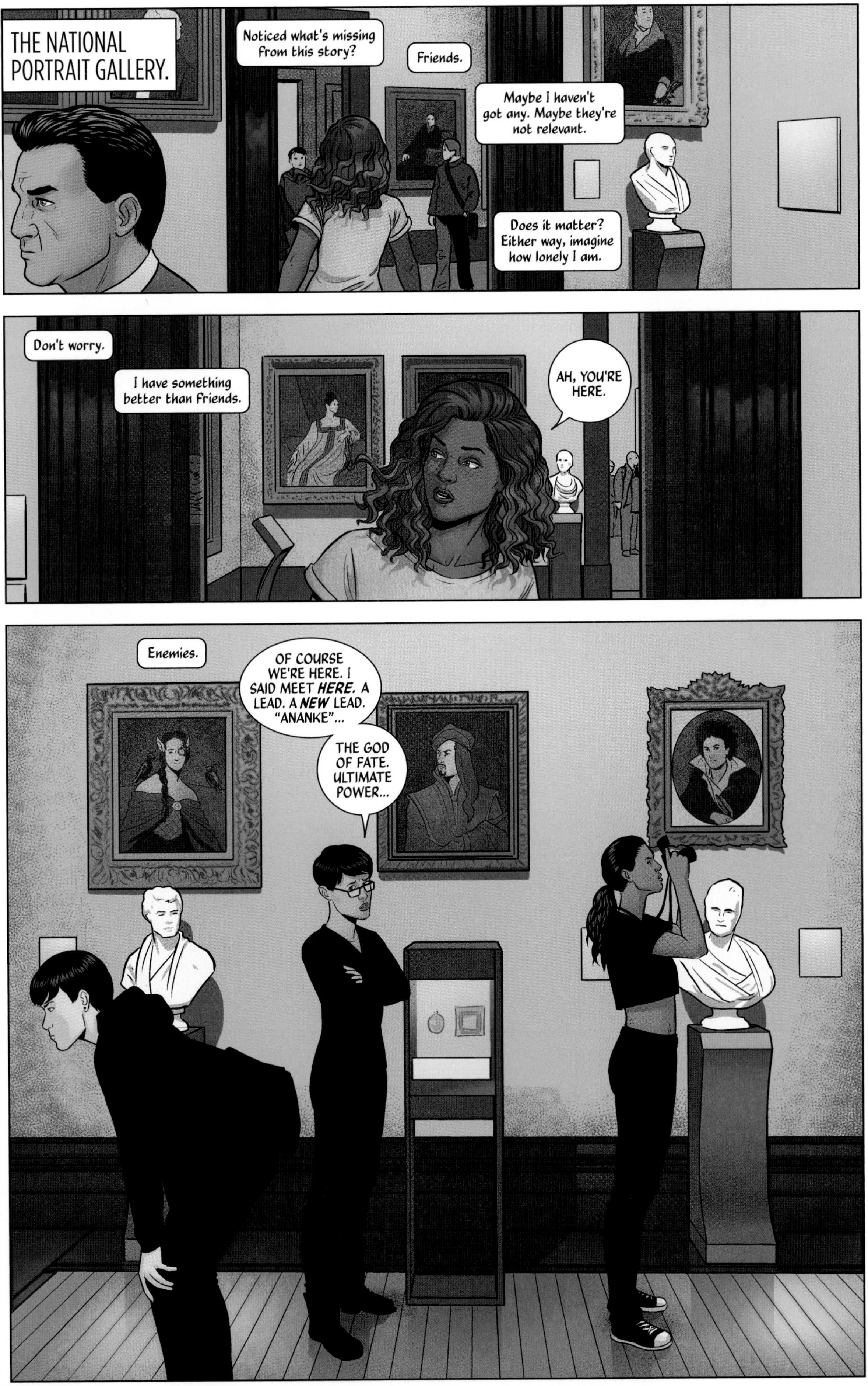
THE NATIONAL PORTRAIT GALLERY.
Noticed what's missing from this story?
Friends.
Maybe I haven't got any. Maybe they're not relevant.
Does it matter? Either way, imagine how lonely I am.
Don't worry.
I have something better than friends.
AH, YOU'RE HERE.
Enemies.
OF COURSE WE'RE HERE. I SAID MEET *HERE.* A LEAD. A *NEW* LEAD. "ANANKE"...
THE GOD OF FATE. ULTIMATE POWER...

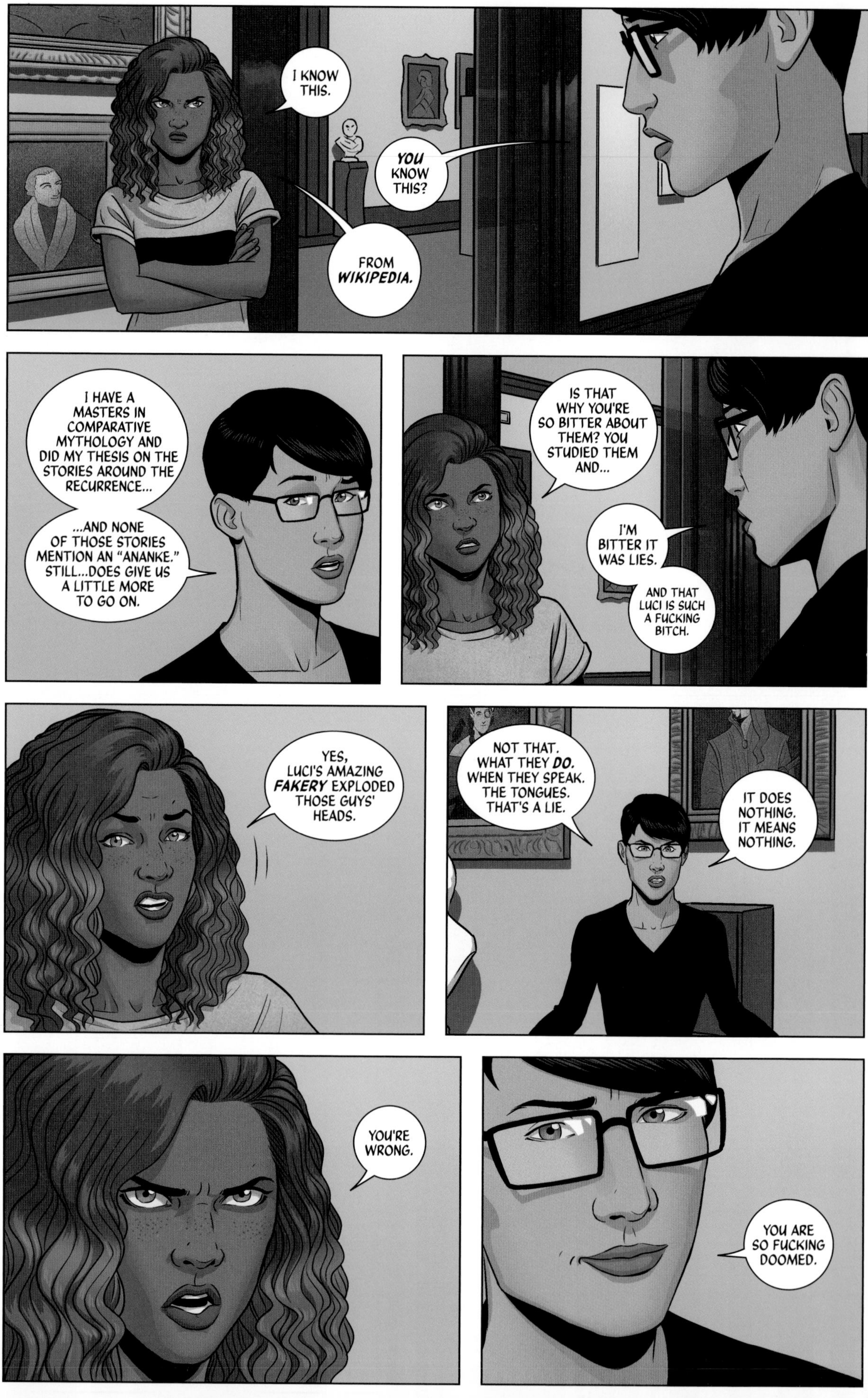
I KNOW THIS.
YOU KNOW THIS?
FROM *WIKIPEDIA.*
I HAVE A MASTERS IN COMPARATIVE MYTHOLOGY AND DID MY THESIS ON THE STORIES AROUND THE RECURRENCE...
...AND NONE OF THOSE STORIES MENTION AN "ANANKE." STILL...DOES GIVE US A LITTLE MORE TO GO ON.
IS THAT WHY YOU'RE SO BITTER ABOUT THEM? YOU STUDIED THEM AND...
I'M BITTER IT WAS LIES.
AND THAT LUCI IS SUCH A FUCKING BITCH.
YES, LUCI'S AMAZING *FAKERY* EXPLODED THOSE GUYS' HEADS.
NOT THAT. WHAT THEY *DO.* WHEN THEY SPEAK. THE TONGUES. THAT'S A LIE.
IT DOES NOTHING. IT MEANS NOTHING.
YOU'RE WRONG.
YOU ARE SO FUCKING DOOMED.

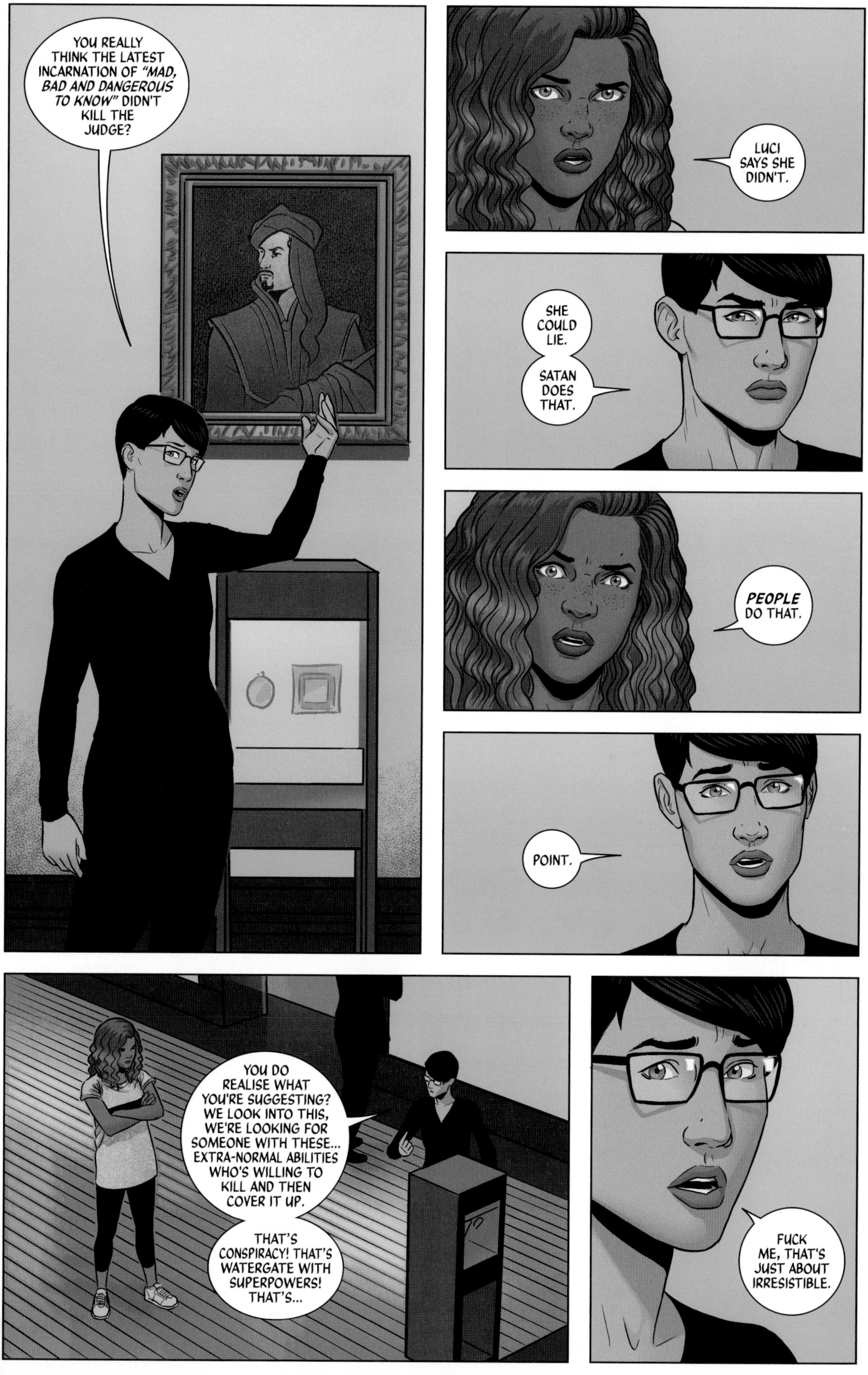
YOU REALLY THINK THE LATEST INCARNATION OF *"MAD, BAD AND DANGEROUS TO KNOW"* DIDN'T KILL THE JUDGE?
LUCI SAYS SHE DIDN'T.
SHE COULD LIE.
SATAN DOES THAT.
PEOPLE DO THAT.
POINT.
YOU DO REALISE WHAT YOU'RE SUGGESTING? WE LOOK INTO THIS, WE'RE LOOKING FOR SOMEONE WITH THESE... EXTRA-NORMAL ABILITIES WHO'S WILLING TO KILL AND THEN COVER IT UP.
THAT'S CONSPIRACY! THAT'S WATERGATE WITH SUPERPOWERS! THAT'S...
FUCK ME, THAT'S JUST ABOUT IRRESISTIBLE.

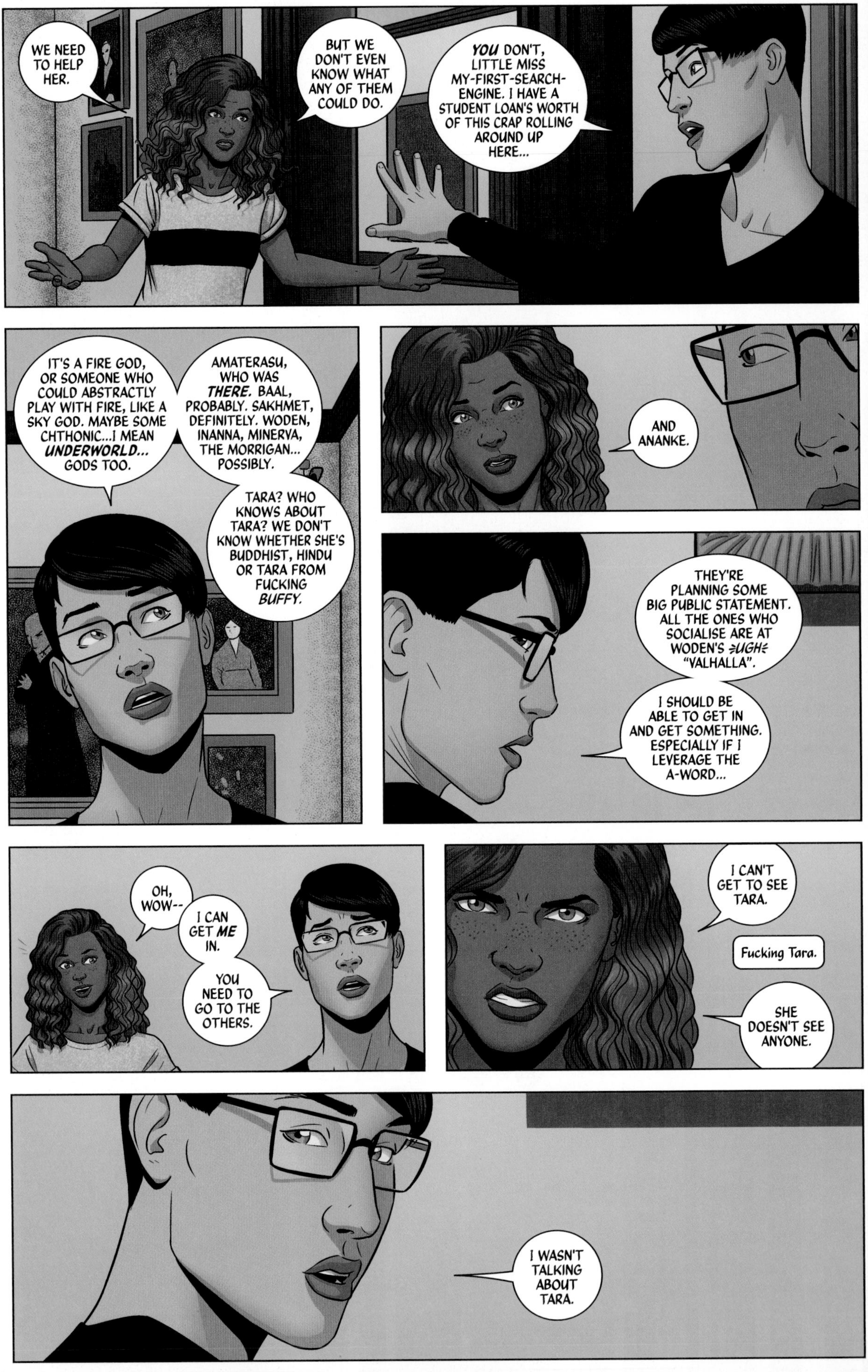
WE NEED TO HELP HER.
BUT WE DON'T EVEN KNOW WHAT ANY OF THEM COULD DO.
YOU DON'T, LITTLE MISS MY-FIRST-SEARCH-ENGINE. I HAVE A STUDENT LOAN'S WORTH OF THIS CRAP ROLLING AROUND UP HERE...
IT'S A FIRE GOD, OR SOMEONE WHO COULD ABSTRACTLY PLAY WITH FIRE, LIKE A SKY GOD. MAYBE SOME CHTHONIC...I MEAN UNDERWORLD... GODS TOO.
AMATERASU, WHO WAS THERE. BAAL, PROBABLY. SAKHMET, DEFINITELY. WODEN, INANNA, MINERVA, THE MORRIGAN... POSSIBLY.
TARA? WHO KNOWS ABOUT TARA? WE DON'T KNOW WHETHER SHE'S BUDDHIST, HINDU OR TARA FROM FUCKING BUFFY.
AND ANANKE.
THEY'RE PLANNING SOME BIG PUBLIC STATEMENT. ALL THE ONES WHO SOCIALISE ARE AT WODEN'S UGH "VALHALLA".
I SHOULD BE ABLE TO GET IN AND GET SOMETHING. ESPECIALLY IF I LEVERAGE THE A-WORD...
OH, WOW--
I CAN GET ME IN.
YOU NEED TO GO TO THE OTHERS.
I CAN'T GET TO SEE TARA.
Fucking Tara.
SHE DOESN'T SEE ANYONE.
I WASN'T TALKING ABOUT TARA.

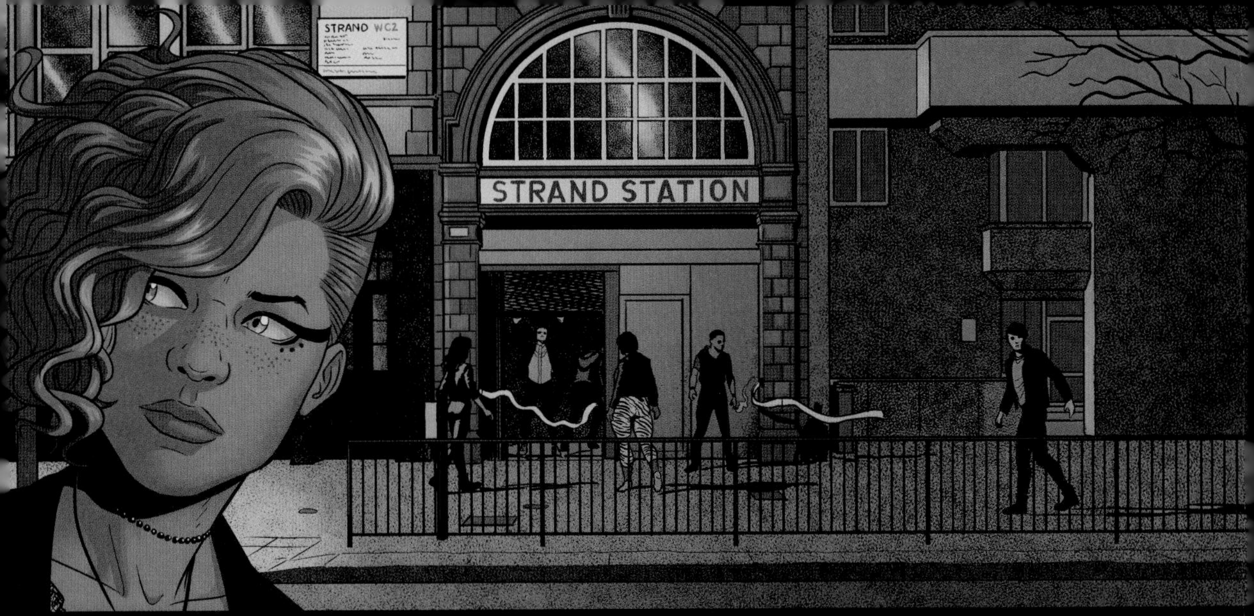
STRAND WC2
STRAND STATION

The Morrigan.

I've seen all the gods...

...except
The Morrigan.

I was at Baal's second gig,
in a warehouse in the middle of
nowhere (i.e. East London).

When Inanna did that
whole week in Camden,
I was crying in the front
row every night.

I've seen Lucifer in Brixton,
Minerva in a cinema in Shepherd's Bush,
Sakhmet at everywhere from Bethnal Green
to the O2, and fucking Tara in
the fucking West End.

I know the names of every
single one of Woden's Valkyries,
and have seen most of them.

But The Morrigan?

She's not like
the others.

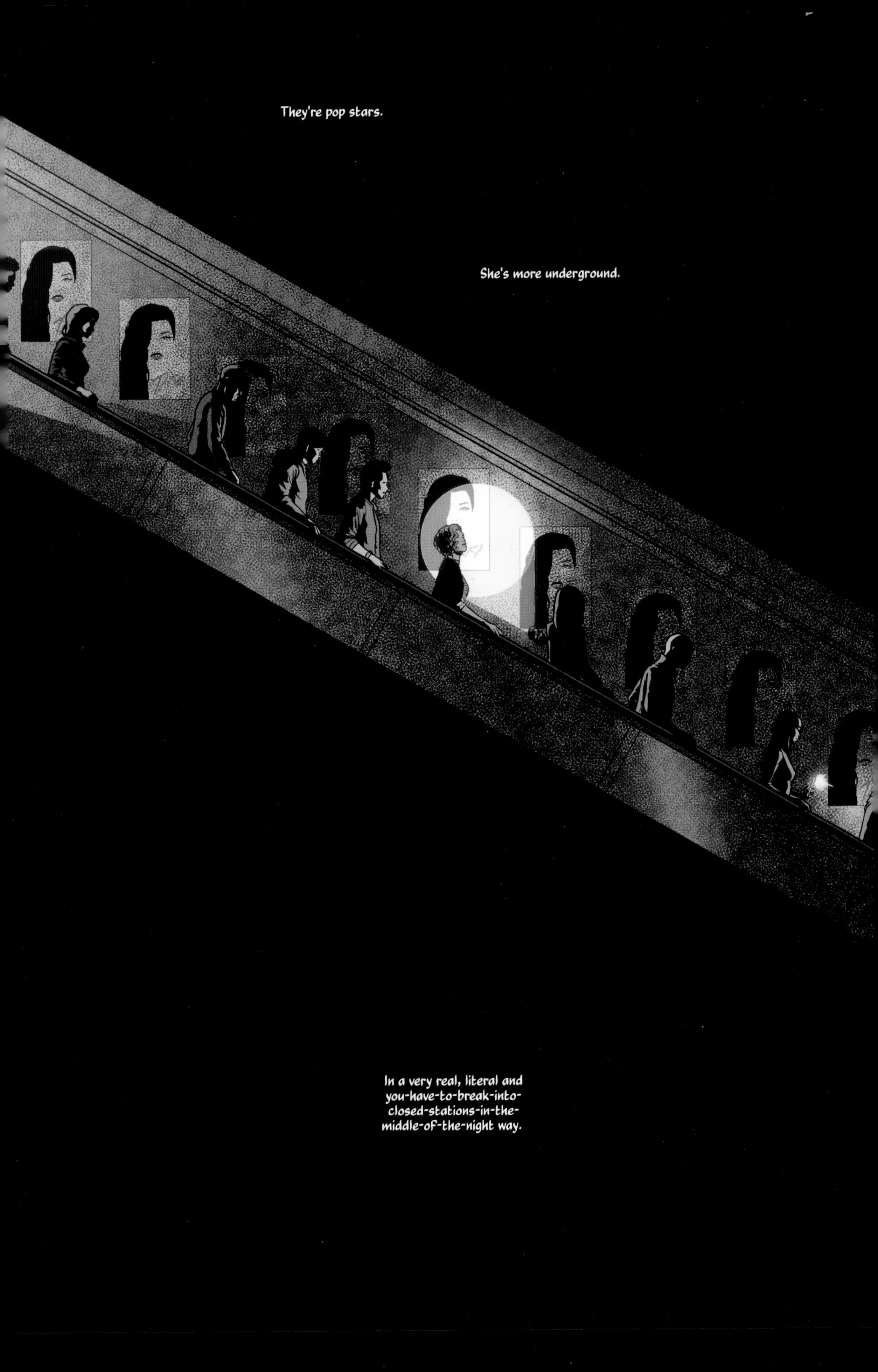
They're pop stars.
She's more underground.
In a very real, literal and you-have-to-break-into-closed-stations-in-the-middle-of-the-night way.

They say if you try and take a photo of her,
when you check the shot, nine times out of ten you'll
see a picture of who you're going to fall in love with...

...at the moment
of their death.

If you're the one in ten who actually
gets a photo of her, and you try to put the shot online,
the "like" button is replaced by a new one reading "DOOM"
and the only woman who's allowed to click it already has.

They say
lots of things.

She sounds like the
worst thing in the world.

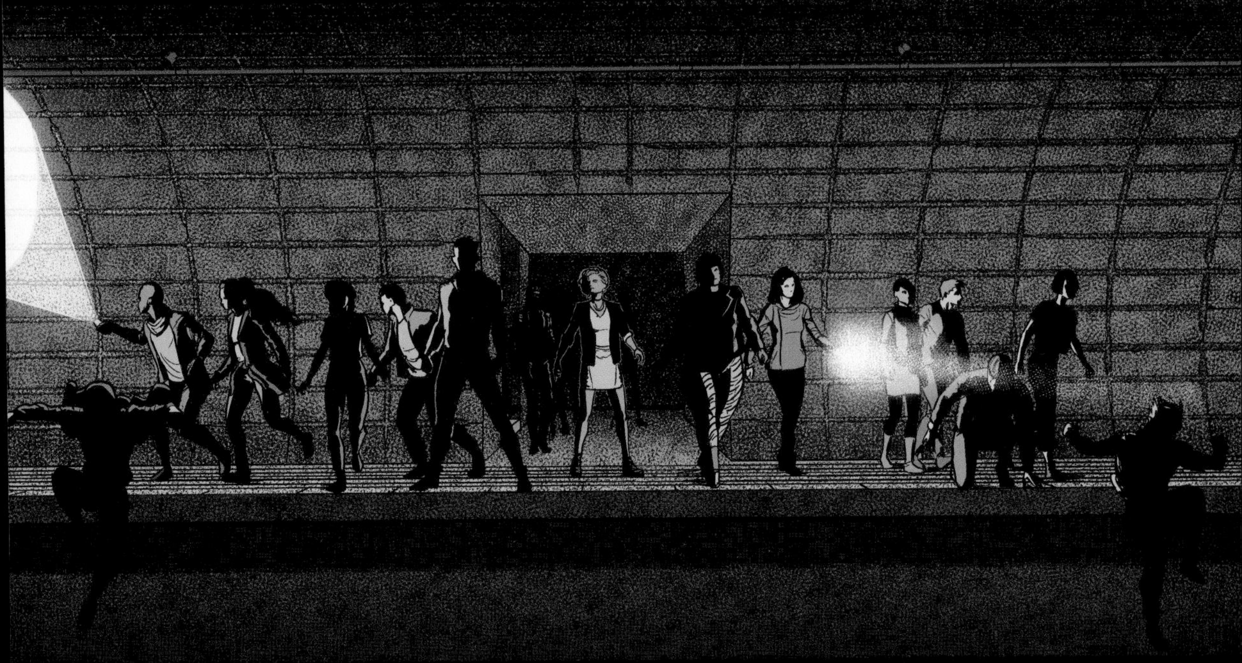

She sounds
perfect.

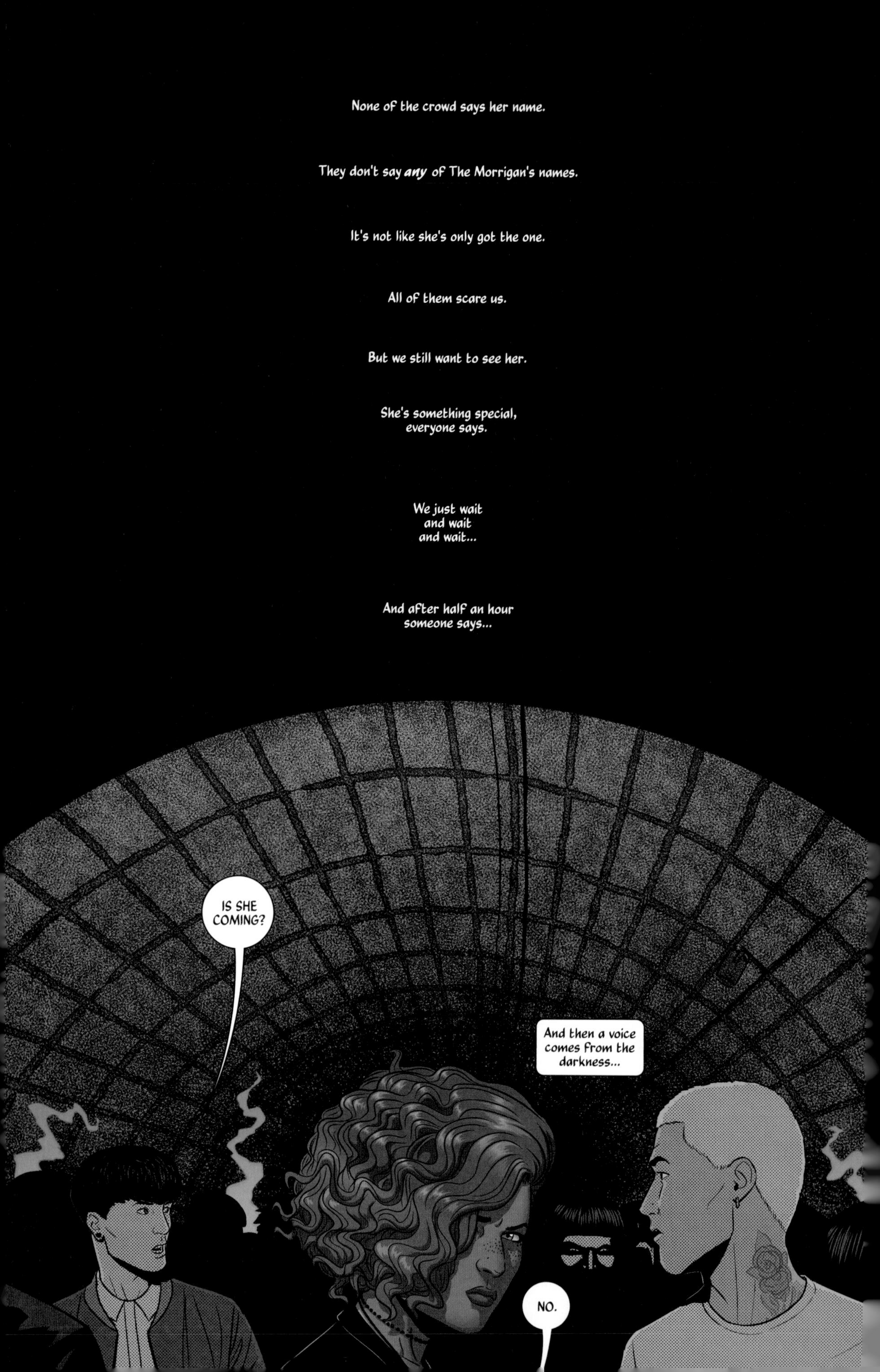
None of the crowd says her name.
They don't say *any* of The Morrigan's names.
It's not like she's only got the one.
All of them scare us.
But we still want to see her.
She's something special, everyone says.
We just wait and wait and wait...
And after half an hour someone says...
IS SHE COMING?
And then a voice comes from the darkness...
NO.

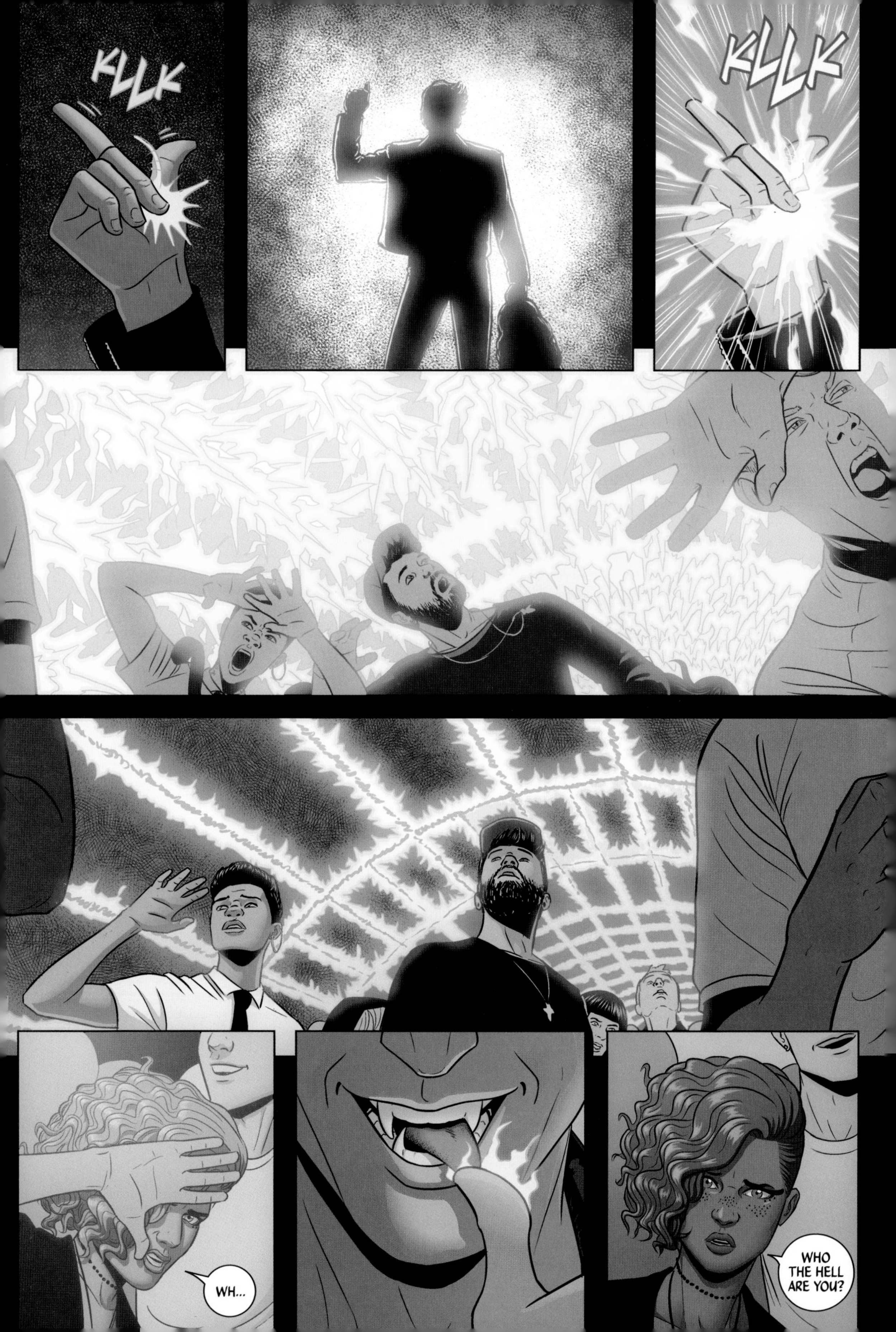
KLLK
KLLK
WH...
WHO THE HELL ARE YOU?

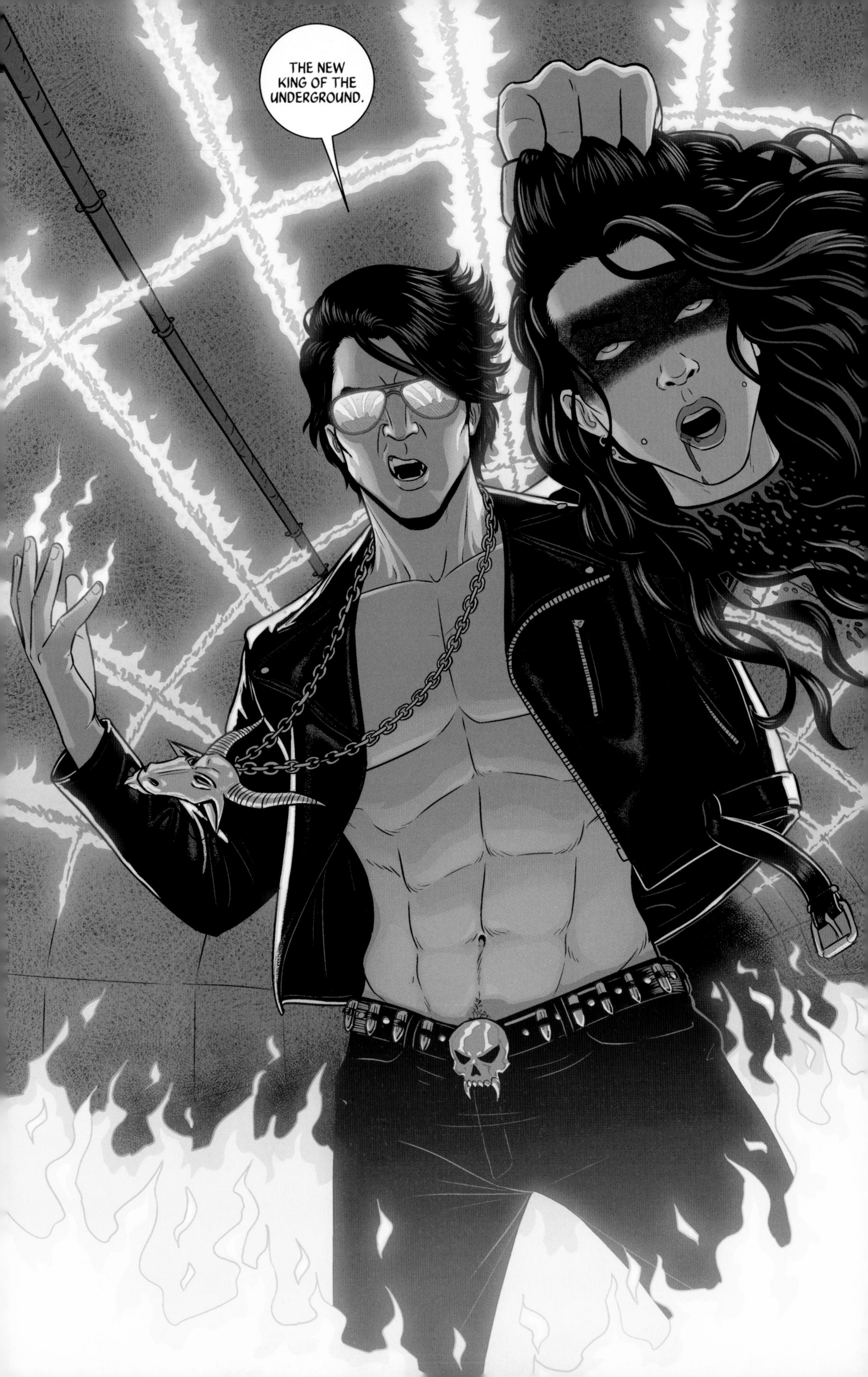
THE NEW KING OF THE UNDERGROUND.

"BAPHOMET"

10 JANUARY 2014

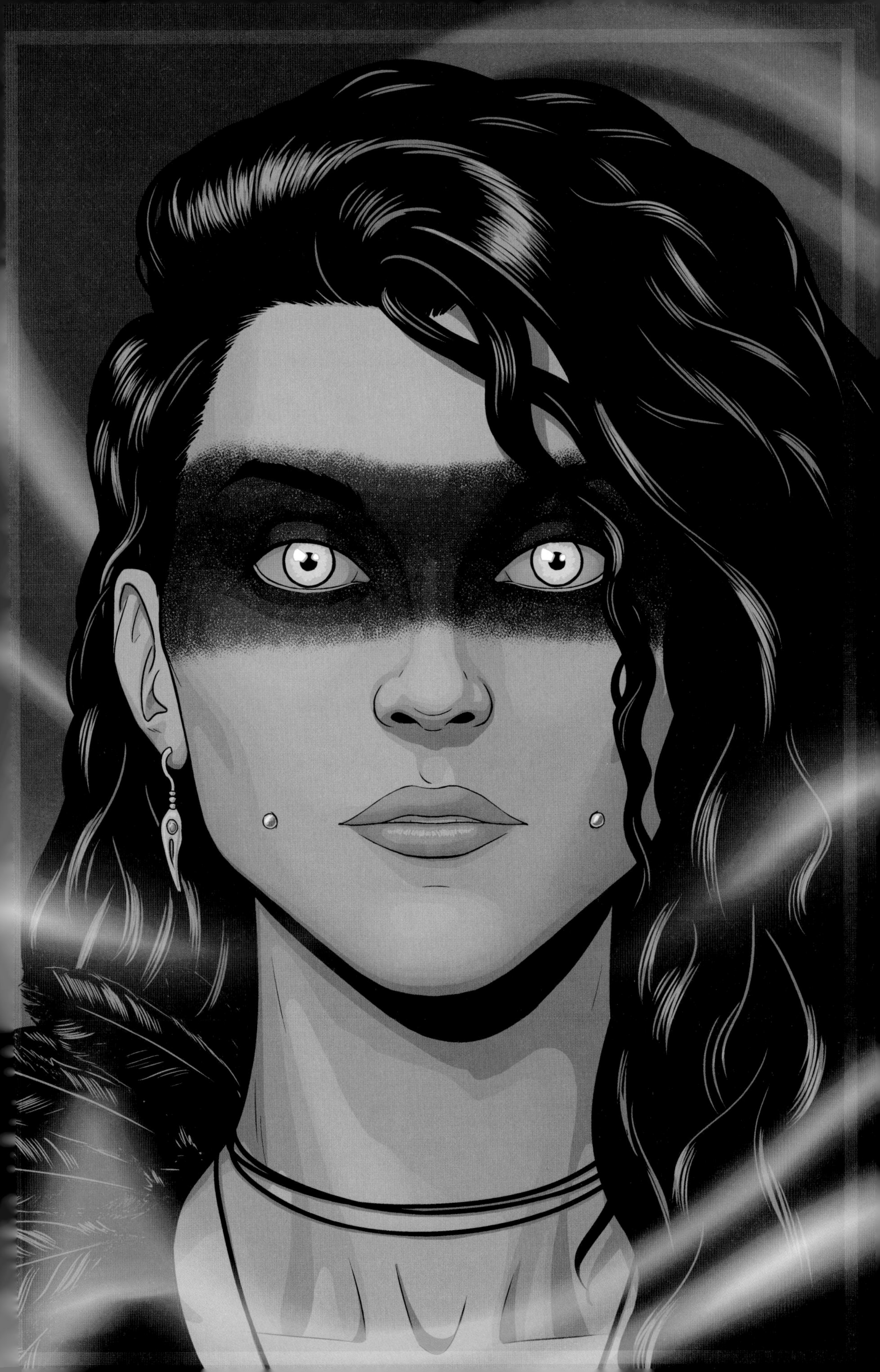

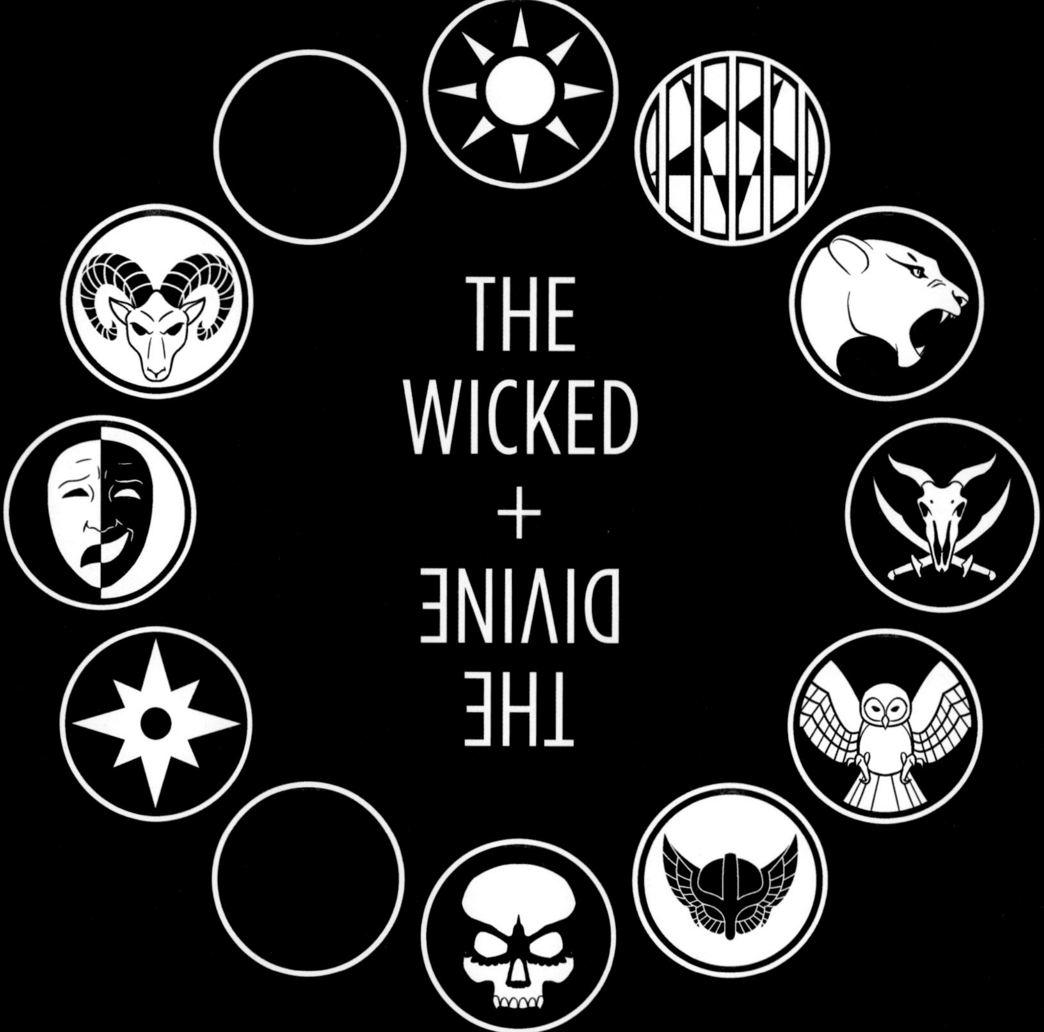
THE
WICKED
+
THE
DIVINE

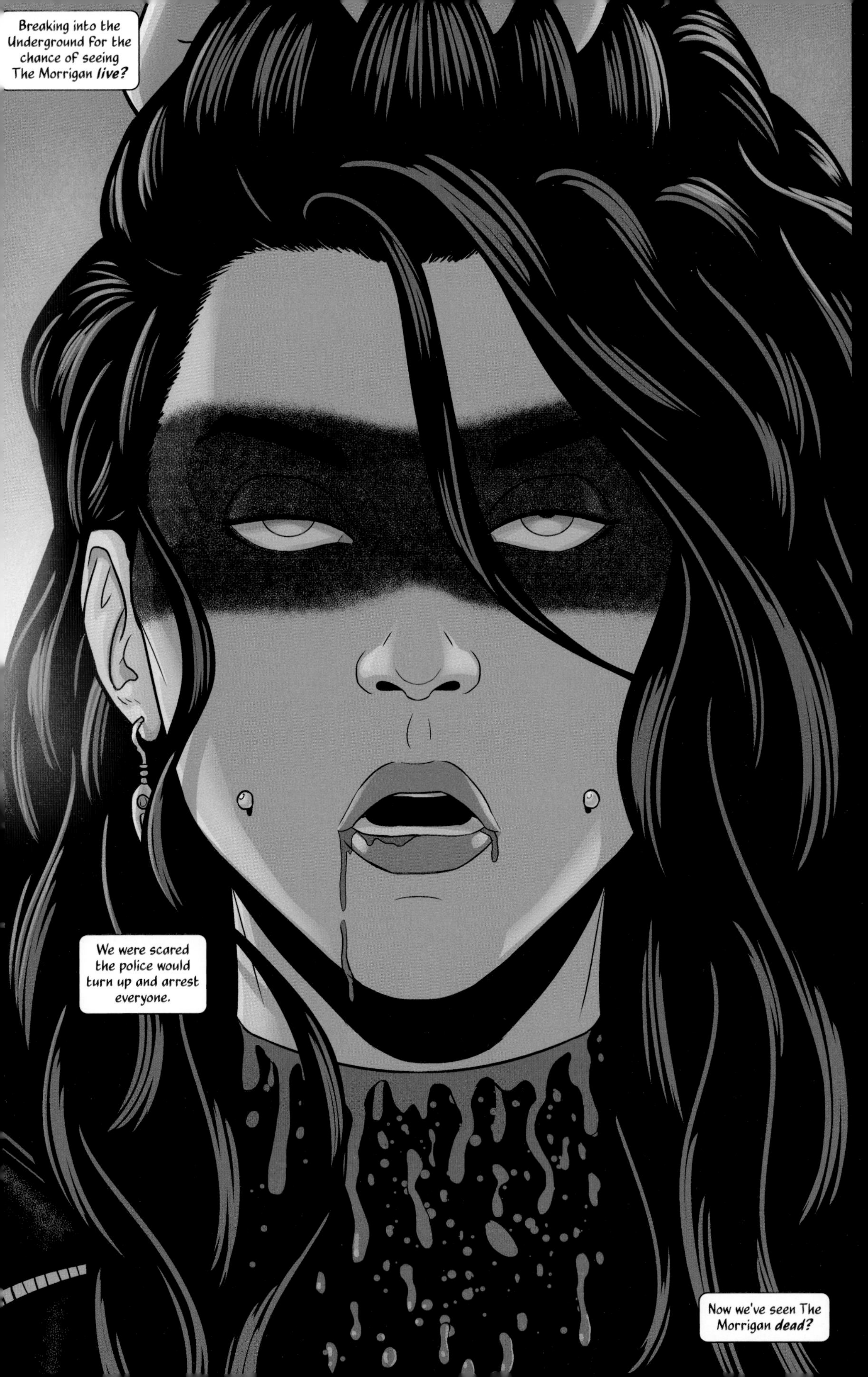
Breaking into the Underground for the chance of seeing The Morrigan *live?*
We were scared the police would turn up and arrest everyone.
Now we've seen The Morrigan *dead?*

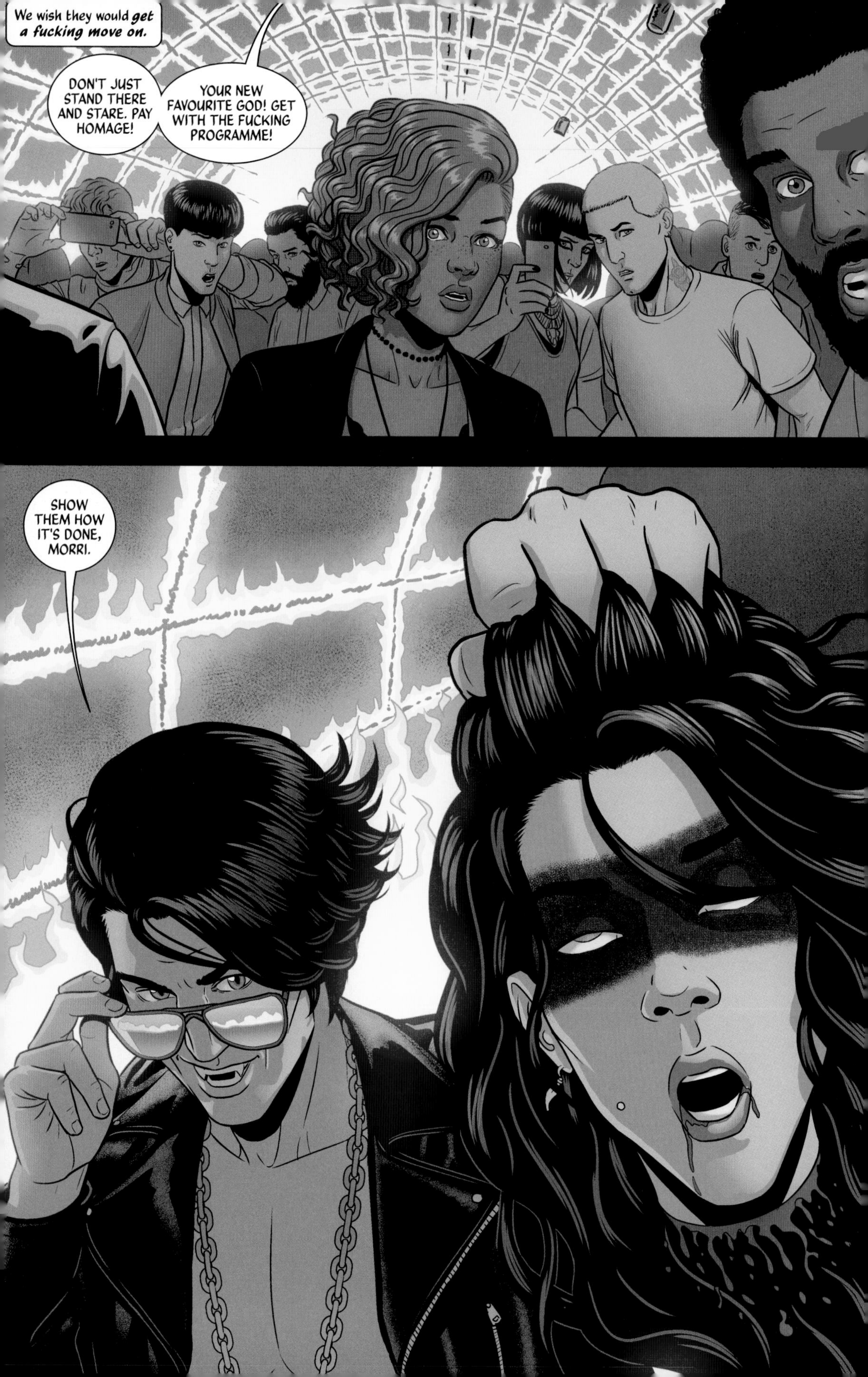
We wish they would *get a fucking move on.*
DON'T JUST STAND THERE AND STARE. PAY HOMAGE!
YOUR NEW FAVOURITE GOD! GET WITH THE FUCKING PROGRAMME!
SHOW THEM HOW IT'S DONE, MORRI.

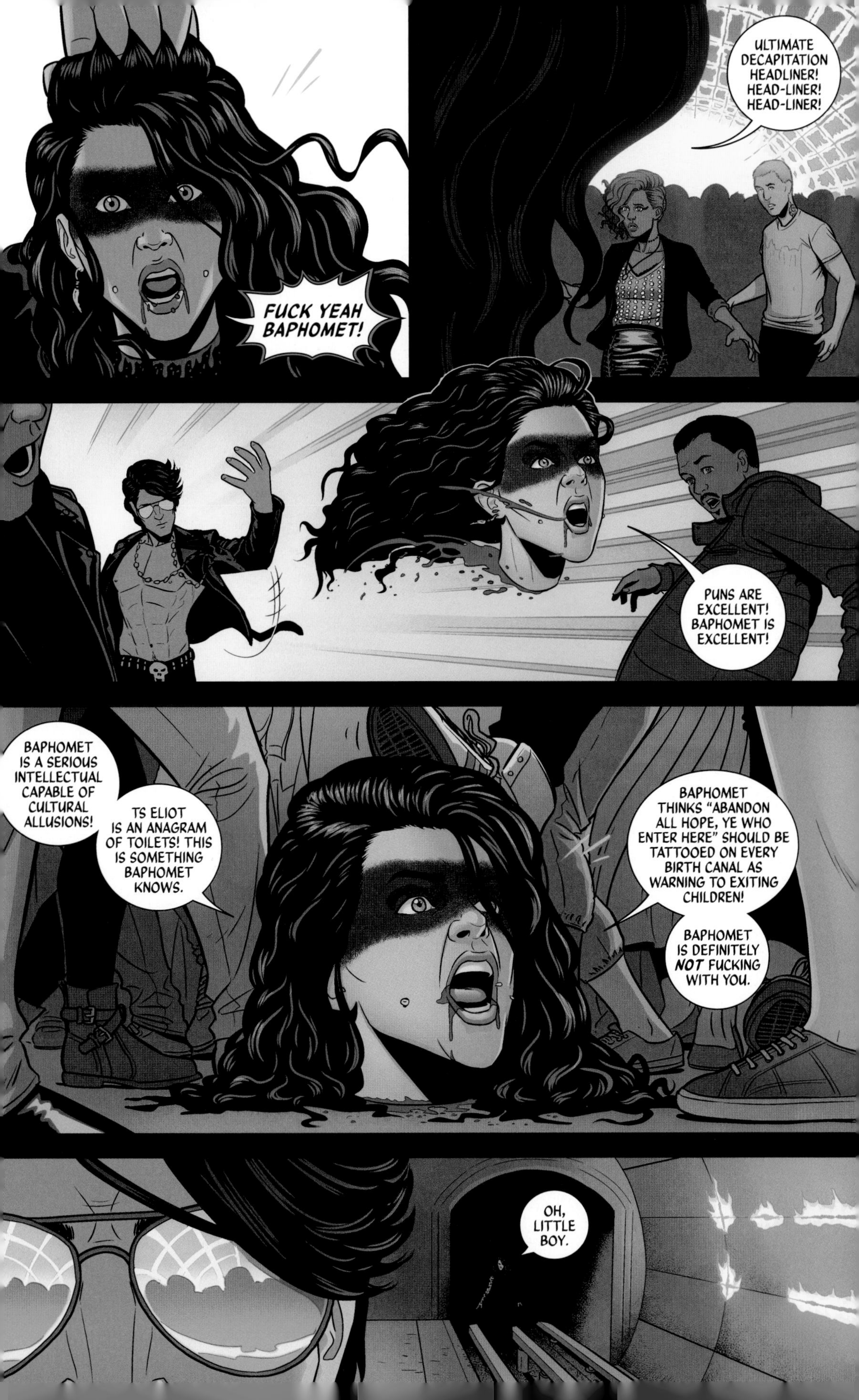
FUCK YEAH BAPHOMET!
ULTIMATE DECAPITATION HEADLINER! HEAD-LINER! HEAD-LINER!
PUNS ARE EXCELLENT! BAPHOMET IS EXCELLENT!
BAPHOMET IS A SERIOUS INTELLECTUAL CAPABLE OF CULTURAL ALLUSIONS!
TS ELIOT IS AN ANAGRAM OF TOILETS! THIS IS SOMETHING BAPHOMET KNOWS.
BAPHOMET THINKS "ABANDON ALL HOPE, YE WHO ENTER HERE" SHOULD BE TATTOOED ON EVERY BIRTH CANAL AS WARNING TO EXITING CHILDREN!
BAPHOMET IS DEFINITELY ***NOT*** FUCKING WITH YOU.
OH, LITTLE BOY.

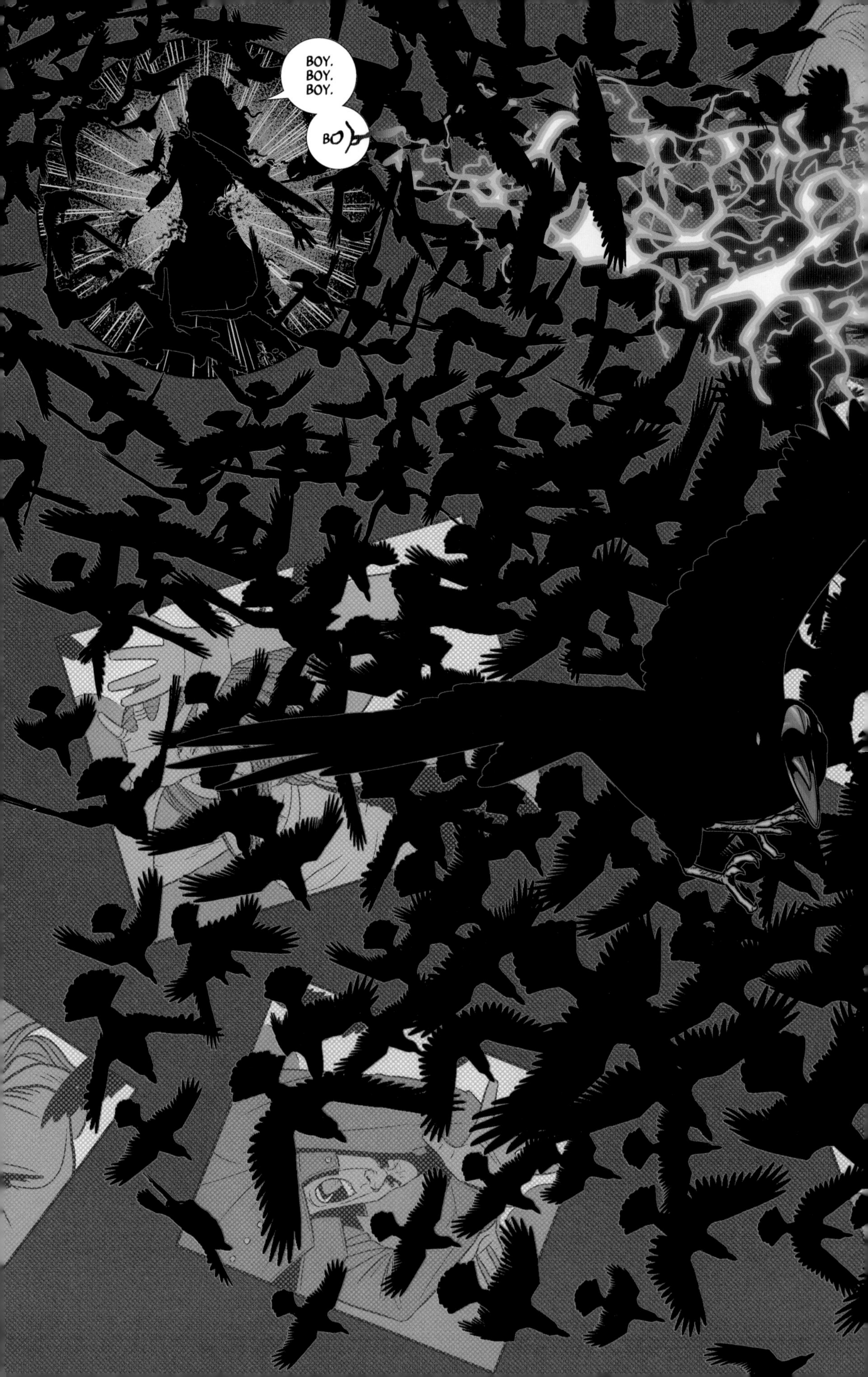
BOY.
BOY.
BOY.
BO

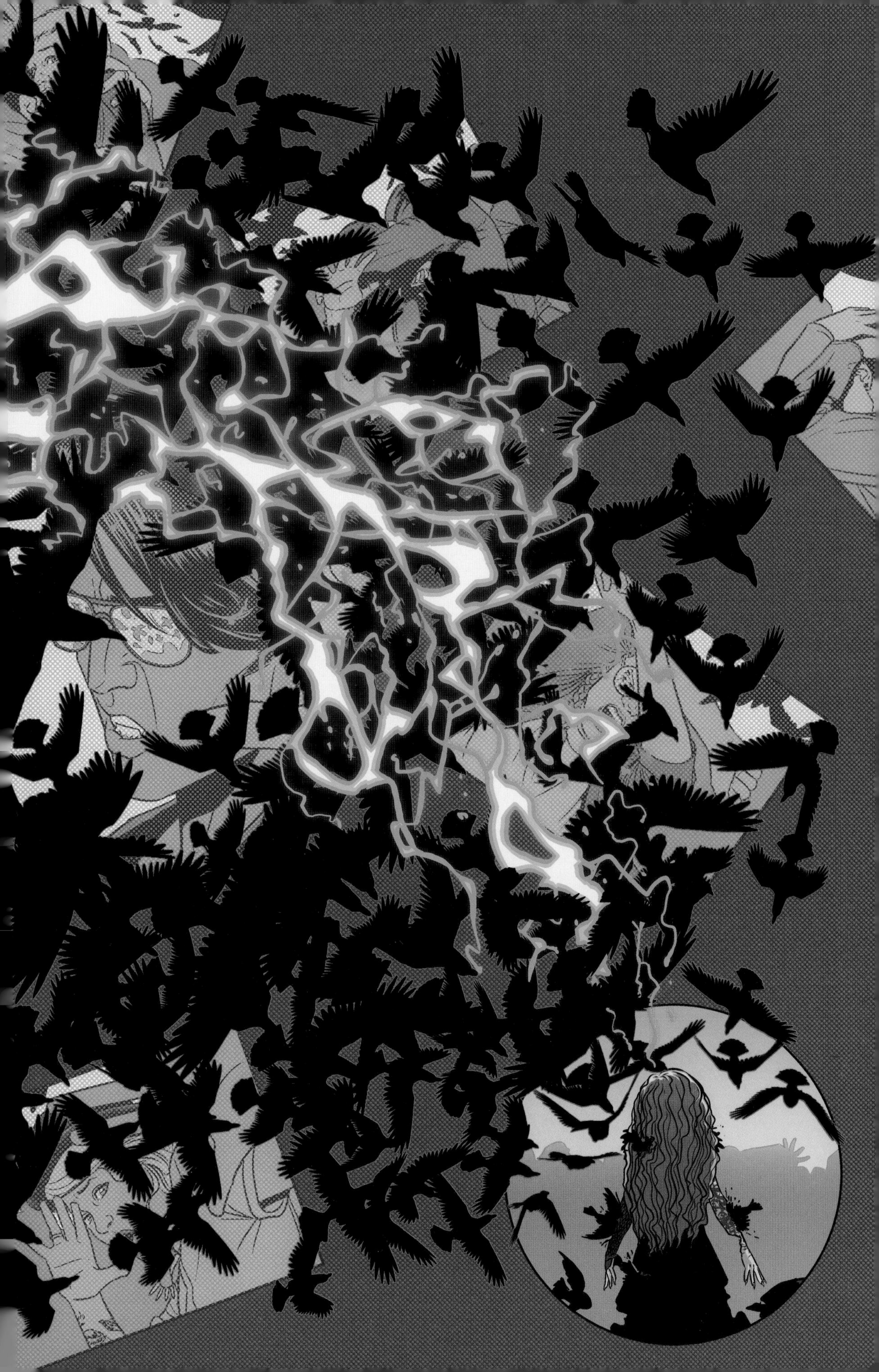

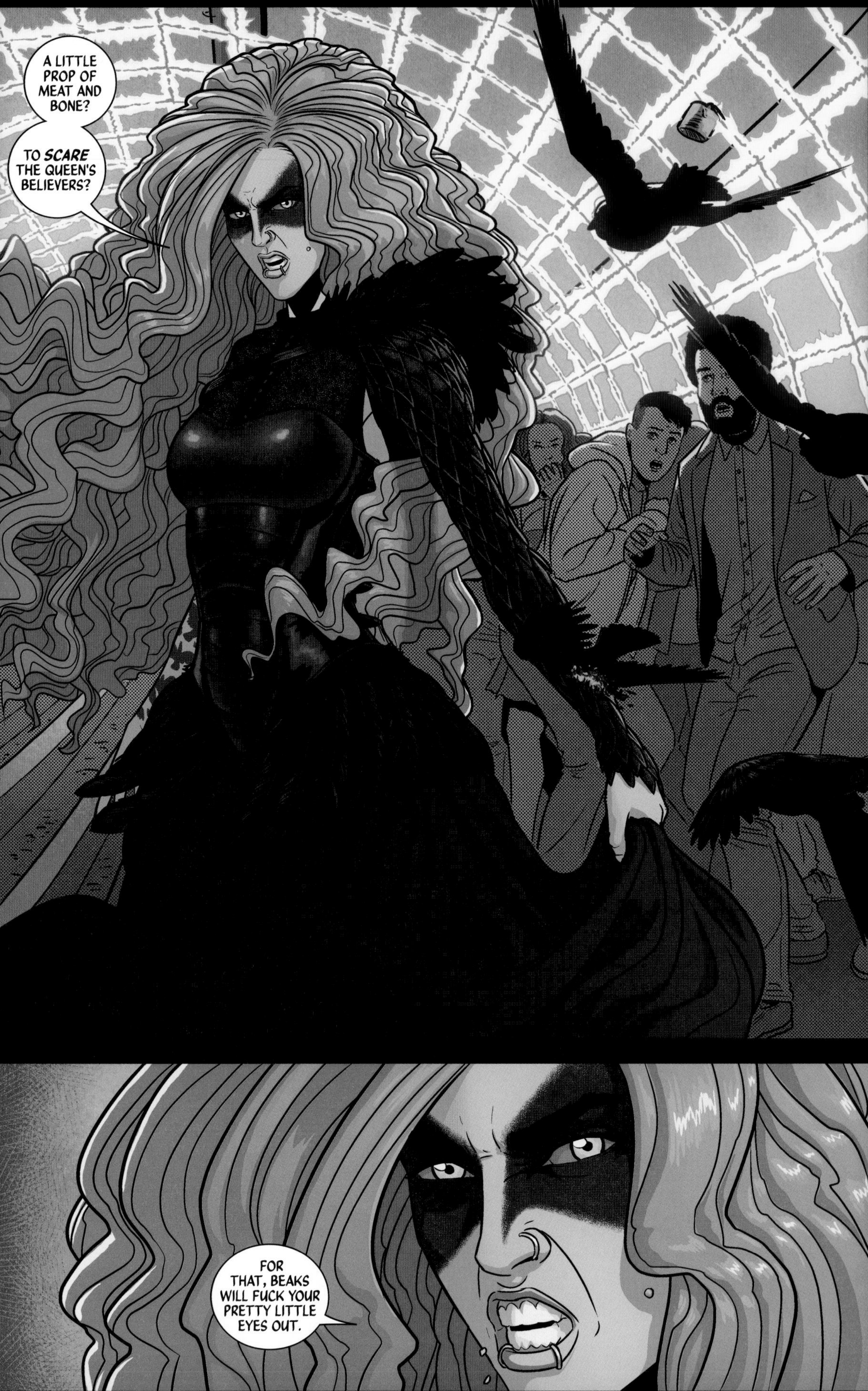
A LITTLE PROP OF MEAT AND BONE?
TO SCARE THE QUEEN'S BELIEVERS?
FOR THAT, BEAKS WILL FUCK YOUR PRETTY LITTLE EYES OUT.

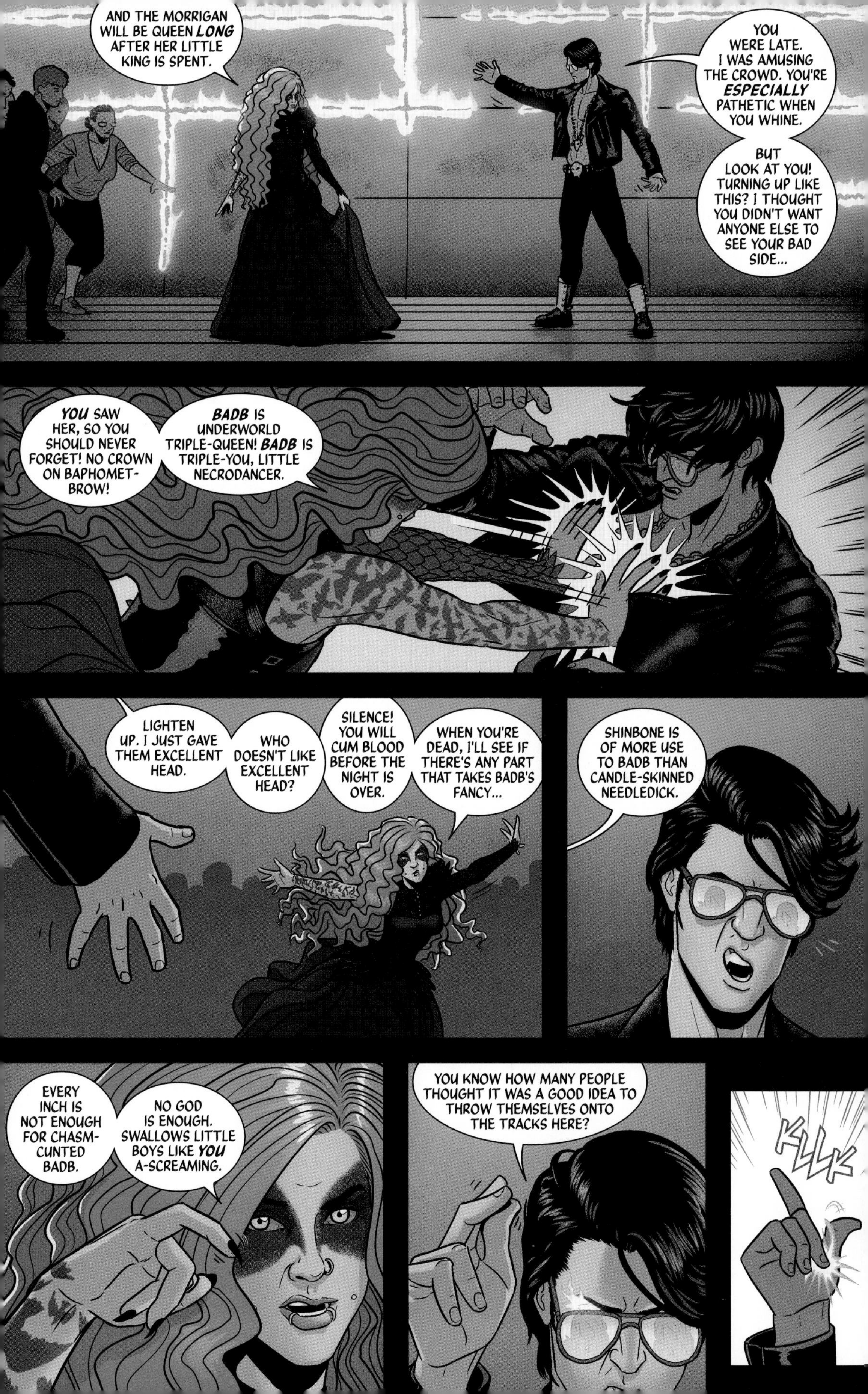
AND THE MORRIGAN WILL BE QUEEN LONG AFTER HER LITTLE KING IS SPENT.
YOU WERE LATE. I WAS AMUSING THE CROWD. YOU'RE ESPECIALLY PATHETIC WHEN YOU WHINE.
BUT LOOK AT YOU! TURNING UP LIKE THIS? I THOUGHT YOU DIDN'T WANT ANYONE ELSE TO SEE YOUR BAD SIDE...
YOU SAW HER, SO YOU SHOULD NEVER FORGET! NO CROWN ON BAPHOMET-BROW!
BADB IS UNDERWORLD TRIPLE-QUEEN! BADB IS TRIPLE-YOU, LITTLE NECRODANCER.
LIGHTEN UP. I JUST GAVE THEM EXCELLENT HEAD.
WHO DOESN'T LIKE EXCELLENT HEAD?
SILENCE! YOU WILL CUM BLOOD BEFORE THE NIGHT IS OVER.
WHEN YOU'RE DEAD, I'LL SEE IF THERE'S ANY PART THAT TAKES BADB'S FANCY...
SHINBONE IS OF MORE USE TO BADB THAN CANDLE-SKINNED NEEDLEDICK.
EVERY INCH IS NOT ENOUGH FOR CHASM-CUNTED BADB.
NO GOD IS ENOUGH. SWALLOWS LITTLE BOYS LIKE YOU A-SCREAMING.
YOU KNOW HOW MANY PEOPLE THOUGHT IT WAS A GOOD IDEA TO THROW THEMSELVES ONTO THE TRACKS HERE?
KLLK

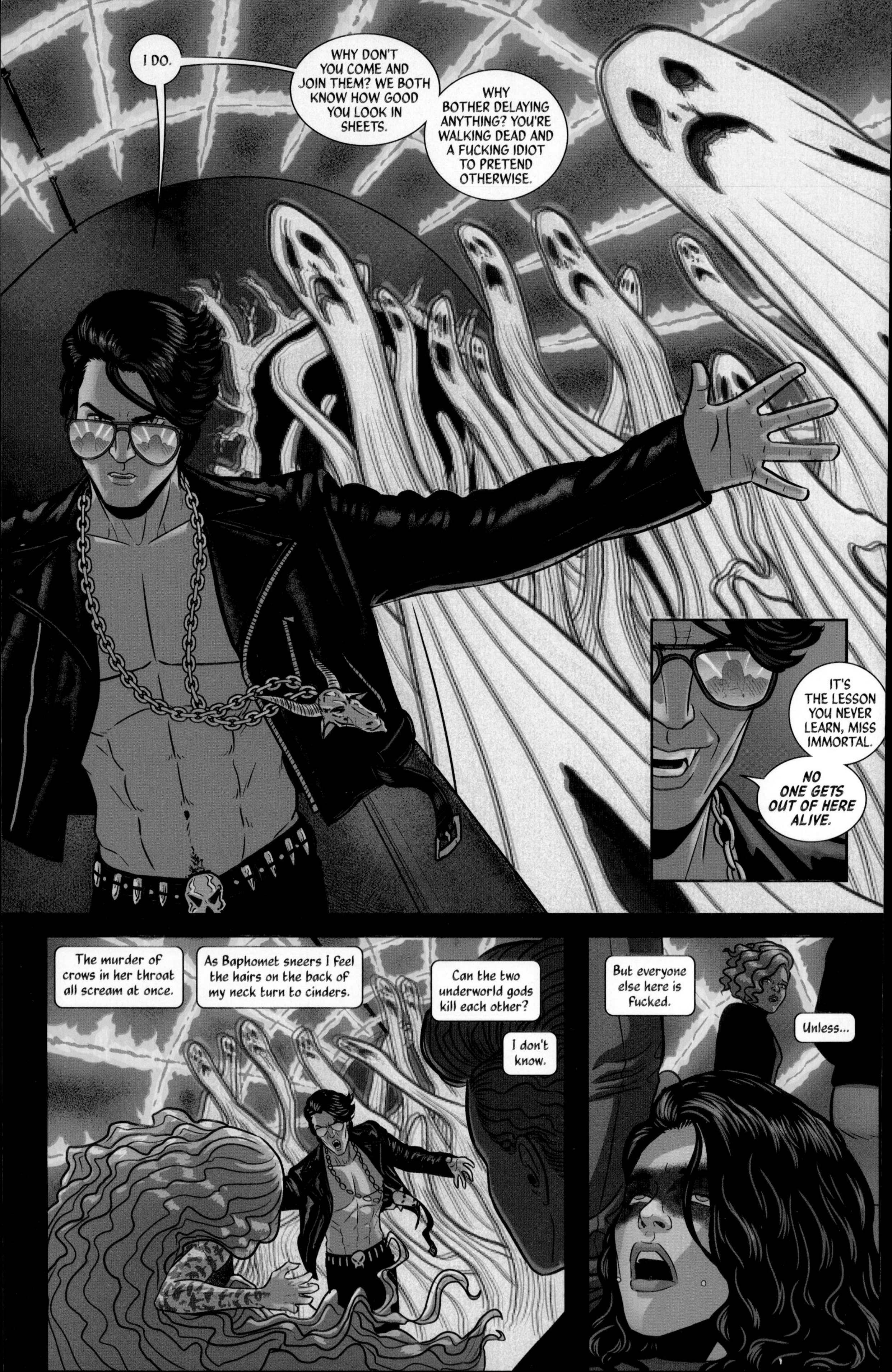
I DO.
WHY DON'T YOU COME AND JOIN THEM? WE BOTH KNOW HOW GOOD YOU LOOK IN SHEETS.
WHY BOTHER DELAYING ANYTHING? YOU'RE WALKING DEAD AND A FUCKING IDIOT TO PRETEND OTHERWISE.
IT'S THE LESSON YOU NEVER LEARN, MISS IMMORTAL.
NO ONE GETS OUT OF HERE ALIVE.
The murder of crows in her throat all scream at once.
As Baphomet sneers I feel the hairs on the back of my neck turn to cinders.
Can the two underworld gods kill each other?
I don't know.
But everyone else here is fucked.
Unless...

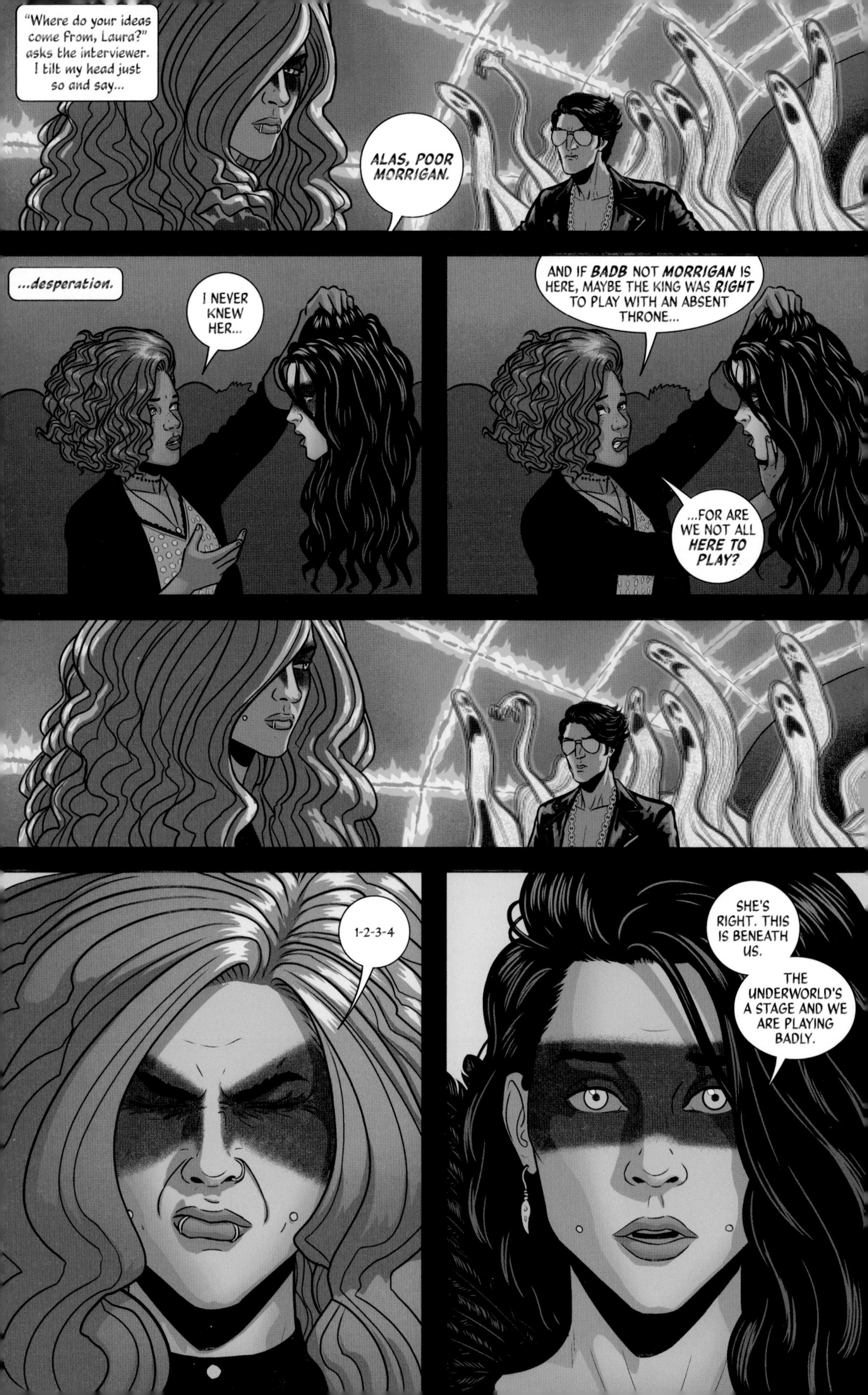
"Where do your ideas come from, Laura?" asks the interviewer. I tilt my head just so and say...
ALAS, POOR MORRIGAN.
...desperation.
I NEVER KNEW HER...
AND IF BADB NOT MORRIGAN IS HERE, MAYBE THE KING WAS RIGHT TO PLAY WITH AN ABSENT THRONE...
...FOR ARE WE NOT ALL HERE TO PLAY?
1-2-3-4
SHE'S RIGHT. THIS IS BENEATH US.
THE UNDERWORLD'S A STAGE AND WE ARE PLAYING BADLY.

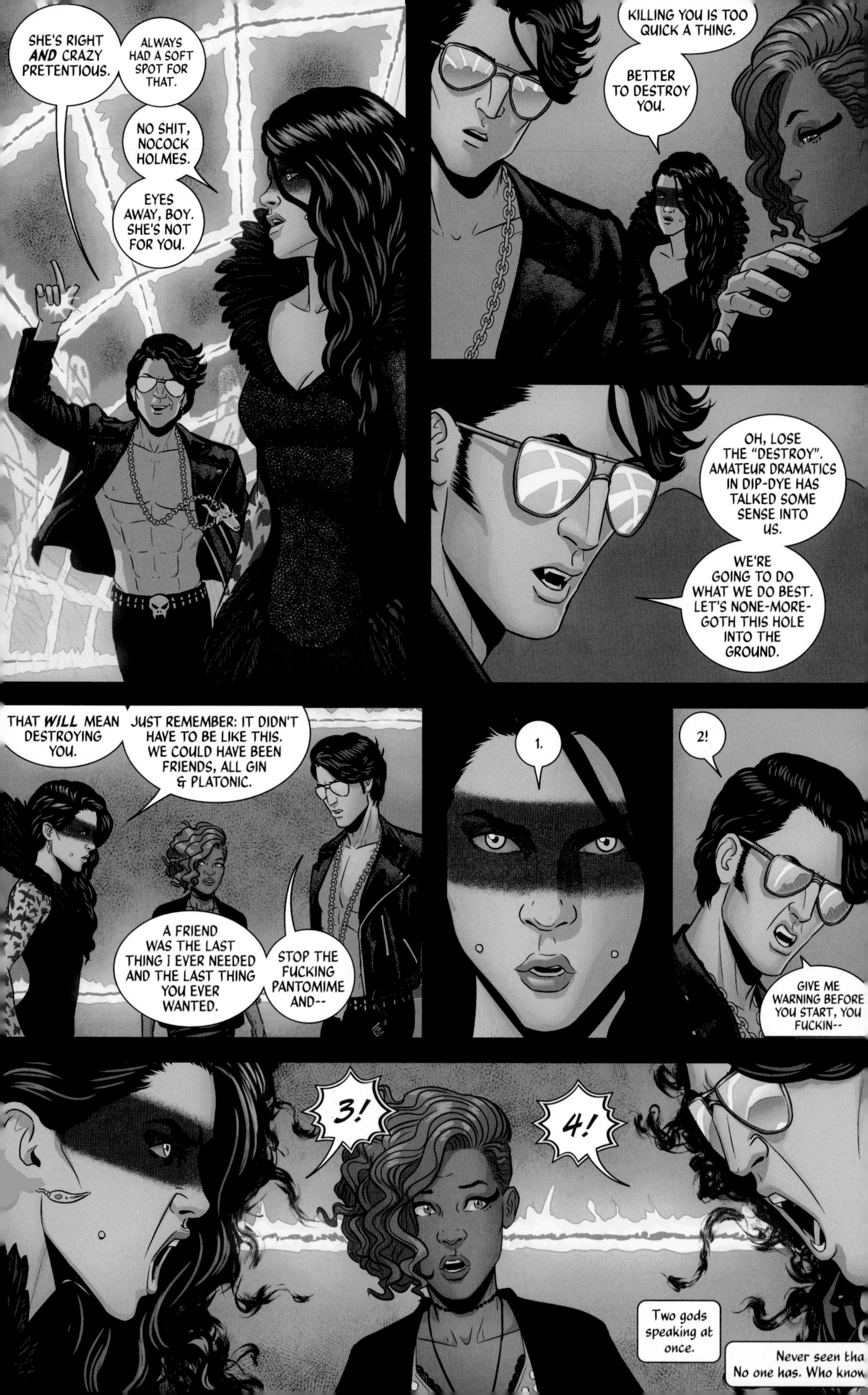

SHE'S RIGHT *AND* CRAZY PRETENTIOUS.
ALWAYS HAD A SOFT SPOT FOR THAT.
NO SHIT, NOCOCK HOLMES.
EYES AWAY, BOY. SHE'S NOT FOR YOU.
KILLING YOU IS TOO QUICK A THING.
BETTER TO DESTROY YOU.
OH, LOSE THE "DESTROY". AMATEUR DRAMATICS IN DIP-DYE HAS TALKED SOME SENSE INTO US.
WE'RE GOING TO DO WHAT WE DO BEST. LET'S NONE-MORE-GOTH THIS HOLE INTO THE GROUND.
THAT *WILL* MEAN DESTROYING YOU.
JUST REMEMBER: IT DIDN'T HAVE TO BE LIKE THIS. WE COULD HAVE BEEN FRIENDS, ALL GIN & PLATONIC.
A FRIEND WAS THE LAST THING I EVER NEEDED AND THE LAST THING YOU EVER WANTED.
STOP THE FUCKING PANTOMIME AND--
1.
2!
GIVE ME WARNING BEFORE YOU START, YOU FUCKIN--
3!
4!
Two gods speaking at once.
Never seen tha
No one has. Who know

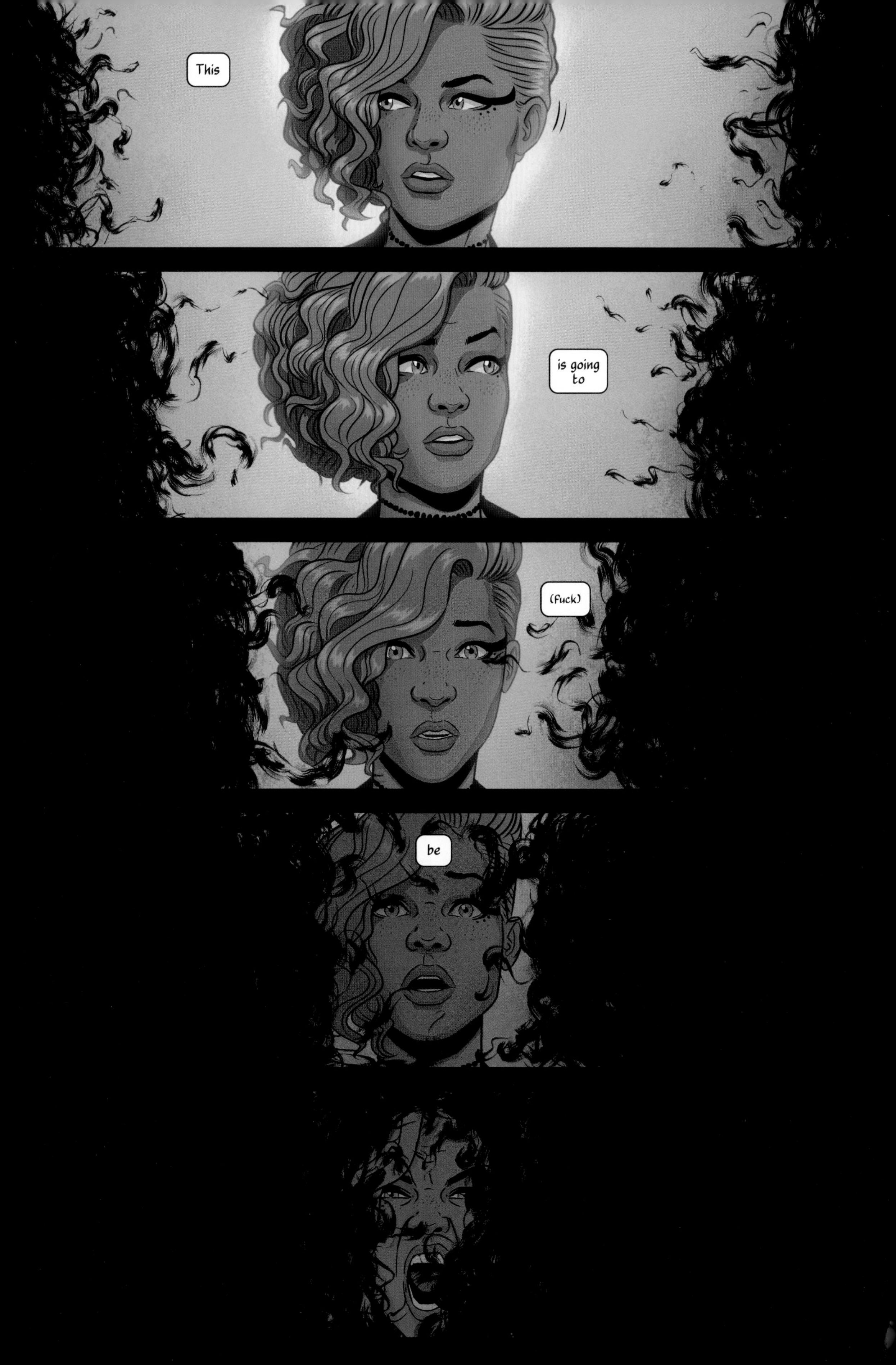
This
is going to
(fuck)
be

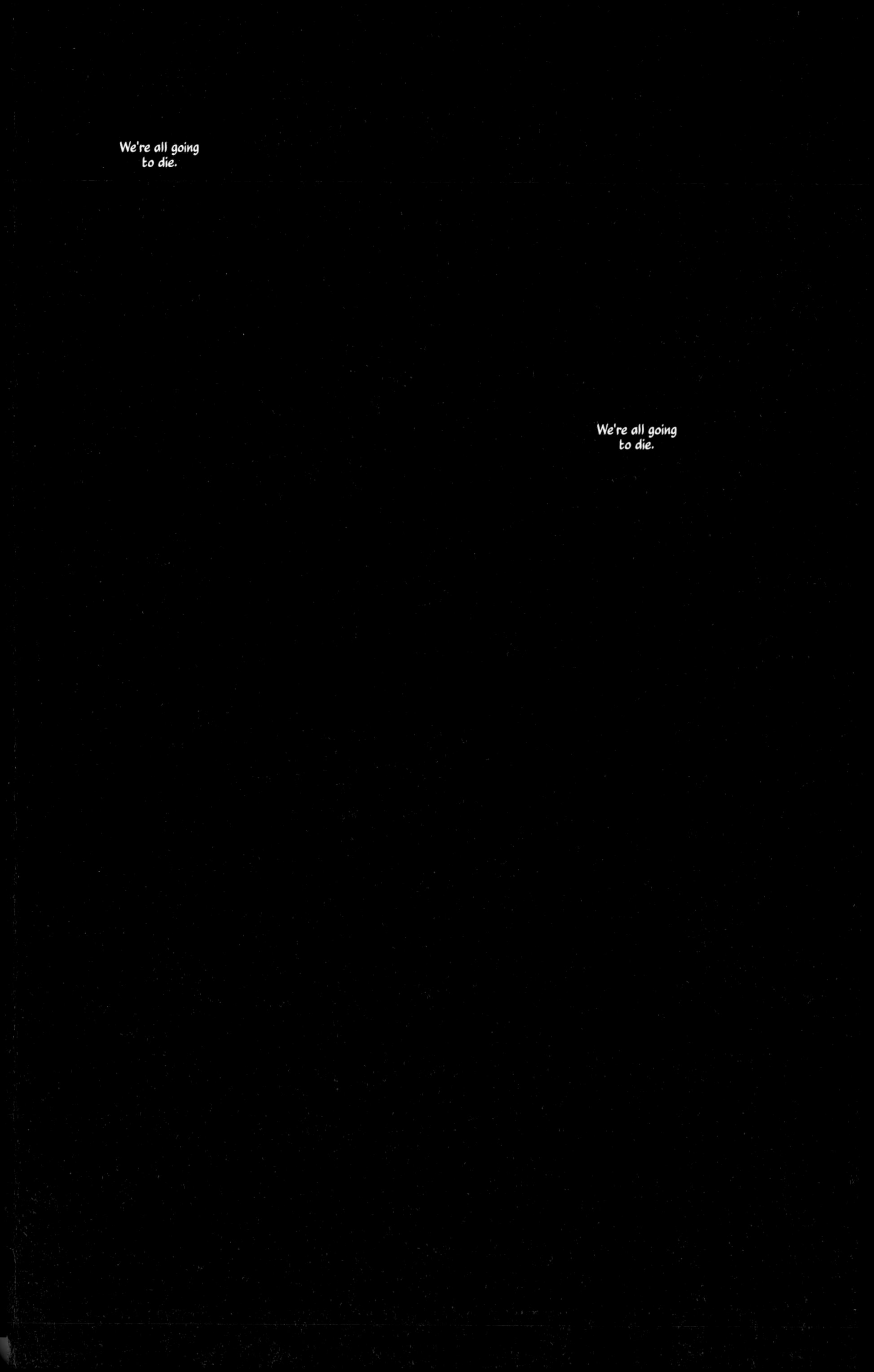
We're all going to die.
We're all going to die.

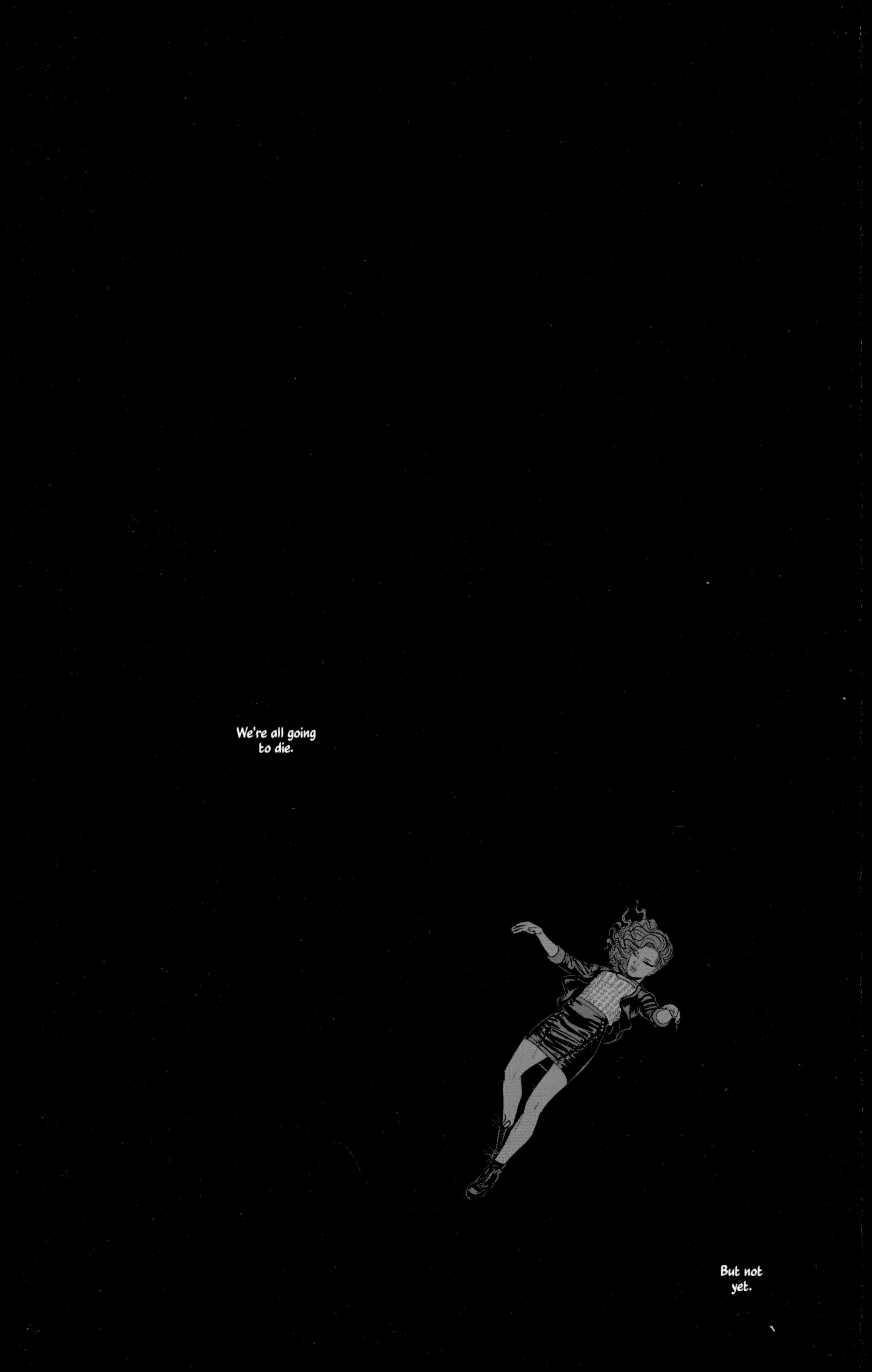
We're all going to die.
But not yet.

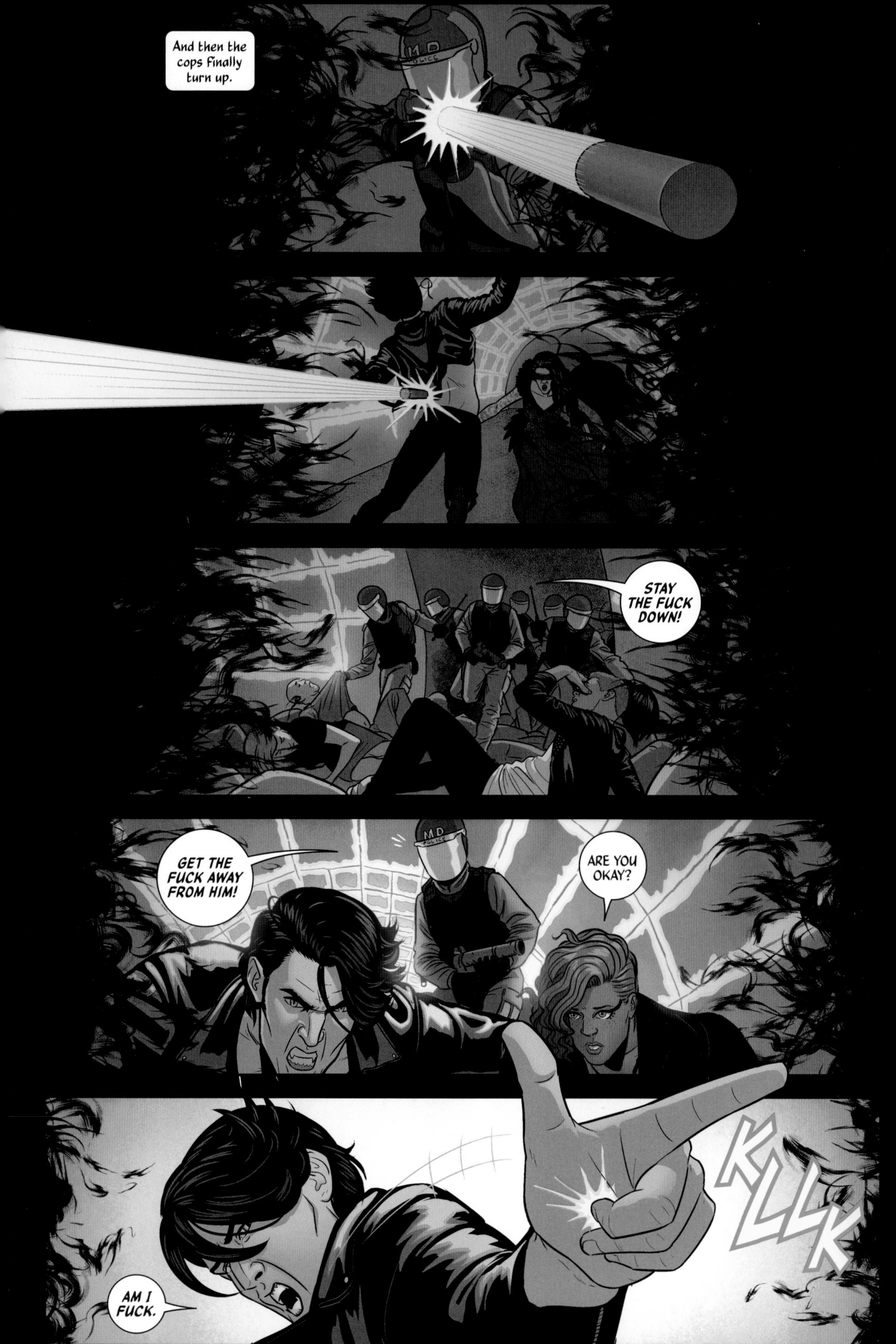
And then the cops finally turn up.
STAY THE FUCK DOWN!
GET THE FUCK AWAY FROM HIM!
ARE YOU OKAY?
AM I FUCK.
KLLK

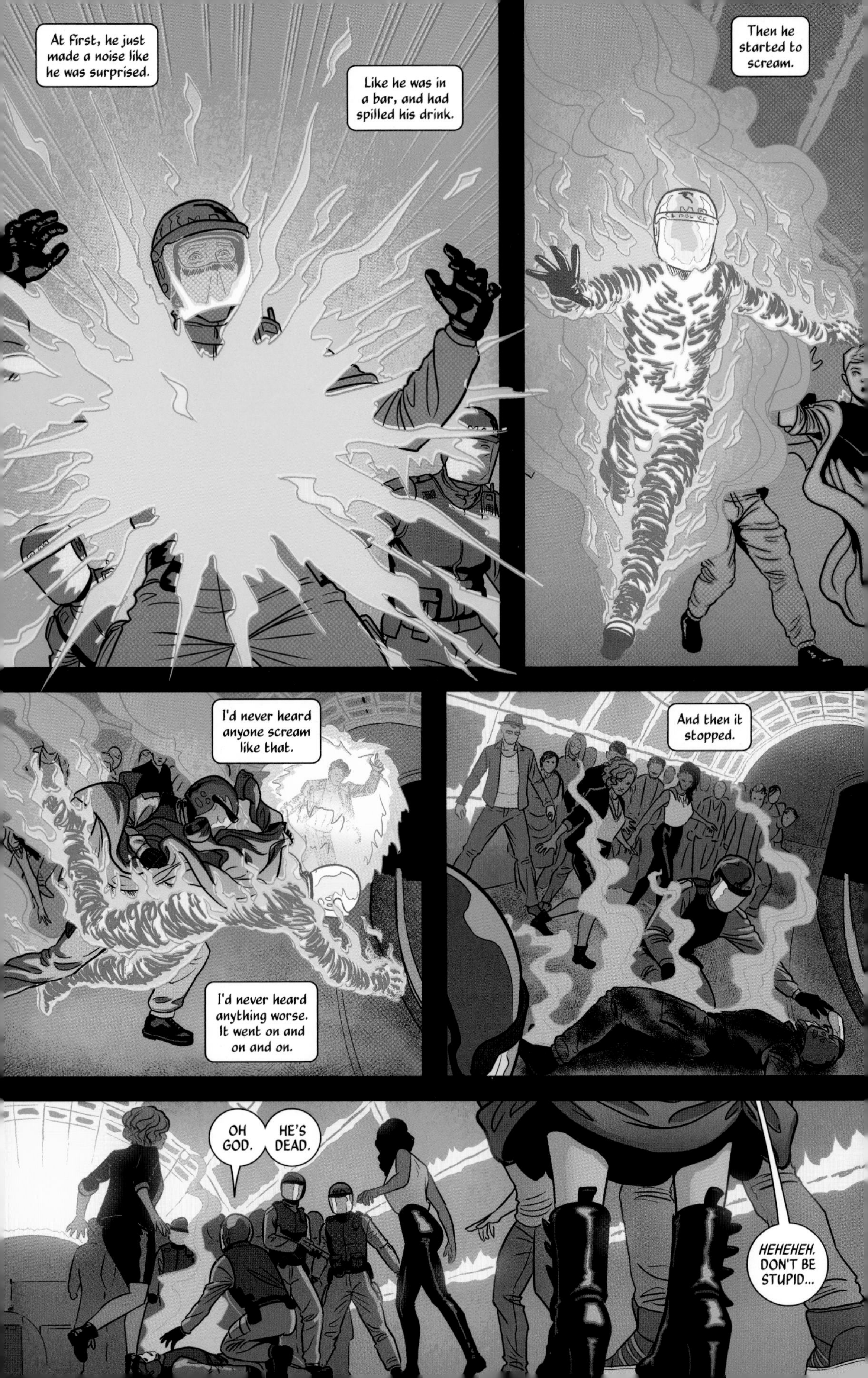
At first, he just made a noise like he was surprised.
Like he was in a bar, and had spilled his drink.
Then he started to scream.
I'd never heard anyone scream like that.
I'd never heard anything worse. It went on and on and on.
And then it stopped.
OH GOD.
HE'S DEAD.
HEHEHEH. DON'T BE STUPID...

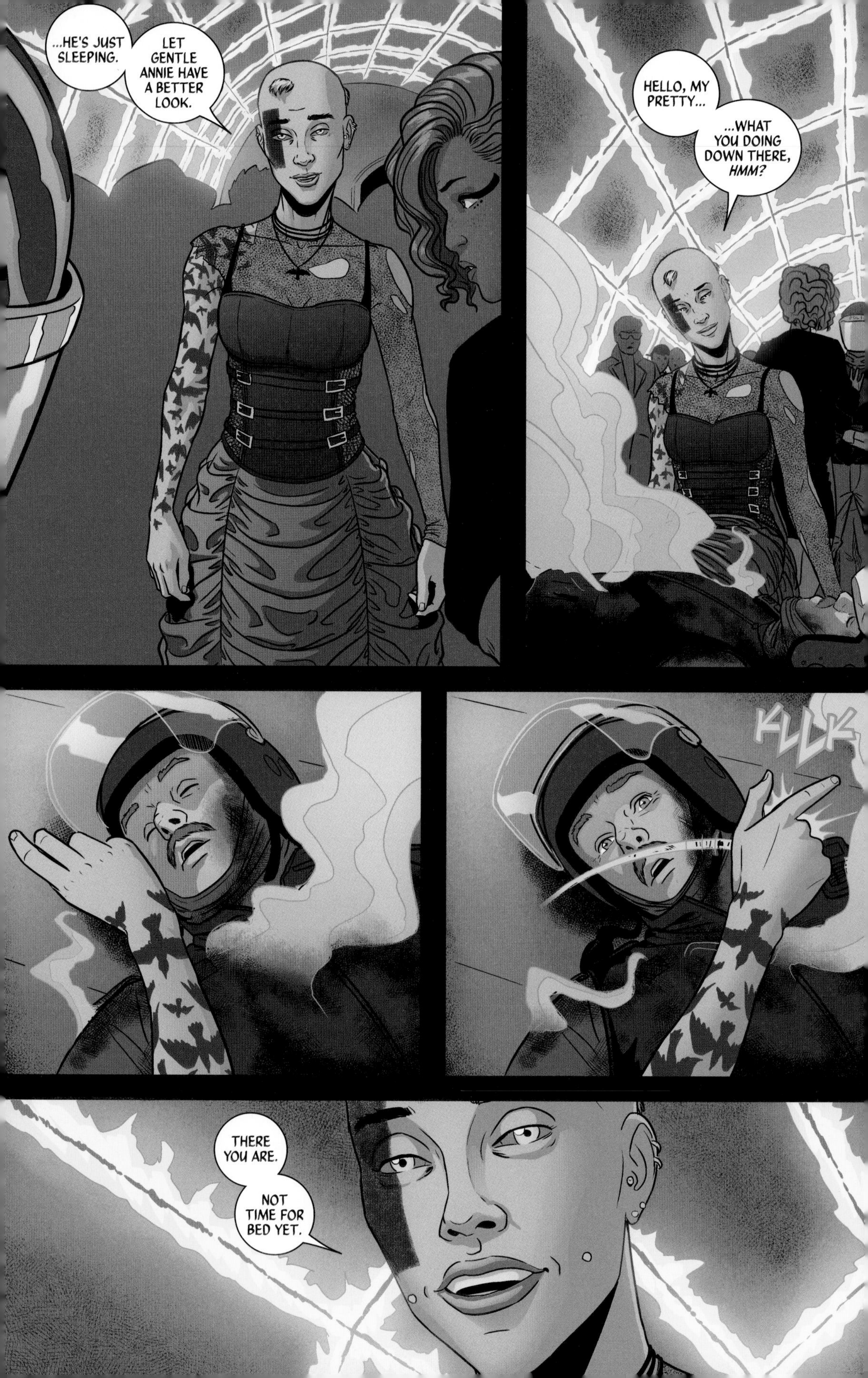
...HE'S JUST SLEEPING.
LET GENTLE ANNIE HAVE A BETTER LOOK.
HELLO, MY PRETTY...
...WHAT YOU DOING DOWN THERE, *HMM?*
KLLK
THERE YOU ARE.
NOT TIME FOR BED YET.

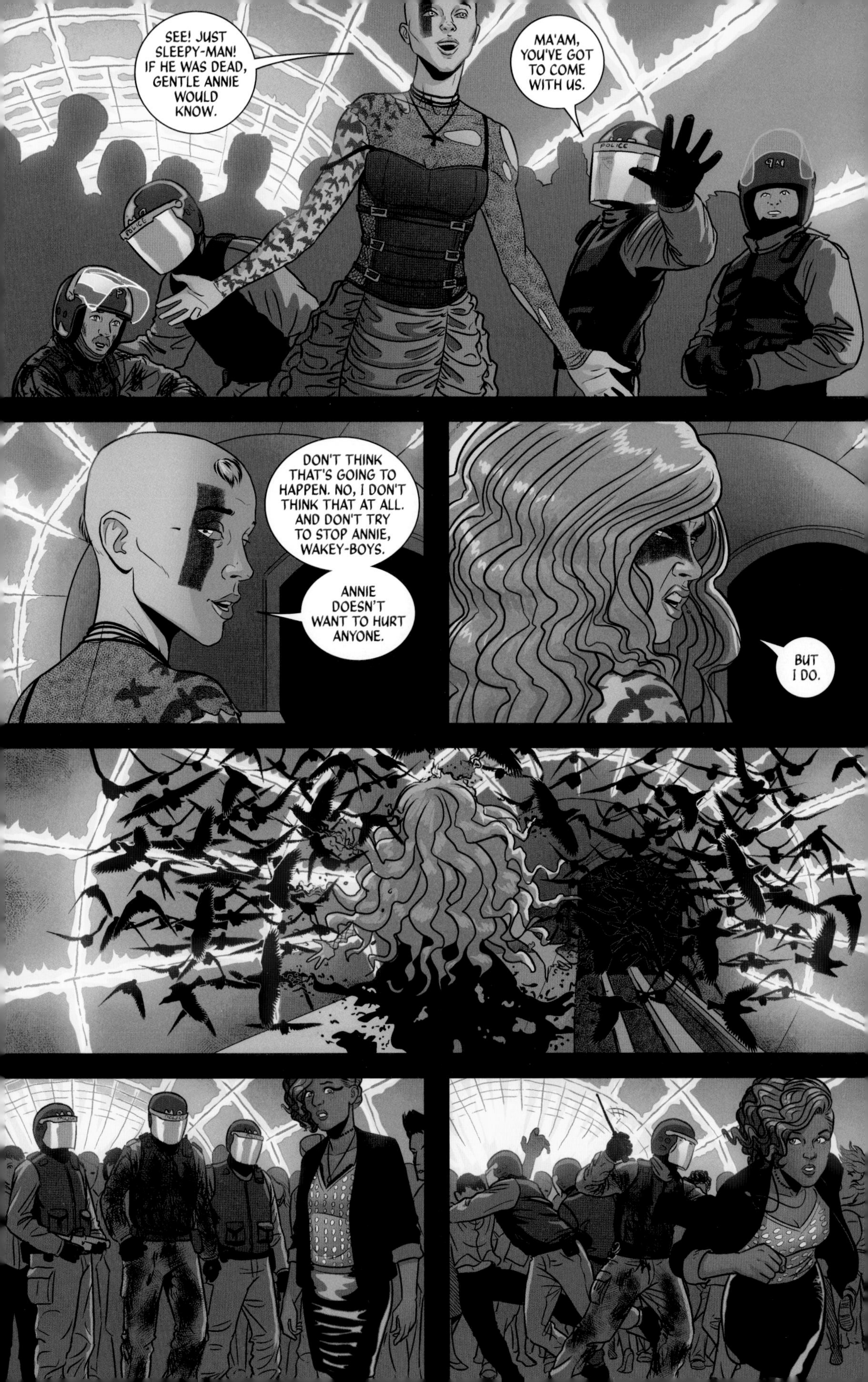
SEE! JUST SLEEPY-MAN! IF HE WAS DEAD, GENTLE ANNIE WOULD KNOW.
MA'AM, YOU'VE GOT TO COME WITH US.
POLICE
POLICE
DON'T THINK THAT'S GOING TO HAPPEN. NO, I DON'T THINK THAT AT ALL. AND DON'T TRY TO STOP ANNIE, WAKEY-BOYS.
ANNIE DOESN'T WANT TO HURT ANYONE.
BUT I DO.

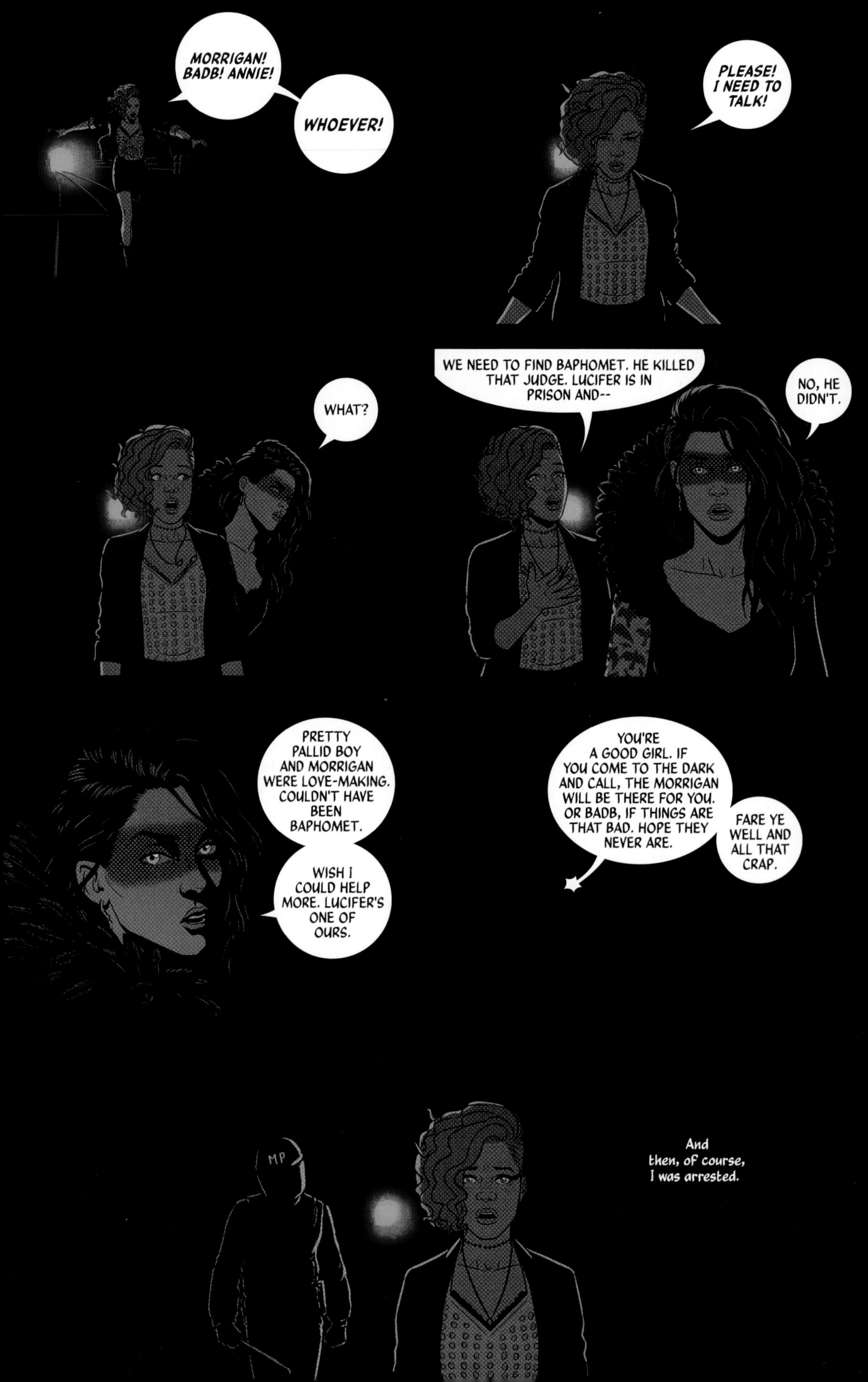
MORRIGAN! BADB! ANNIE!
WHOEVER!
PLEASE! I NEED TO TALK!
WHAT?
WE NEED TO FIND BAPHOMET. HE KILLED THAT JUDGE. LUCIFER IS IN PRISON AND--
NO, HE DIDN'T.
PRETTY PALLID BOY AND MORRIGAN WERE LOVE-MAKING. COULDN'T HAVE BEEN BAPHOMET.
WISH I COULD HELP MORE. LUCIFER'S ONE OF OURS.
YOU'RE A GOOD GIRL. IF YOU COME TO THE DARK AND CALL, THE MORRIGAN WILL BE THERE FOR YOU. OR BADB, IF THINGS ARE THAT BAD. HOPE THEY NEVER ARE.
FARE YE WELL AND ALL THAT CRAP.
MP
And then, of course, I was arrested.

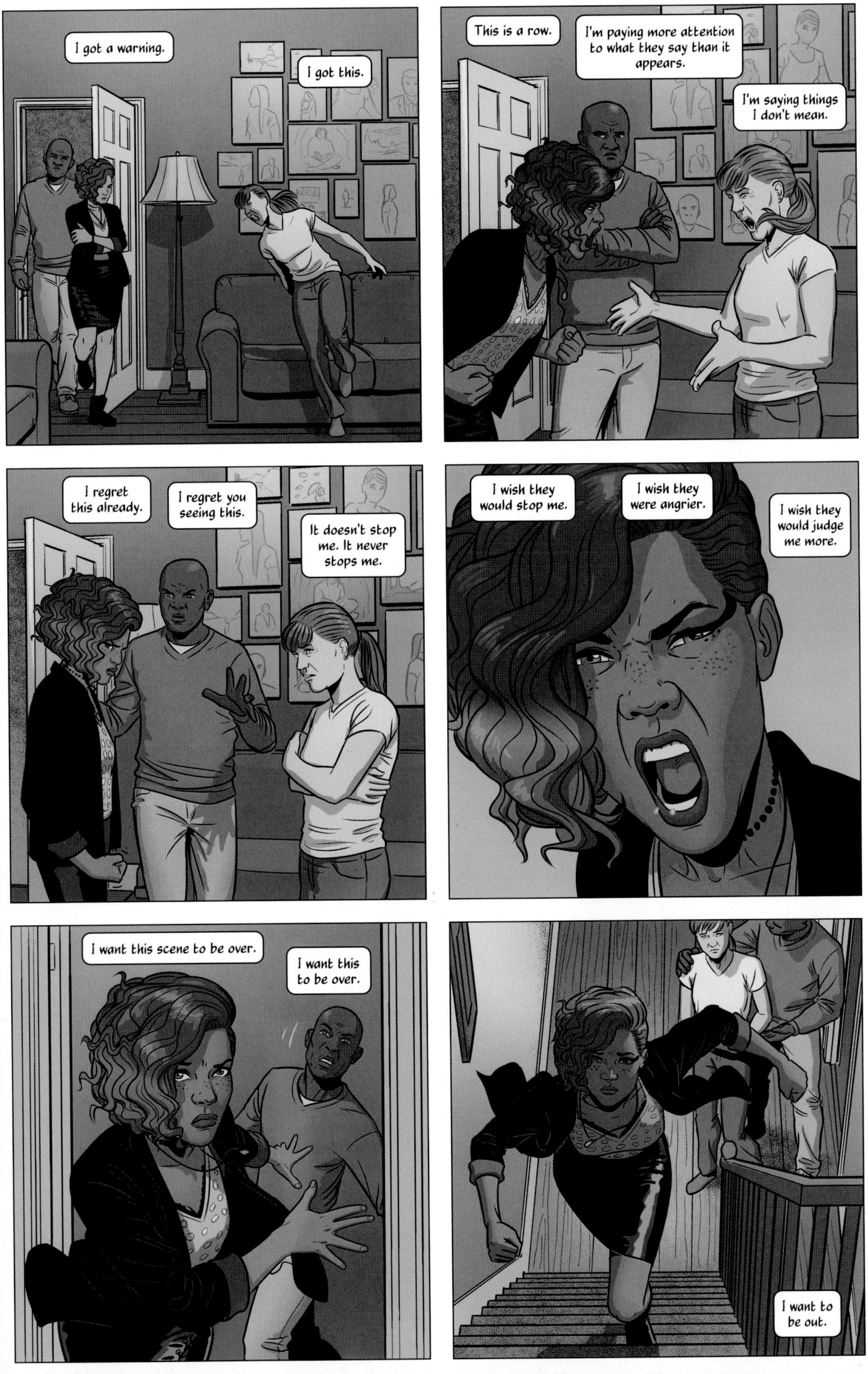
I got a warning.
I got this.
This is a row.
I'm paying more attention to what they say than it appears.
I'm saying things I don't mean.
I regret this already.
I regret you seeing this.
It doesn't stop me. It never stops me.
I wish they would stop me.
I wish they were angrier.
I wish they would judge me more.
I want this scene to be over.
I want this to be over.
I want to be out.

CHTHONIC
HOMESICK BLUES

10 JANUARY 2014

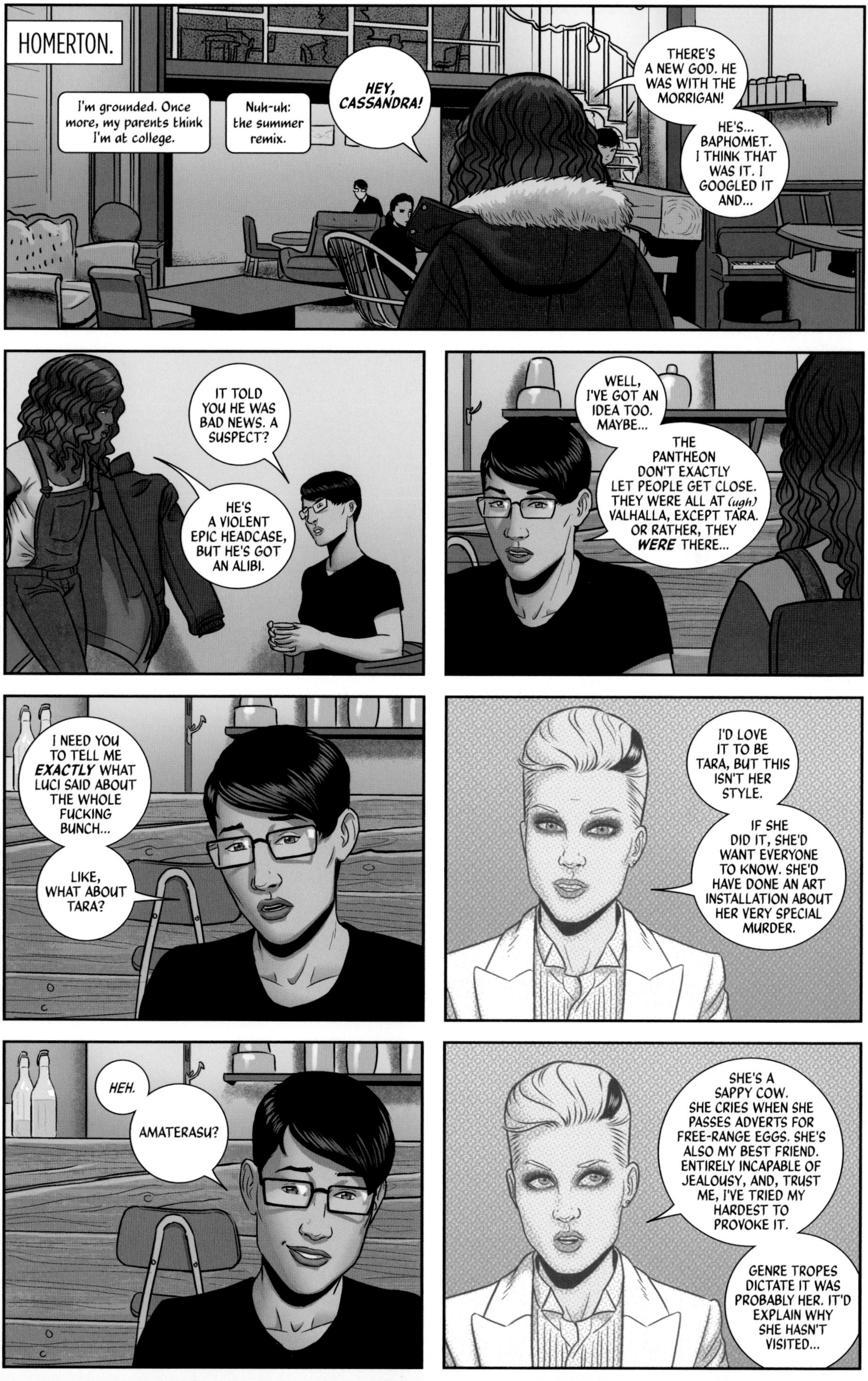
HOMERTON.
I'm grounded. Once more, my parents think I'm at college.
Nuh-uh: the summer remix.
HEY, CASSANDRA!
THERE'S A NEW GOD. HE WAS WITH THE MORRIGAN!
HE'S... BAPHOMET. I THINK THAT WAS IT. I GOOGLED IT AND...
IT TOLD YOU HE WAS BAD NEWS. A SUSPECT?
HE'S A VIOLENT EPIC HEADCASE, BUT HE'S GOT AN ALIBI.
WELL, I'VE GOT AN IDEA TOO. MAYBE...
THE PANTHEON DON'T EXACTLY LET PEOPLE GET CLOSE. THEY WERE ALL AT (ugh) VALHALLA, EXCEPT TARA. OR RATHER, THEY WERE THERE...
I NEED YOU TO TELL ME EXACTLY WHAT LUCI SAID ABOUT THE WHOLE FUCKING BUNCH...
LIKE, WHAT ABOUT TARA?
I'D LOVE IT TO BE TARA, BUT THIS ISN'T HER STYLE.
IF SHE DID IT, SHE'D WANT EVERYONE TO KNOW. SHE'D HAVE DONE AN ART INSTALLATION ABOUT HER VERY SPECIAL MURDER.
HEH.
AMATERASU?
SHE'S A SAPPY COW. SHE CRIES WHEN SHE PASSES ADVERTS FOR FREE-RANGE EGGS. SHE'S ALSO MY BEST FRIEND. ENTIRELY INCAPABLE OF JEALOUSY, AND, TRUST ME, I'VE TRIED MY HARDEST TO PROVOKE IT.
GENRE TROPES DICTATE IT WAS PROBABLY HER. IT'D EXPLAIN WHY SHE HASN'T VISITED...

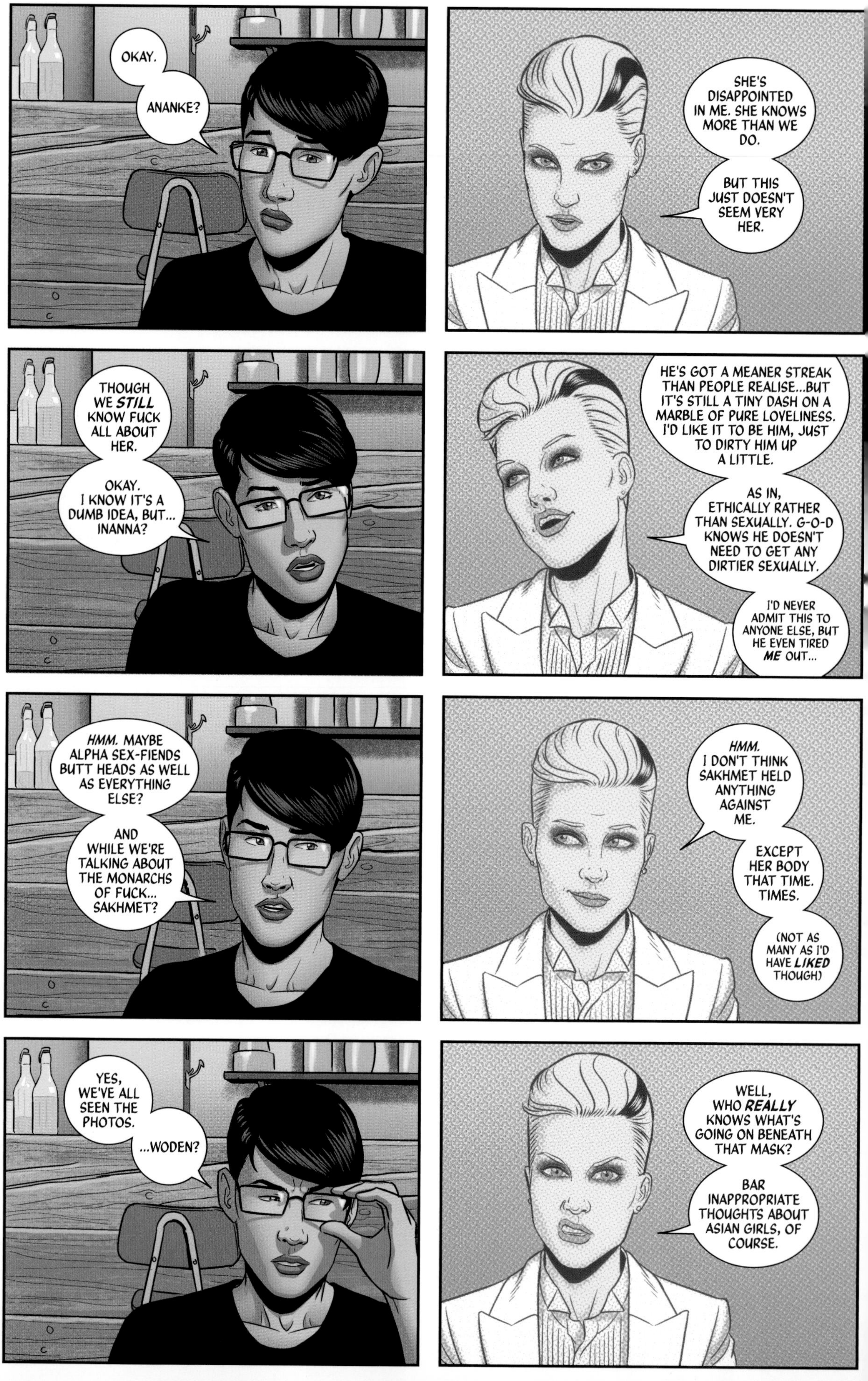
OKAY.
ANANKE?
SHE'S DISAPPOINTED IN ME. SHE KNOWS MORE THAN WE DO.
BUT THIS JUST DOESN'T SEEM VERY HER.
THOUGH WE *STILL* KNOW FUCK ALL ABOUT HER.
OKAY. I KNOW IT'S A DUMB IDEA, BUT... INANNA?
HE'S GOT A MEANER STREAK THAN PEOPLE REALISE...BUT IT'S STILL A TINY DASH ON A MARBLE OF PURE LOVELINESS. I'D LIKE IT TO BE HIM, JUST TO DIRTY HIM UP A LITTLE.
AS IN, ETHICALLY RATHER THAN SEXUALLY. G-O-D KNOWS HE DOESN'T NEED TO GET ANY DIRTIER SEXUALLY.
I'D NEVER ADMIT THIS TO ANYONE ELSE, BUT HE EVEN TIRED *ME* OUT...
HMM. MAYBE ALPHA SEX-FIENDS BUTT HEADS AS WELL AS EVERYTHING ELSE?
AND WHILE WE'RE TALKING ABOUT THE MONARCHS OF FUCK... SAKHMET?
HMM. I DON'T THINK SAKHMET HELD ANYTHING AGAINST ME.
EXCEPT HER BODY THAT TIME. TIMES.
(NOT AS MANY AS I'D HAVE *LIKED* THOUGH)
YES, WE'VE ALL SEEN THE PHOTOS.
...WODEN?
WELL, WHO *REALLY* KNOWS WHAT'S GOING ON BENEATH THAT MASK?
BAR INAPPROPRIATE THOUGHTS ABOUT ASIAN GIRLS, OF COURSE.

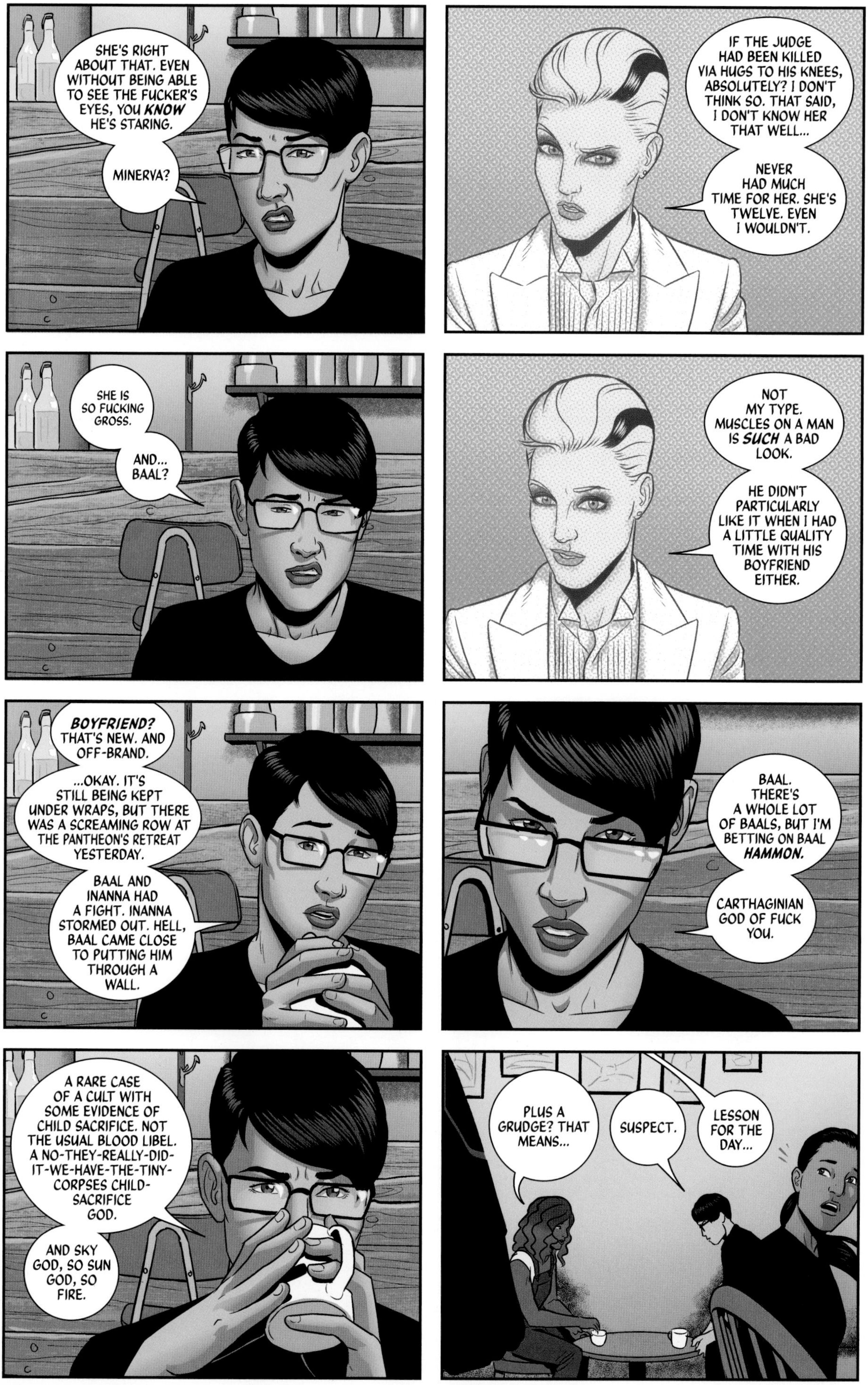
SHE'S RIGHT ABOUT THAT. EVEN WITHOUT BEING ABLE TO SEE THE FUCKER'S EYES, YOU KNOW HE'S STARING.
MINERVA?
IF THE JUDGE HAD BEEN KILLED VIA HUGS TO HIS KNEES, ABSOLUTELY? I DON'T THINK SO. THAT SAID, I DON'T KNOW HER THAT WELL...
NEVER HAD MUCH TIME FOR HER. SHE'S TWELVE. EVEN I WOULDN'T.
SHE IS SO FUCKING GROSS.
AND... BAAL?
NOT MY TYPE. MUSCLES ON A MAN IS SUCH A BAD LOOK.
HE DIDN'T PARTICULARLY LIKE IT WHEN I HAD A LITTLE QUALITY TIME WITH HIS BOYFRIEND EITHER.
BOYFRIEND? THAT'S NEW. AND OFF-BRAND.
...OKAY. IT'S STILL BEING KEPT UNDER WRAPS, BUT THERE WAS A SCREAMING ROW AT THE PANTHEON'S RETREAT YESTERDAY.
BAAL AND INANNA HAD A FIGHT. INANNA STORMED OUT. HELL, BAAL CAME CLOSE TO PUTTING HIM THROUGH A WALL.
BAAL. THERE'S A WHOLE LOT OF BAALS, BUT I'M BETTING ON BAAL HAMMON.
CARTHAGINIAN GOD OF FUCK YOU.
A RARE CASE OF A CULT WITH SOME EVIDENCE OF CHILD SACRIFICE. NOT THE USUAL BLOOD LIBEL. A NO-THEY-REALLY-DID-IT-WE-HAVE-THE-TINY-CORPSES CHILD-SACRIFICE GOD.
AND SKY GOD, SO SUN GOD, SO FIRE.
PLUS A GRUDGE? THAT MEANS...
SUSPECT.
LESSON FOR THE DAY...

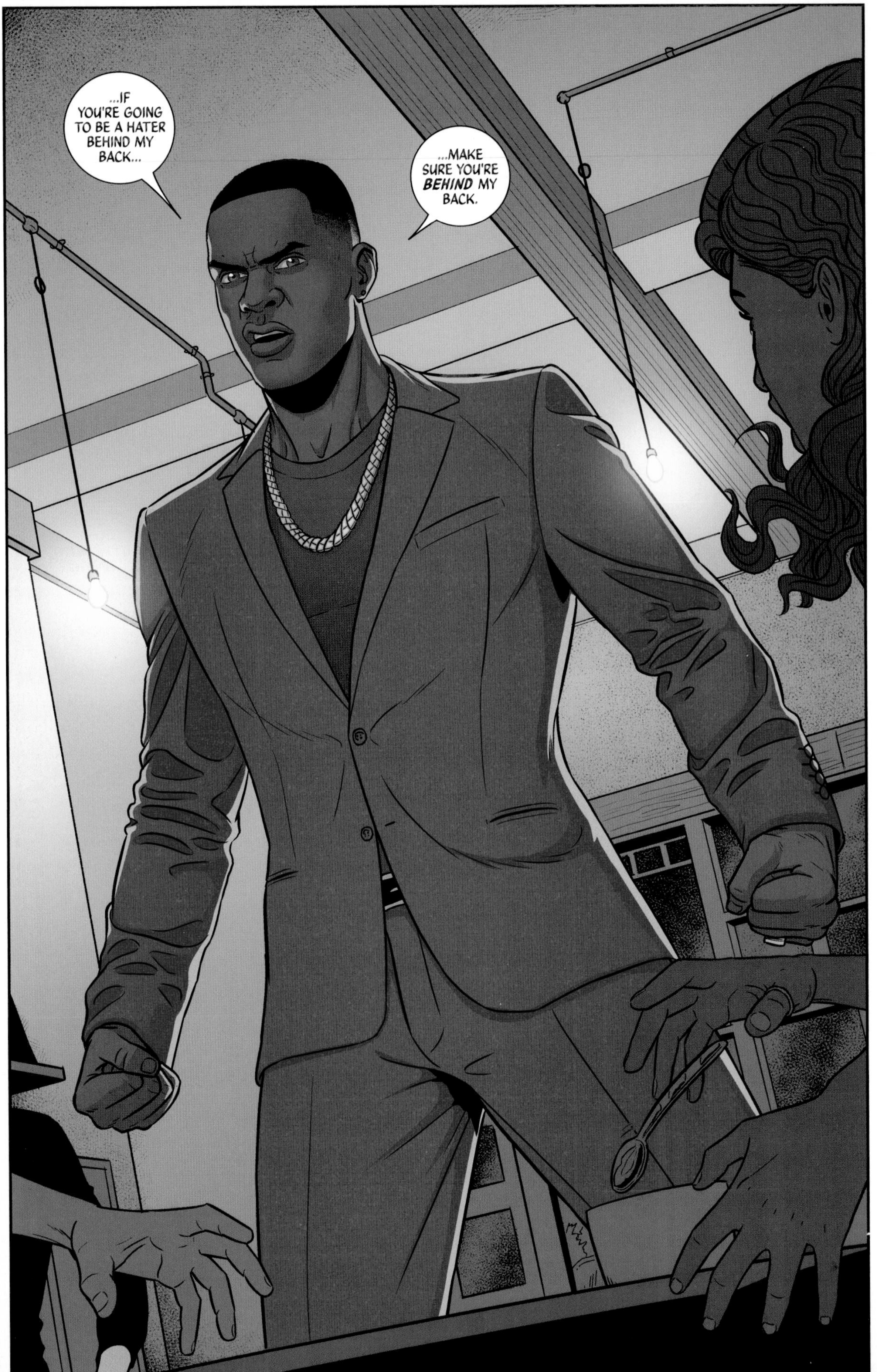
...IF YOU'RE GOING TO BE A HATER BEHIND MY BACK...
...MAKE SURE YOU'RE *BEHIND* MY BACK.

REVENGE IS THE
MOST IMPORTANT
MEAL OF THE DAY

10 JANUARY 2014

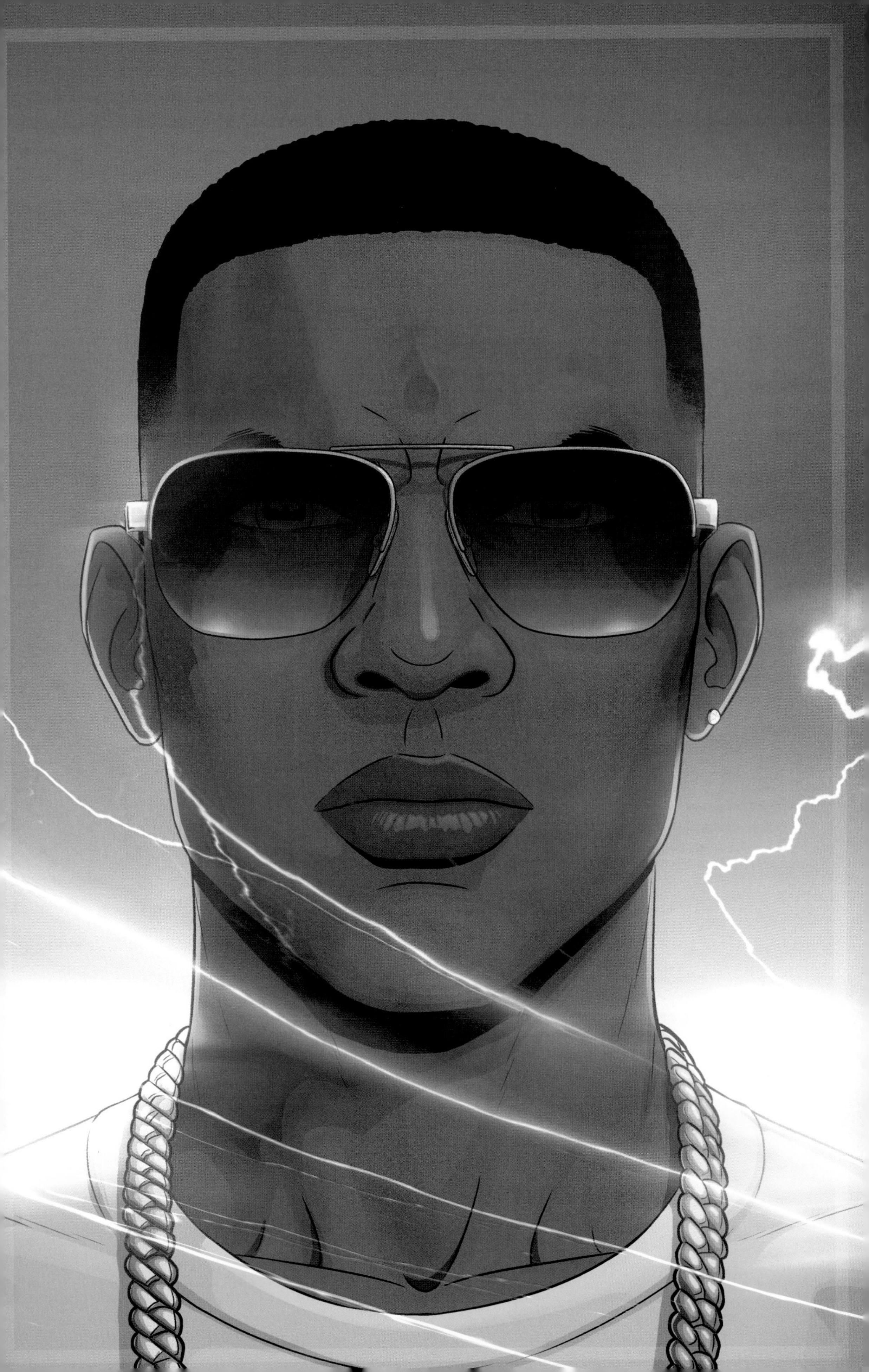

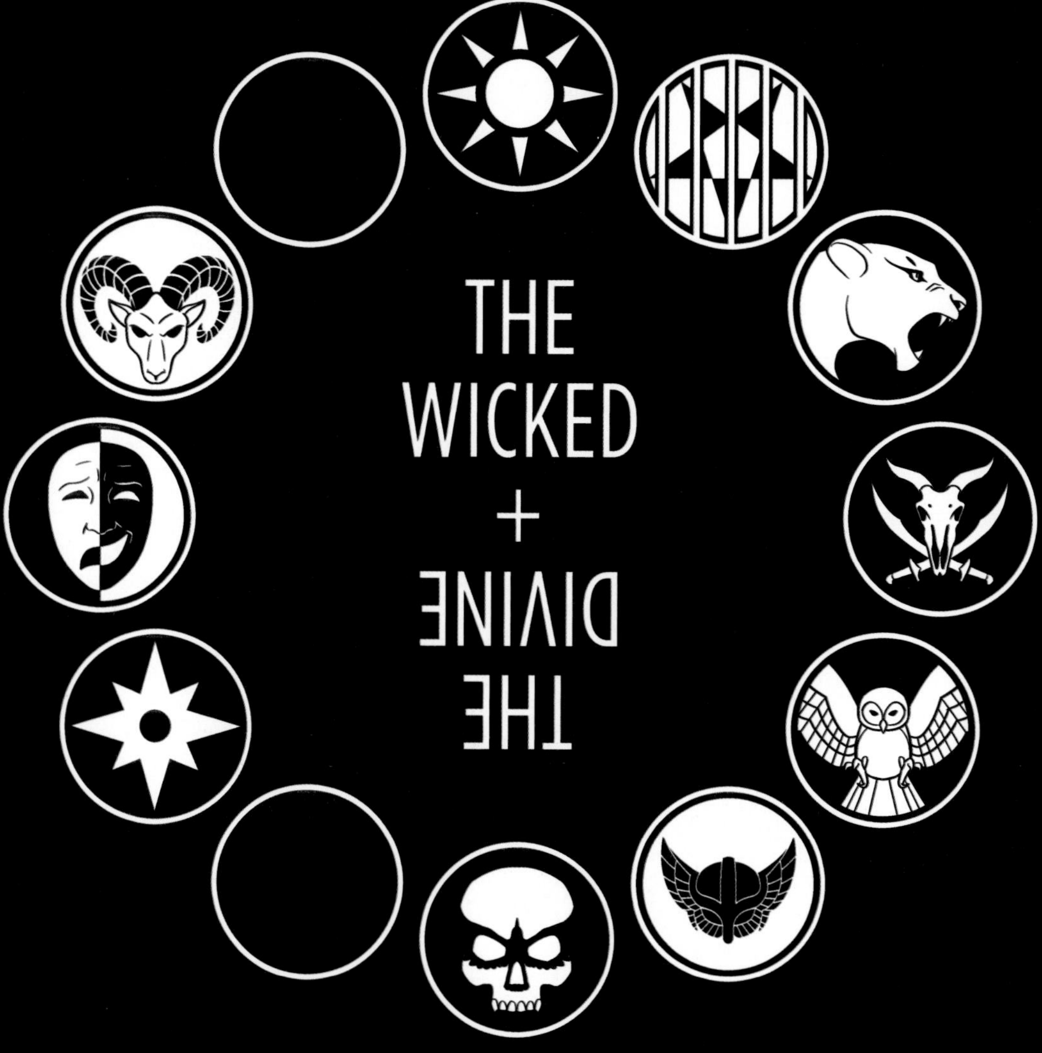
THE
WICKED
+
THE
DIVINE

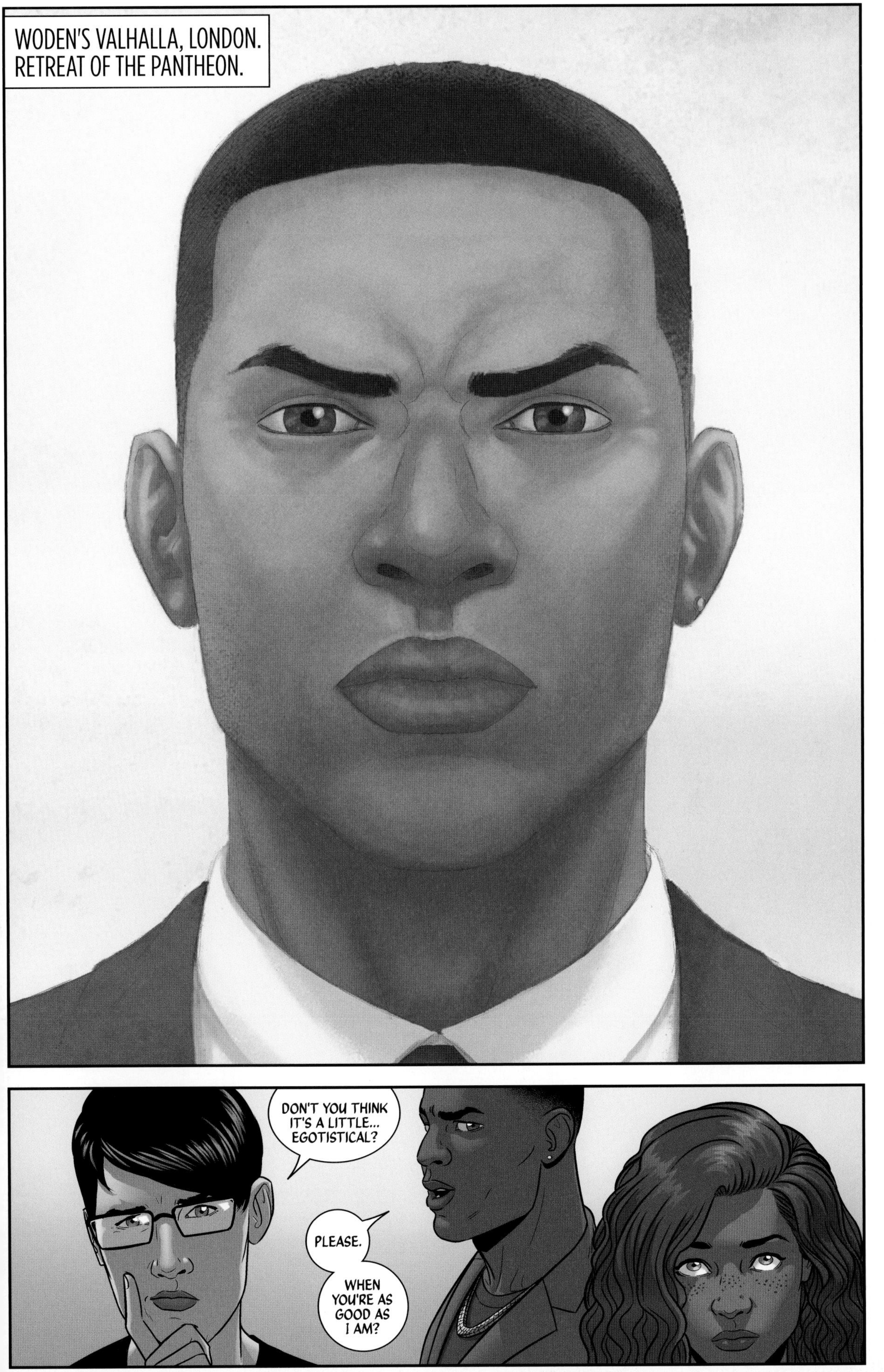
WODEN'S VALHALLA, LONDON.
RETREAT OF THE PANTHEON.
DON'T YOU THINK IT'S A LITTLE... EGOTISTICAL?
PLEASE.
WHEN YOU'RE AS GOOD AS I AM?

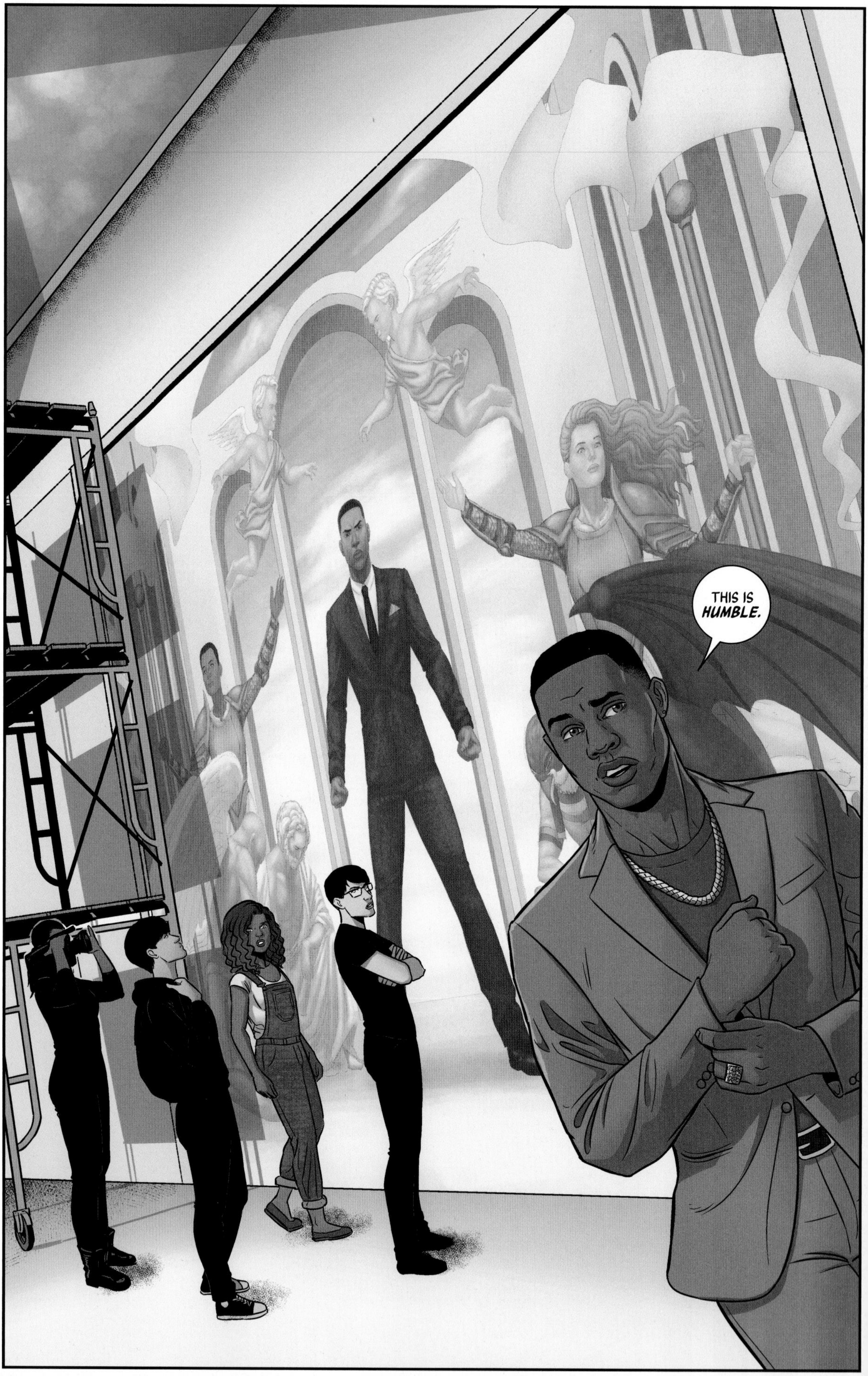
THIS IS *HUMBLE.*

THE IMMORAL
OF THE TALE

10 JANUARY 2014

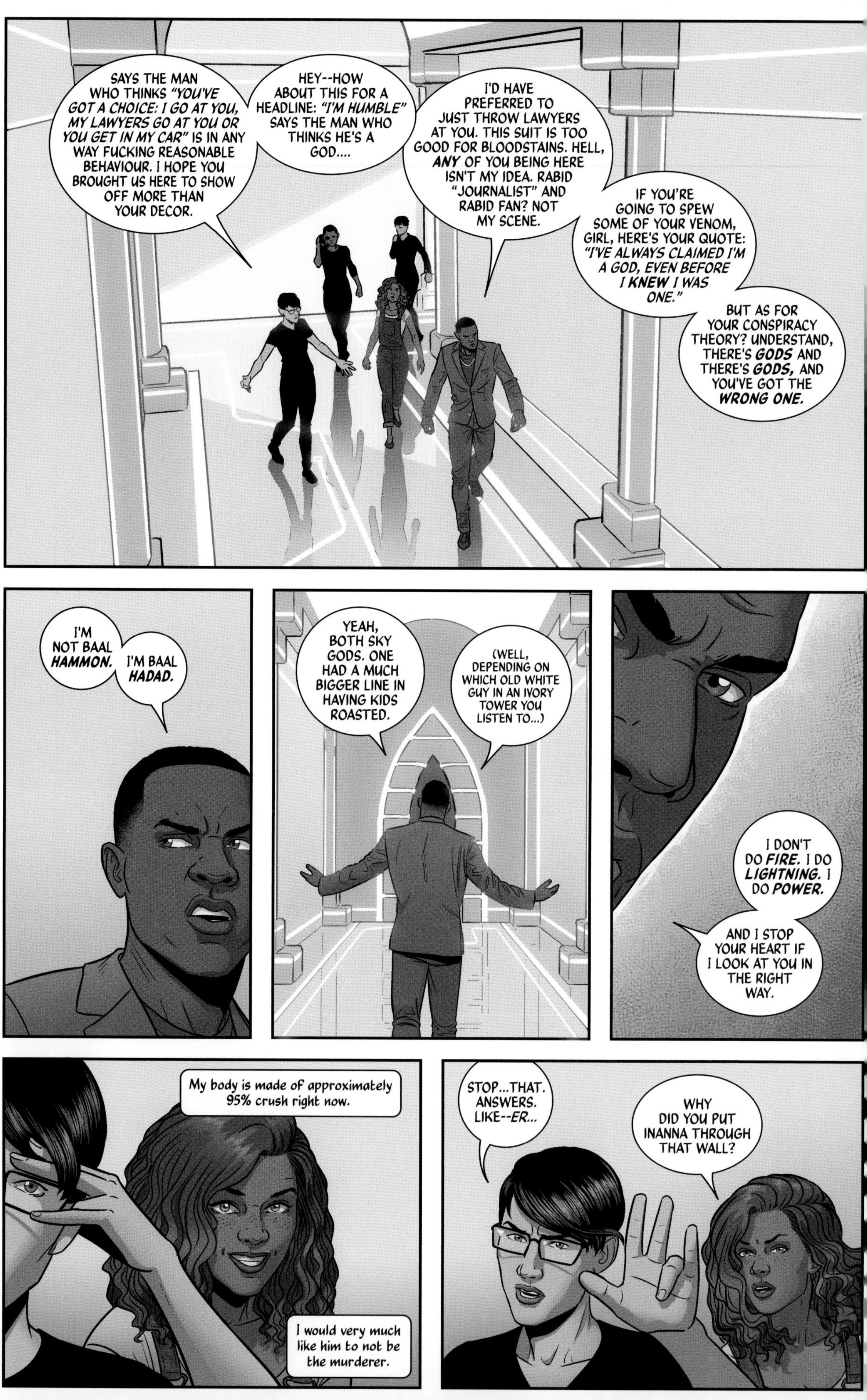
SAYS THE MAN WHO THINKS "YOU'VE GOT A CHOICE: I GO AT YOU, MY LAWYERS GO AT YOU OR YOU GET IN MY CAR" IS IN ANY WAY FUCKING REASONABLE BEHAVIOUR. I HOPE YOU BROUGHT US HERE TO SHOW OFF MORE THAN YOUR DECOR.
HEY--HOW ABOUT THIS FOR A HEADLINE: "I'M HUMBLE" SAYS THE MAN WHO THINKS HE'S A GOD....
I'D HAVE PREFERRED TO JUST THROW LAWYERS AT YOU. THIS SUIT IS TOO GOOD FOR BLOODSTAINS. HELL, ANY OF YOU BEING HERE ISN'T MY IDEA. RABID "JOURNALIST" AND RABID FAN? NOT MY SCENE.
IF YOU'RE GOING TO SPEW SOME OF YOUR VENOM, GIRL, HERE'S YOUR QUOTE: "I'VE ALWAYS CLAIMED I'M A GOD, EVEN BEFORE I KNEW I WAS ONE."
BUT AS FOR YOUR CONSPIRACY THEORY? UNDERSTAND, THERE'S GODS AND THERE'S GODS, AND YOU'VE GOT THE WRONG ONE.
I'M NOT BAAL HAMMON.
I'M BAAL HADAD.
YEAH, BOTH SKY GODS. ONE HAD A MUCH BIGGER LINE IN HAVING KIDS ROASTED.
(WELL, DEPENDING ON WHICH OLD WHITE GUY IN AN IVORY TOWER YOU LISTEN TO...)
I DON'T DO FIRE. I DO LIGHTNING. I DO POWER.
AND I STOP YOUR HEART IF I LOOK AT YOU IN THE RIGHT WAY.
My body is made of approximately 95% crush right now.
I would very much like him to not be the murderer.
STOP...THAT. ANSWERS. LIKE--ER...
WHY DID YOU PUT INANNA THROUGH THAT WALL?

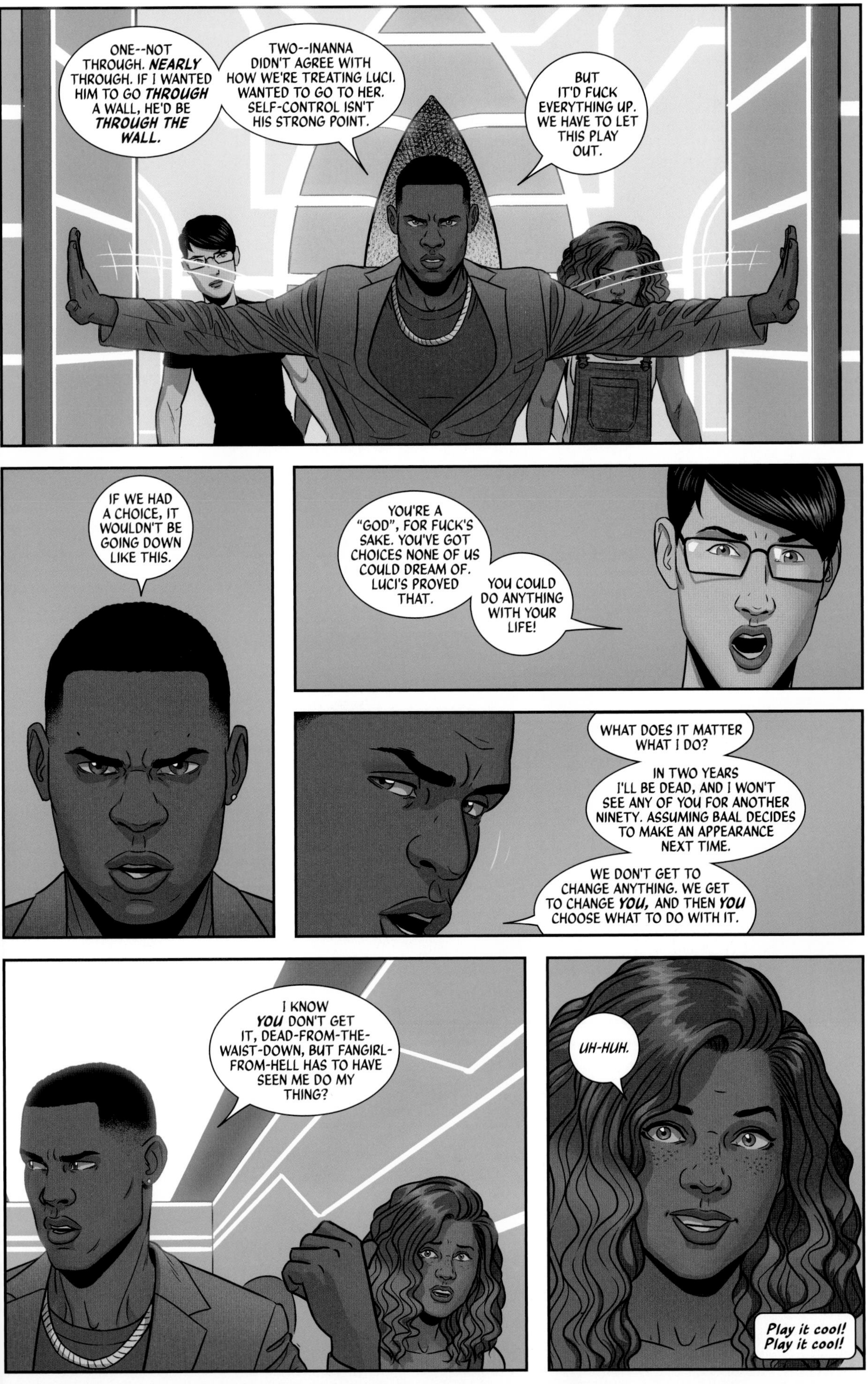
ONE--NOT THROUGH. NEARLY THROUGH. IF I WANTED HIM TO GO THROUGH A WALL, HE'D BE THROUGH THE WALL.
TWO--INANNA DIDN'T AGREE WITH HOW WE'RE TREATING LUCI. WANTED TO GO TO HER. SELF-CONTROL ISN'T HIS STRONG POINT.
BUT IT'D FUCK EVERYTHING UP. WE HAVE TO LET THIS PLAY OUT.
IF WE HAD A CHOICE, IT WOULDN'T BE GOING DOWN LIKE THIS.
YOU'RE A "GOD", FOR FUCK'S SAKE. YOU'VE GOT CHOICES NONE OF US COULD DREAM OF. LUCI'S PROVED THAT.
YOU COULD DO ANYTHING WITH YOUR LIFE!
WHAT DOES IT MATTER WHAT I DO?
IN TWO YEARS I'LL BE DEAD, AND I WON'T SEE ANY OF YOU FOR ANOTHER NINETY. ASSUMING BAAL DECIDES TO MAKE AN APPEARANCE NEXT TIME.
WE DON'T GET TO CHANGE ANYTHING. WE GET TO CHANGE YOU, AND THEN YOU CHOOSE WHAT TO DO WITH IT.
I KNOW YOU DON'T GET IT, DEAD-FROM-THE-WAIST-DOWN, BUT FANGIRL-FROM-HELL HAS TO HAVE SEEN ME DO MY THING?
UH-HUH.
Play it cool! Play it cool!

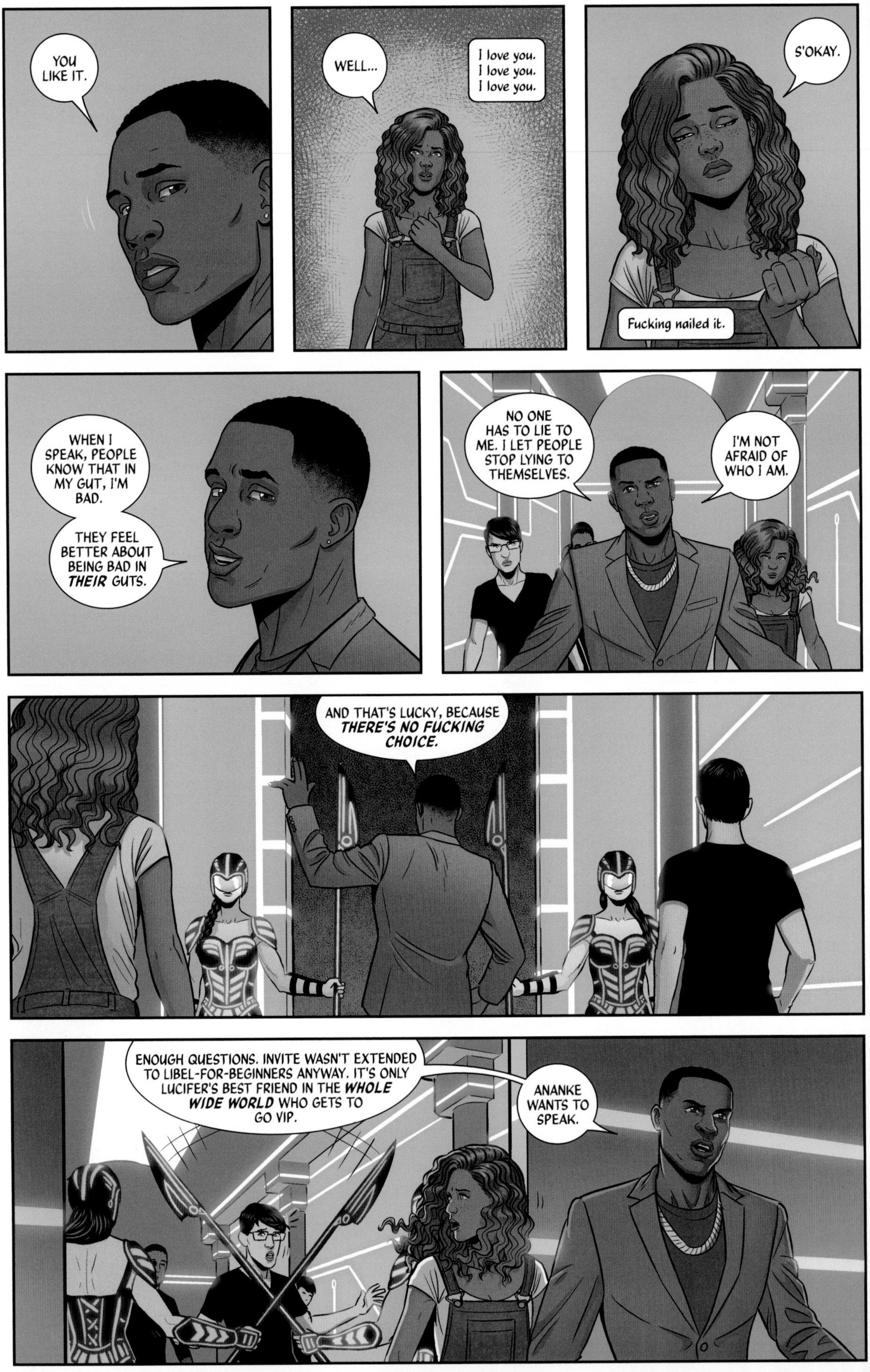
YOU LIKE IT.
WELL...
I love you. I love you. I love you.
S'OKAY.
Fucking nailed it.
WHEN I SPEAK, PEOPLE KNOW THAT IN MY GUT, I'M BAD.
THEY FEEL BETTER ABOUT BEING BAD IN *THEIR* GUTS.
NO ONE HAS TO LIE TO ME. I LET PEOPLE STOP LYING TO THEMSELVES.
I'M NOT AFRAID OF WHO I AM.
AND THAT'S LUCKY, BECAUSE *THERE'S NO FUCKING CHOICE.*
ENOUGH QUESTIONS. INVITE WASN'T EXTENDED TO LIBEL-FOR-BEGINNERS ANYWAY. IT'S ONLY LUCIFER'S BEST FRIEND IN THE *WHOLE WIDE WORLD* WHO GETS TO GO VIP.
ANANKE WANTS TO SPEAK.

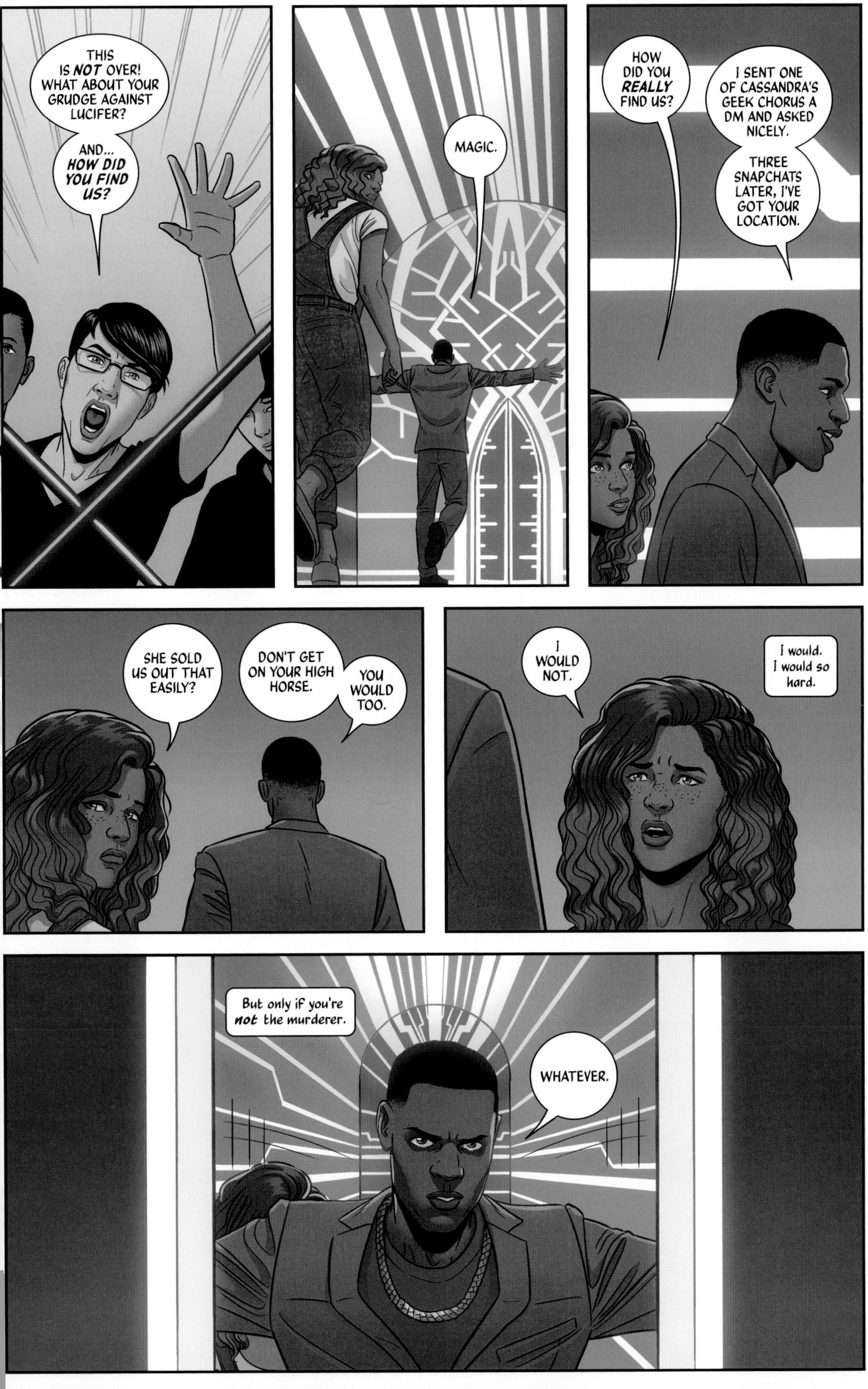
THIS IS NOT OVER! WHAT ABOUT YOUR GRUDGE AGAINST LUCIFER?
AND... HOW DID YOU FIND US?
MAGIC.
HOW DID YOU REALLY FIND US?
I SENT ONE OF CASSANDRA'S GEEK CHORUS A DM AND ASKED NICELY.
THREE SNAPCHATS LATER, I'VE GOT YOUR LOCATION.
SHE SOLD US OUT THAT EASILY?
DON'T GET ON YOUR HIGH HORSE.
YOU WOULD TOO.
I WOULD NOT.
I would. I would so hard.
But only if you're not the murderer.
WHATEVER.

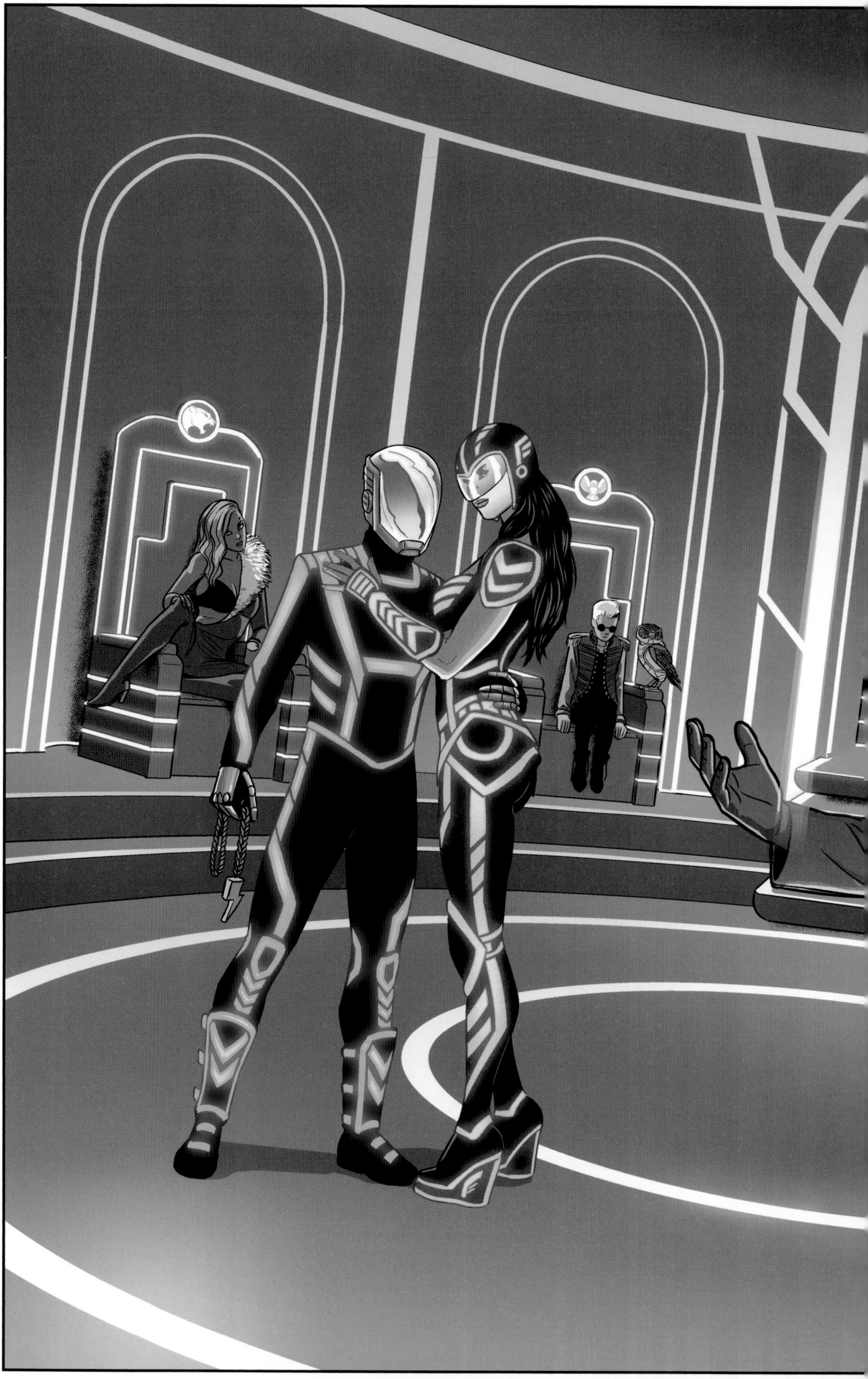

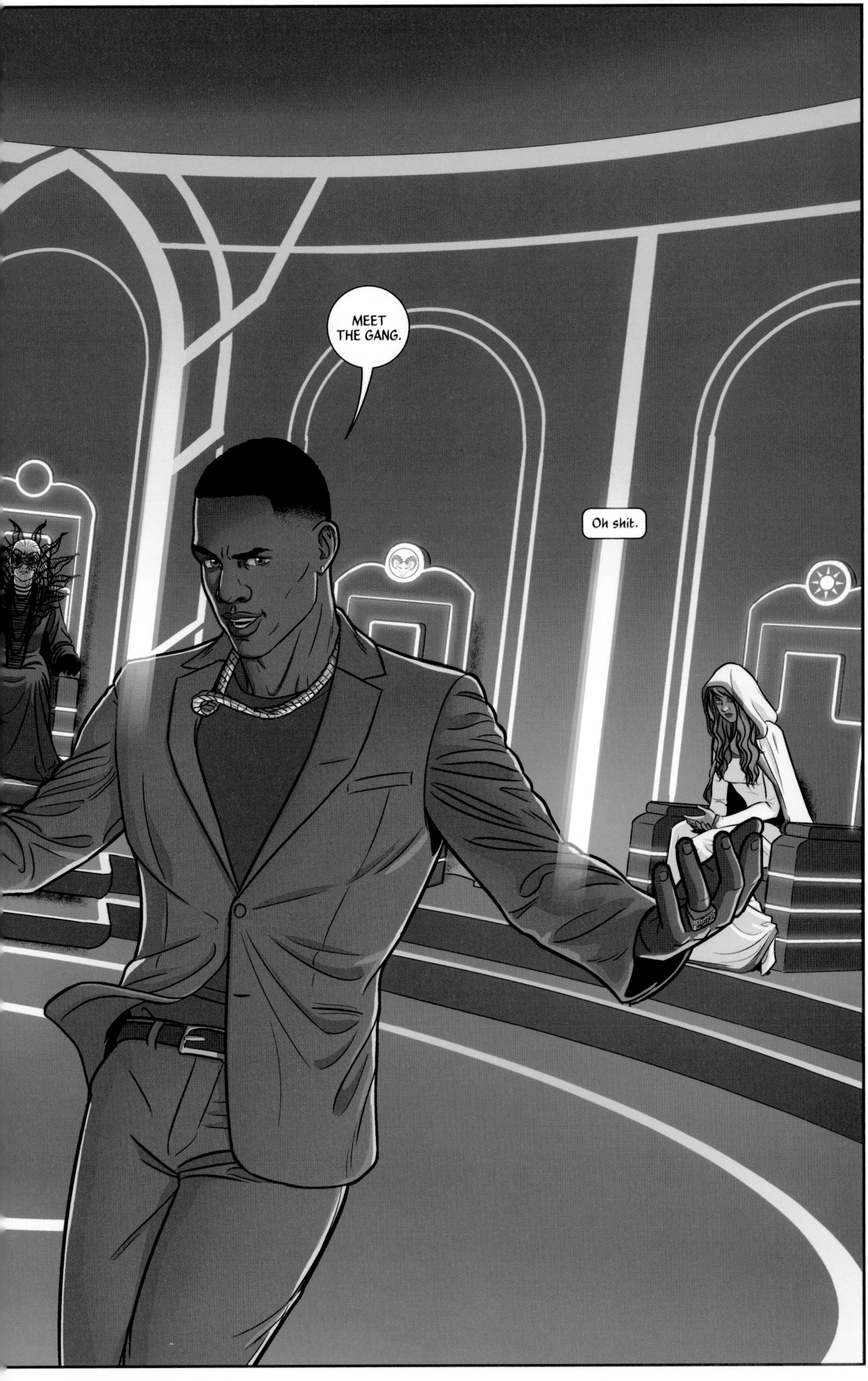
MEET THE GANG.
Oh shit.

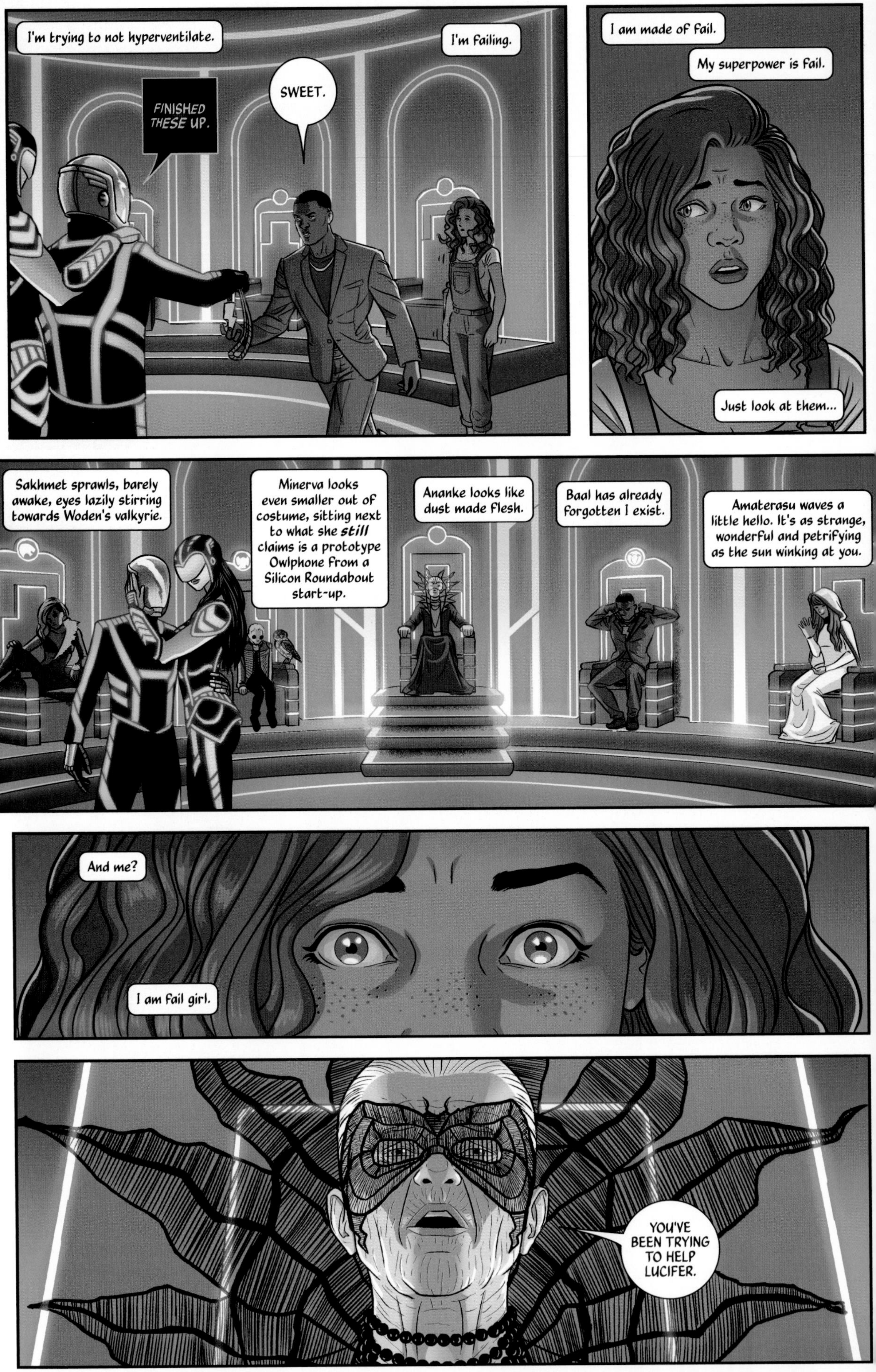
I'm trying to not hyperventilate.
FINISHED THESE UP.
SWEET.
I'm failing.
I am made of fail.
My superpower is fail.
Just look at them...
Sakhmet sprawls, barely awake, eyes lazily stirring towards Woden's valkyrie.
Minerva looks even smaller out of costume, sitting next to what she *still* claims is a prototype Owlphone from a Silicon Roundabout start-up.
Ananke looks like dust made flesh.
Baal has already forgotten I exist.
Amaterasu waves a little hello. It's as strange, wonderful and petrifying as the sun winking at you.
And me?
I am fail girl.
YOU'VE BEEN TRYING TO HELP LUCIFER.

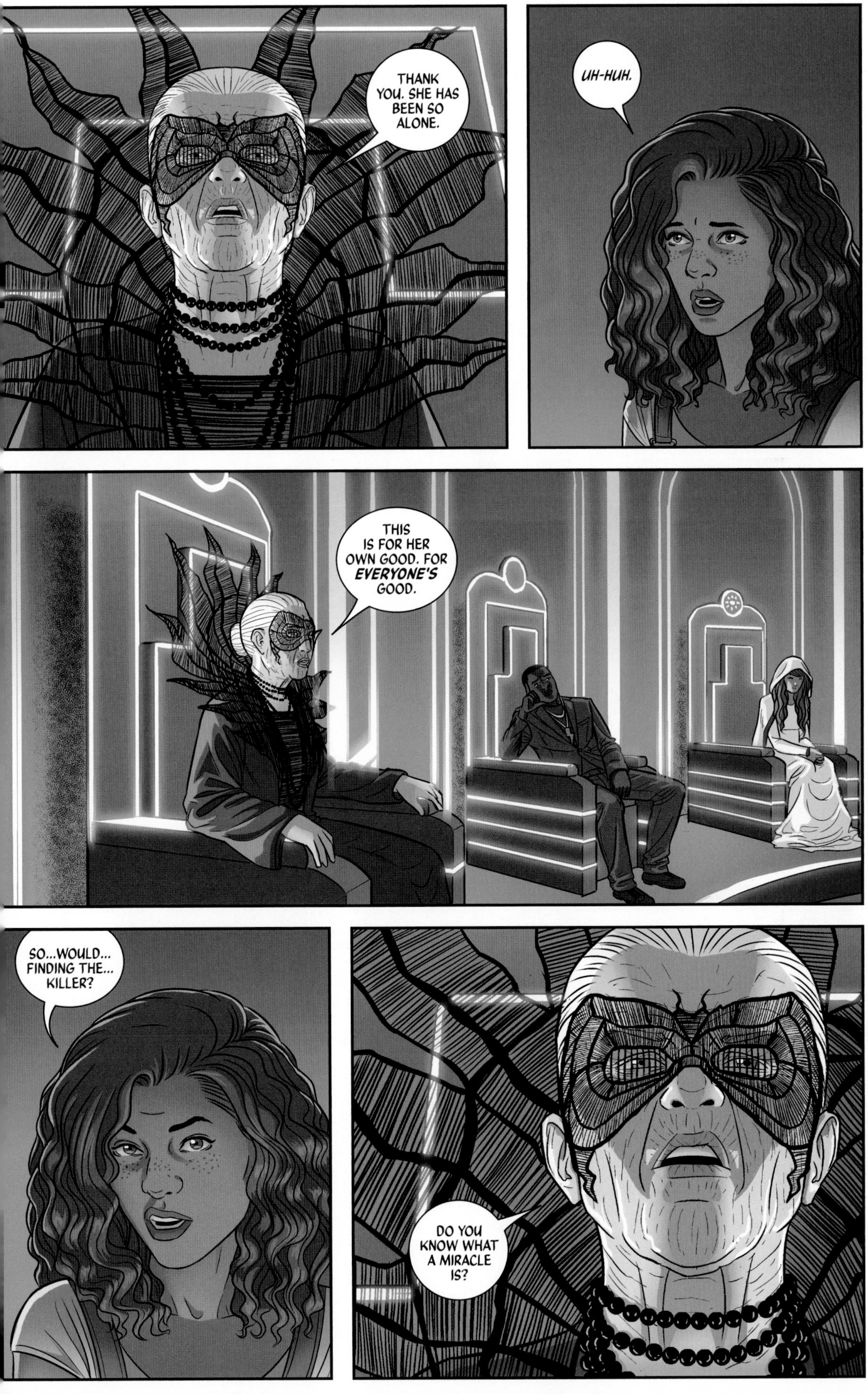
THANK YOU. SHE HAS BEEN SO ALONE.
UH-HUH.
THIS IS FOR HER OWN GOOD. FOR EVERYONE'S GOOD.
SO...WOULD... FINDING THE... KILLER?
DO YOU KNOW WHAT A MIRACLE IS?

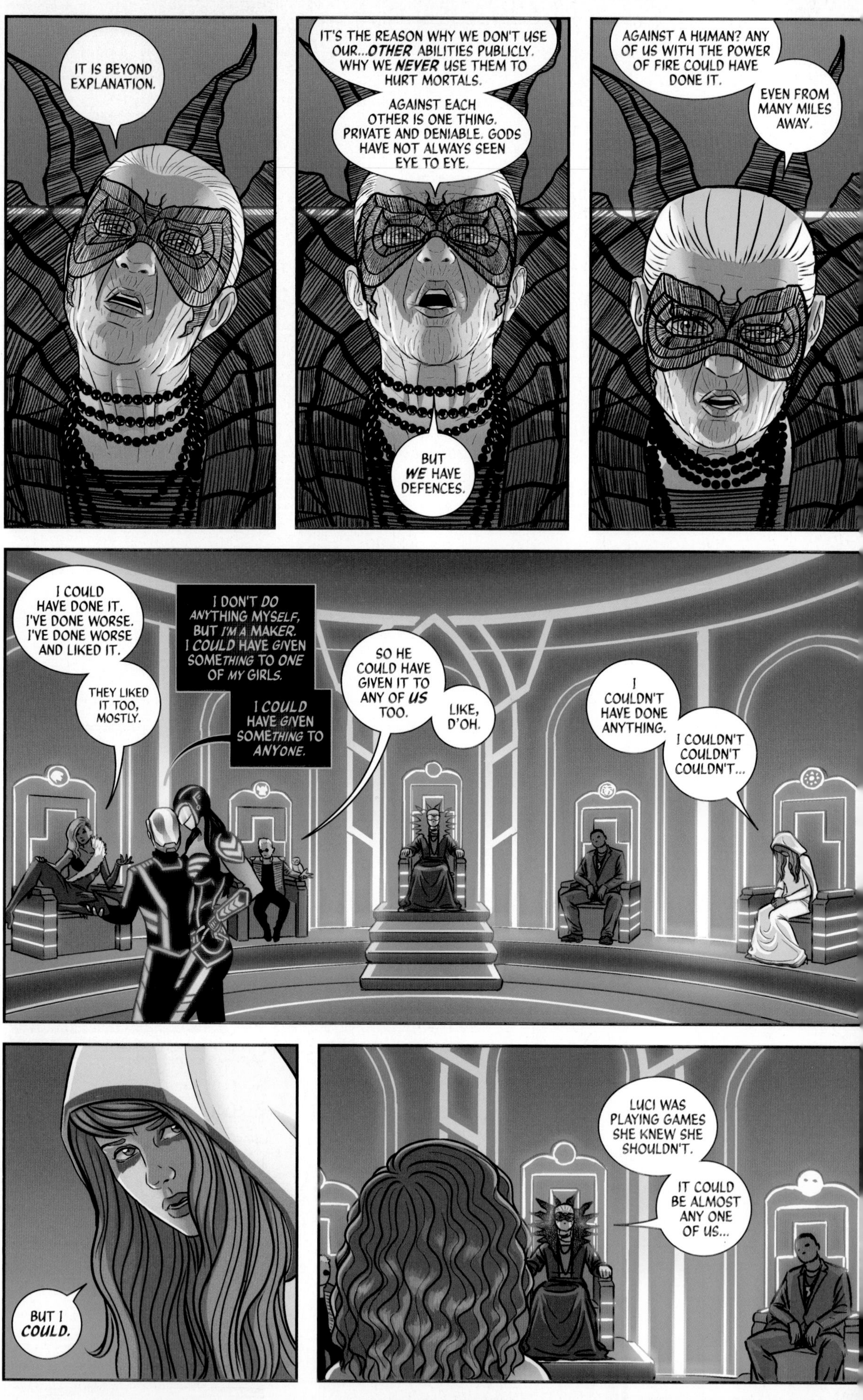
IT IS BEYOND EXPLANATION.
IT'S THE REASON WHY WE DON'T USE OUR...OTHER ABILITIES PUBLICLY. WHY WE NEVER USE THEM TO HURT MORTALS.
AGAINST EACH OTHER IS ONE THING. PRIVATE AND DENIABLE. GODS HAVE NOT ALWAYS SEEN EYE TO EYE.
BUT WE HAVE DEFENCES.
AGAINST A HUMAN? ANY OF US WITH THE POWER OF FIRE COULD HAVE DONE IT.
EVEN FROM MANY MILES AWAY.
I COULD HAVE DONE IT. I'VE DONE WORSE. I'VE DONE WORSE AND LIKED IT.
THEY LIKED IT TOO, MOSTLY.
I DON'T DO ANYTHING MYSELF, BUT I'M A MAKER. I COULD HAVE GIVEN SOMETHING TO ONE OF MY GIRLS.
I COULD HAVE GIVEN SOMETHING TO ANYONE.
SO HE COULD HAVE GIVEN IT TO ANY OF US TOO.
LIKE, D'OH.
I COULDN'T HAVE DONE ANYTHING.
I COULDN'T COULDN'T COULDN'T...
BUT I COULD.
LUCI WAS PLAYING GAMES SHE KNEW SHE SHOULDN'T.
IT COULD BE ALMOST ANY ONE OF US...

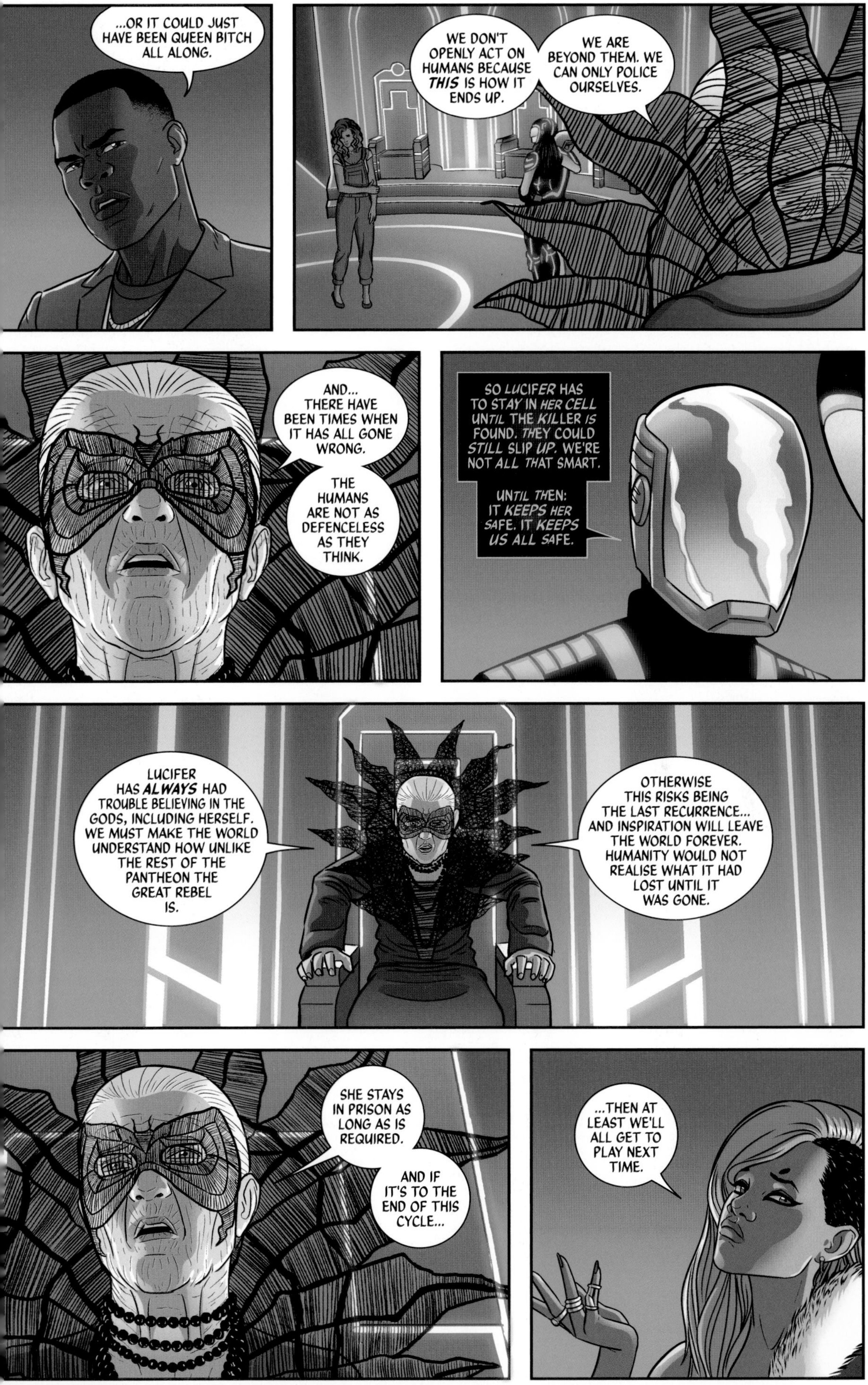
...OR IT COULD JUST HAVE BEEN QUEEN BITCH ALL ALONG.
WE DON'T OPENLY ACT ON HUMANS BECAUSE *THIS* IS HOW IT ENDS UP.
WE ARE BEYOND THEM. WE CAN ONLY POLICE OURSELVES.
AND... THERE HAVE BEEN TIMES WHEN IT HAS ALL GONE WRONG.
THE HUMANS ARE NOT AS DEFENCELESS AS THEY THINK.
SO *LUCIFER* HAS TO STAY IN *HER CELL* UN*TIL* THE *KILLER IS* FOUND. *THEY* COULD *STILL SLIP UP*. WE'RE NOT *ALL THAT* SMART.
UN*TIL* T*HEN*: IT *KEEPS* HER SAFE. IT *KEEPS US ALL* SAFE.
LUCIFER HAS ***ALWAYS*** HAD TROUBLE BELIEVING IN THE GODS, INCLUDING HERSELF. WE MUST MAKE THE WORLD UNDERSTAND HOW UNLIKE THE REST OF THE PANTHEON THE GREAT REBEL IS.
OTHERWISE THIS RISKS BEING THE LAST RECURRENCE... AND INSPIRATION WILL LEAVE THE WORLD FOREVER. HUMANITY WOULD NOT REALISE WHAT IT HAD LOST UNTIL IT WAS GONE.
SHE STAYS IN PRISON AS LONG AS IS REQUIRED.
AND IF IT'S TO THE END OF THIS CYCLE...
...THEN AT LEAST WE'LL ALL GET TO PLAY NEXT TIME.

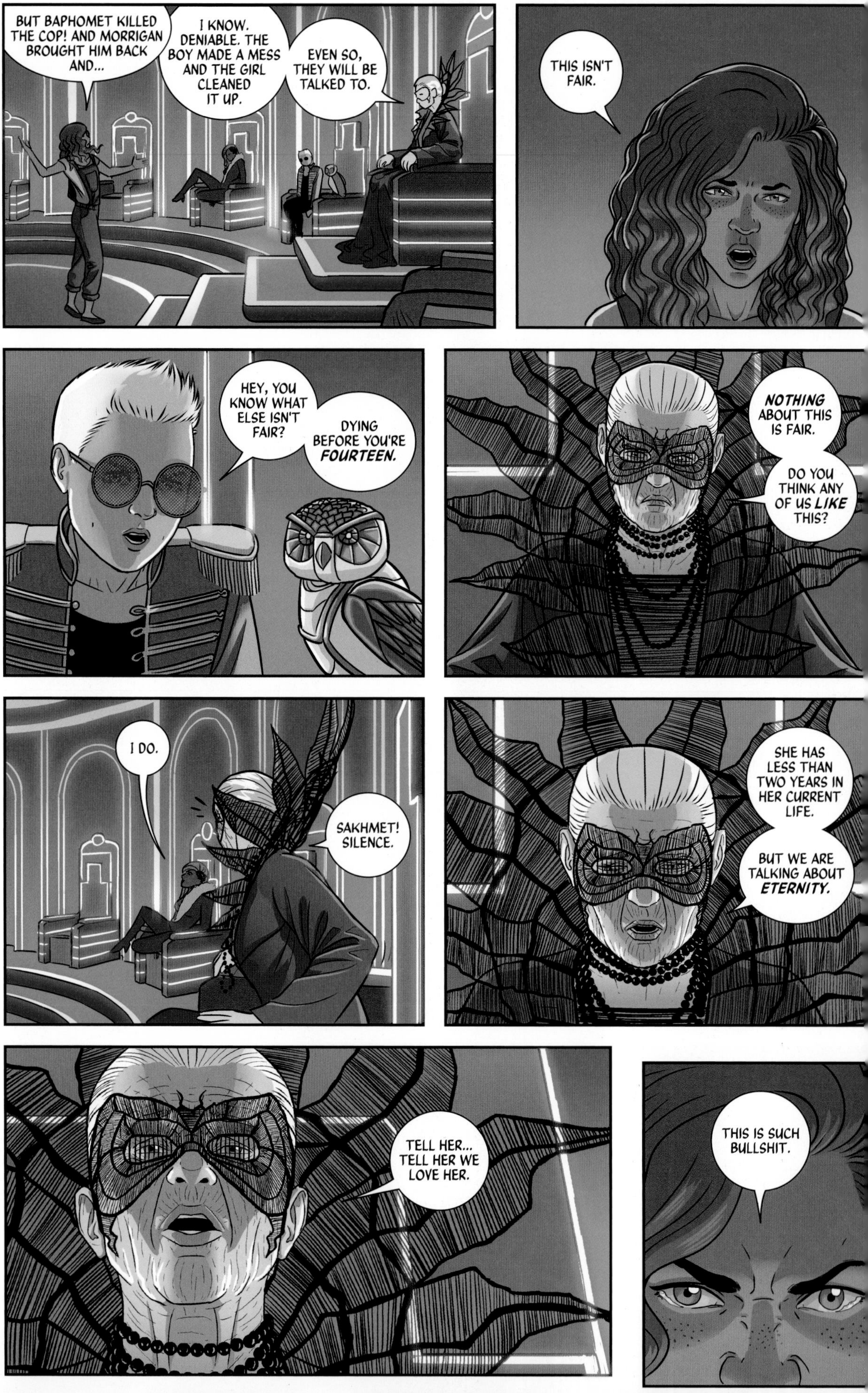
BUT BAPHOMET KILLED THE COP! AND MORRIGAN BROUGHT HIM BACK AND...
I KNOW. DENIABLE. THE BOY MADE A MESS AND THE GIRL CLEANED IT UP.
EVEN SO, THEY WILL BE TALKED TO.
THIS ISN'T FAIR.
HEY, YOU KNOW WHAT ELSE ISN'T FAIR?
DYING BEFORE YOU'RE *FOURTEEN.*
NOTHING ABOUT THIS IS FAIR.
DO YOU THINK ANY OF US *LIKE* THIS?
I DO.
SAKHMET! SILENCE.
SHE HAS LESS THAN TWO YEARS IN HER CURRENT LIFE.
BUT WE ARE TALKING ABOUT *ETERNITY.*
TELL HER... TELL HER WE LOVE HER.
THIS IS SUCH BULLSHIT.

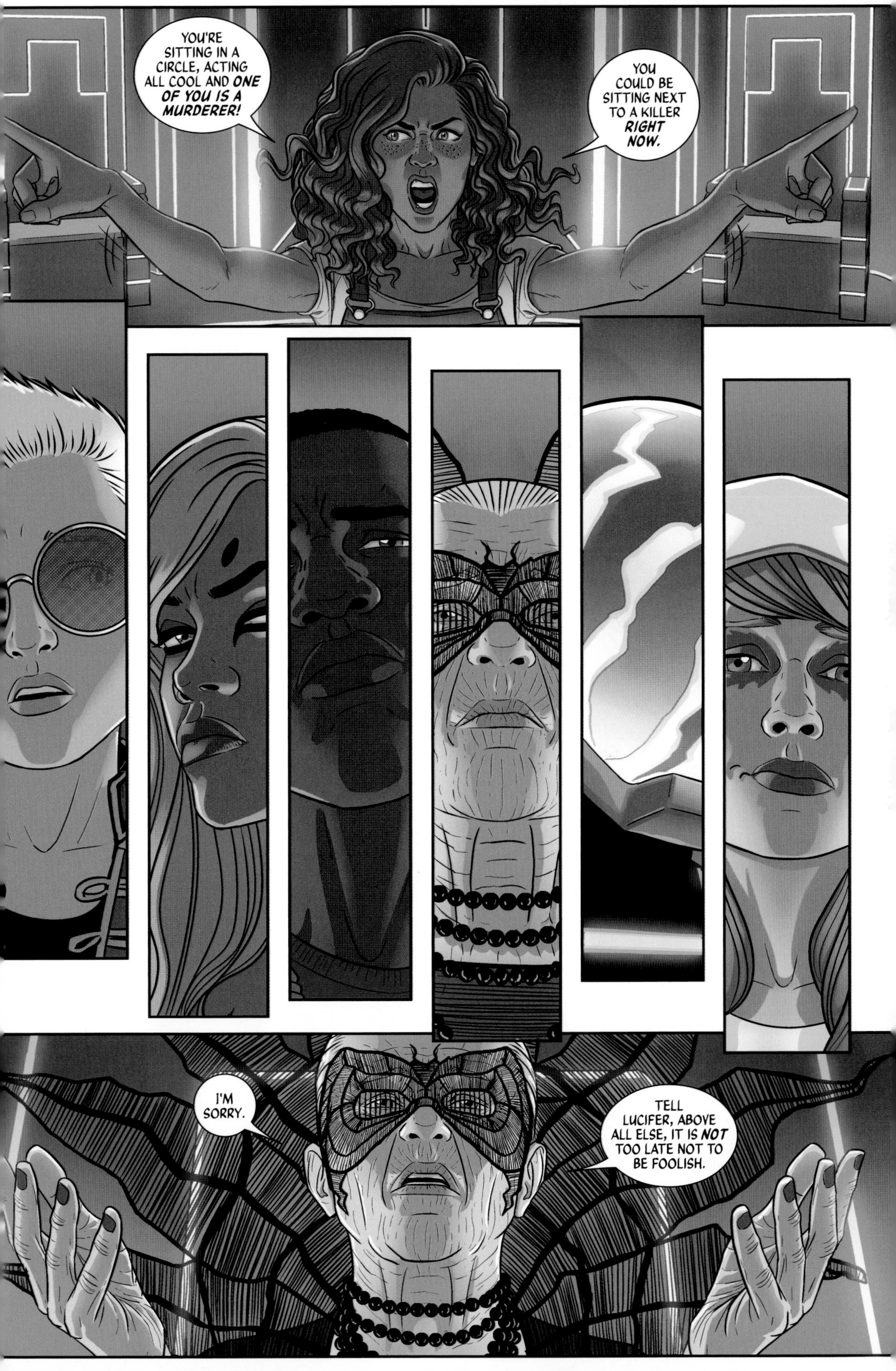
YOU'RE SITTING IN A CIRCLE, ACTING ALL COOL AND *ONE OF YOU IS A MURDERER!*
YOU COULD BE SITTING NEXT TO A KILLER *RIGHT NOW.*
I'M SORRY.
TELL LUCIFER, ABOVE ALL ELSE, IT IS *NOT* TOO LATE NOT TO BE FOOLISH.

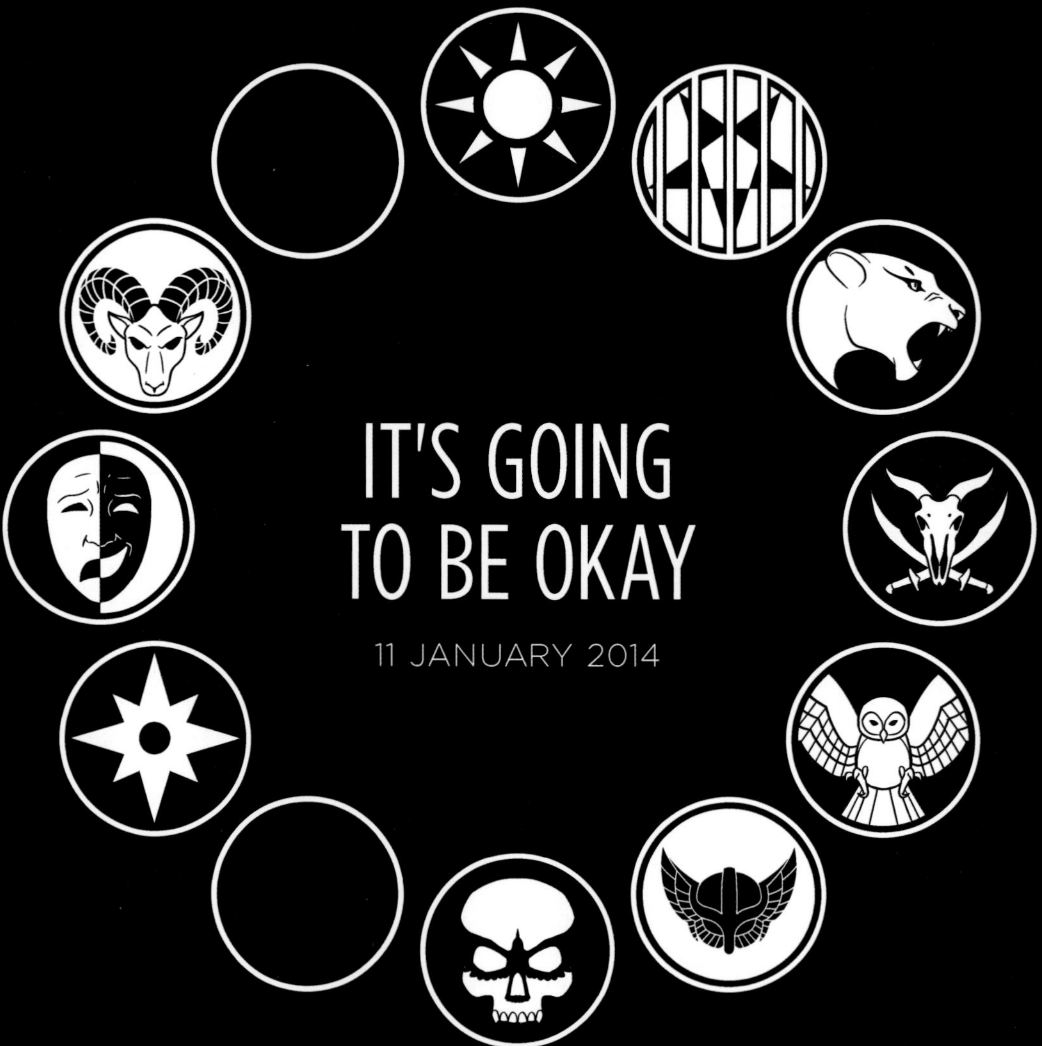
IT'S GOING
TO BE OKAY
11 JANUARY 2014

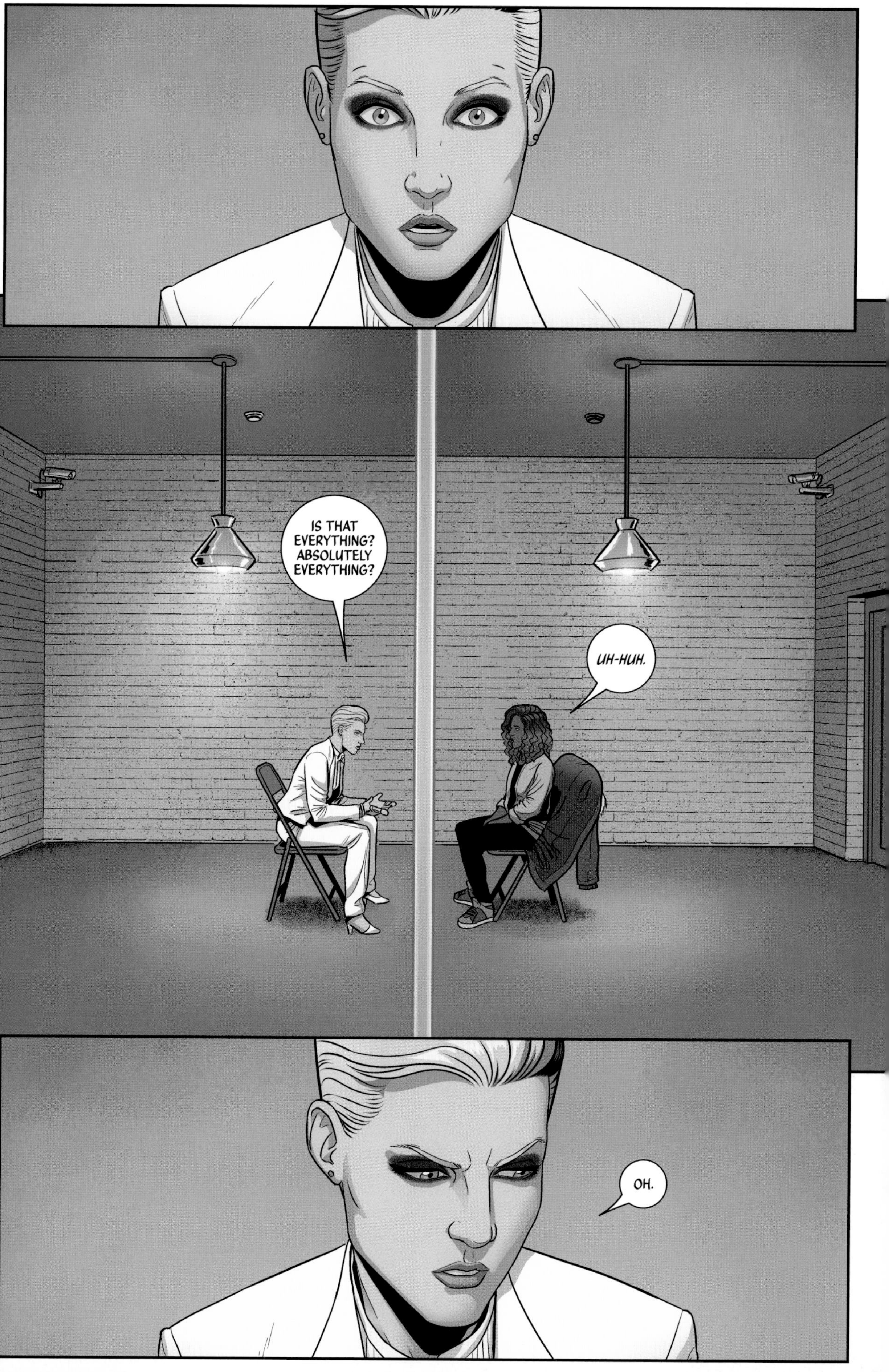
IS THAT EVERYTHING? ABSOLUTELY EVERYTHING?
UH-HUH.
OH.

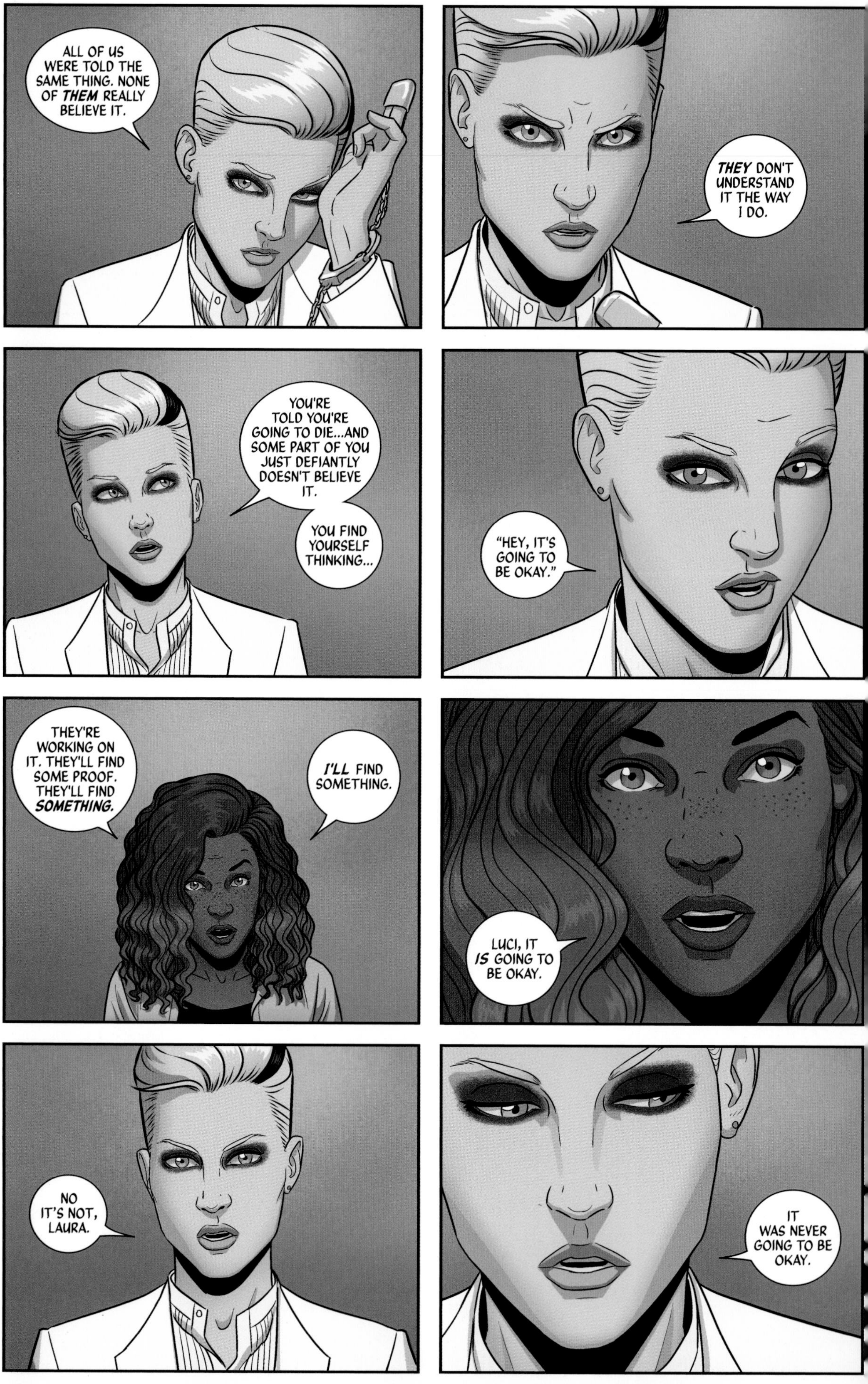
ALL OF US WERE TOLD THE SAME THING. NONE OF *THEM* REALLY BELIEVE IT.
THEY DON'T UNDERSTAND IT THE WAY I DO.
YOU'RE TOLD YOU'RE GOING TO DIE...AND SOME PART OF YOU JUST DEFIANTLY DOESN'T BELIEVE IT.
YOU FIND YOURSELF THINKING...
"HEY, IT'S GOING TO BE OKAY."
THEY'RE WORKING ON IT. THEY'LL FIND SOME PROOF. THEY'LL FIND *SOMETHING.*
I'LL FIND SOMETHING.
LUCI, IT *IS* GOING TO BE OKAY.
NO IT'S NOT, LAURA.
IT WAS NEVER GOING TO BE OKAY.

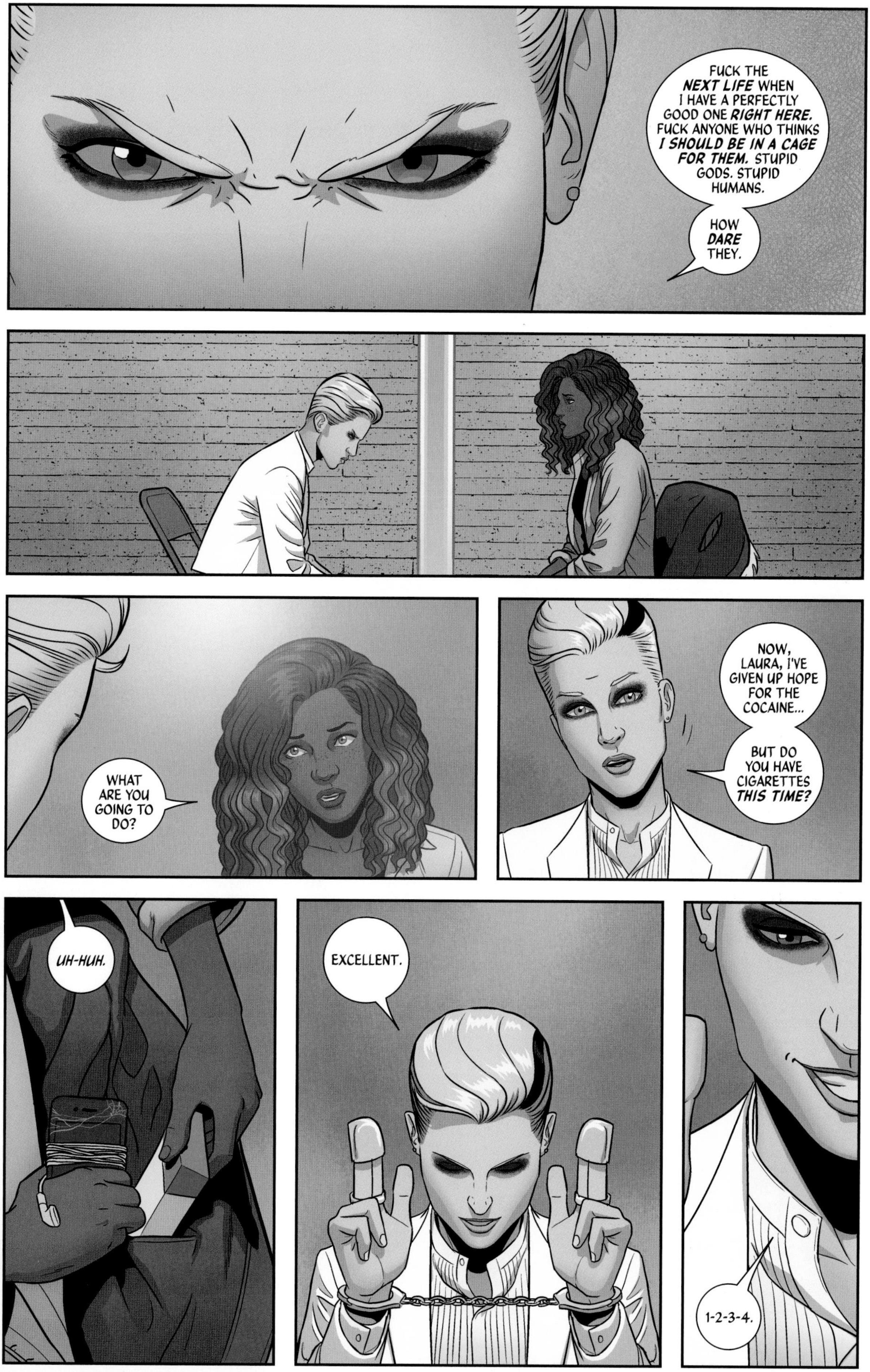
FUCK THE **NEXT LIFE** WHEN I HAVE A PERFECTLY GOOD ONE **RIGHT HERE.** FUCK ANYONE WHO THINKS ***I SHOULD BE IN A CAGE FOR THEM.*** STUPID GODS. STUPID HUMANS.
HOW ***DARE*** THEY.
WHAT ARE YOU GOING TO DO?
NOW, LAURA, I'VE GIVEN UP HOPE FOR THE COCAINE...
BUT DO YOU HAVE CIGARETTES ***THIS TIME?***
UH-HUH.
EXCELLENT.
1-2-3-4.

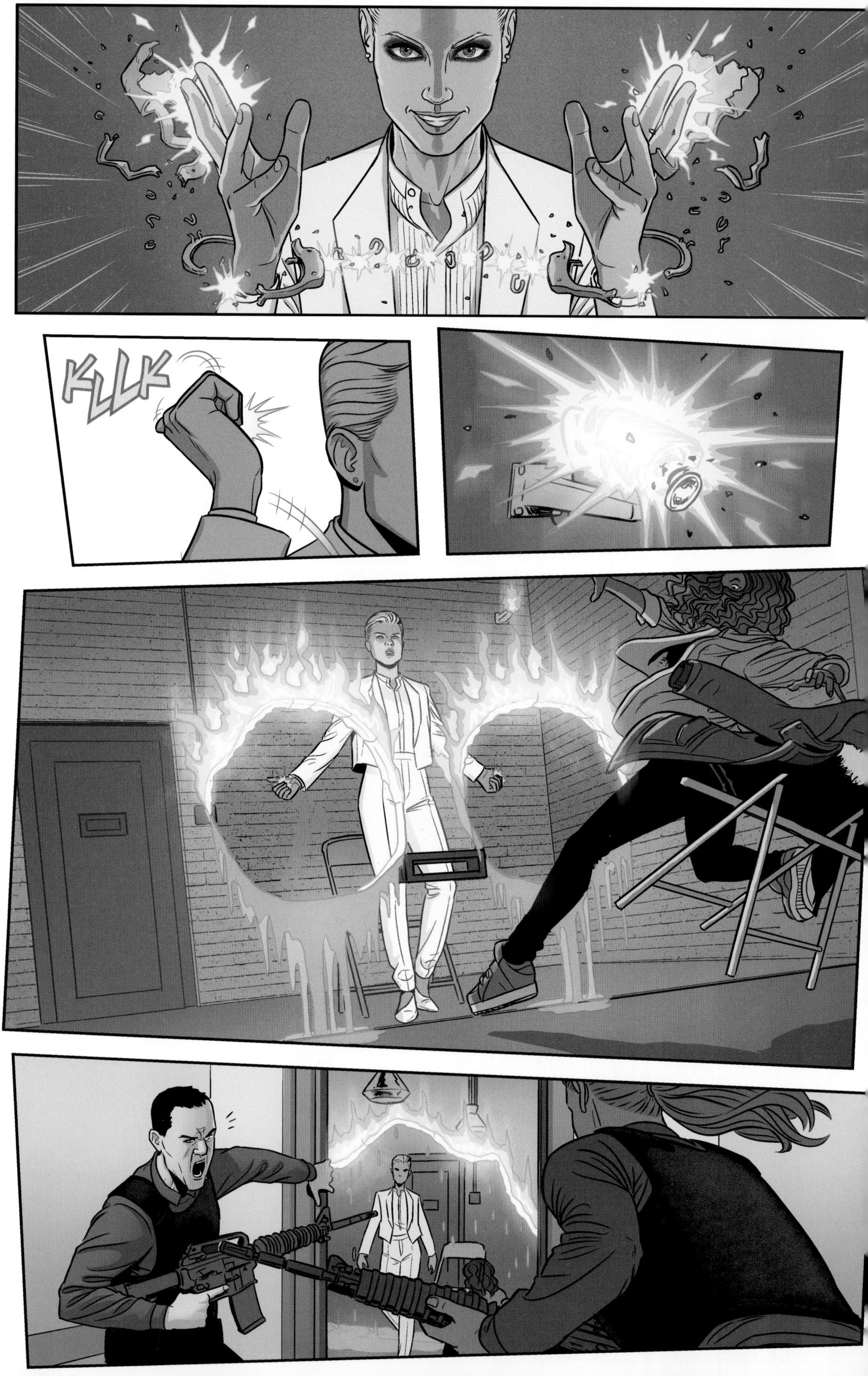
KLLK

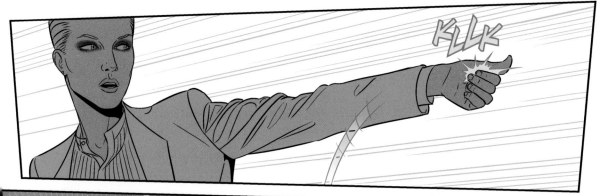

KLLK

WHAT AM I GOING TO DO?

I'M GOING TO SMOKE.

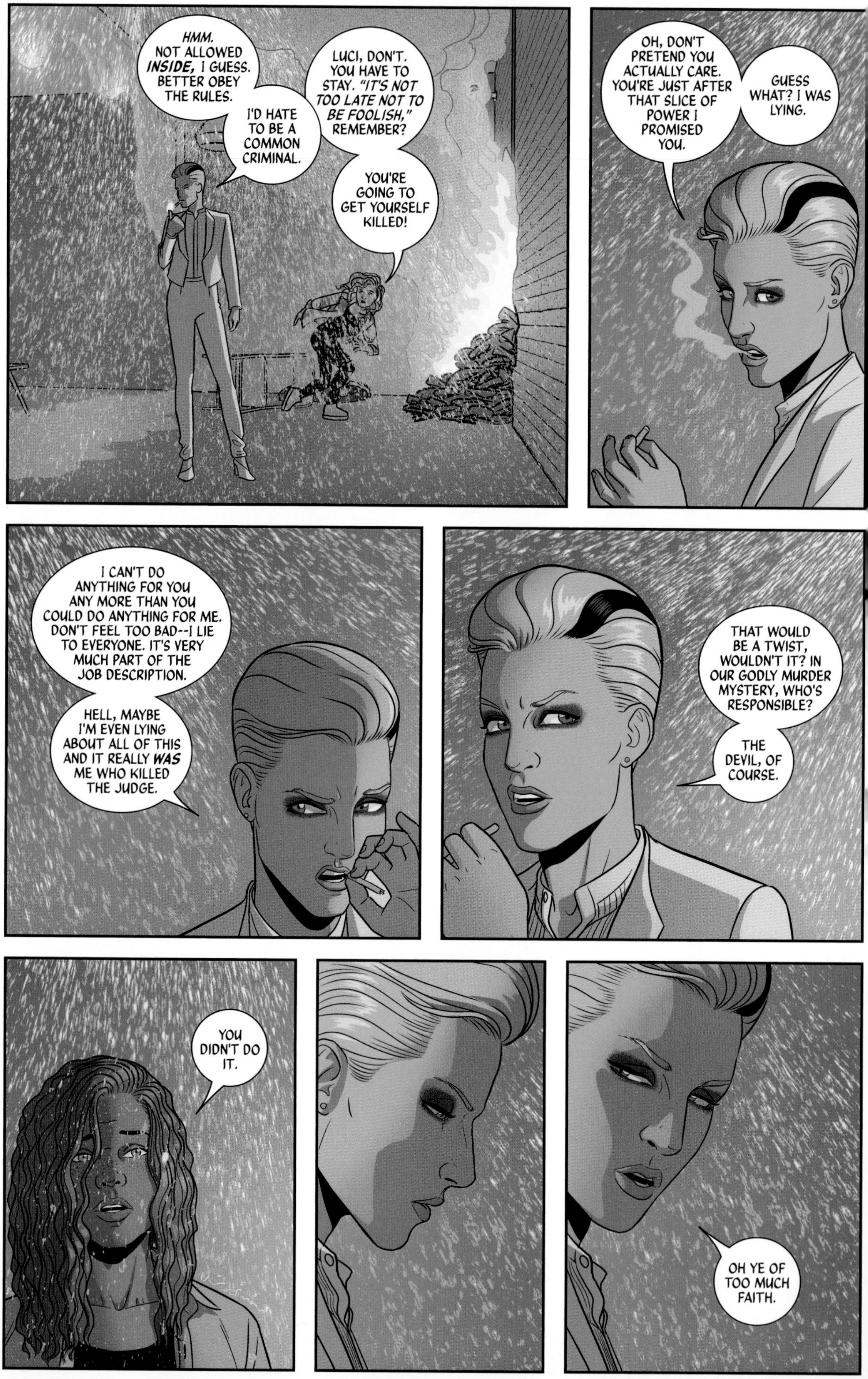
HMM. NOT ALLOWED *INSIDE,* I GUESS. BETTER OBEY THE RULES.
I'D HATE TO BE A COMMON CRIMINAL.
LUCI, DON'T. YOU HAVE TO STAY. *"IT'S NOT TOO LATE NOT TO BE FOOLISH,"* REMEMBER?
YOU'RE GOING TO GET YOURSELF KILLED!
OH, DON'T PRETEND YOU ACTUALLY CARE. YOU'RE JUST AFTER THAT SLICE OF POWER I PROMISED YOU.
GUESS WHAT? I WAS LYING.
I CAN'T DO ANYTHING FOR YOU ANY MORE THAN YOU COULD DO ANYTHING FOR ME. DON'T FEEL TOO BAD--I LIE TO EVERYONE. IT'S VERY MUCH PART OF THE JOB DESCRIPTION.
HELL, MAYBE I'M EVEN LYING ABOUT ALL OF THIS AND IT REALLY *WAS* ME WHO KILLED THE JUDGE.
THAT WOULD BE A TWIST, WOULDN'T IT? IN OUR GODLY MURDER MYSTERY, WHO'S RESPONSIBLE?
THE DEVIL, OF COURSE.
YOU DIDN'T DO IT.
OH YE OF TOO MUCH FAITH.

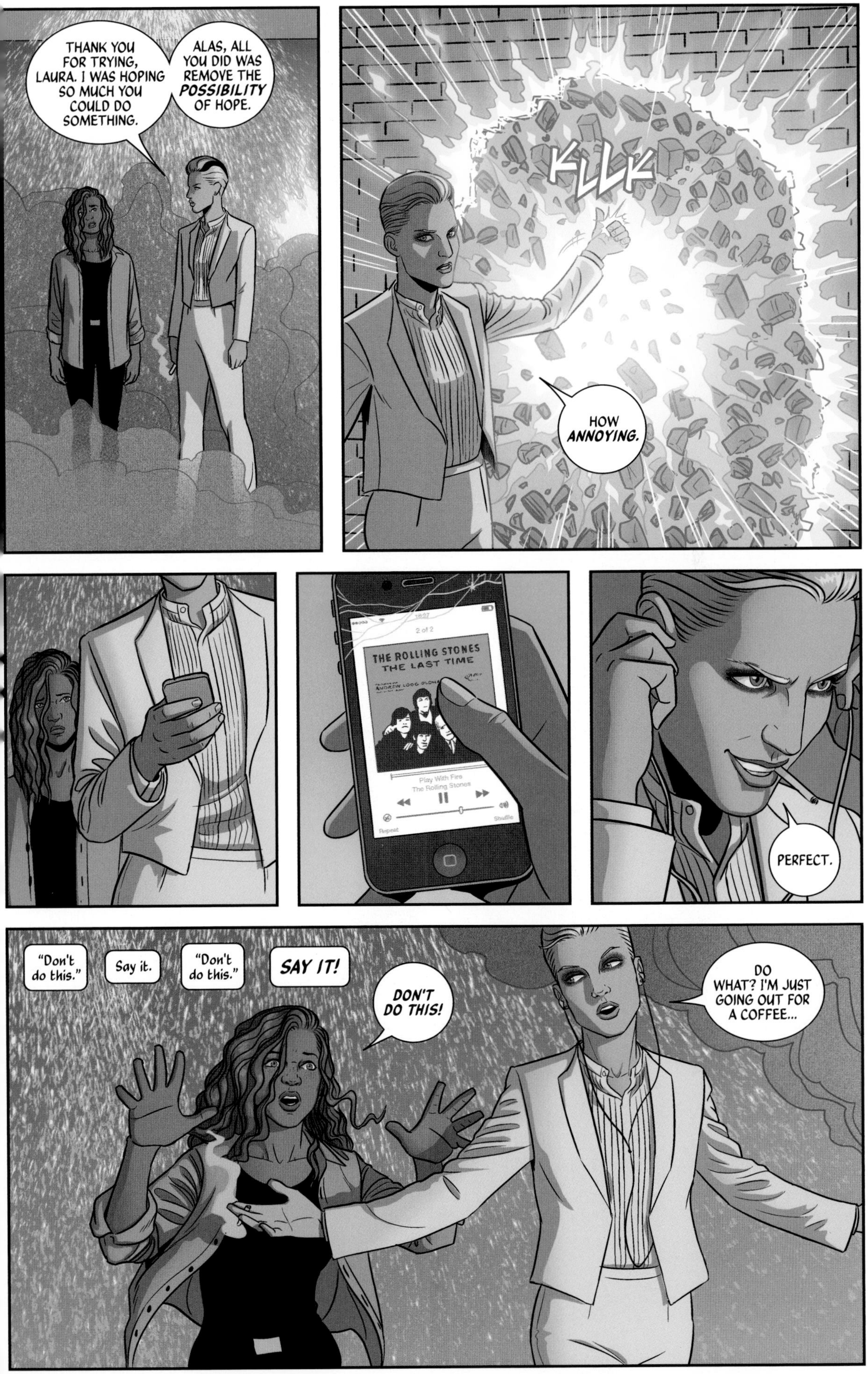
THANK YOU FOR TRYING, LAURA. I WAS HOPING SO MUCH YOU COULD DO SOMETHING.
ALAS, ALL YOU DID WAS REMOVE THE *POSSIBILITY* OF HOPE.
KLLK
HOW *ANNOYING.*
THE ROLLING STONES
THE LAST TIME
2 of 2
Play With Fire
The Rolling Stones
Repeat
Shuffle
PERFECT.
"Don't do this."
Say it.
"Don't do this."
SAY IT!
DON'T DO THIS!
DO WHAT? I'M JUST GOING OUT FOR A COFFEE...

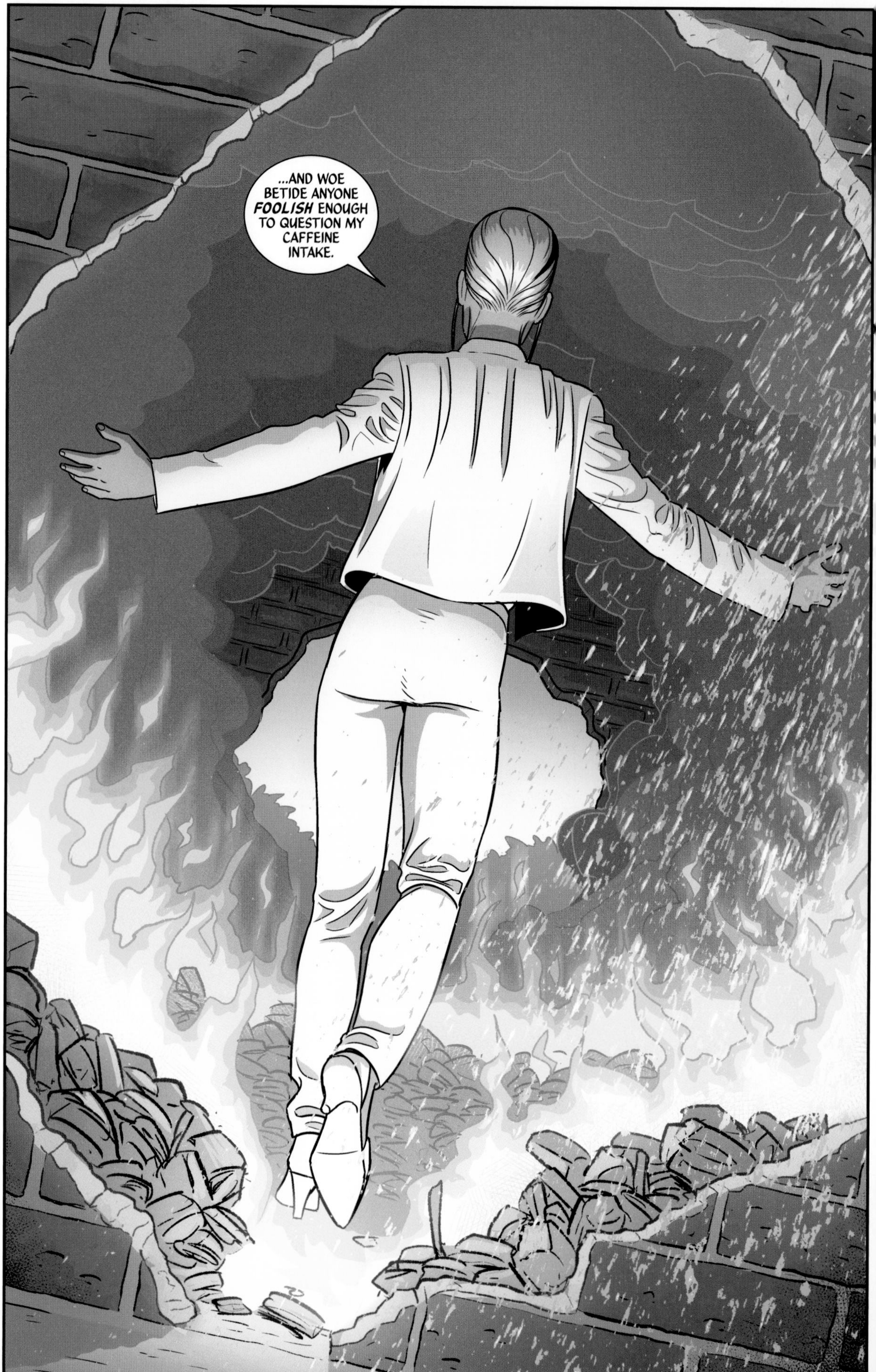
...AND WOE BETIDE ANYONE FOOLISH ENOUGH TO QUESTION MY CAFFEINE INTAKE.

THE
WICKED
+
DIVINE
THE

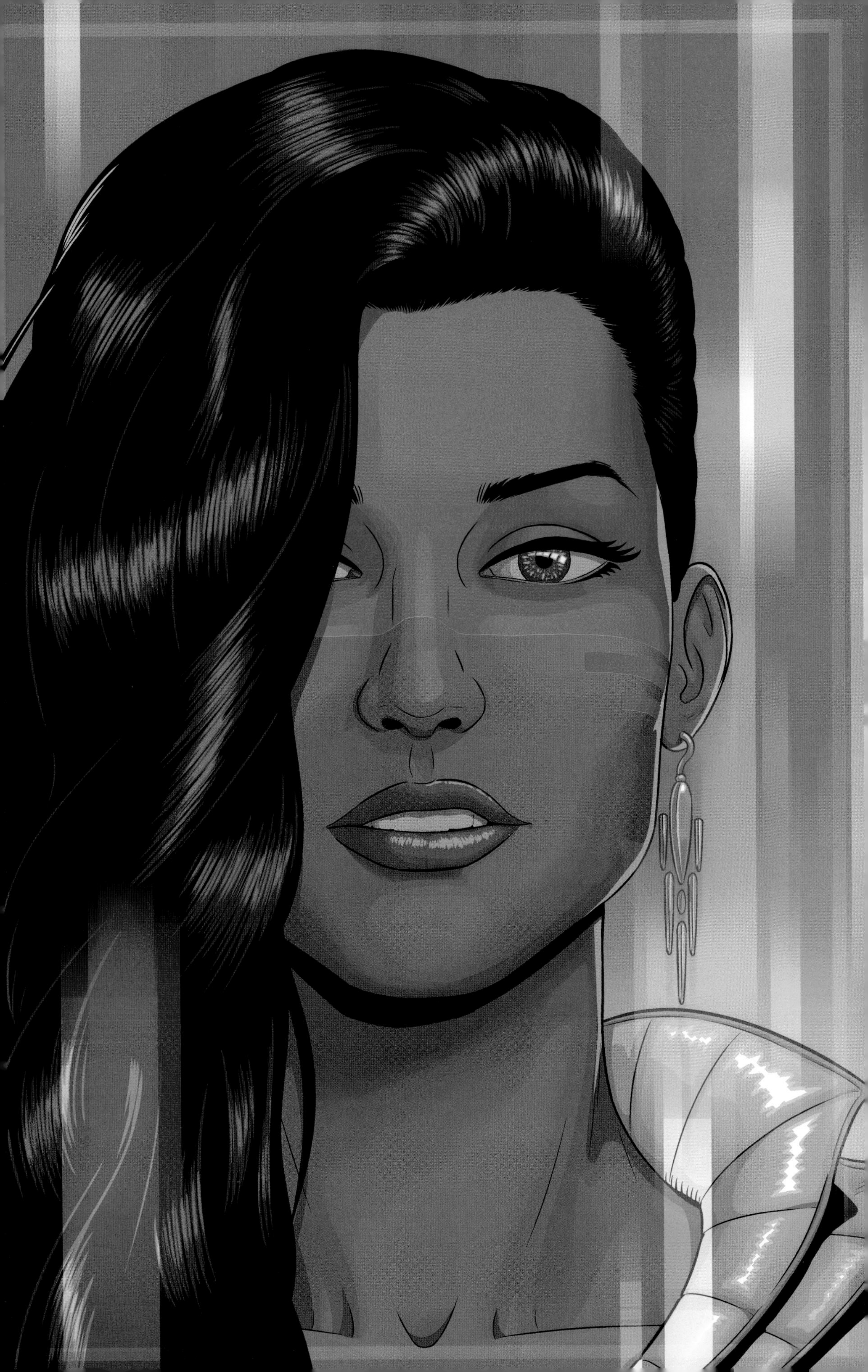

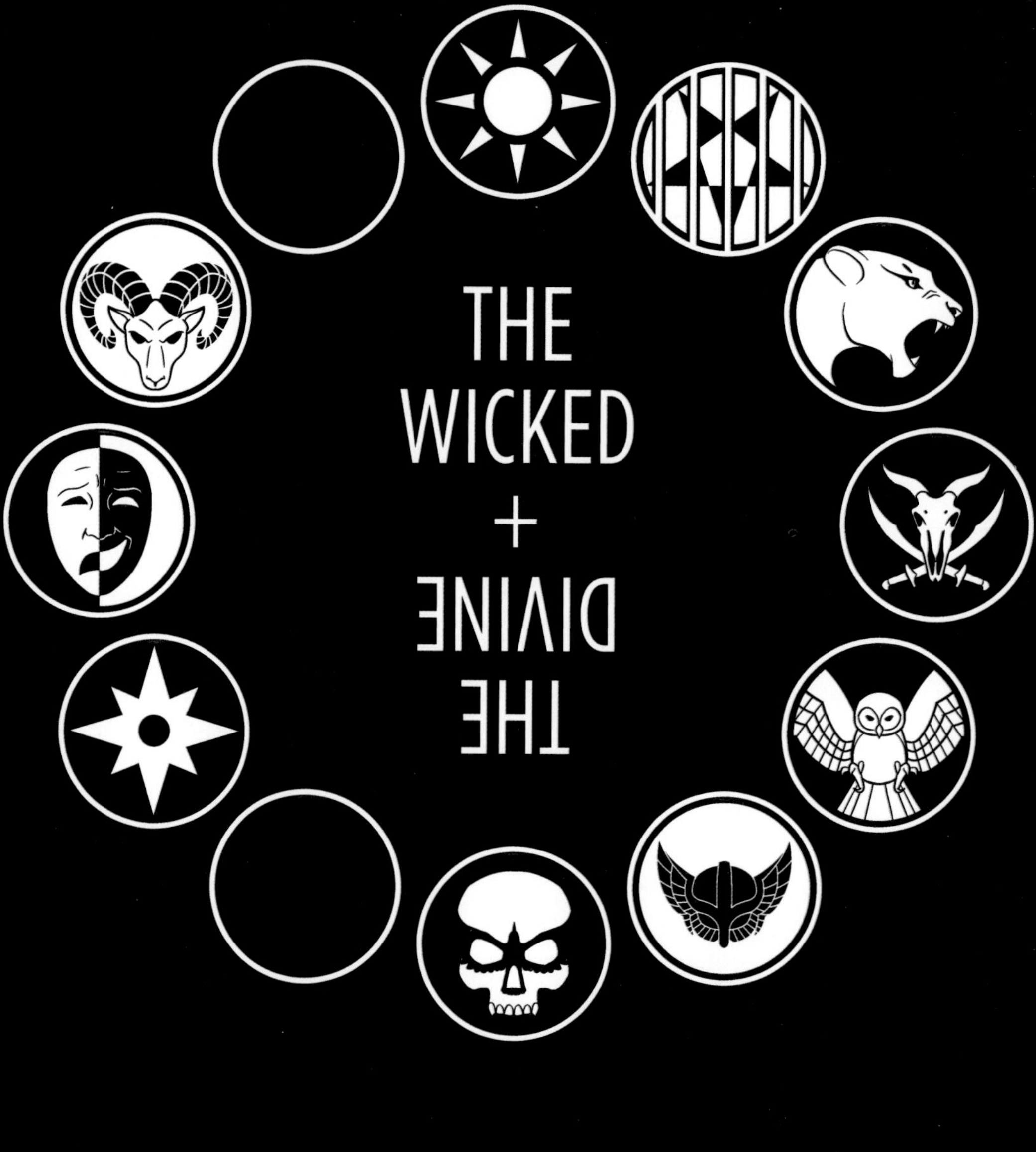
THE
WICKED
+
THE
DIVINE

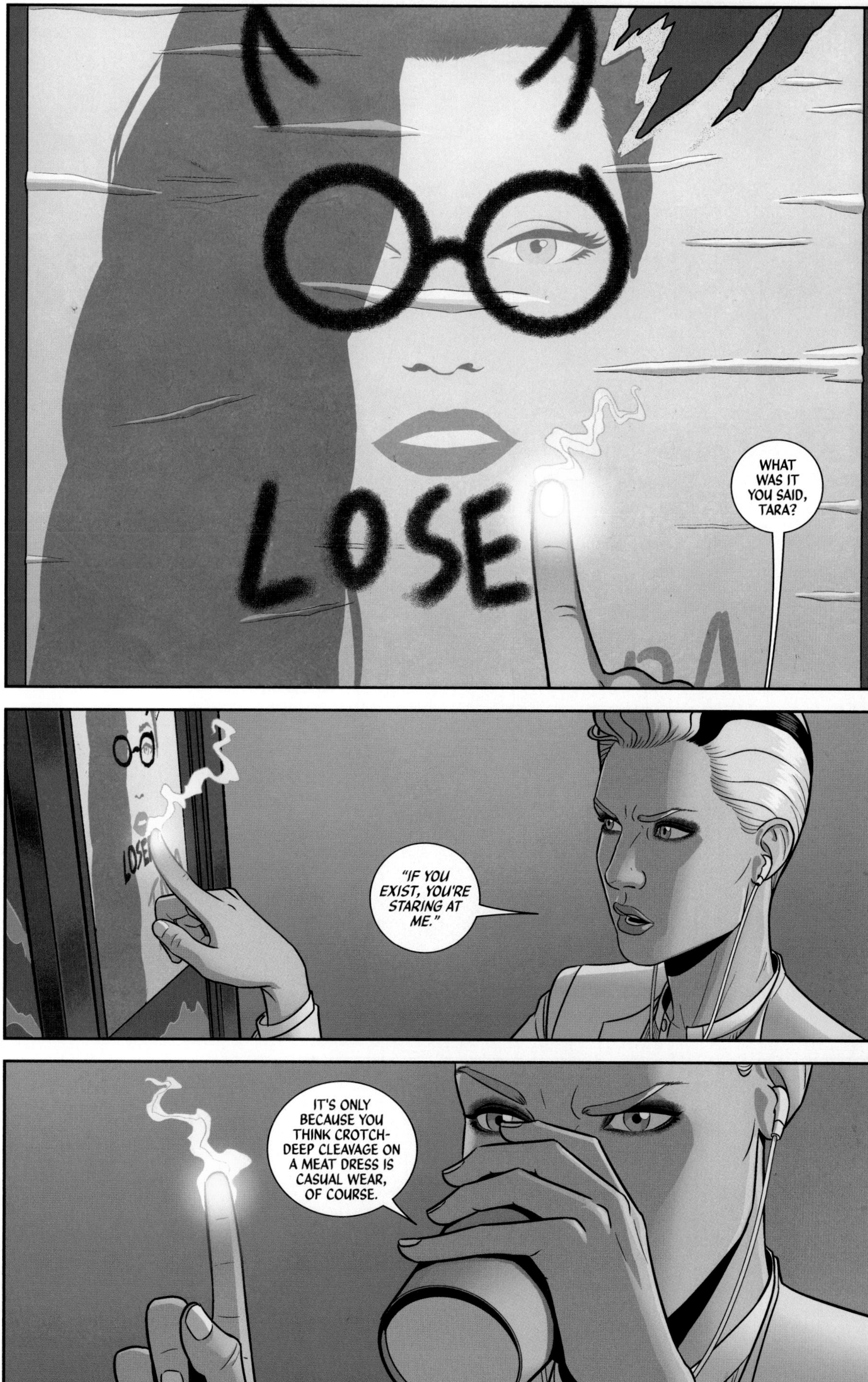
LOSE
WHAT WAS IT YOU SAID, TARA?
LOSER
"IF YOU EXIST, YOU'RE STARING AT ME."
IT'S ONLY BECAUSE YOU THINK CROTCH-DEEP CLEAVAGE ON A MEAT DRESS IS CASUAL WEAR, OF COURSE.

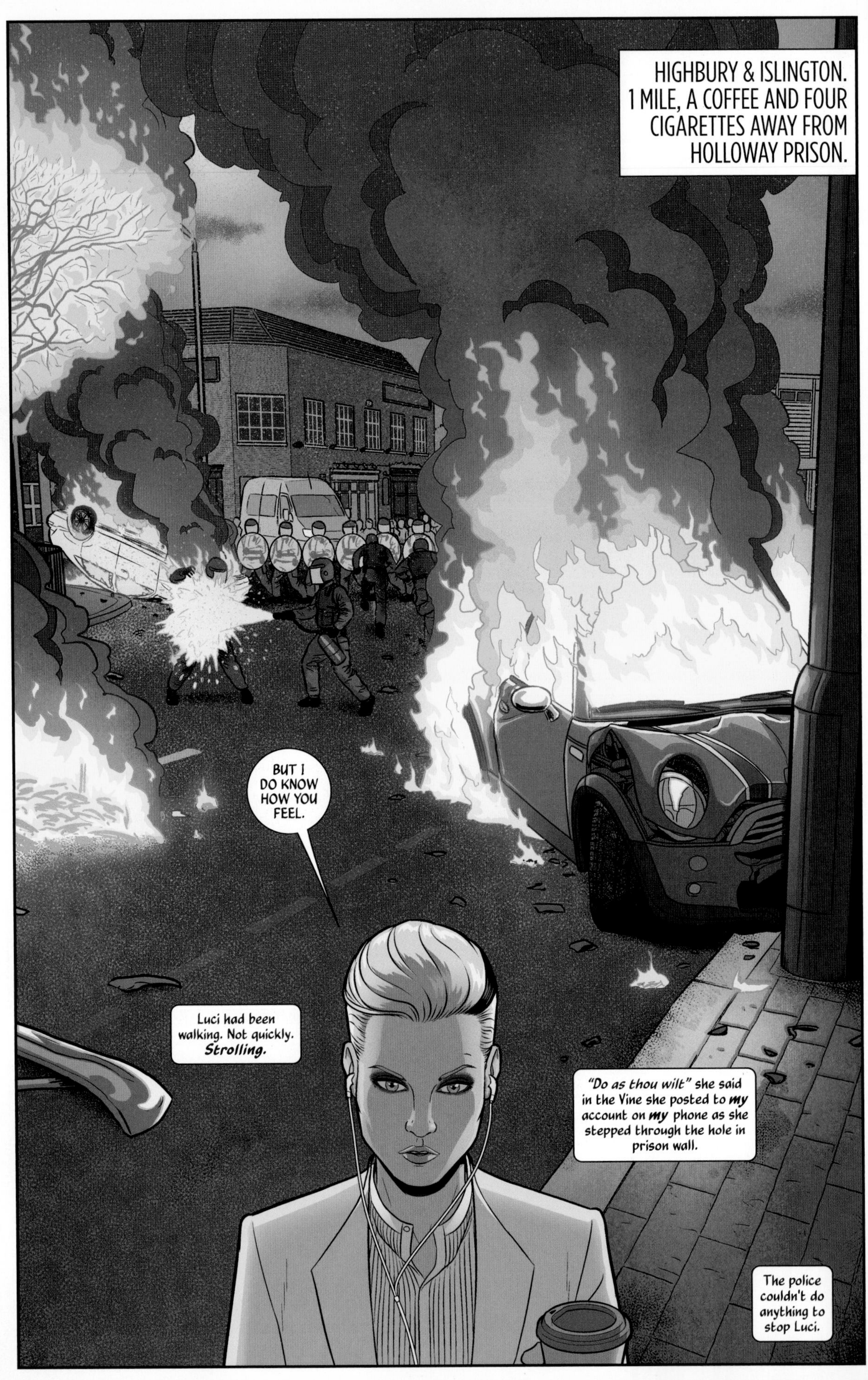
HIGHBURY & ISLINGTON. 1 MILE, A COFFEE AND FOUR CIGARETTES AWAY FROM HOLLOWAY PRISON.
BUT I DO KNOW HOW YOU FEEL.
Luci had been walking. Not quickly. Strolling.
"Do as thou wilt" she said in the Vine she posted to my account on my phone as she stepped through the hole in prison wall.
The police couldn't do anything to stop Luci.

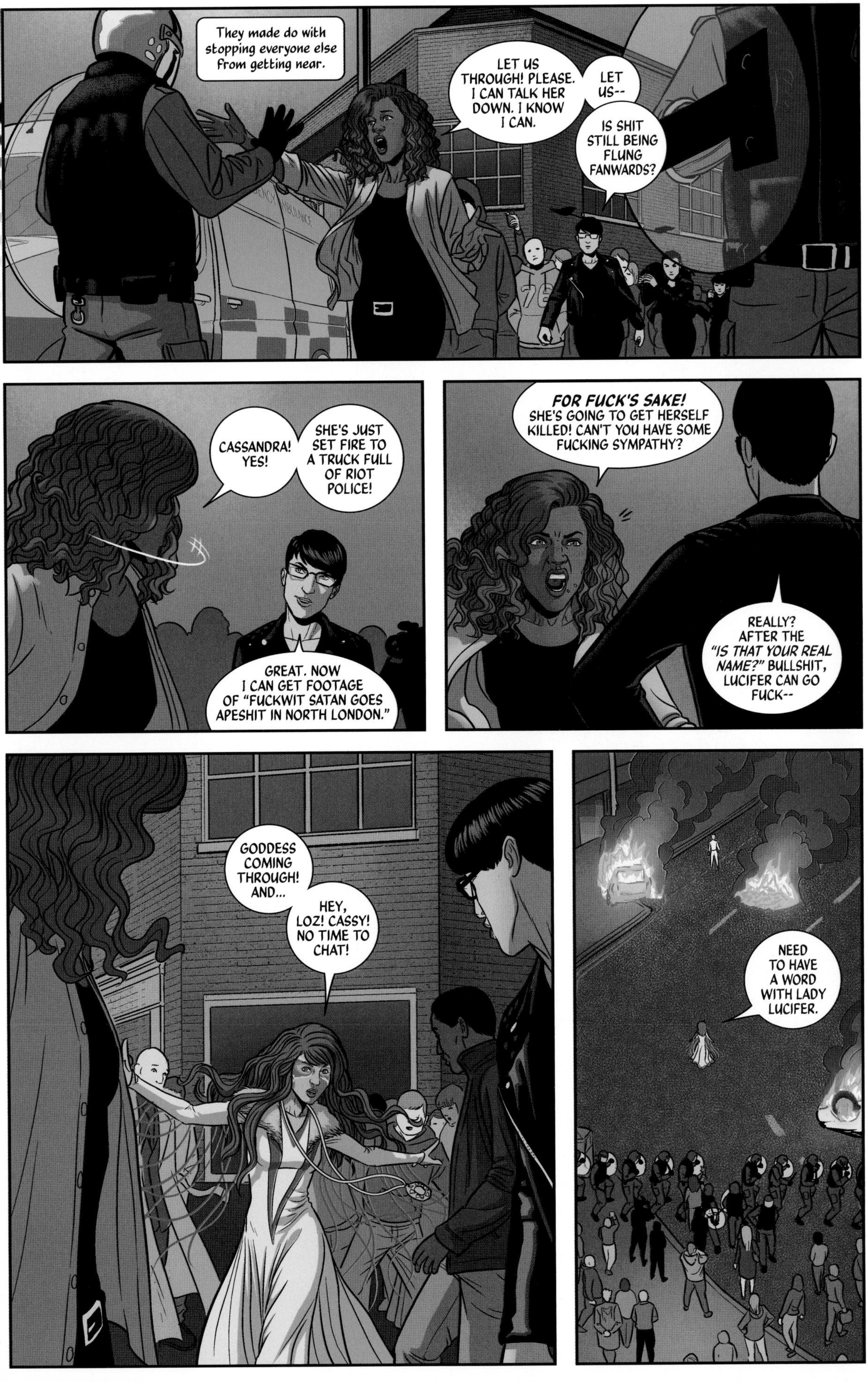
They made do with stopping everyone else from getting near.
LET US THROUGH! PLEASE. I CAN TALK HER DOWN. I KNOW I CAN.
LET US--
IS SHIT STILL BEING FLUNG FANWARDS?
CASSANDRA! YES!
SHE'S JUST SET FIRE TO A TRUCK FULL OF RIOT POLICE!
GREAT. NOW I CAN GET FOOTAGE OF "FUCKWIT SATAN GOES APESHIT IN NORTH LONDON."
FOR FUCK'S SAKE! SHE'S GOING TO GET HERSELF KILLED! CAN'T YOU HAVE SOME FUCKING SYMPATHY?
REALLY? AFTER THE "IS THAT YOUR REAL NAME?" BULLSHIT, LUCIFER CAN GO FUCK--
GODDESS COMING THROUGH! AND...
HEY, LOZ! CASSY! NO TIME TO CHAT!
NEED TO HAVE A WORD WITH LADY LUCIFER.

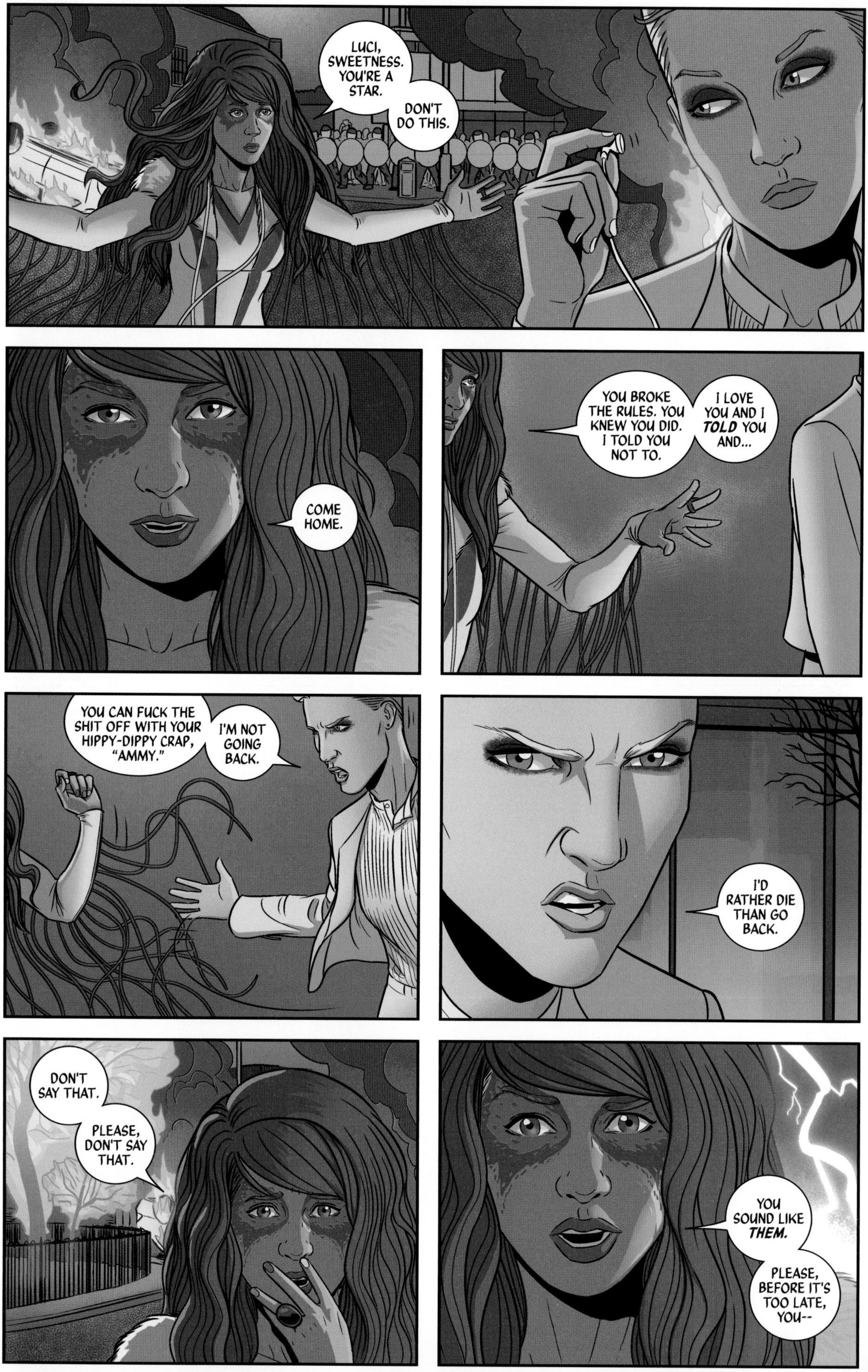
LUCI, SWEETNESS. YOU'RE A STAR.
DON'T DO THIS.
COME HOME.
YOU BROKE THE RULES. YOU KNEW YOU DID. I TOLD YOU NOT TO.
I LOVE YOU AND I *TOLD* YOU AND...
YOU CAN FUCK THE SHIT OFF WITH YOUR HIPPY-DIPPY CRAP, "AMMY."
I'M NOT GOING BACK.
I'D RATHER DIE THAN GO BACK.
DON'T SAY THAT.
PLEASE, DON'T SAY THAT.
YOU SOUND LIKE *THEM.*
PLEASE, BEFORE IT'S TOO LATE, YOU--

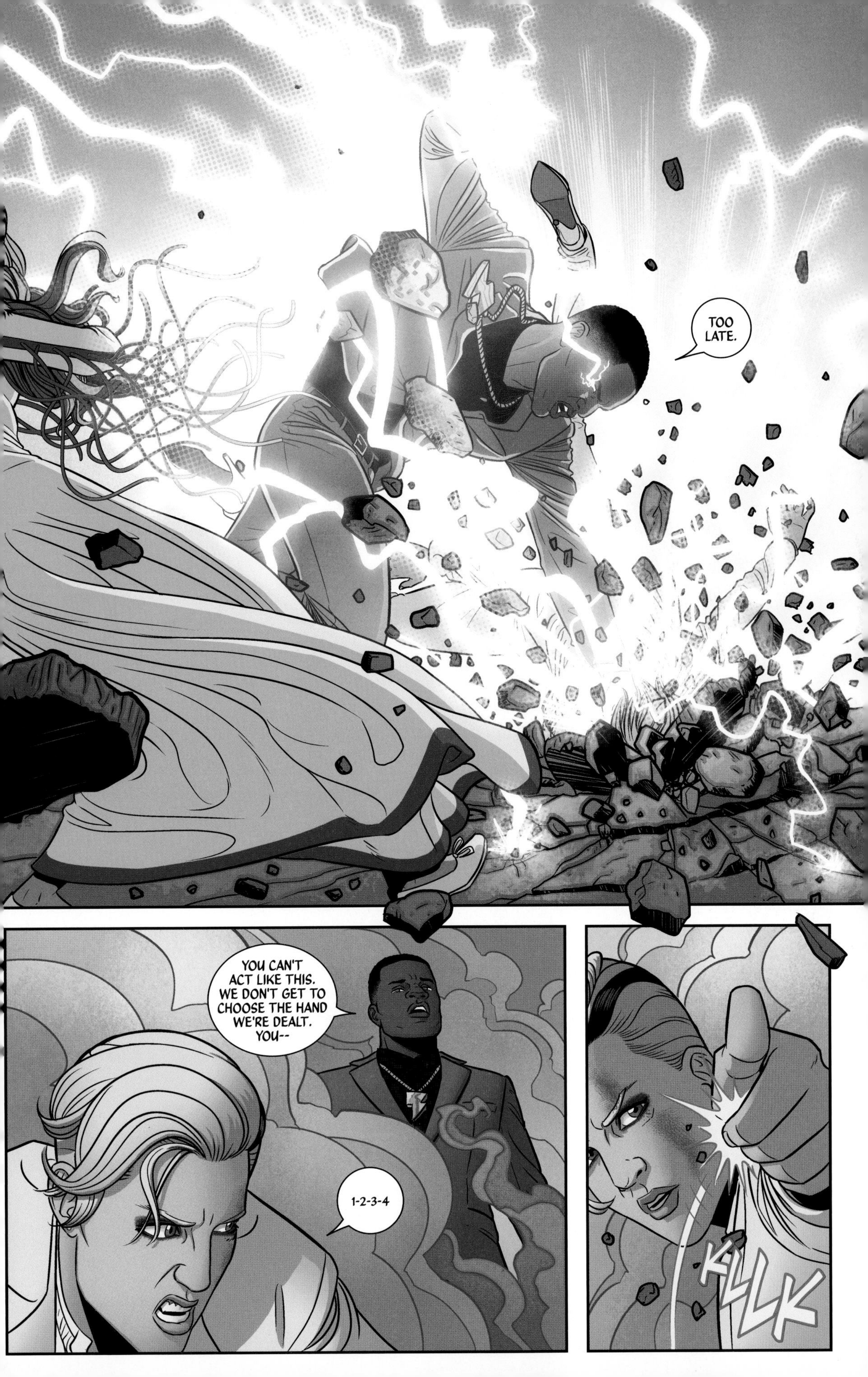
TOO LATE.
YOU CAN'T ACT LIKE THIS. WE DON'T GET TO CHOOSE THE HAND WE'RE DEALT. YOU--
1-2-3-4
KLLK

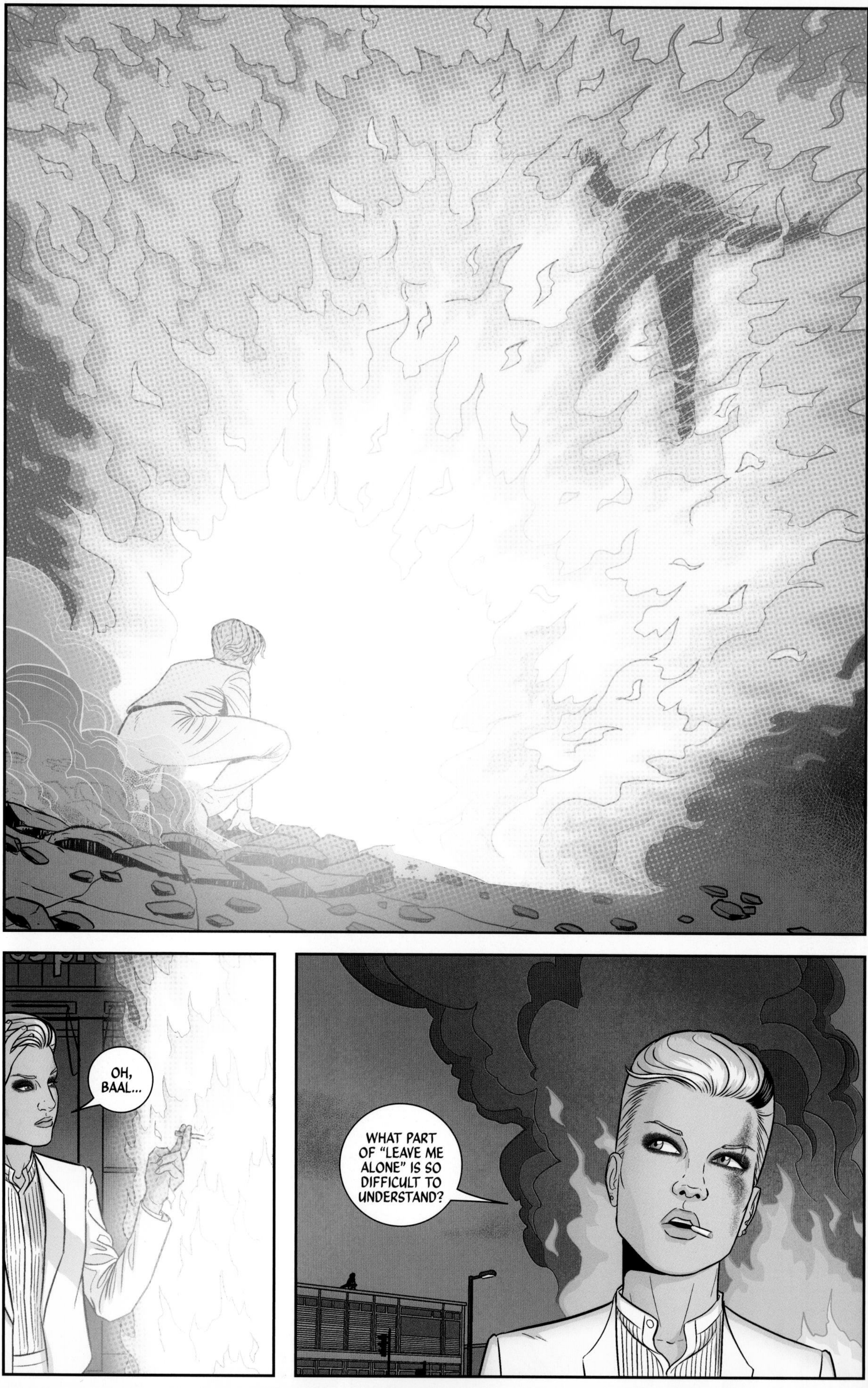
OH, BAAL...
WHAT PART OF "LEAVE ME ALONE" IS SO DIFFICULT TO UNDERSTAND?

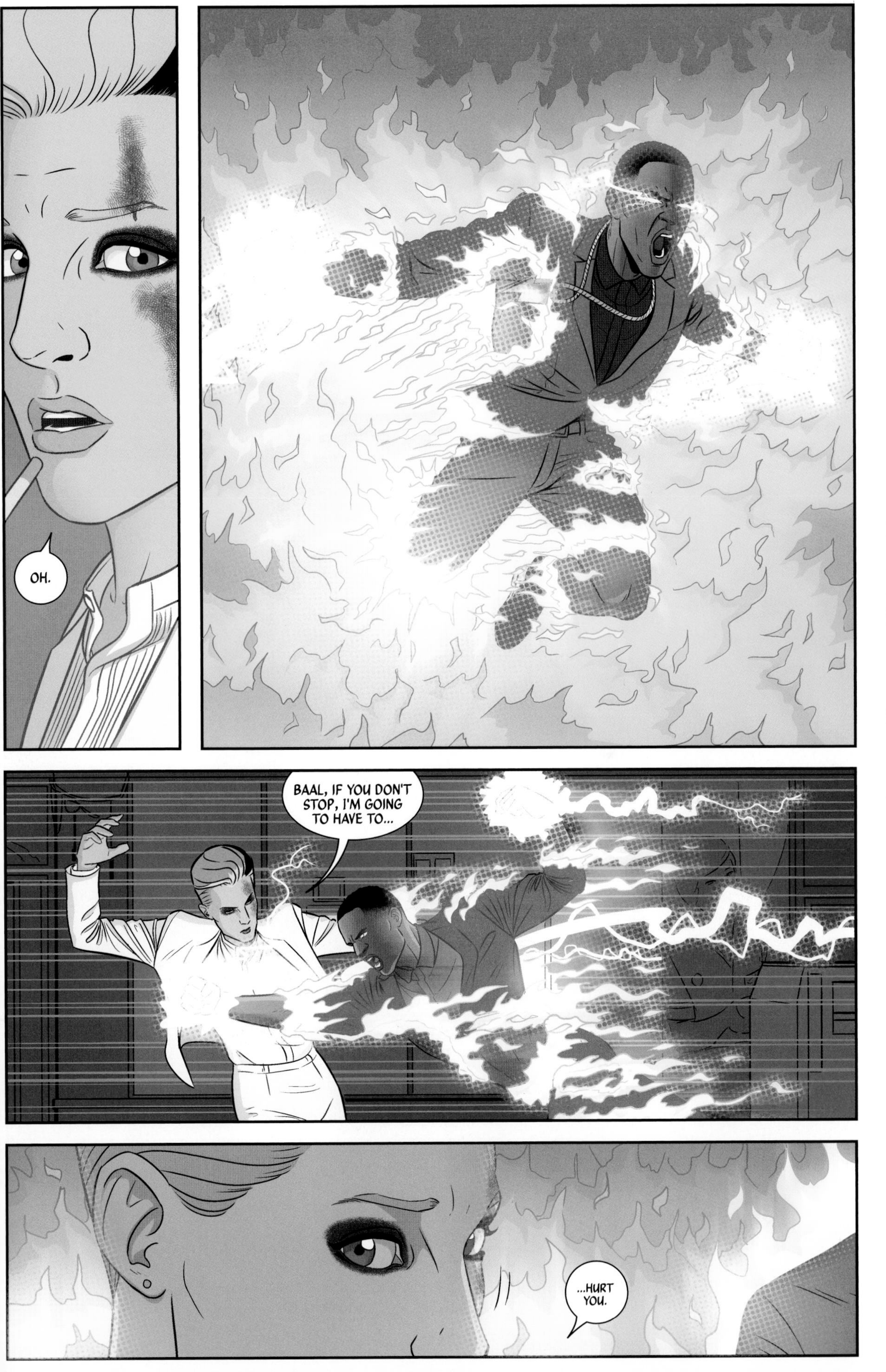
OH.
BAAL, IF YOU DON'T STOP, I'M GOING TO HAVE TO...
...HURT YOU.

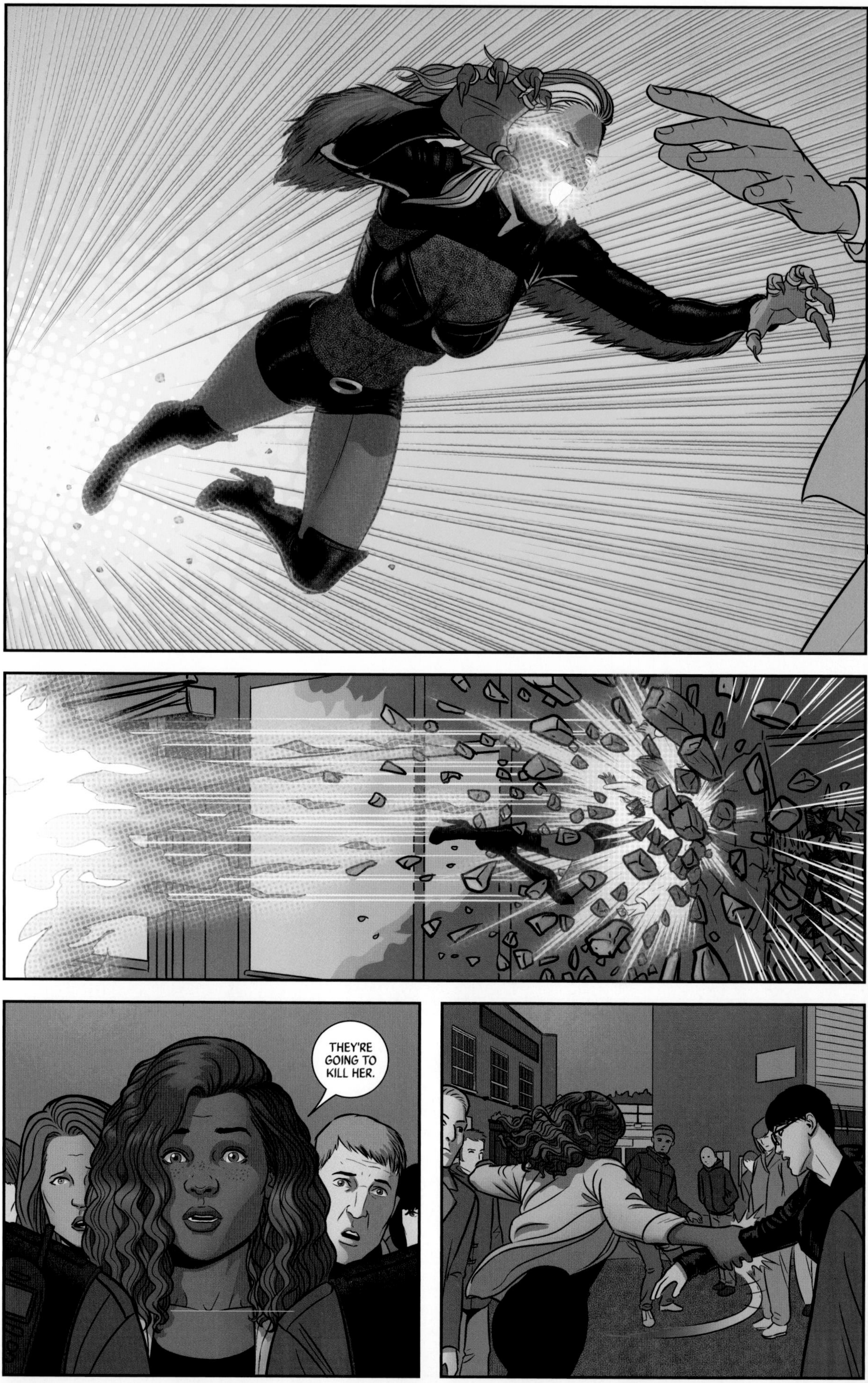
THEY'RE GOING TO KILL HER.

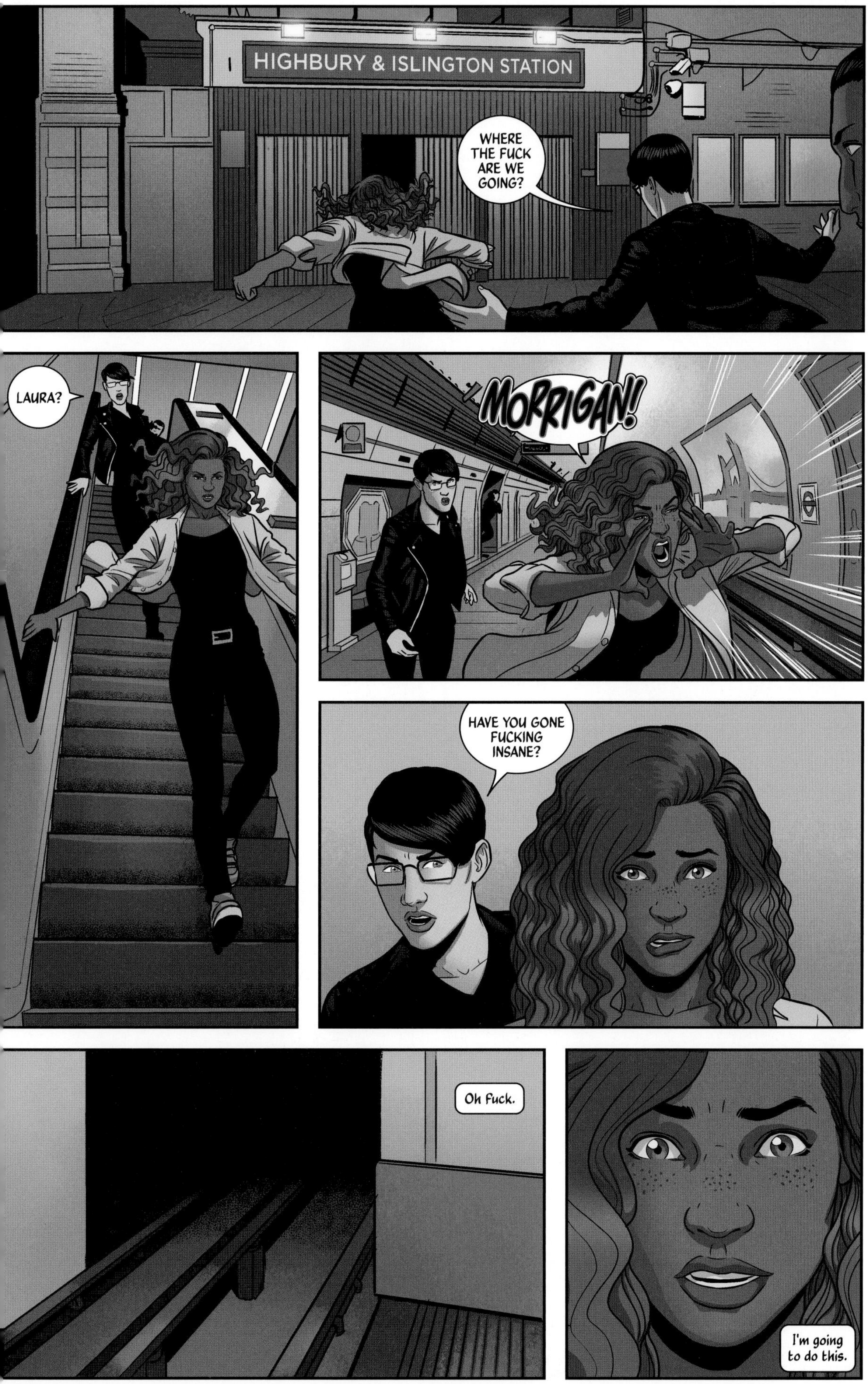
HIGHBURY & ISLINGTON STATION
WHERE THE FUCK ARE WE GOING?
LAURA?
MORRIGAN!
HAVE YOU GONE FUCKING INSANE?
Oh fuck.
I'm going to do this.

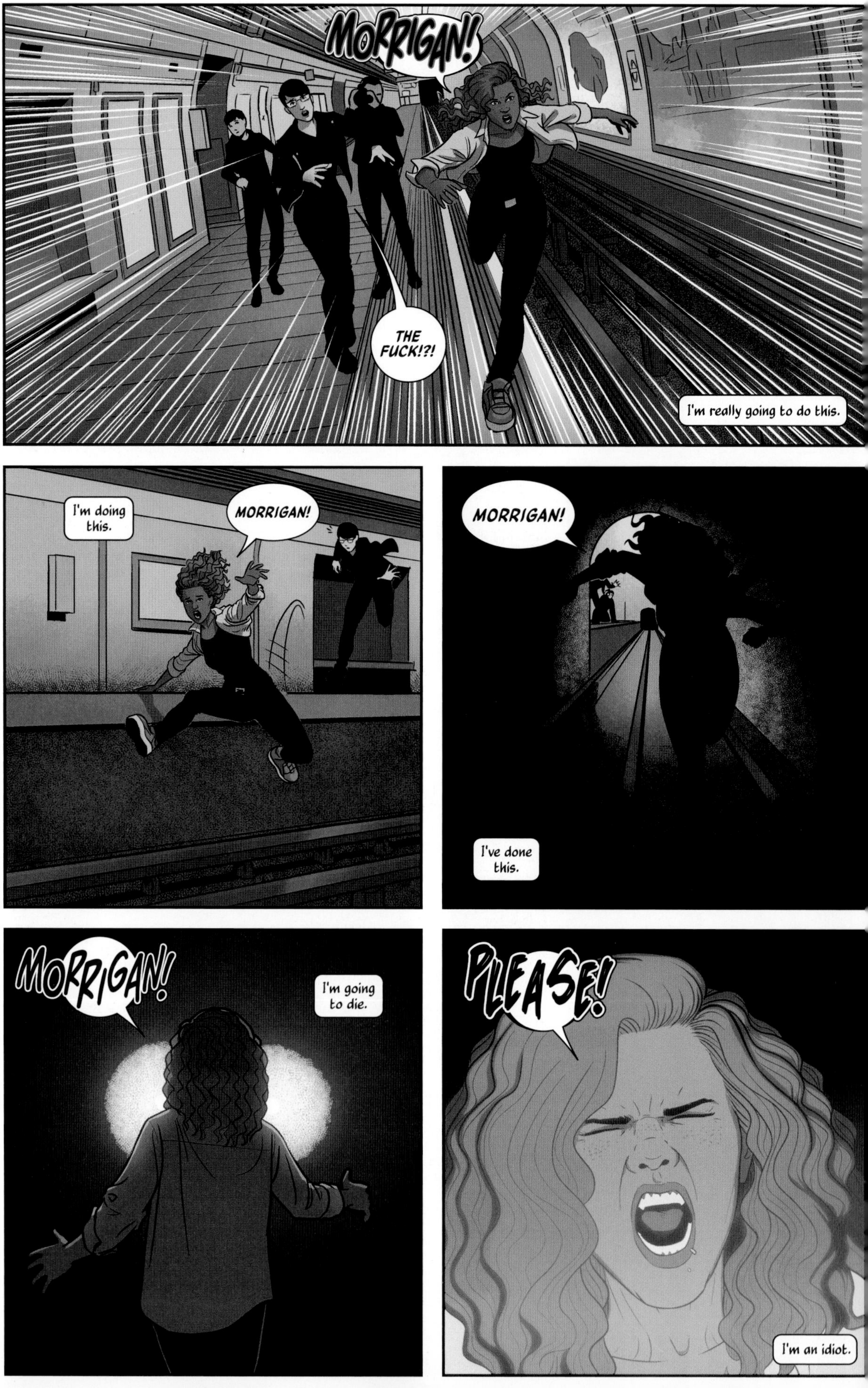
MORRIGAN!
THE FUCK!?!
I'm really going to do this.
I'm doing this.
MORRIGAN!
MORRIGAN!
I've done this.
MORRIGAN!
I'm going to die.
PLEASE!
I'm an idiot.

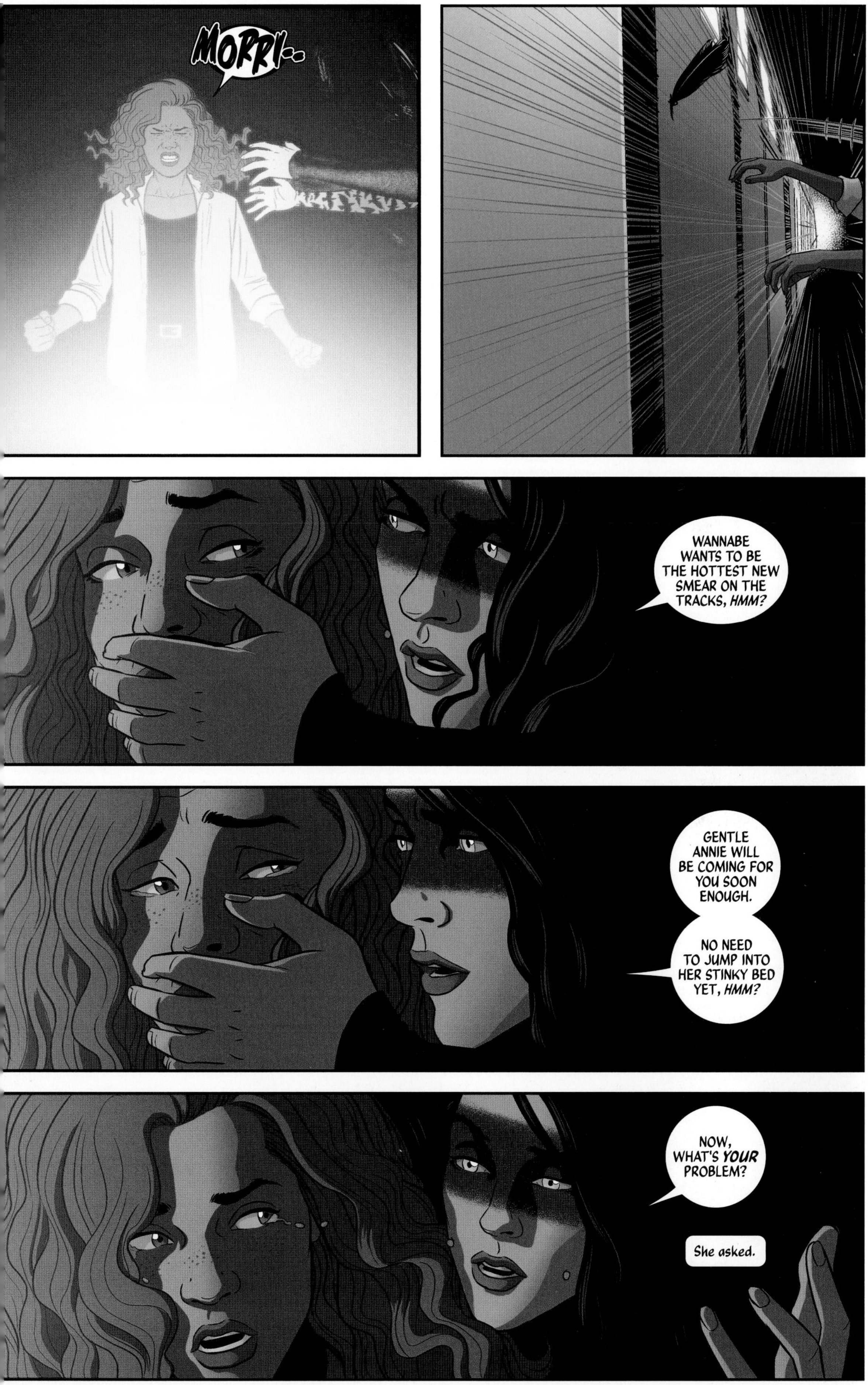
MORRI--
WANNABE WANTS TO BE THE HOTTEST NEW SMEAR ON THE TRACKS, HMM?
GENTLE ANNIE WILL BE COMING FOR YOU SOON ENOUGH.
NO NEED TO JUMP INTO HER STINKY BED YET, HMM?
NOW, WHAT'S YOUR PROBLEM?
She asked.

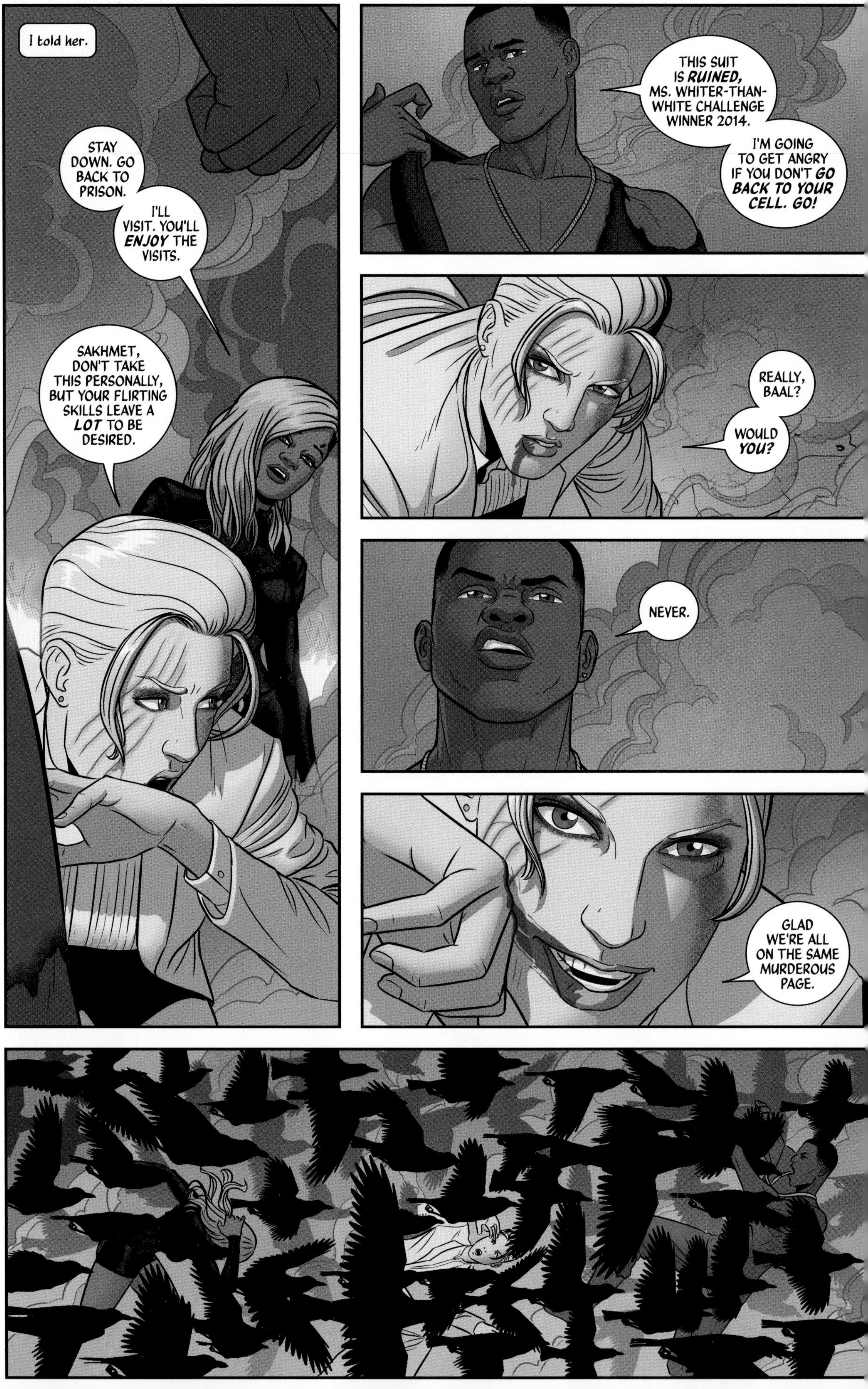
I told her.
STAY DOWN. GO BACK TO PRISON.
I'LL VISIT. YOU'LL ENJOY THE VISITS.
SAKHMET, DON'T TAKE THIS PERSONALLY, BUT YOUR FLIRTING SKILLS LEAVE A LOT TO BE DESIRED.
THIS SUIT IS RUINED, MS. WHITER-THAN-WHITE CHALLENGE WINNER 2014.
I'M GOING TO GET ANGRY IF YOU DON'T GO BACK TO YOUR CELL. GO!
REALLY, BAAL?
WOULD YOU?
NEVER.
GLAD WE'RE ALL ON THE SAME MURDEROUS PAGE.

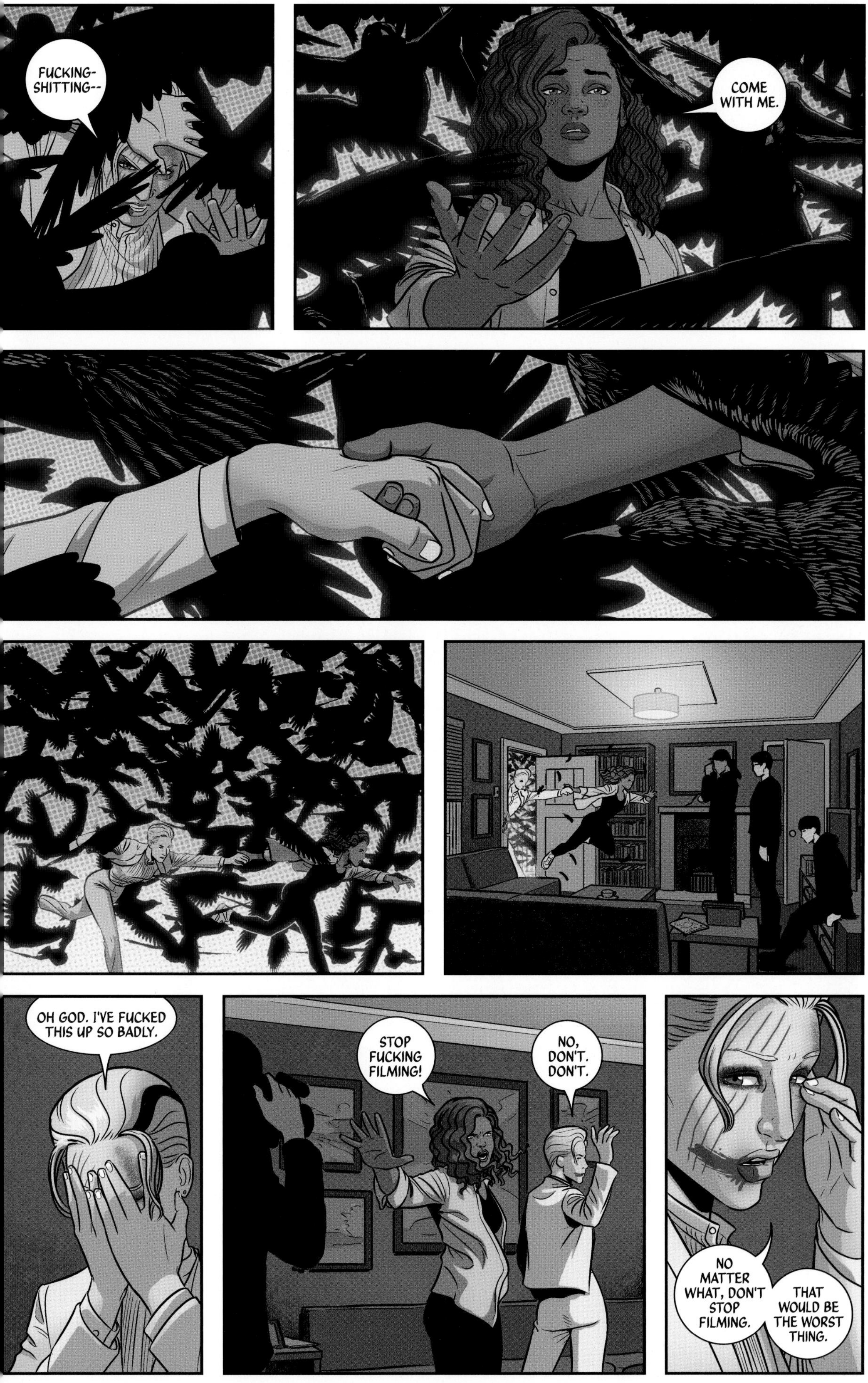
FUCKING-
SHITTING--
COME WITH ME.
OH GOD. I'VE FUCKED THIS UP SO BADLY.
STOP FUCKING FILMING!
NO, DON'T. DON'T.
NO MATTER WHAT, DON'T STOP FILMING.
THAT WOULD BE THE WORST THING.

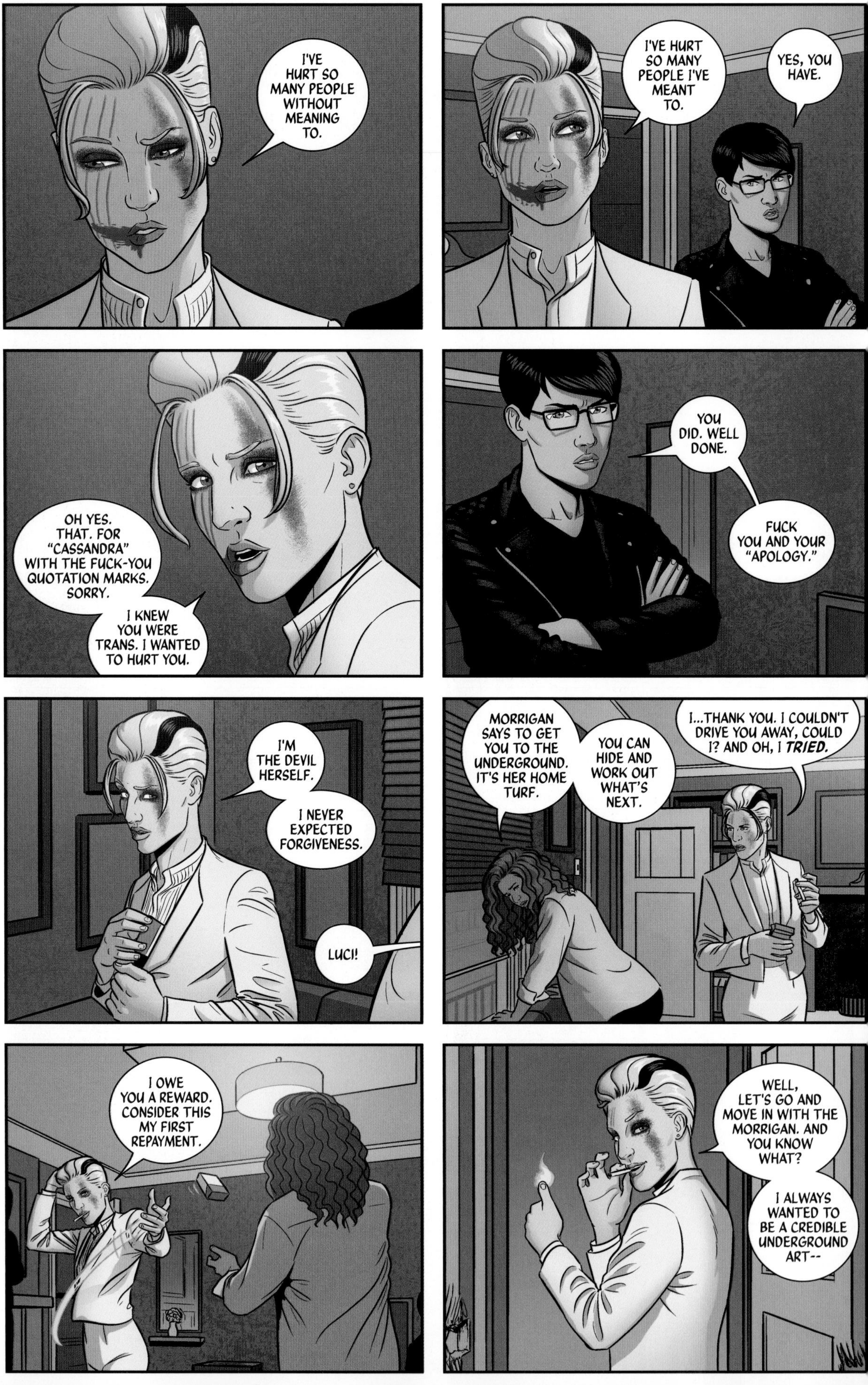
I'VE HURT SO MANY PEOPLE WITHOUT MEANING TO.
I'VE HURT SO MANY PEOPLE I'VE MEANT TO.
YES, YOU HAVE.
OH YES. THAT. FOR "CASSANDRA" WITH THE FUCK-YOU QUOTATION MARKS. SORRY.
I KNEW YOU WERE TRANS. I WANTED TO HURT YOU.
YOU DID. WELL DONE.
FUCK YOU AND YOUR "APOLOGY."
I'M THE DEVIL HERSELF.
I NEVER EXPECTED FORGIVENESS.
LUCI!
MORRIGAN SAYS TO GET YOU TO THE UNDERGROUND. IT'S HER HOME TURF.
YOU CAN HIDE AND WORK OUT WHAT'S NEXT.
I...THANK YOU. I COULDN'T DRIVE YOU AWAY, COULD I? AND OH, I *TRIED.*
I OWE YOU A REWARD. CONSIDER THIS MY FIRST REPAYMENT.
WELL, LET'S GO AND MOVE IN WITH THE MORRIGAN. AND YOU KNOW WHAT?
I ALWAYS WANTED TO BE A CREDIBLE UNDERGROUND ART--

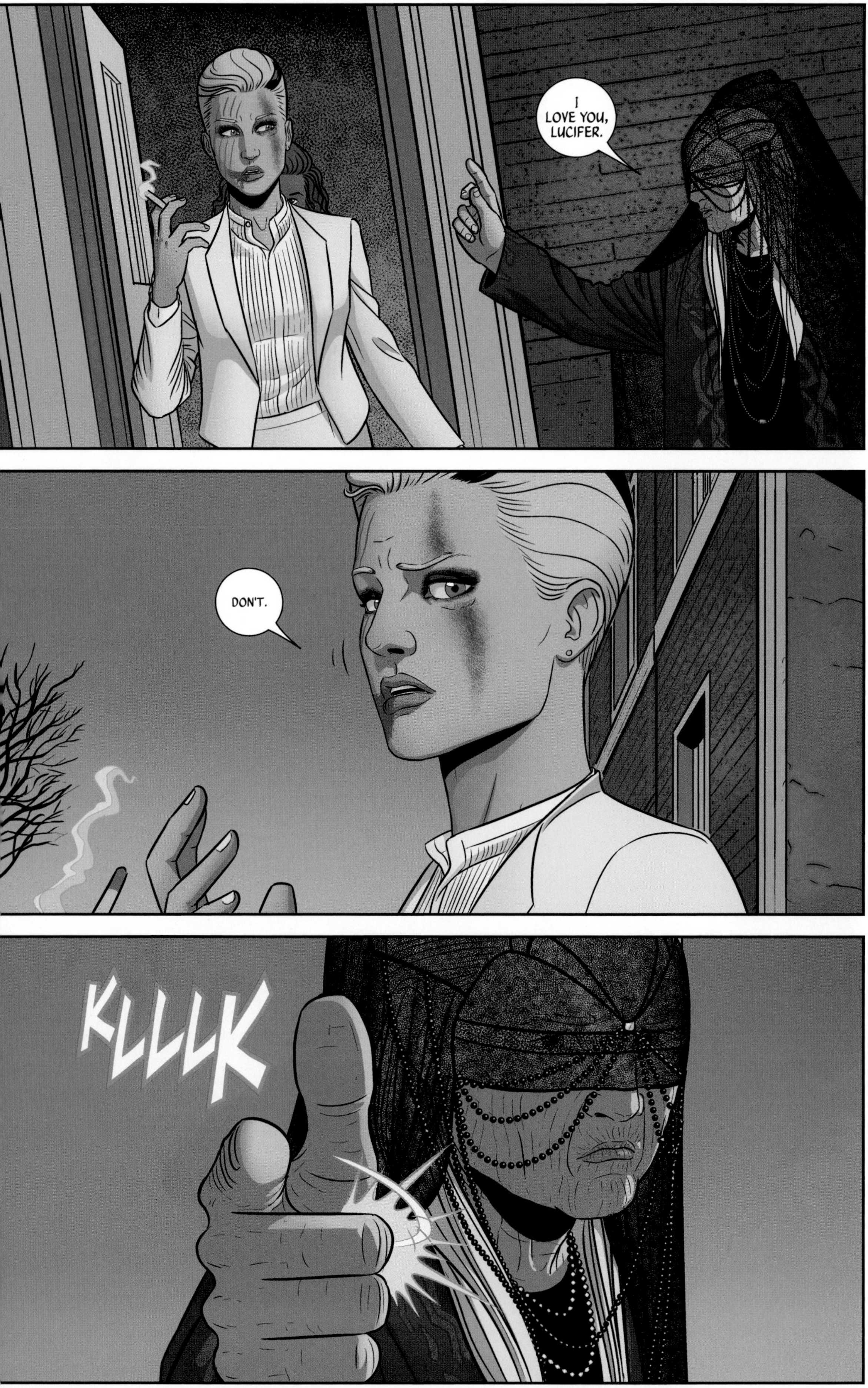
I LOVE YOU, LUCIFER.
DON'T.
KLLLK

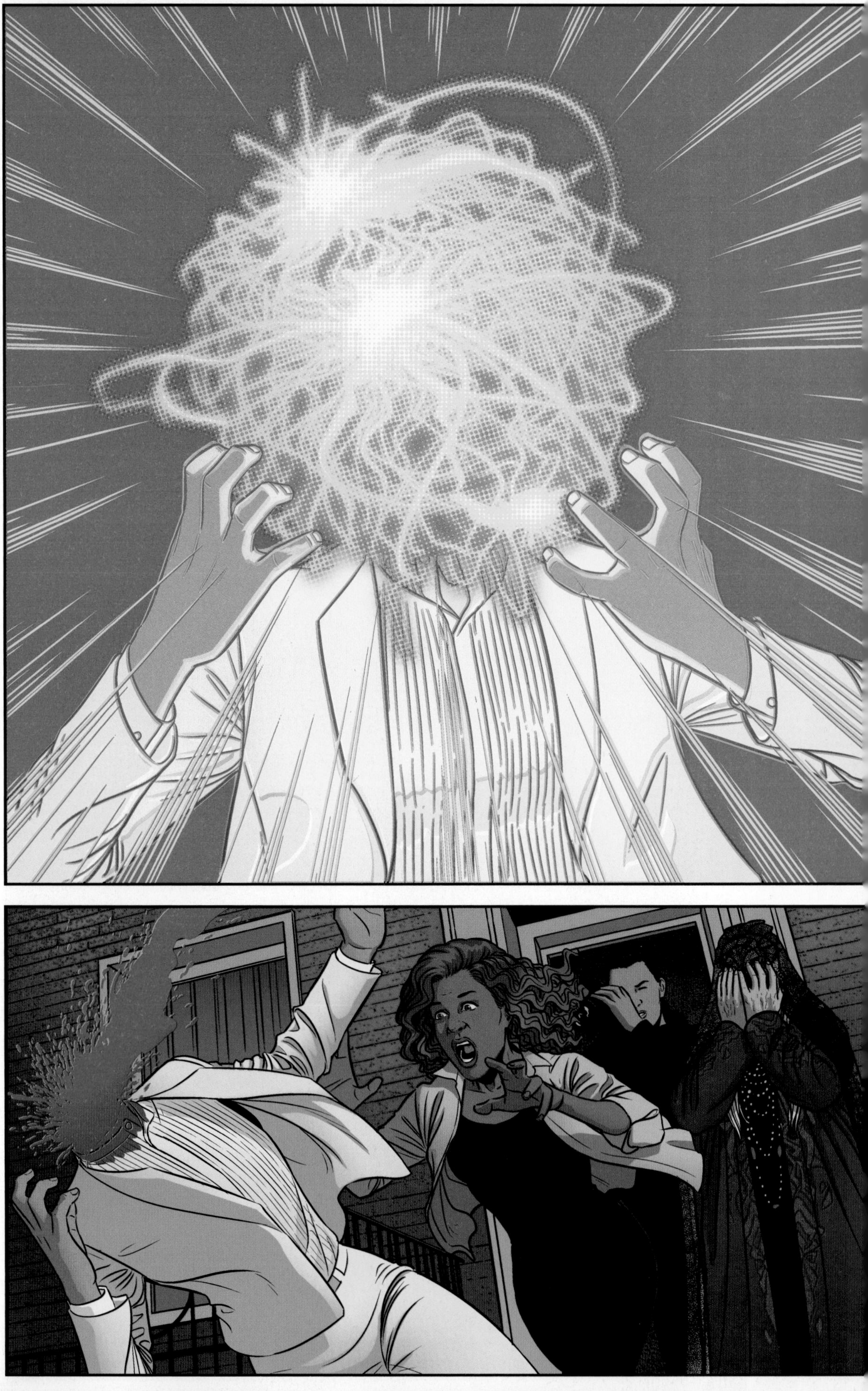

I don't remember anything
about the next few minutes.

I guess I'm grateful for that.

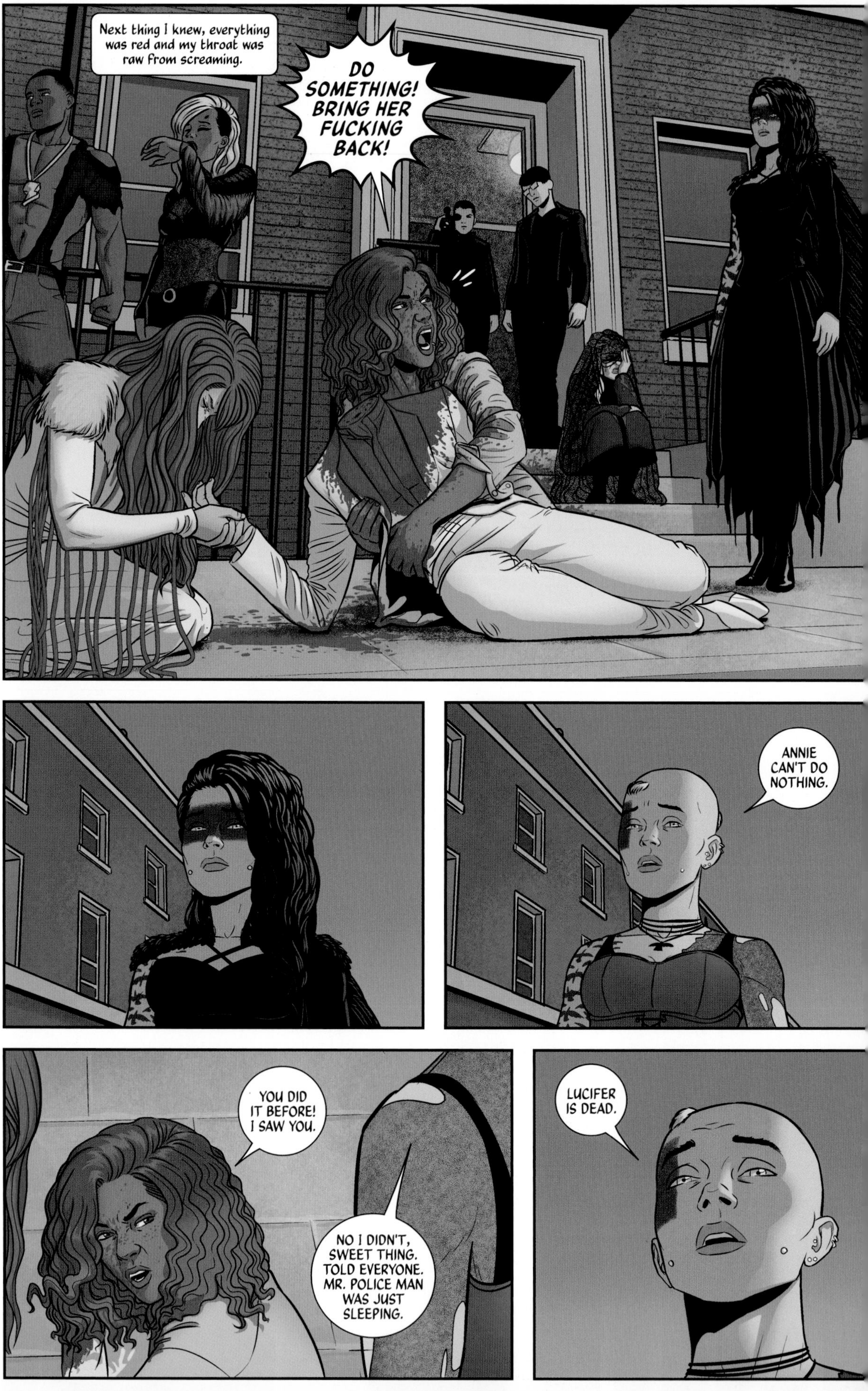
Next thing I knew, everything was red and my throat was raw from screaming.
DO SOMETHING! BRING HER FUCKING BACK!
ANNIE CAN'T DO NOTHING.
YOU DID IT BEFORE! I SAW YOU.
NO I DIDN'T, SWEET THING. TOLD EVERYONE. MR. POLICE MAN WAS JUST SLEEPING.
LUCIFER IS DEAD.

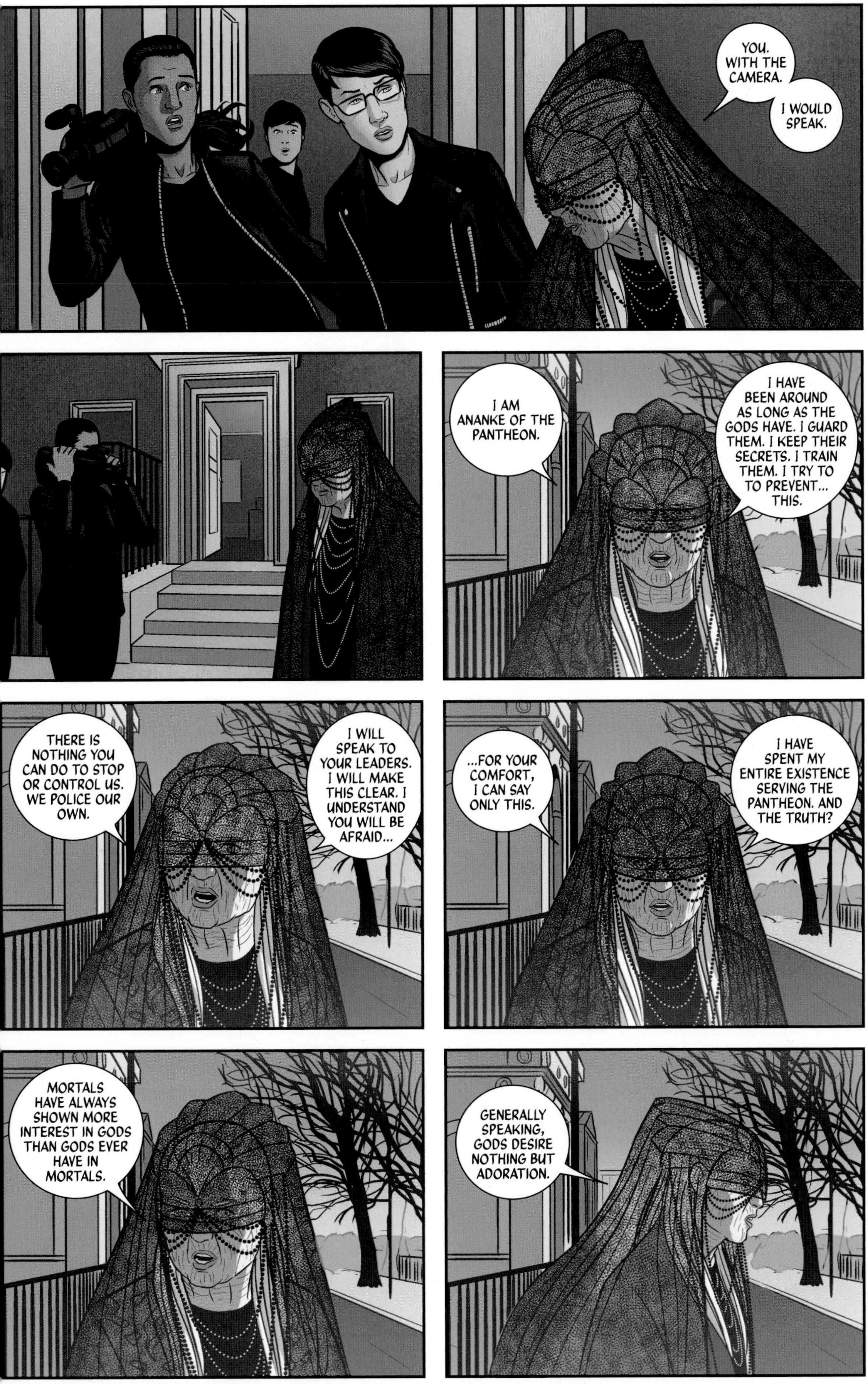
YOU. WITH THE CAMERA.
I WOULD SPEAK.
I AM ANANKE OF THE PANTHEON.
I HAVE BEEN AROUND AS LONG AS THE GODS HAVE. I GUARD THEM. I KEEP THEIR SECRETS. I TRAIN THEM. I TRY TO TO PREVENT... THIS.
THERE IS NOTHING YOU CAN DO TO STOP OR CONTROL US. WE POLICE OUR OWN.
I WILL SPEAK TO YOUR LEADERS. I WILL MAKE THIS CLEAR. I UNDERSTAND YOU WILL BE AFRAID...
...FOR YOUR COMFORT, I CAN SAY ONLY THIS.
I HAVE SPENT MY ENTIRE EXISTENCE SERVING THE PANTHEON. AND THE TRUTH?
MORTALS HAVE ALWAYS SHOWN MORE INTEREST IN GODS THAN GODS EVER HAVE IN MORTALS.
GENERALLY SPEAKING, GODS DESIRE NOTHING BUT ADORATION.

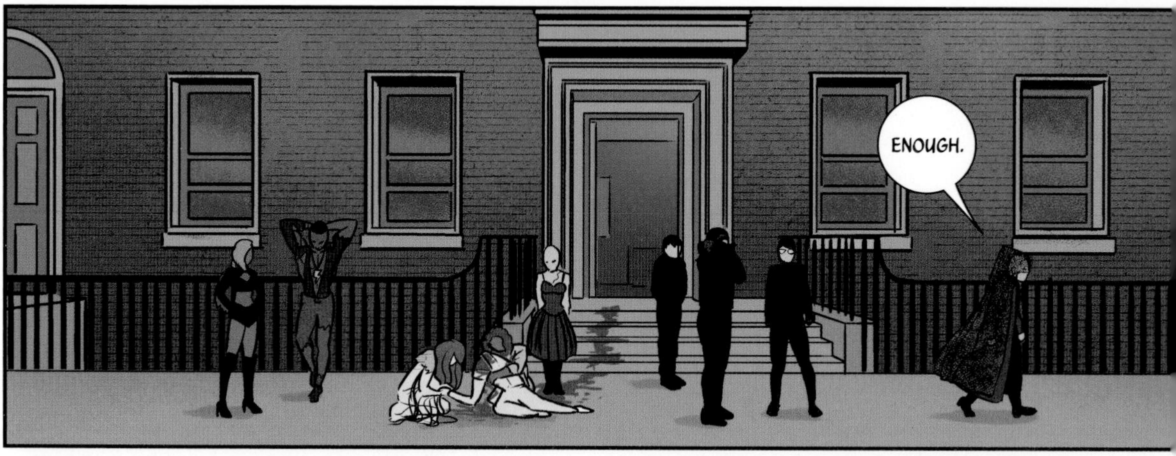
ENOUGH.

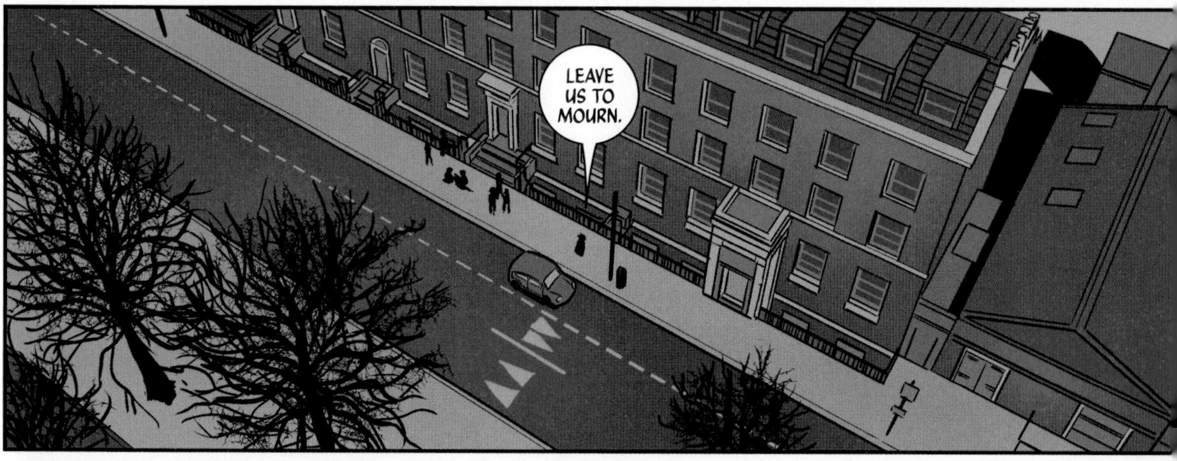
LEAVE US TO MOURN.

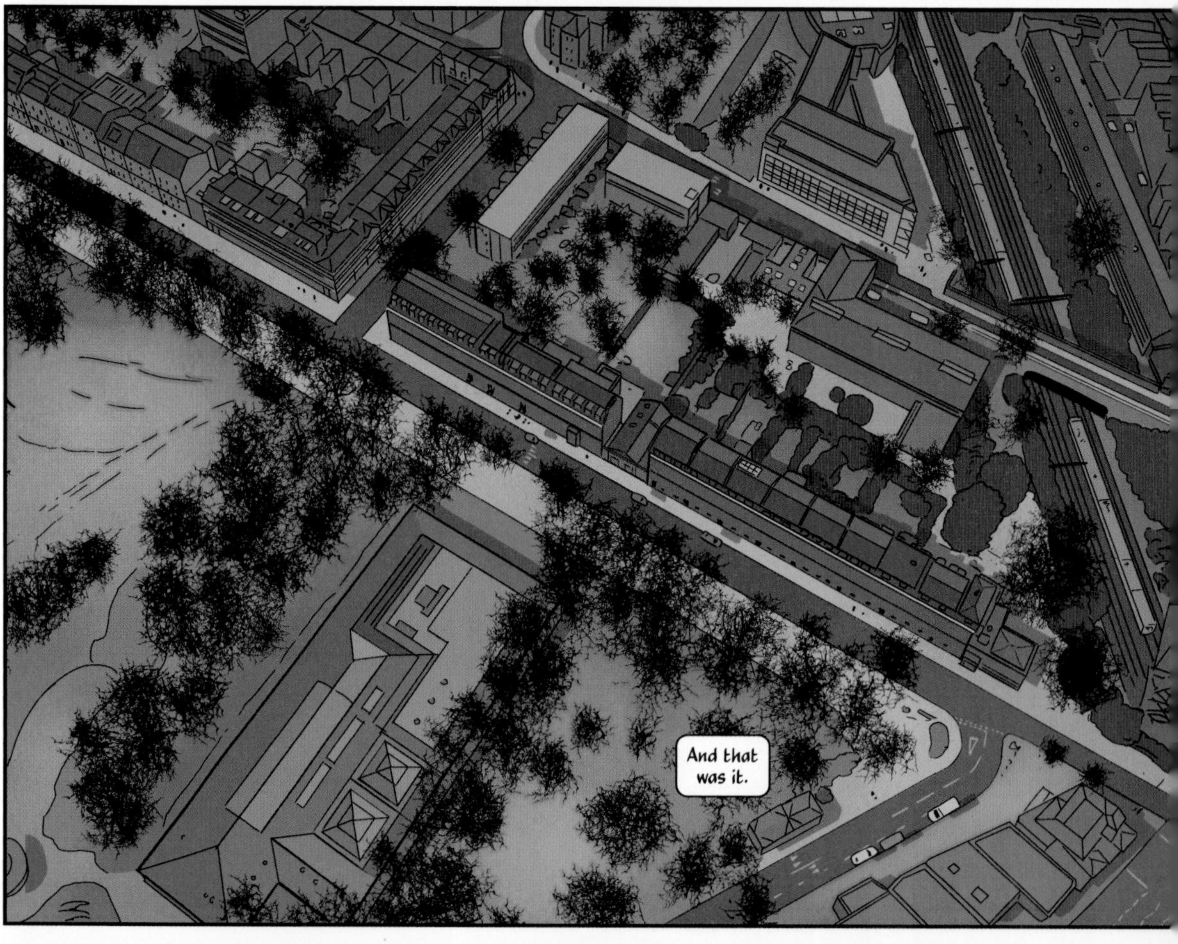
And that was it.

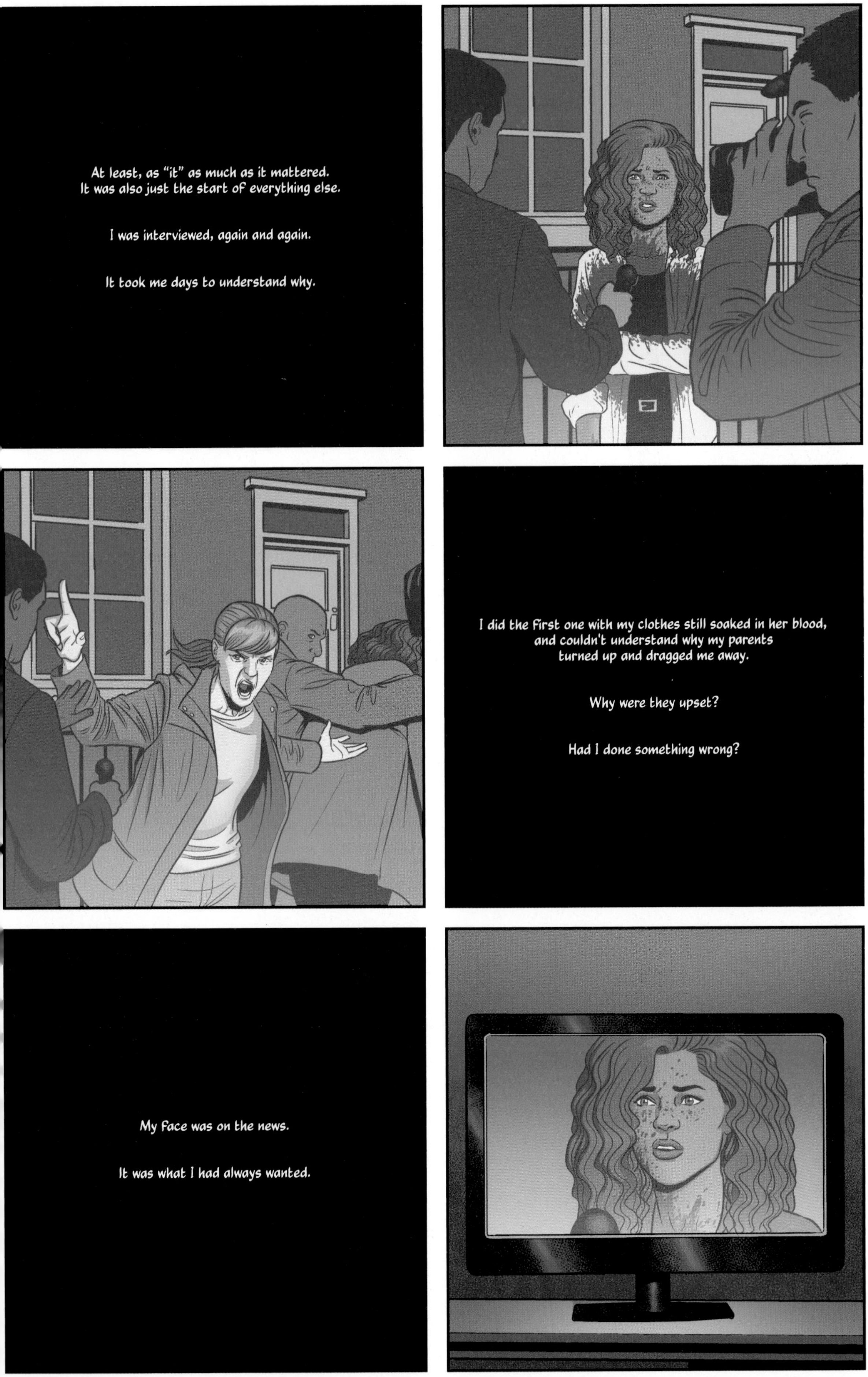
At least, as "it" as much as it mattered.
It was also just the start of everything else.
I was interviewed, again and again.
It took me days to understand why.
I did the first one with my clothes still soaked in her blood, and couldn't understand why my parents turned up and dragged me away.
Why were they upset?
Had I done something wrong?
My face was on the news.
It was what I had always wanted.

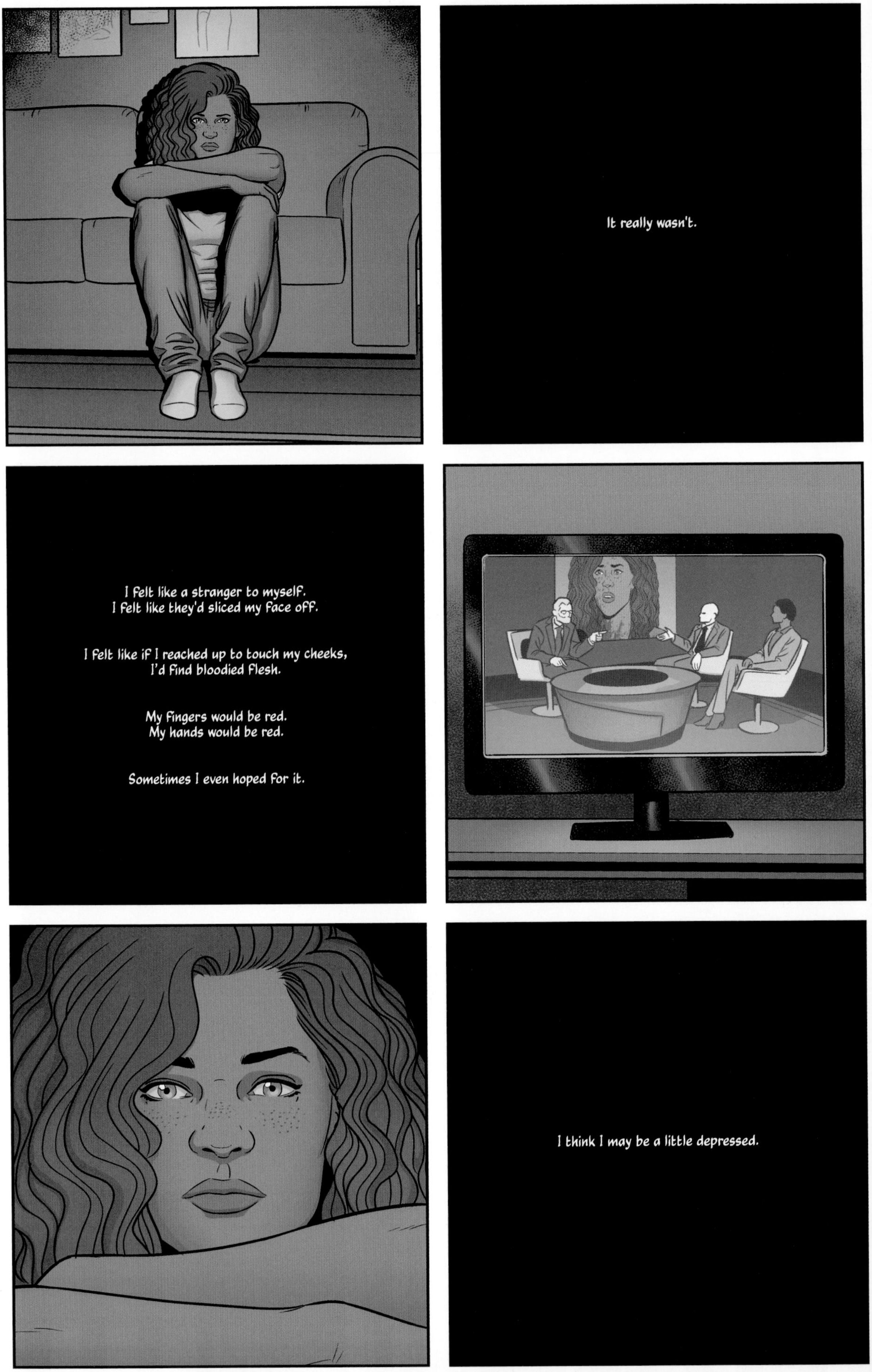
It really wasn't.
I felt like a stranger to myself.
I felt like they'd sliced my face off.
I felt like if I reached up to touch my cheeks,
I'd find bloodied flesh.
My fingers would be red.
My hands would be red.
Sometimes I even hoped for it.
I think I may be a little depressed.

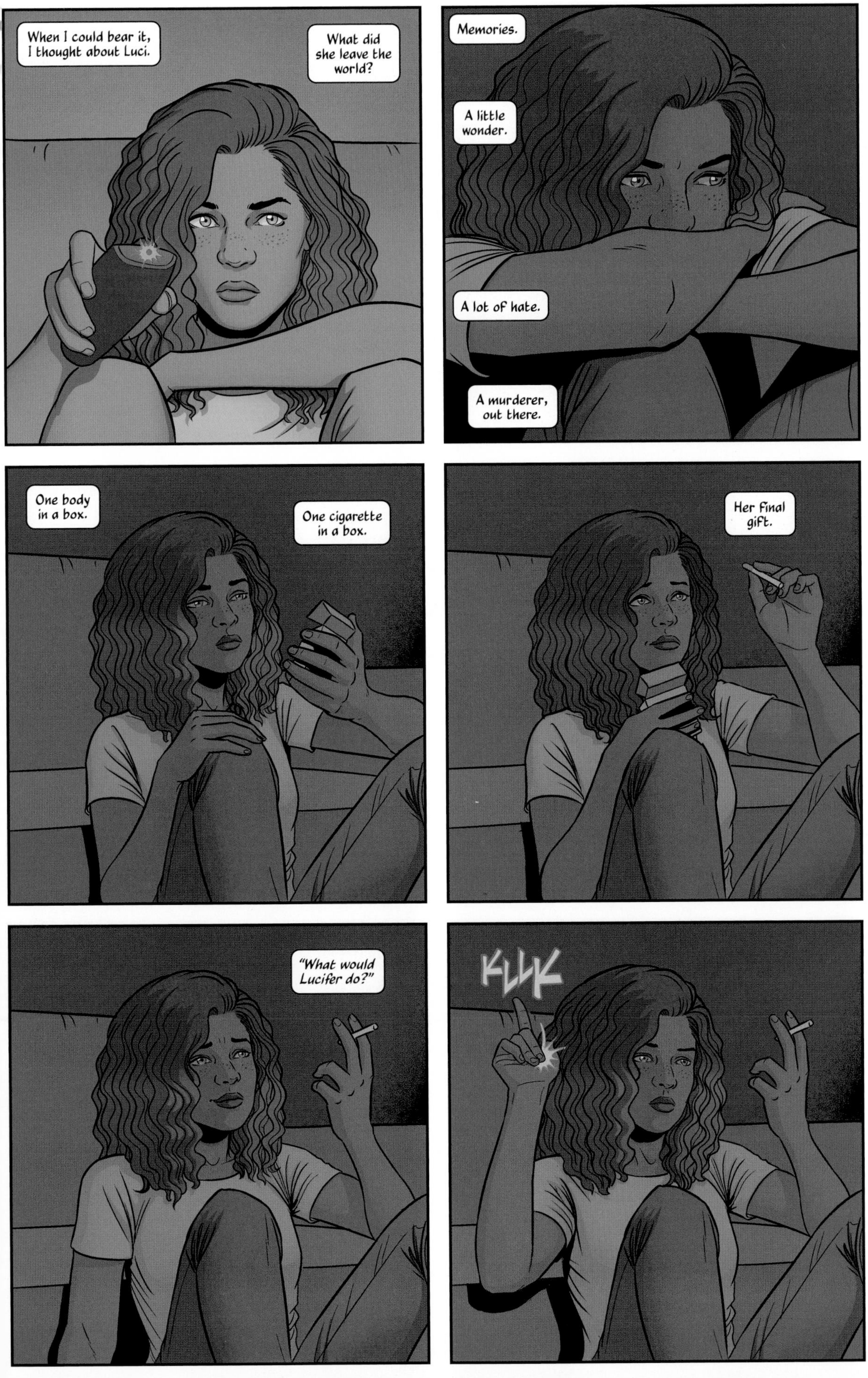

When I could bear it, I thought about Luci.
What did she leave the world?
Memories.
A little wonder.
A lot of hate.
A murderer, out there.
One body in a box.
One cigarette in a box.
Her final gift.
"What would Lucifer do?"
KLIK

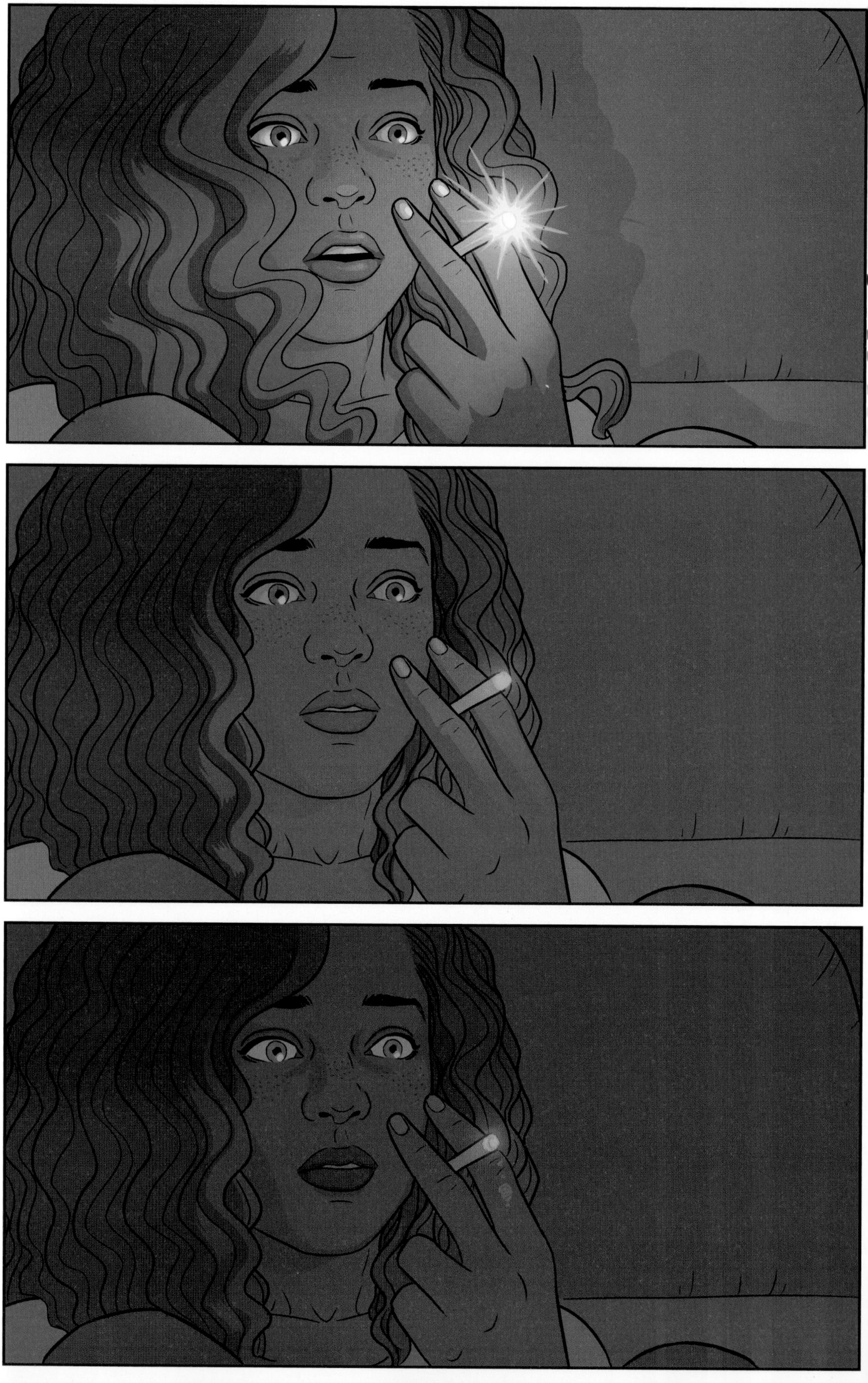

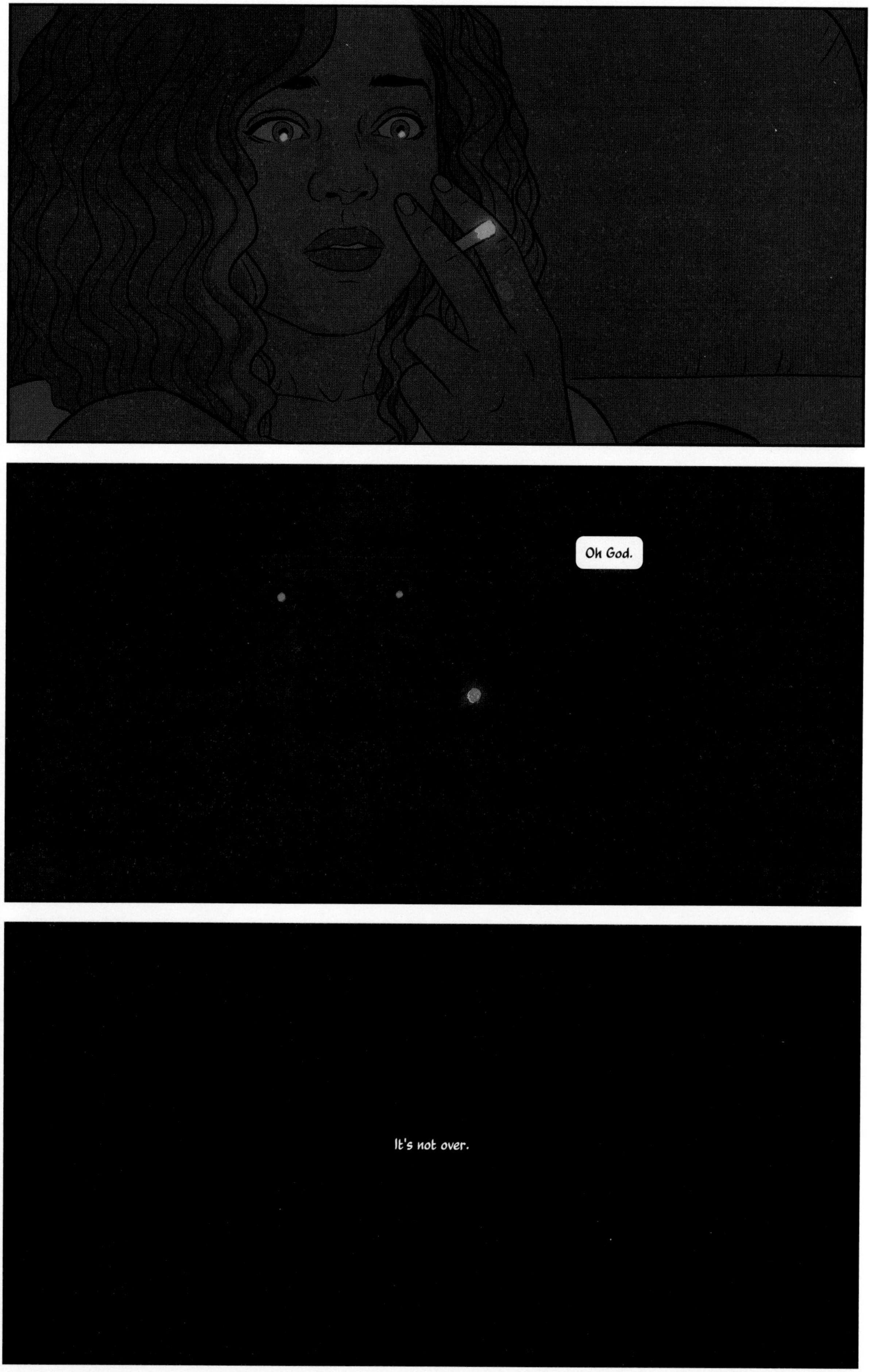
Oh God.
It's not over.

SYMPATHY

19 JANUARY 2014

THE
WICKED
+
DIVINE
THE

VARIANT ART

We're lucky that we have talented friends. To be honest, when you're as awful as we are, we're lucky to have friends. Relevantly, when doing a book where image is such a central aspect, we thought it would be a fantastic opportunity to get them to go and strut their stuff with our characters. The results were astounding, and well worth including in some manner of cover art gallery in this book, but we don't have any room and...

...oh my. Look what we've just found.

Jamie McKelvie
Issue one cover (Coloured by Matthew Wilson)

Bryan Lee O'Malley
Issue one cover

Matthew Wilson, Jordie Bellaire
Issue one colour variants (Bellaire bottom right)

Matthew Wilson, Jamie McKelvie
Issue one and two colour variants (McKelvie bottom right)

Jamie McKelvie
Issue two cover

Chip Zdarsky
Issue two cover

Jamie McKelvie
Issue three cover

Stephanie Hans
Issue three cover

Kevin Wada
Issue four cover

Jamie McKelvie
Issue five cover

Becky Cloonan
Issue five cover

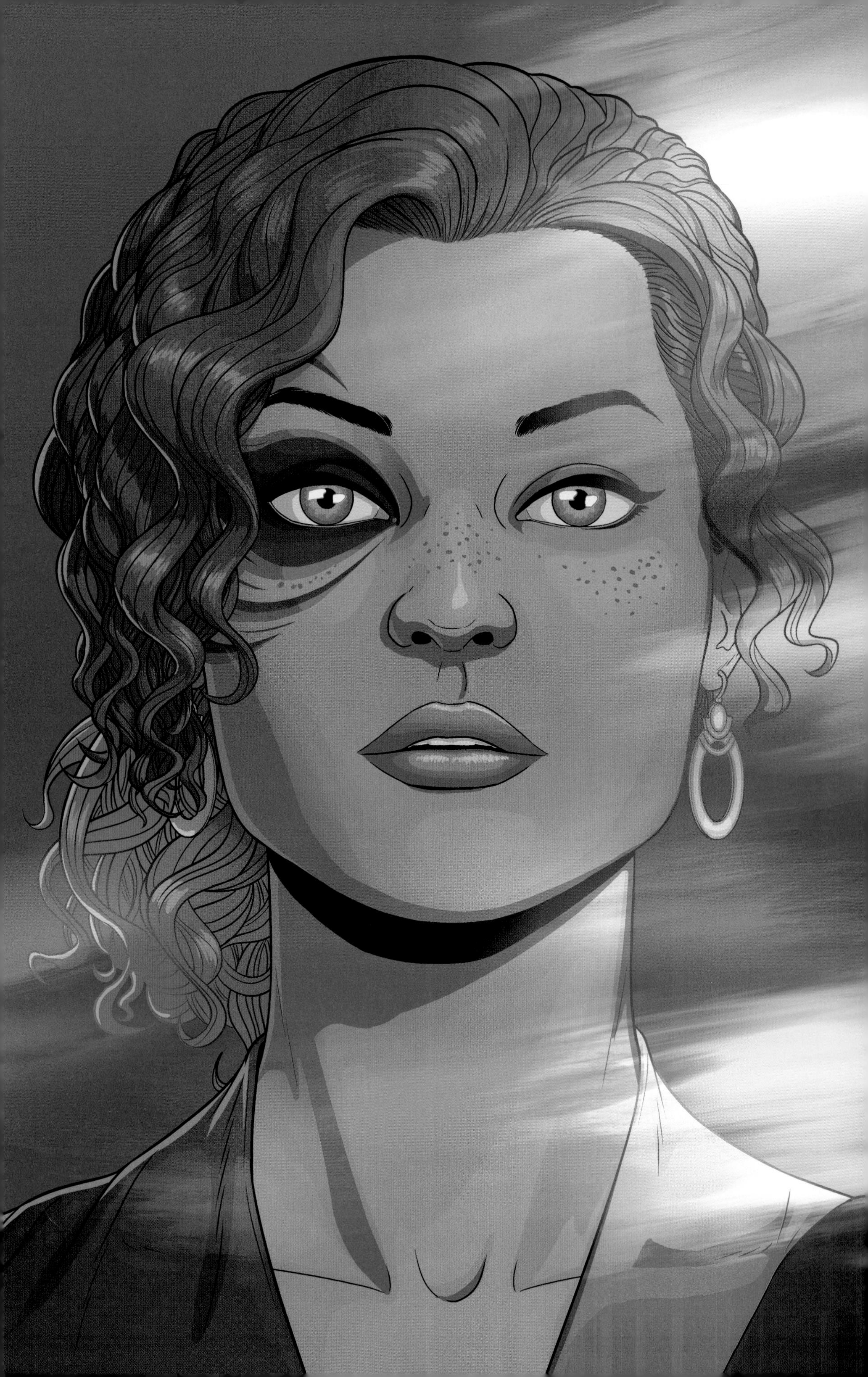

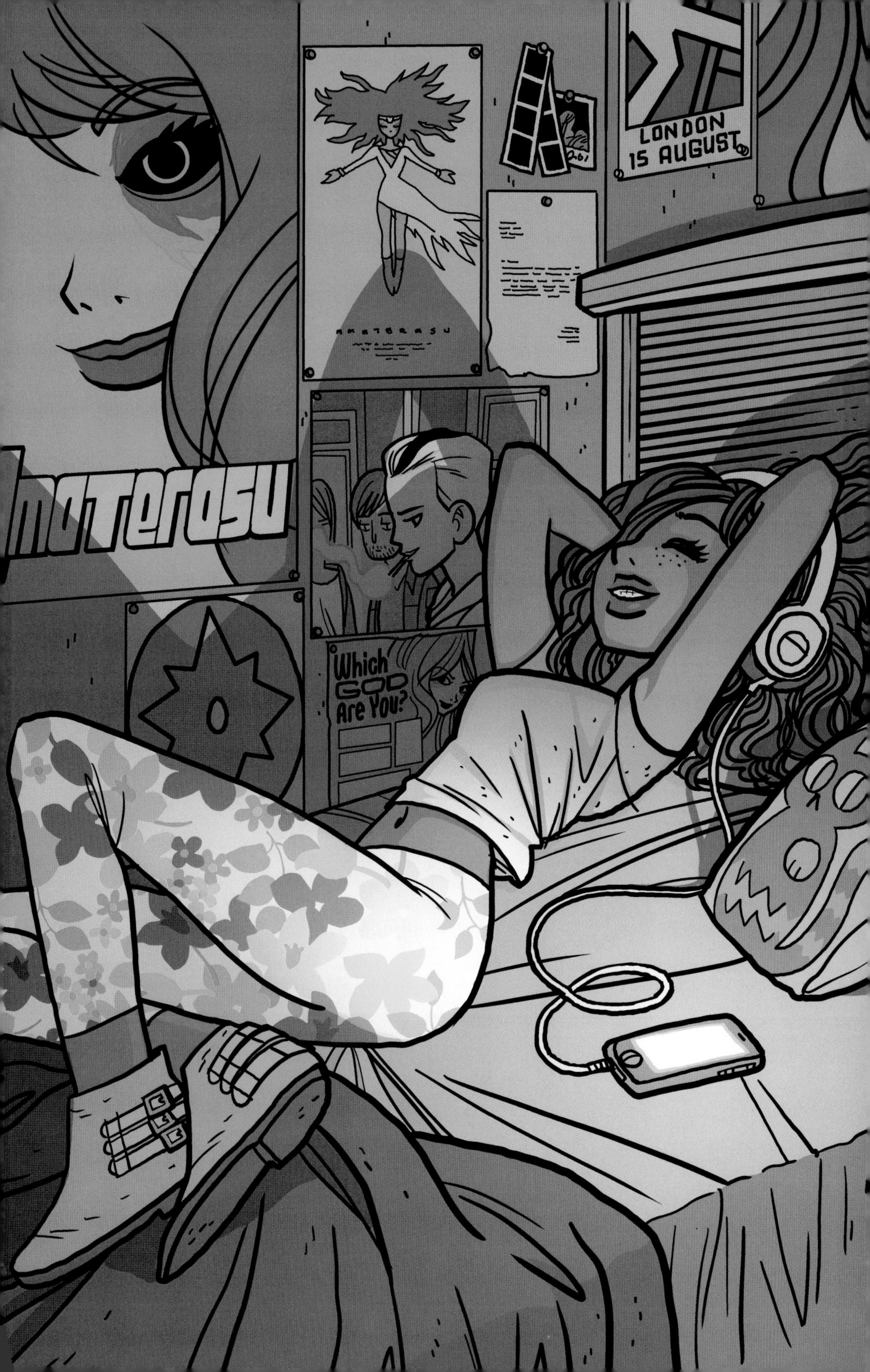

LONDON
15 AUGUST
materasu
Which GOD Are You?

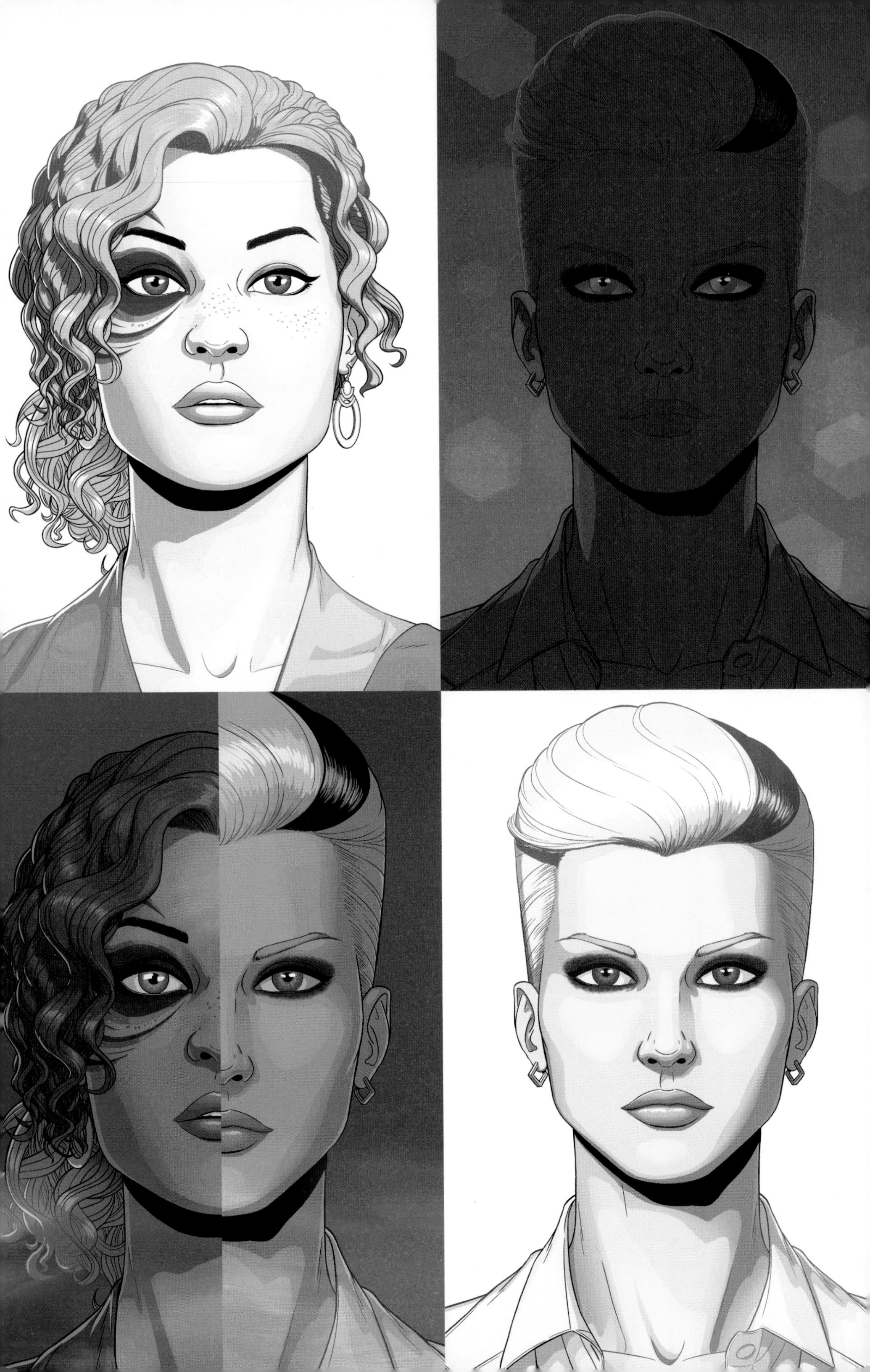

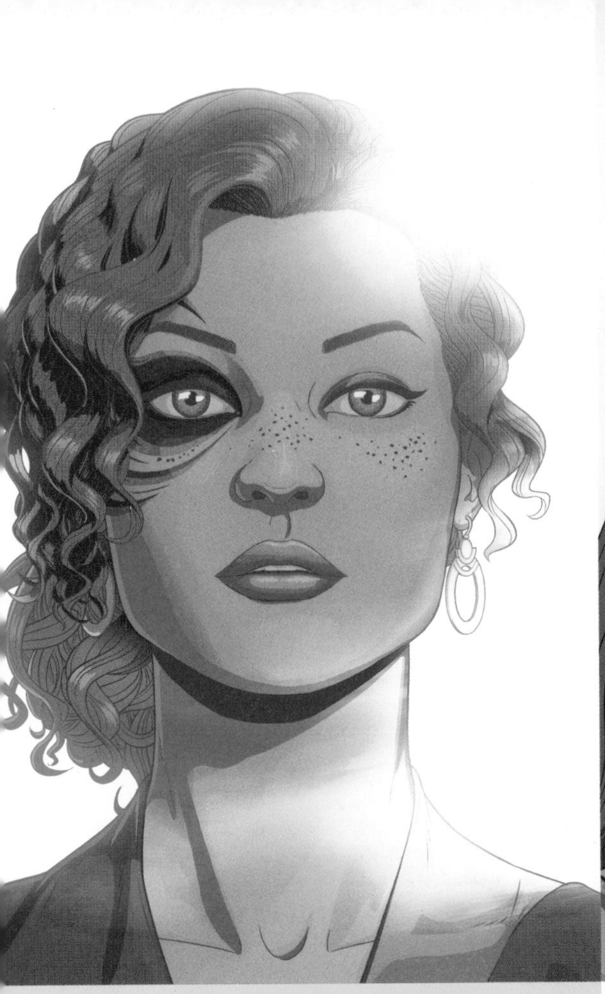
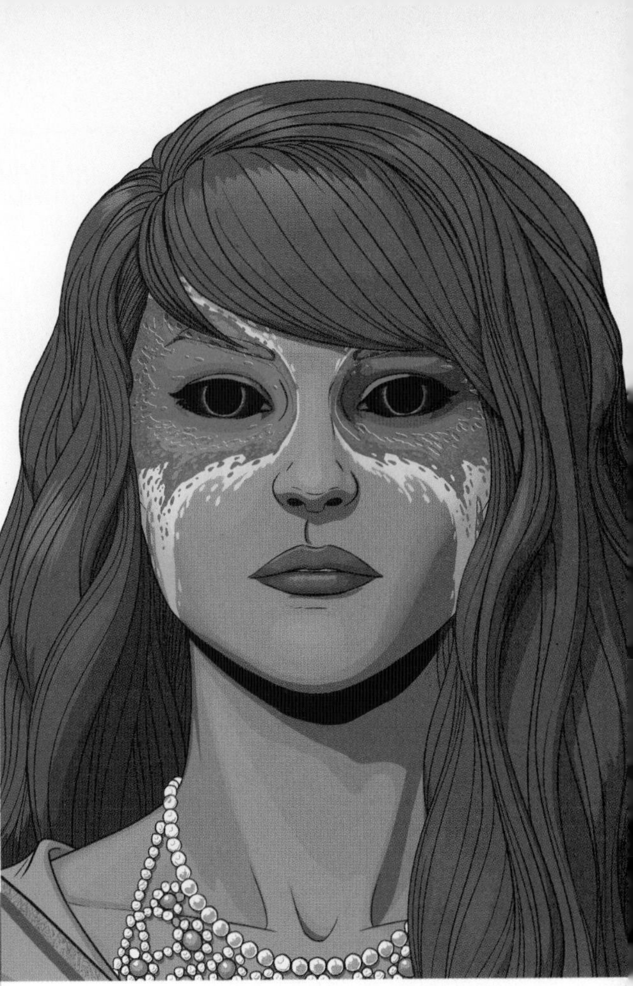
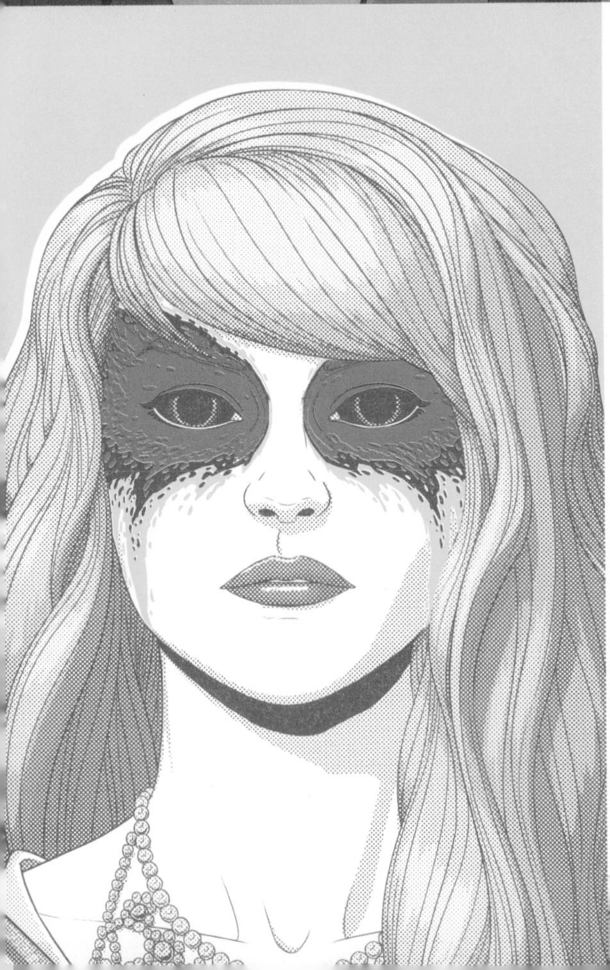
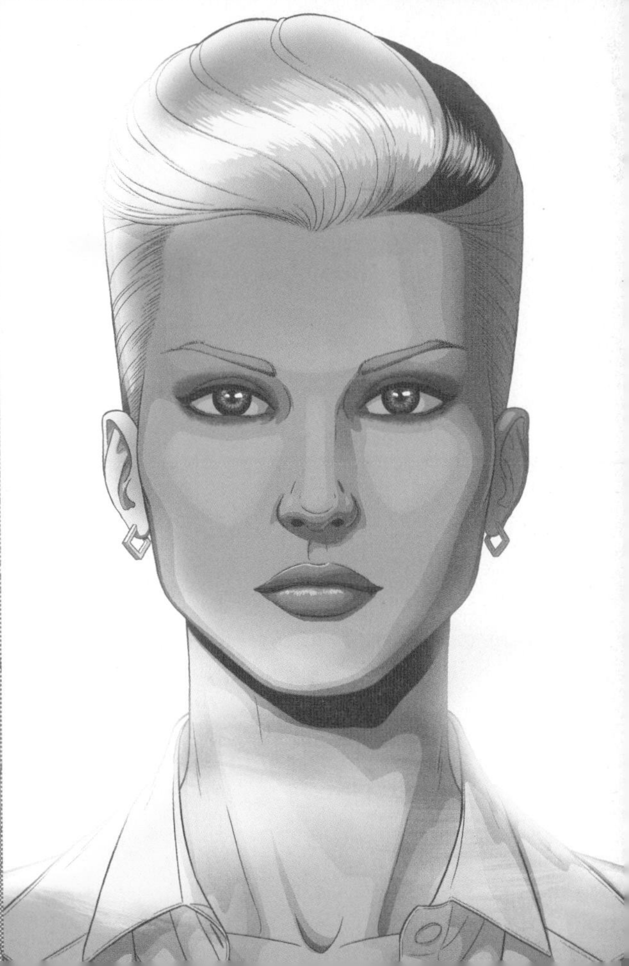

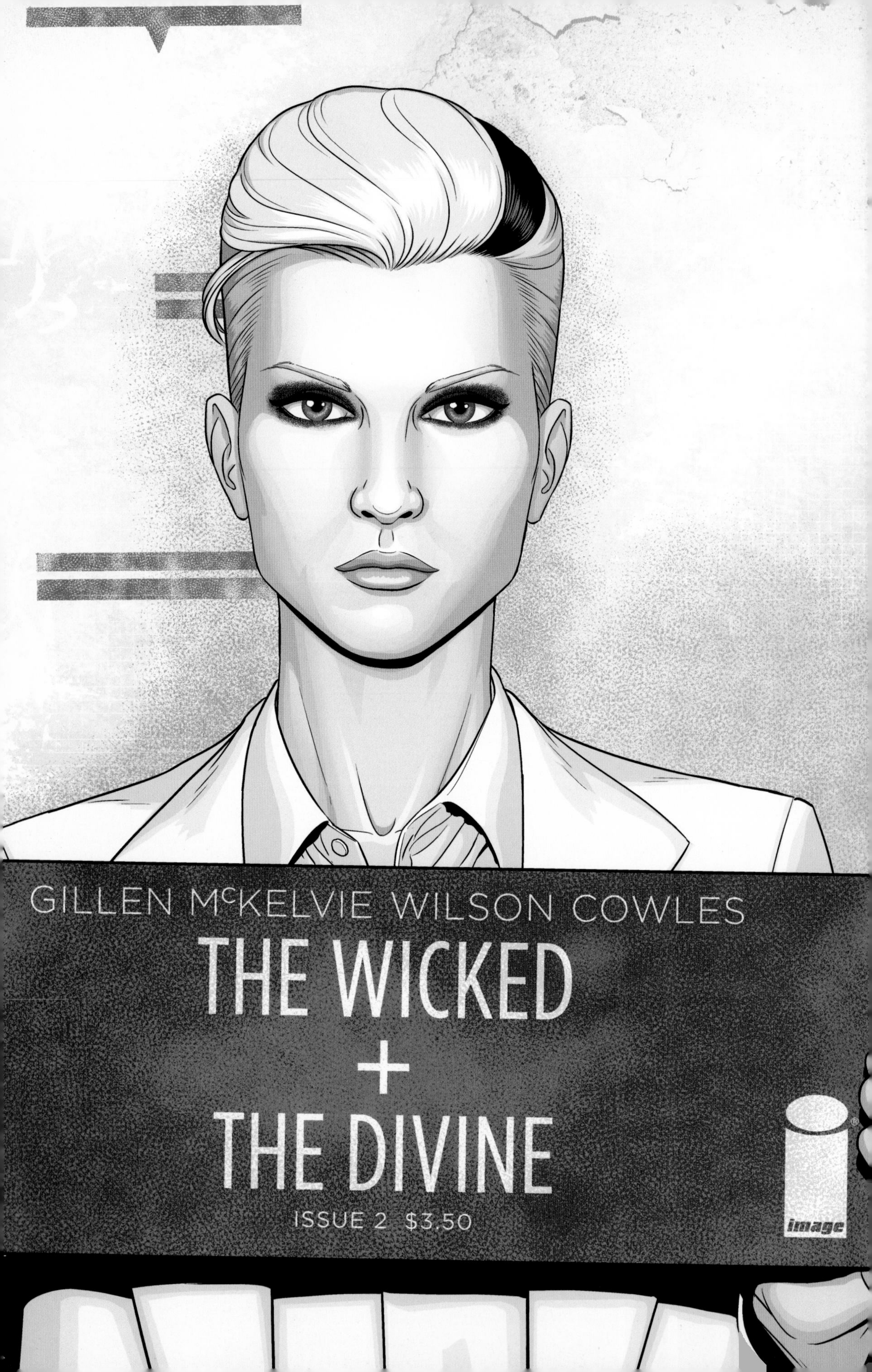
GILLEN McKELVIE WILSON COWLES
THE WICKED + THE DIVINE
ISSUE 2 $3.50
image

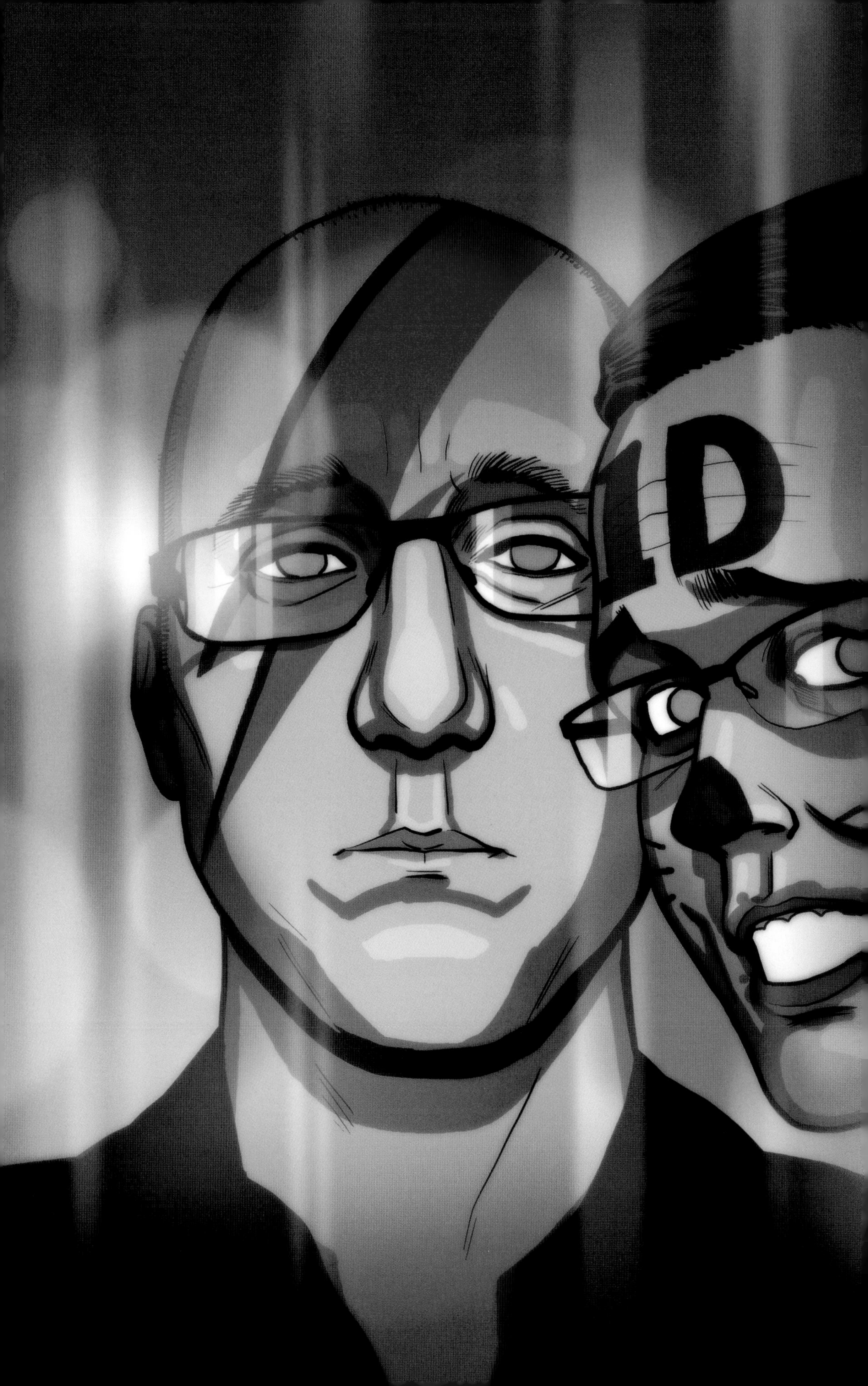

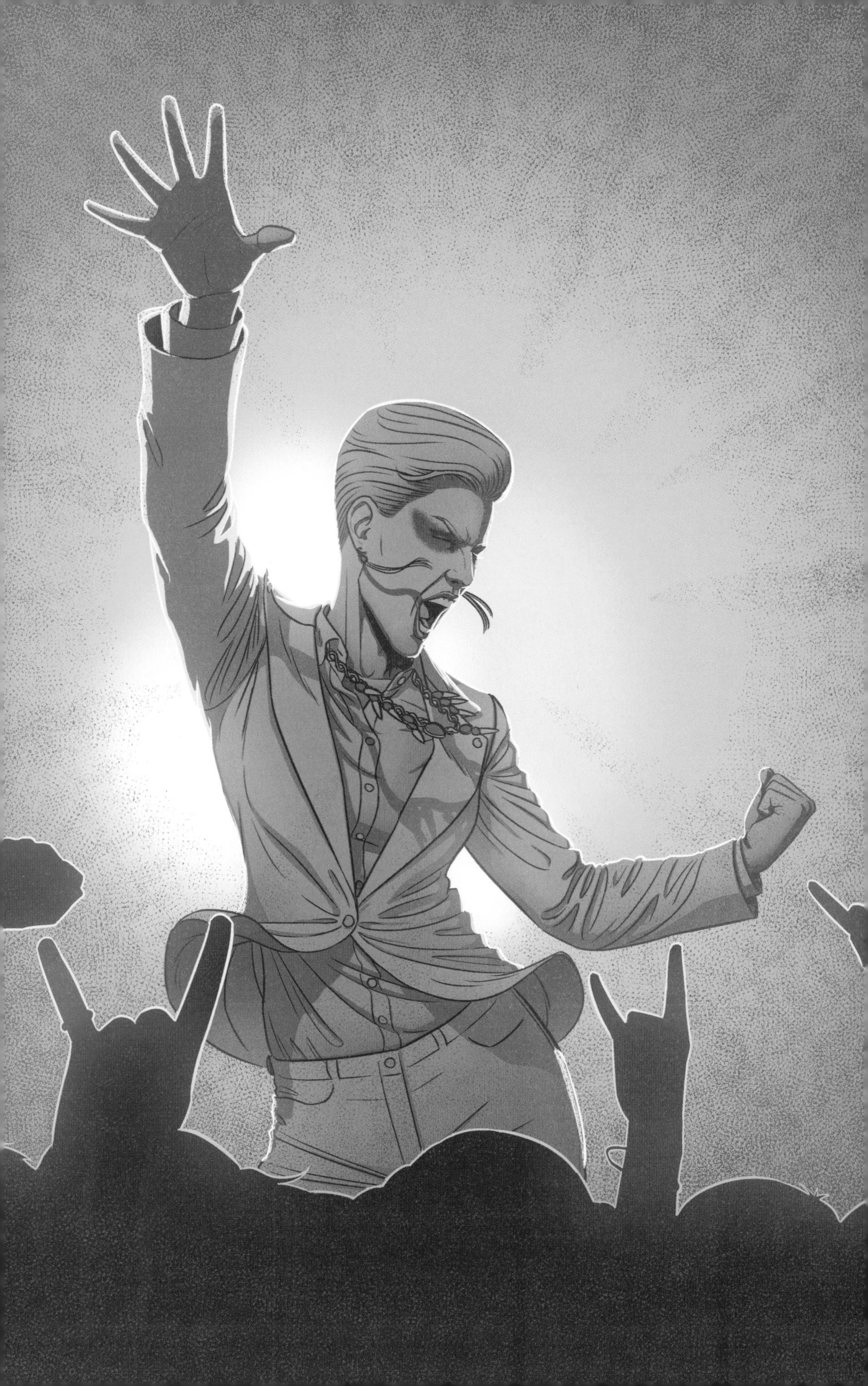

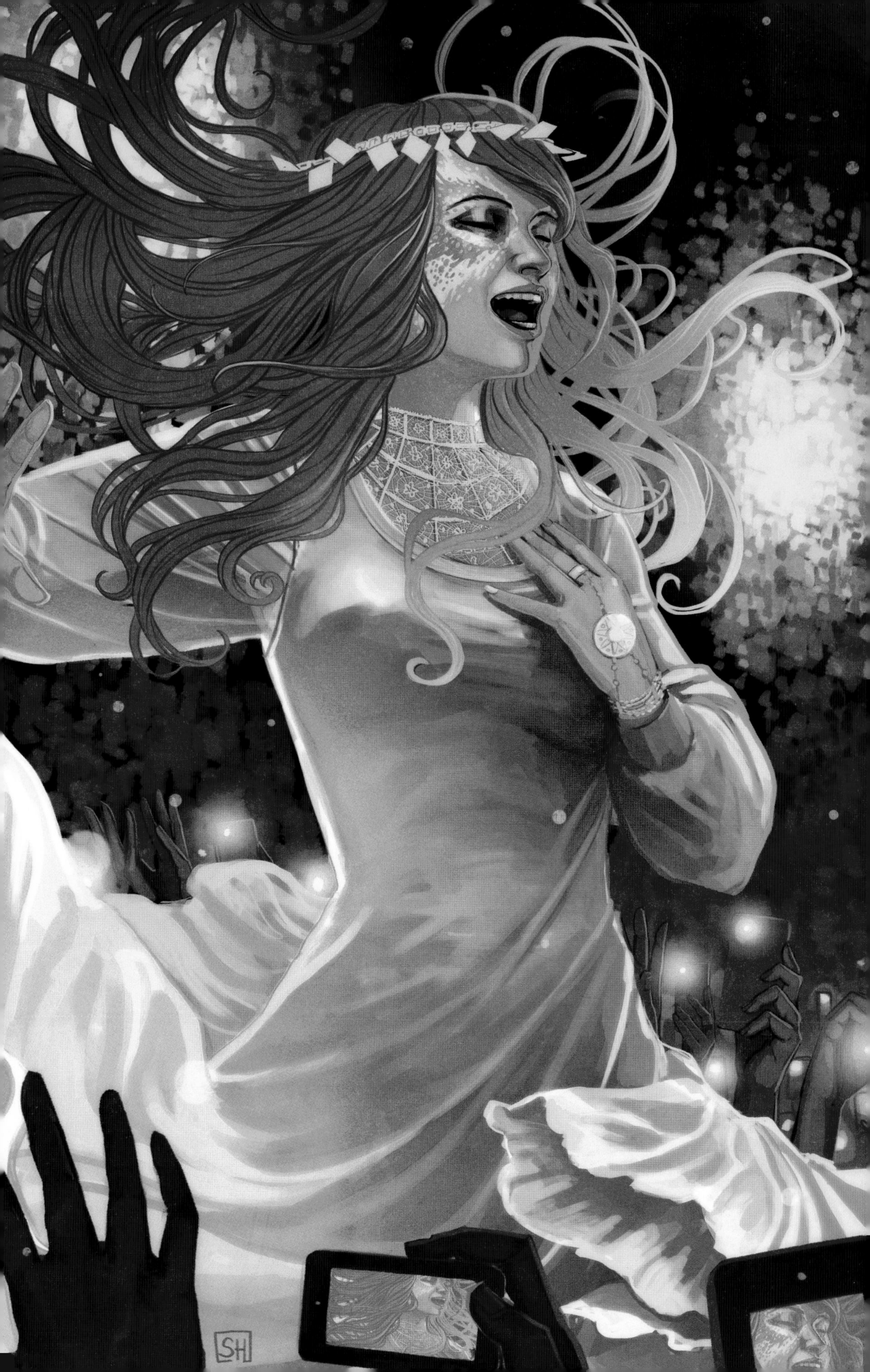

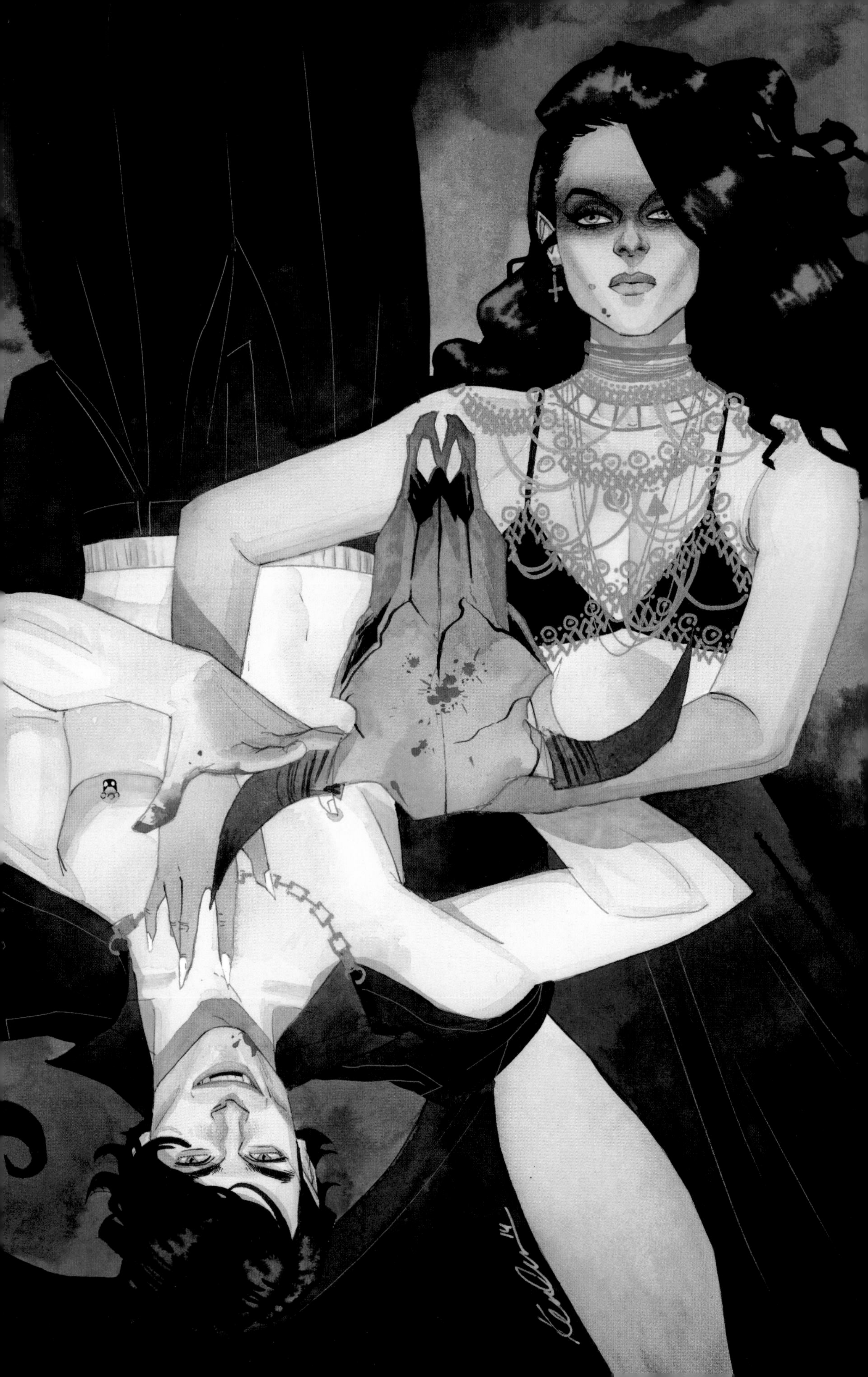

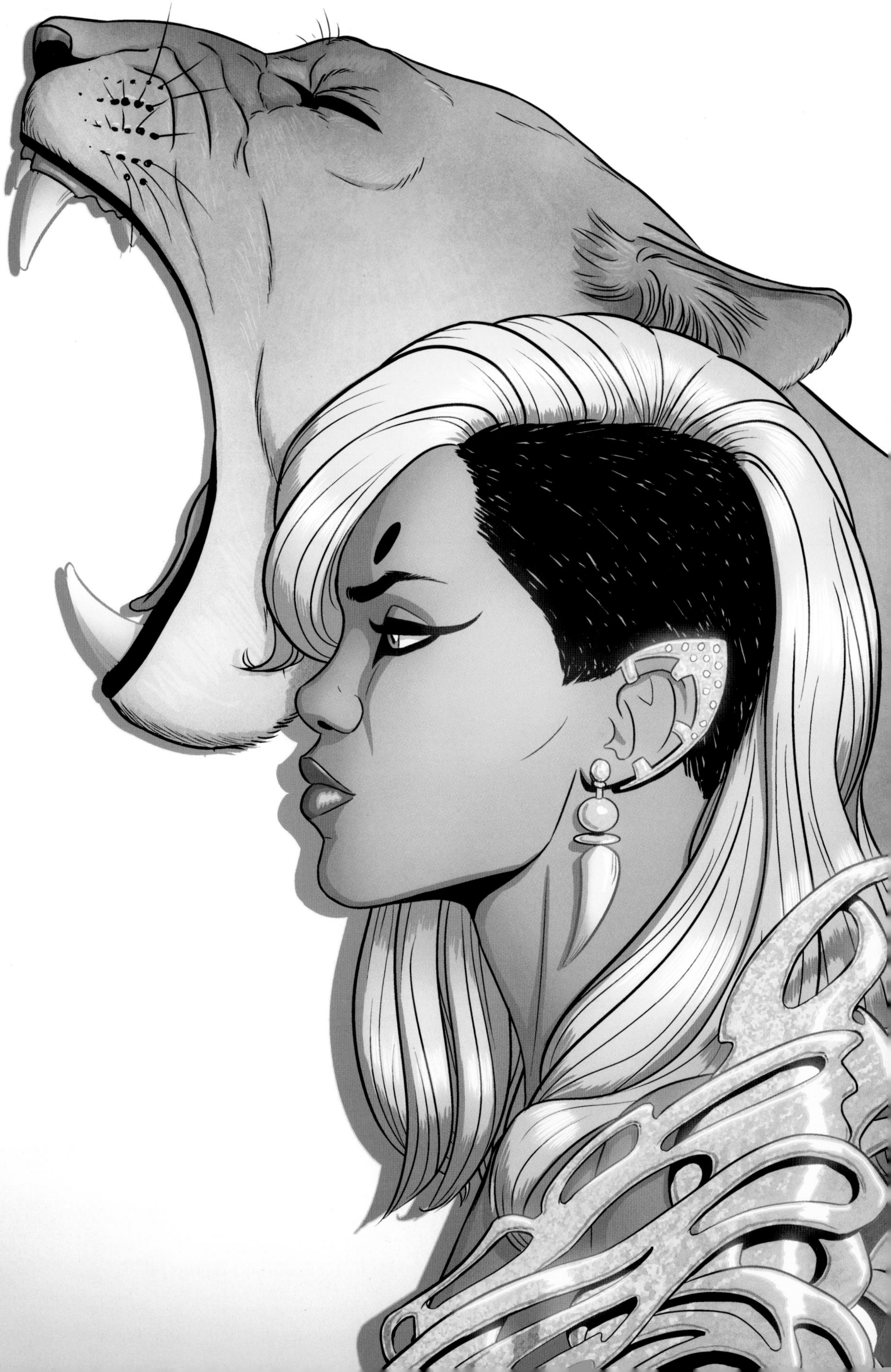

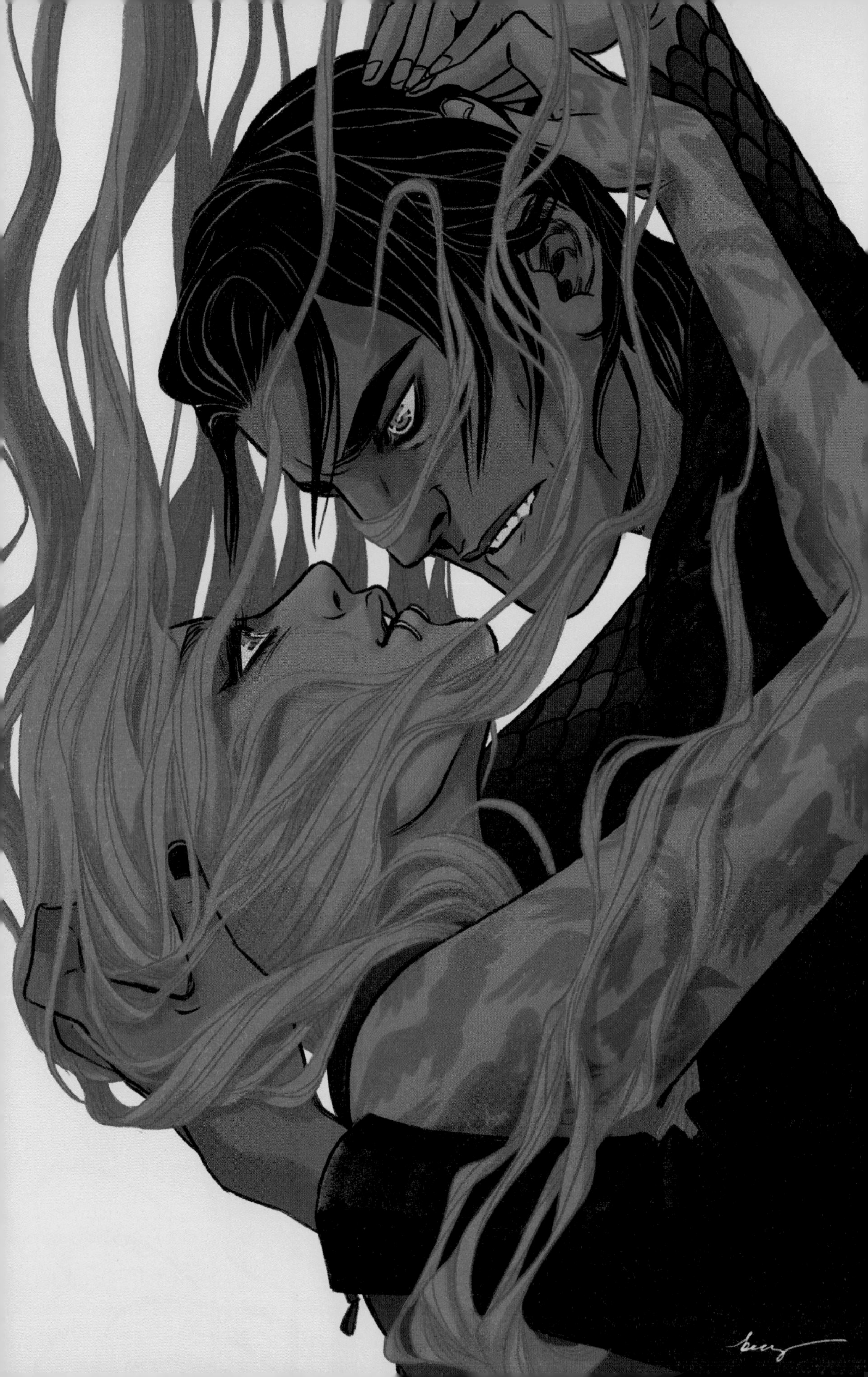

APOCRYPHA

Well, it includes some things that could be termed "Apocrypha" anyway, and we'll jump at any excuse to drop the word "apocrypha." Yes, as you can imagine, we're very popular and not at all lonely most of the time.

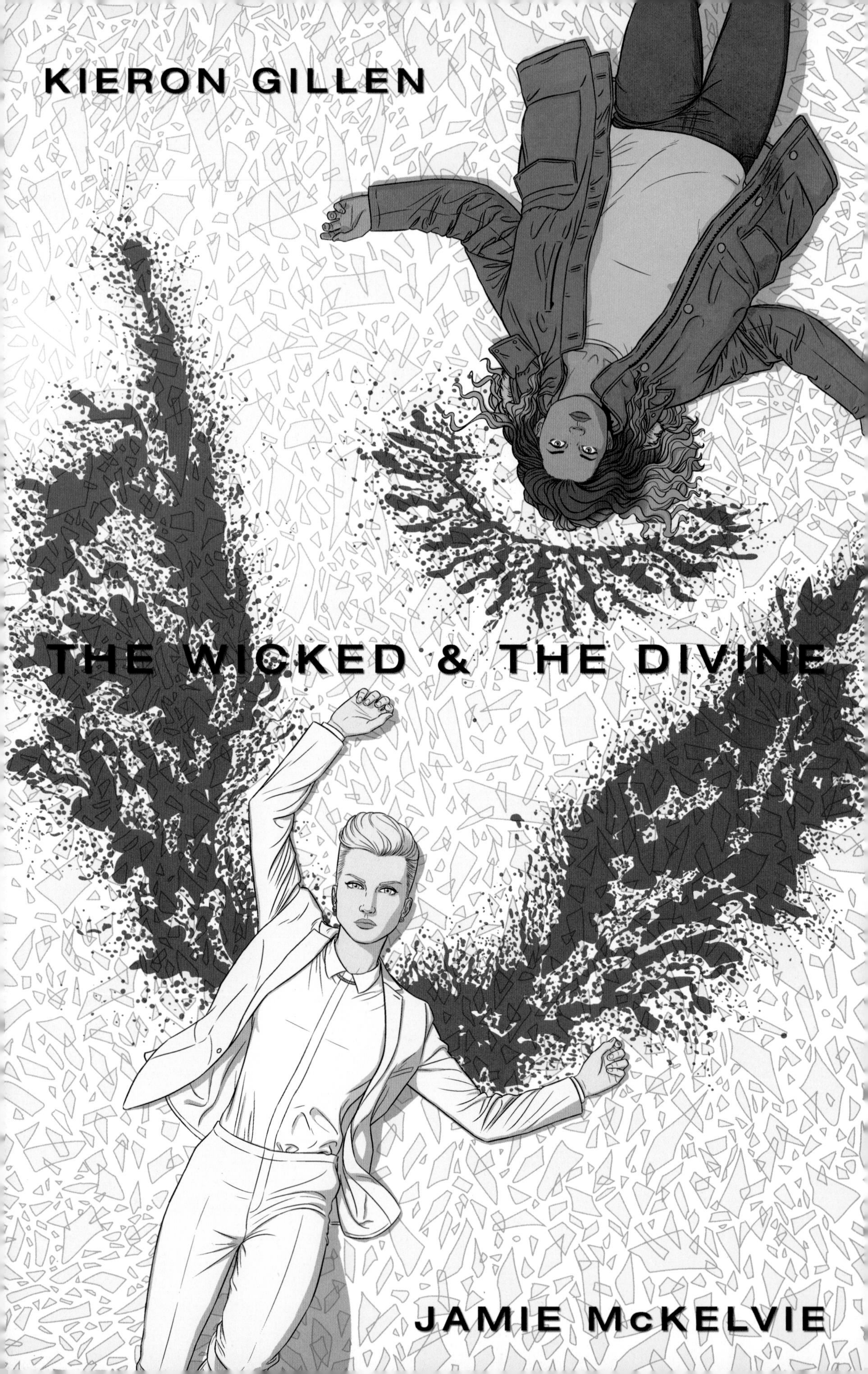
KIERON GILLEN
THE WICKED & THE DIVINE
JAMIE McKELVIE

ANNOUNCEMENT (left)

We announced *The Wicked + The Divine* at the Image Expo in San Francisco on January 9th. This was the first piece of art produced for the comic. As the relationship between Laura and Luci was so core to the book, we wanted to focus on them. Jamie instantly regretted having all that broken glass, as he had to ink it all.

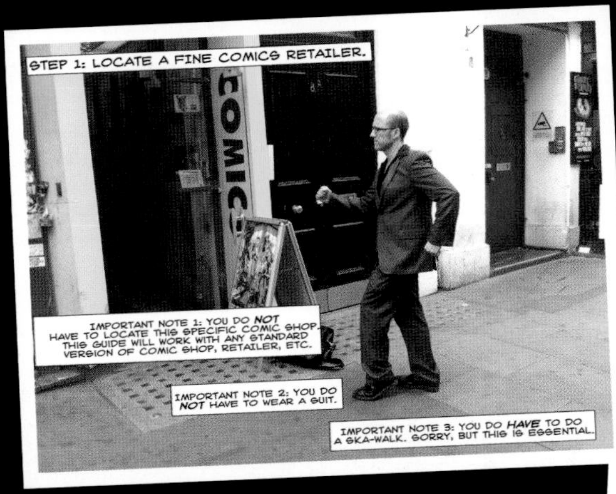
STEP 1: LOCATE A FINE COMICS RETAILER.
IMPORTANT NOTE 1: YOU DO NOT HAVE TO LOCATE THIS SPECIFIC COMIC SHOP. THIS GUIDE WILL WORK WITH ANY STANDARD VERSION OF COMIC SHOP, RETAILER, ETC.
IMPORTANT NOTE 2: YOU DO NOT HAVE TO WEAR A SUIT.
IMPORTANT NOTE 3: YOU DO HAVE TO DO A SKA-WALK. SORRY, BUT THIS IS ESSENTIAL.

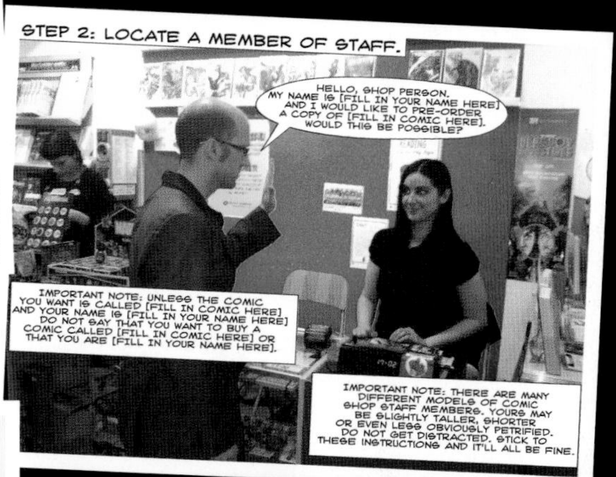
STEP 2: LOCATE A MEMBER OF STAFF.
HELLO, SHOP PERSON. MY NAME IS [FILL IN YOUR NAME HERE] AND I WOULD LIKE TO PRE-ORDER A COPY OF [FILL IN COMIC HERE]. WOULD THIS BE POSSIBLE?
IMPORTANT NOTE: UNLESS THE COMIC YOU WANT IS CALLED [FILL IN COMIC HERE] AND YOUR NAME IS [FILL IN YOUR NAME HERE] DO NOT SAY THAT YOU WANT TO BUY A COMIC CALLED [FILL IN COMIC HERE] OR THAT YOU ARE [FILL IN YOUR NAME HERE].
IMPORTANT NOTE: THERE ARE MANY DIFFERENT MODELS OF COMIC SHOP STAFF MEMBERS. YOURS MAY BE SLIGHTLY TALLER, SHORTER OR EVEN LESS OBVIOUSLY PETRIFIED. DO NOT GET DISTRACTED. STICK TO THESE INSTRUCTIONS AND IT'LL ALL BE FINE.

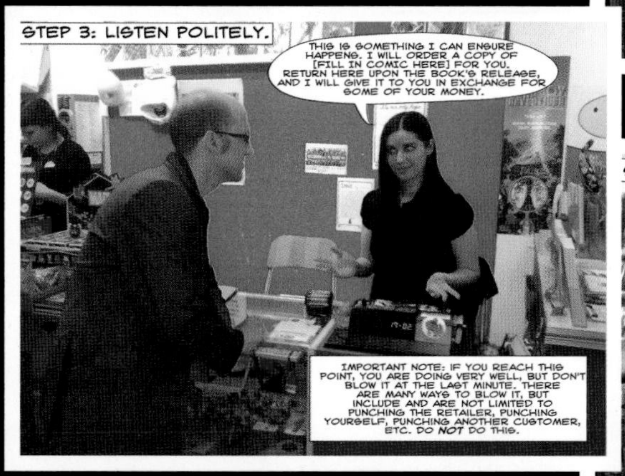
STEP 3: LISTEN POLITELY.
THIS IS SOMETHING I CAN ENSURE HAPPENS. I WILL ORDER A COPY OF [FILL IN COMIC HERE] FOR YOU. RETURN HERE UPON THE BOOK'S RELEASE, AND I WILL GIVE IT TO YOU IN EXCHANGE FOR SOME OF YOUR MONEY.
IMPORTANT NOTE: IF YOU REACH THIS POINT, YOU ARE DOING VERY WELL, BUT DON'T BLOW IT AT THE LAST MINUTE. THERE ARE MANY WAYS TO BLOW IT, BUT INCLUDE AND ARE NOT LIMITED TO PUNCHING THE RETAILER, PUNCHING YOURSELF, PUNCHING ANOTHER CUSTOMER, ETC. DO NOT DO THIS.

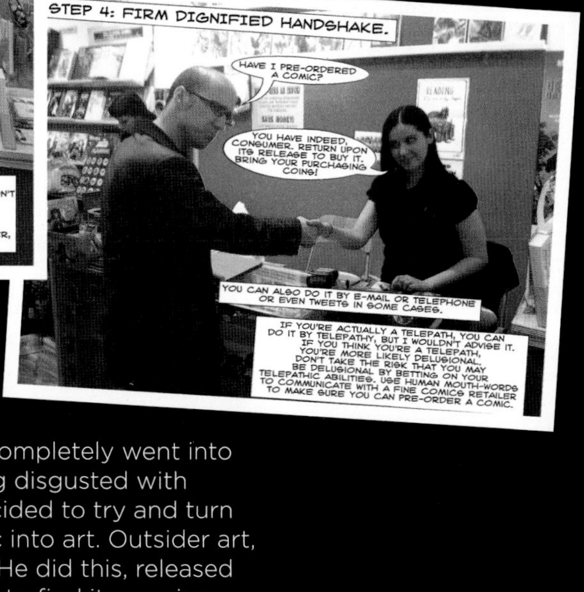
STEP 4: FIRM DIGNIFIED HANDSHAKE.
HAVE I PRE-ORDERED A COMIC?
YOU HAVE INDEED, CONSUMER. RETURN UPON ITS RELEASE TO BUY IT. BRING YOUR PURCHASING COINS!
YOU CAN ALSO DO IT BY E-MAIL OR TELEPHONE OR EVEN TWEETS IN SOME CASES.
IF YOU'RE ACTUALLY A TELEPATH, YOU CAN DO IT BY TELEPATHY, BUT I WOULDN'T ADVISE IT. IF YOU THINK YOU'RE A TELEPATH, YOU'RE MORE LIKELY DELUSIONAL. DON'T TAKE THE RISK THAT YOU MAY BE DELUSIONAL BY BETTING ON YOUR TELEPATHIC ABILITIES. USE HUMAN MOUTH-WORDS TO COMMUNICATE WITH A FINE COMICS RETAILER TO MAKE SURE YOU CAN PRE-ORDER A COMIC.

HOW TO PRE-ORDER COMICS

As this book was such a big deal for us, we completely went into hype-monster mode. In the final week, feeling disgusted with himself and somewhat demented, Kieron decided to try and turn his exhortations on how to pre-order a comic into art. Outsider art, admittedly, but that's neither here nor there. He did this, released it with all the typos, and the Internet seemed to find it amusing. Hurrah, etc.

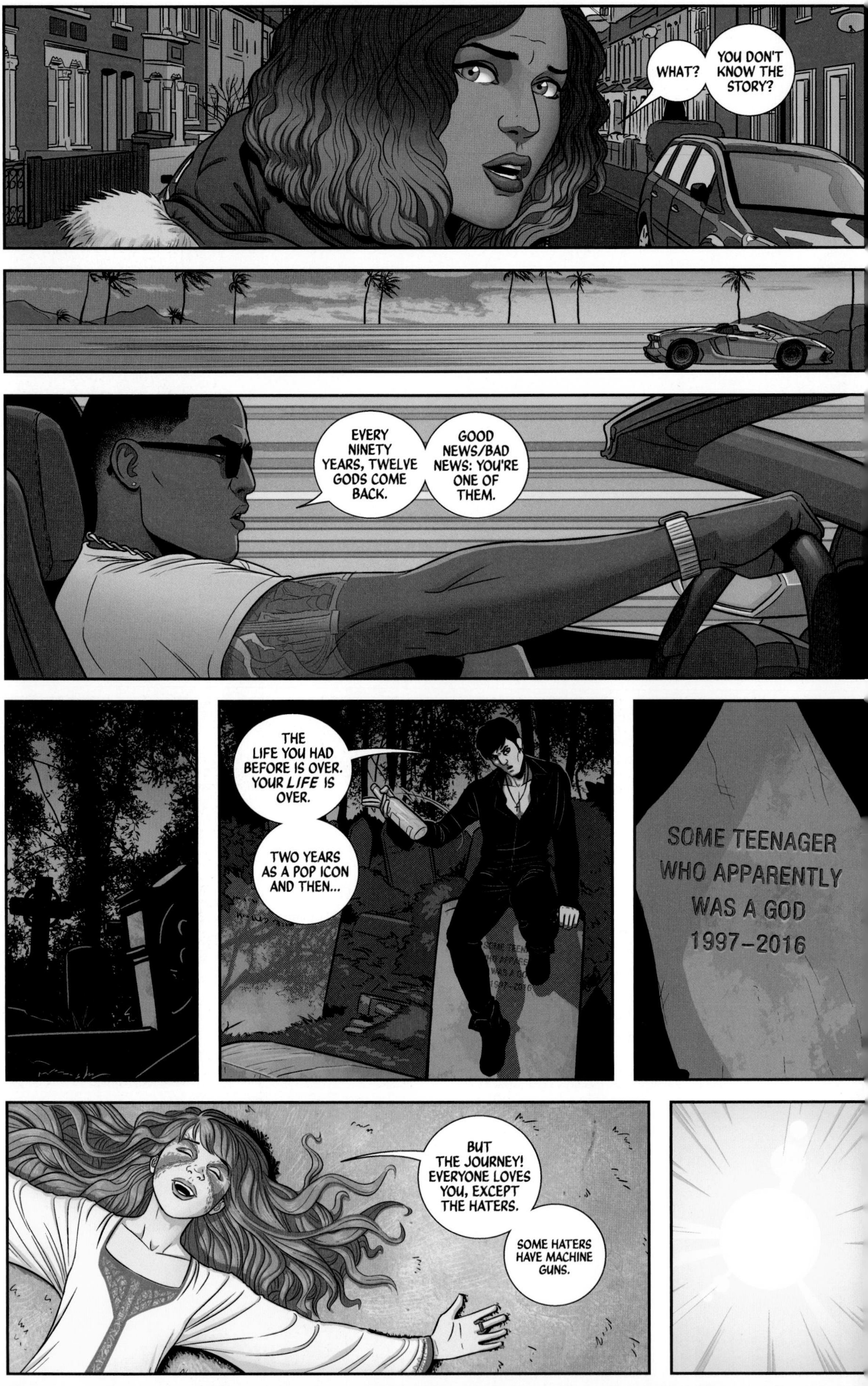
WHAT?
YOU DON'T KNOW THE STORY?
EVERY NINETY YEARS, TWELVE GODS COME BACK.
GOOD NEWS/BAD NEWS: YOU'RE ONE OF THEM.
THE LIFE YOU HAD BEFORE IS OVER. YOUR *LIFE* IS OVER.
TWO YEARS AS A POP ICON AND THEN...
SOME TEENAGER WHO APPARENTLY WAS A GOD 1997–2016
BUT THE JOURNEY! EVERYONE LOVES YOU, EXCEPT THE HATERS.
SOME HATERS HAVE MACHINE GUNS.

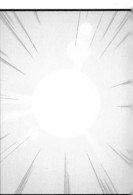

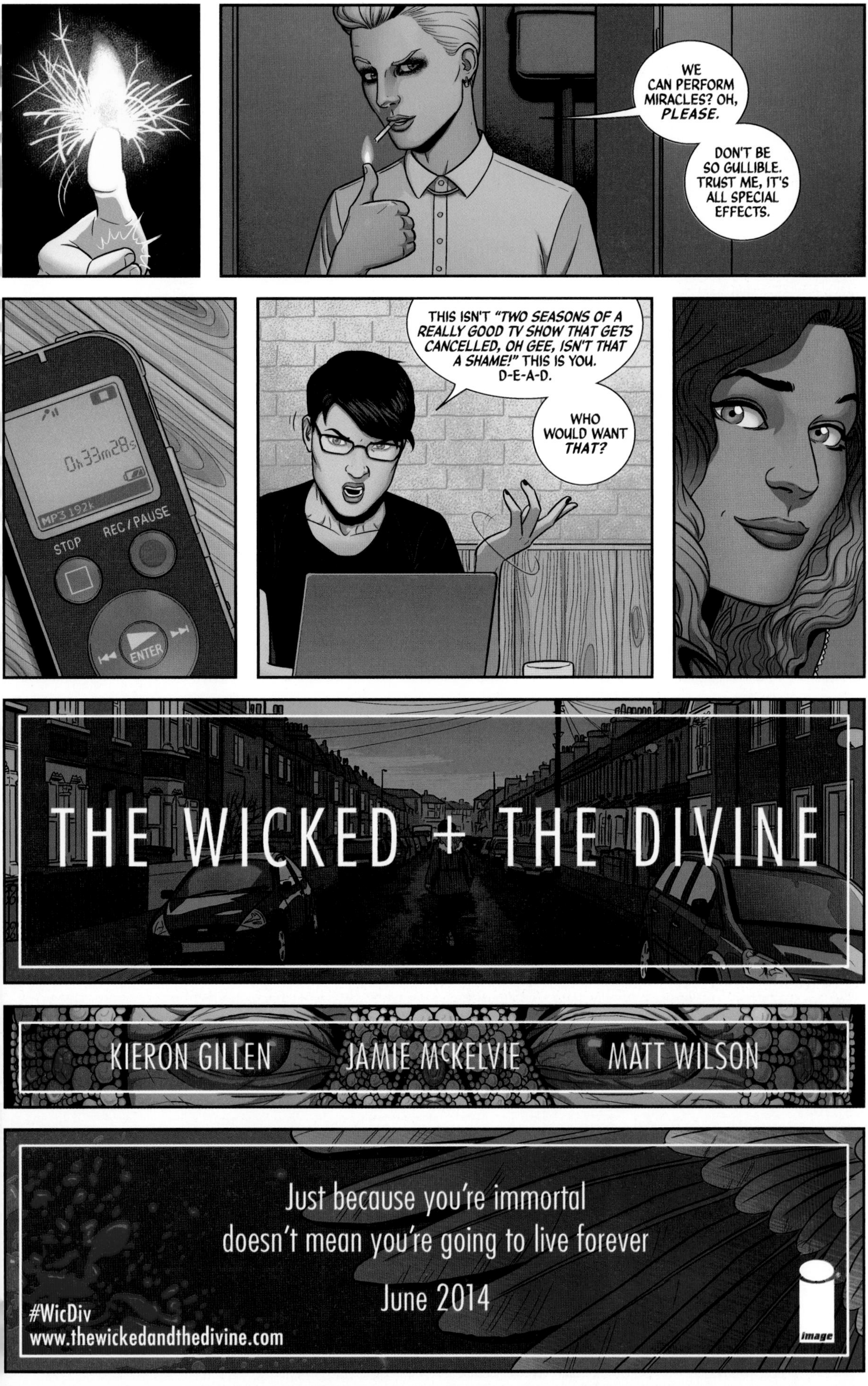

WE CAN PERFORM MIRACLES? OH, PLEASE.
DON'T BE SO GULLIBLE. TRUST ME, IT'S ALL SPECIAL EFFECTS.
REC / PAUSE
STOP
ENTER
THIS ISN'T "TWO SEASONS OF A REALLY GOOD TV SHOW THAT GETS CANCELLED, OH GEE, ISN'T THAT A SHAME!" THIS IS YOU. D-E-A-D.
WHO WOULD WANT THAT?
THE WICKED + THE DIVINE
KIERON GILLEN
JAMIE McKELVIE
MATT WILSON
Just because you're immortal
doesn't mean you're going to live forever
June 2014
#WicDiv
www.thewickedandthedivine.com
image

TEASER (previous pages)

One part of *Phonogram* we always were kind of happy with was
the short advert teaser. Rather than repurposing panels from the
book or dropping a preview, we created a bespoke one-page
story that introduced the concepts. We decided to do it again
for *The Wicked + The Divine*, except when seeing the script,
Jamie decided it'd be better on two pages. This is the first sign
that Team *Phonogram* were entering their opulent phase.

NATHAN FAIRBAIRN FRESCO

When seeing the script for issue four, Jamie had the bright
idea that rather than Matt colouring the fresco, we reach out to
another colourist with a very different style. Nathan Fairbairn
was up for it, rendering over Jamie's art in a fully painted
style, leading to this wonderful image. We're very happy. That
said, us paying a completely different colourist to do a small
piece of an issue's art is another example of us going into
the aforementioned decadent phase. We look forward to the
Barbarians arriving and killing us all. It's more than we deserve.

MORE TITLES BY THE CREATORS

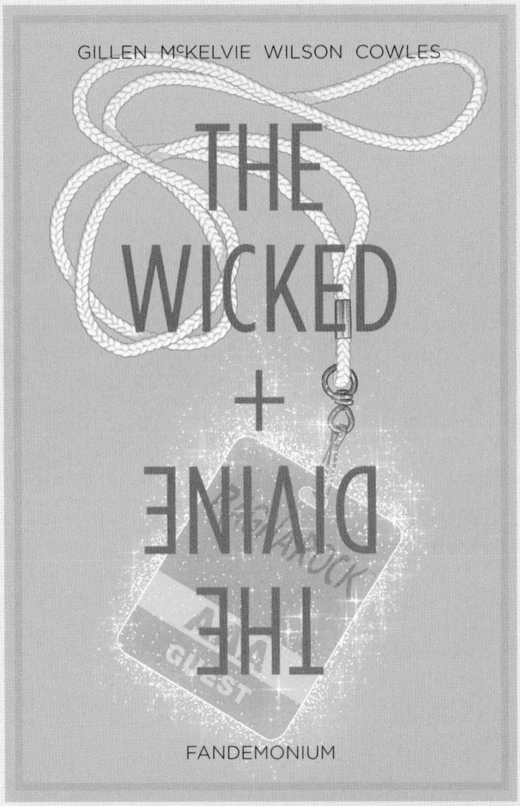
GILLEN McKELVIE WILSON COWLES
THE WICKED + THE DIVINE
FANDEMONIUM

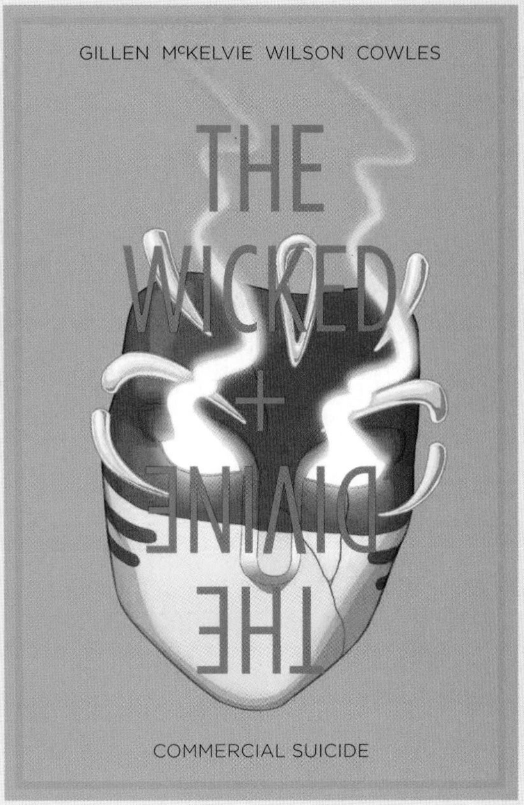
GILLEN McKELVIE WILSON COWLES
THE WICKED + THE DIVINE
COMMERCIAL SUICIDE

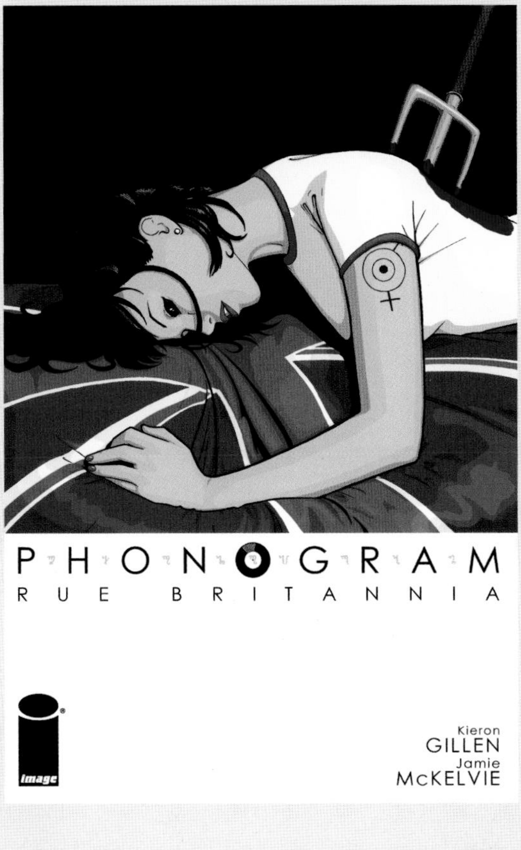
PHONOGRAM
RUE BRITANNIA
Kieron GILLEN
Jamie McKELVIE

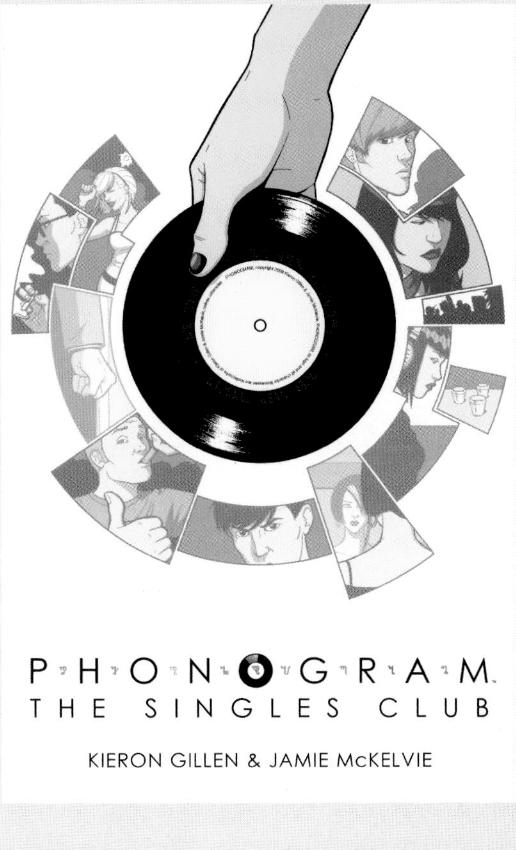
PHONOGRAM
THE SINGLES CLUB
KIERON GILLEN & JAMIE McKELVIE

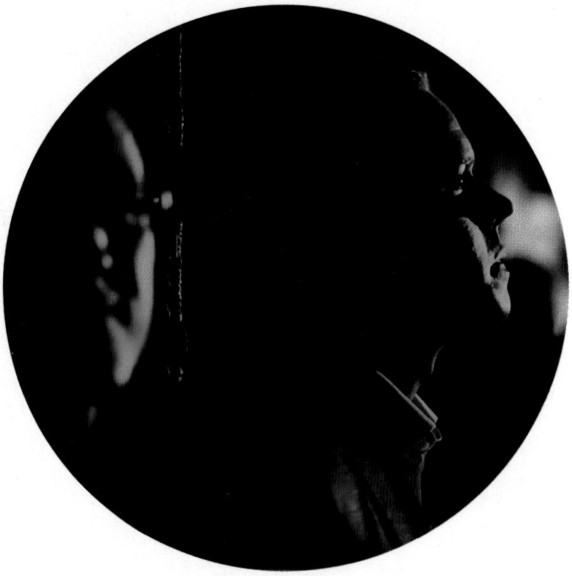

Kieron Gillen is out of focus. He writes.
Jamie McKelvie is in focus. He draws.
Matthew Wilson isn't pictured. He colours.

Photo by Dan Griliopoulos